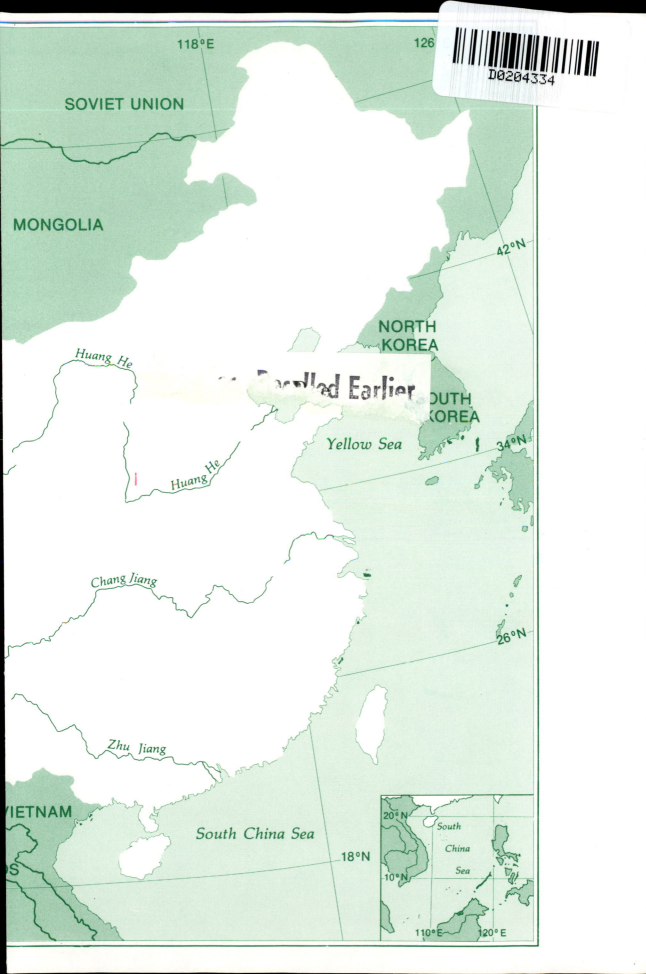

SOVIET UNION

MONGOLIA

42°N

NORTH
KOREA

Huang He

Recalled Earlier

OUTH
KOREA

Yellow Sea

34°N

Huang He

Chang Jiang

26°N

Zhu Jiang

VIETNAM

South China Sea

18°N

20°N

South

China

Sea

10°N

110°E   120°E

118°E

126

FEEDING A BILLION

FRONTIERS
OF
CHINESE AGRICULTURE

by

Sylvan Wittwer
Yu Youtai
Sun Han
Wang Lianzheng

Michigan State University Press
1987

© Michigan State University Press 1987
Printed in the United States of America

The paper used in this publication meets the minimum
requirements of American National Standard for Information Sciences--Permanence of Paper for Printed
Library Materials ANSI Z39.48-1984.

Library of Congress Catloging-in-Publication Data

Feeding a billion.

   Includes bibliographies.
   1. Agriculture--Economic aspects--China. 2. Food
supply--China. I. Sun, Han. II. Wittwer, S. H.
(Sylvan Harold), 1917-
HD2098.F45   1987   338.1'9'51   87-60024
ISBN 0-87013-246-6

Michigan State University Press
East Lansing, Michigan 48823-5202

To Maurine--my loving and understanding wife, who for more than fifty years, has stood by my side with support and encouragement for all worthy activities.

Design and production - Julie Loehr
Cover - Lynne Brown, Media Graphics
Cartography - Ellen White
Typeset and Keyline - Forsberg Advertising
Color Design - Jerry Gates
Color Separations - Image Arts

CONTENTS

ACKNOWLEDGEMENTS

Specific debts of gratitude in the production of this volume are extended to institutions as well as to people--to Michigan State University and its College of Agriculture and Natural Resources for partially supporting my five trips to China, (1980, 1981, 1983, 1985, 1987) and providing release time and the provision of an office and secretary for four years as an emeritus professor; to the Michigan State University Press for unusual editorial assistance and design expertise; and the Michigan State University Foundation for underwriting the cost of publication; and to many institutions in China which welcomed and financed my travels and arranged field trips into many provinces, municipalities, autonomous regions and remote areas. Of special note were the Ministry of Agriculture, Animal Husbandry and Fishery, the Chinese Academy of Agricultural Sciences, the Jiangsu Academy of Agricultural Sciences, the Heilongjiang Academy of Agricultural Sciences and the Northeast Agricultural College.

Early encouragement and editorial assistance for the book was provided by Lyle and Jean Blair, former directors of the Michigan State University Press, and later by Richard Chapin, current director. During the final stages of preparation and for editorial assistance, design and graphics and ultimate production, our thanks go to the untiring efforts of Ellen Link, Julie L. Loehr, Lynne A. Brown and Ellen R. White and especially for the word processing assistance of Shelly Jean Hamelink, who over a four year period typed and re-typed chapter after chapter. Without their help and tolerance of imperfections, this book would not have been possible. Finally, I thank Maurine Wittwer for her constant encouragement, proofing of chapters and her companionship on four of the trips to China, and her untiring support of this project from its beginning to completion.

Invaluable assistance in making available statistics and timely literature citations, reports, reprints and preprints and critiques was given by Joyce A. Madancy and Halsey L. Beemer Jr. of the Committee of Scholarly Communication with the Peoples Republic of China; National Academy of Sciences; Bruce Stone of the International Food Policy Research Institute; Francis Tuan of the Economic Research Service of the

U.S. Department of Agriculture; Norton D. Strommen of the World Outlook and Situation Board of the U.S. Department of Agriculture; M. R. Bilbeise of the Food and Agriculture Organization of United Nations; Hank Fitzhugh of Winrock International; Douglas R. Dewey of the Agricultural Research Service, U.S. Department of Agriculture; Vernon W. Ruttan, University of Minnesota; Philip F. Low of Purdue University; Sarah Greene of the MacMillan Publishing Co.; the World Bank and Rodale Press. I also thank Nicholas R. Lardy, of the University of Washington and Vaclav Smil of the University of Manitoba for generously sharing their reprints, preprints and other documents relating to Agricultural development, food production and environmental constraints in China.

Many associates at Michigan State University and elsewhere deserve recognition for careful editing, proofing and suggestions for specific chapters. Thanks go to Frank D'itri, Milo B. Tesar, Everett H. Everson, Thomas G. Isleib, Shigemi Honma, Stanley K. Ries, Timothy S. Chang, William Tai, Merle Esmay, Jacob A. Hoefer, John Kelly, Edward Klos, David Pimentel, T. C. Tso, Emil M. Mrak and Robert D. Munson.

Encouragement for this entire project came especially from present and former clost associates, chief among whom were James H. Anderson, Gordon E. Guyer, John A. Hannah, Irving Wyeth, Patricia Riley, Robert LaPrad, Ralph Smuckler, Warren Cohen, Donald Isleib, K. N. Satyapal, Martha R. Mulder, R. Paul Larsen, Charlie Downs and Laurie Wink. Each contributed significantly in their special way. Others in the community, including Perry Driggs, Nancy Washburne, Kelly Thurston and Jennie Stoddard, were constantly encouraging the effort.

Special thanks are extended to Howard Camden, a former student, who provided a continuing clipping bureau and access to latest news releases concerning developments in China from 1980 to the present.

From the Chinese side significant inputs were provided for many of the chapters. Chief among the contributors were Shao Qiquan, Li Ansheng, Lu Wei and Wei Rongxuan of the Genetic Institute, Academia Sinica; Li Shuxuan and Jiang Cisheng of the Zhejiang Agricultural University and Shen Tsuin of the Beijing Agricultural University; Luo Peng of Sichuan University; Kuo Chunyen of the South China Institute of Botany, Academia Sinica; Ling Yilu, Yuan Congyi, Zhou Xing, Jin Zhewen and Dai Huishan of the Jiangsu Academy of Agricultural Sciences; Zhang Zengmin of the Heilongjiang Academy of Agricultural Sciences; Xu Zhenying, Wang Jinling, Jiang Yiyuen, Li Jinghua, Chen Rensheng and Shi Lansheng of the Northeast Agricultural College; Zhu Zuxiang Director General of the National Rice Research Institute in Hangzhou; Mrs. Chen Hang, Director of the Beijing Vegetable Research

Center; Mrs. Xu Lianfang, Director of the Harbin Vegetable Research Institute and Mrs. Guang Zhongyen of the Horticultural Research Institute of the Heilongjiang Academy of Agricultural Sciences.

This project was endorsed and encouraged from its beginning by He Kang, Minister of Agriculture, Animal Husbandry and Fishery; Lu Liangshu, President of the Chinese Academy of Agricultural Sciences, Shi Bohong, Vice President of the Northeast Agricultural College; Gao Liangzhi, President of the Jiangsu Academy of Agricultural Sciences; and Chu Xin, Vice-President of the Shanghai Academy of Agricultural Sciences. Finally, special recognition, thanks and appreciation are extended to Qu Ningkang of the Bureau of Science and Technology of the Ministry of Agricultural, Animal Husbandry and Fishery and to Zhao Weijun, Information Specialist, of the Chinese Academy of Agricultural Sciences for their untiring efforts in arranging agendas, accomodations, field trips and as interpreters, translators and extenders of knowledge of Chinese agriculture during all five visits in China.

PREFACE

The world is indebted to China for much of its food production capacity. No other country has more varied and illustrious food and agricultural traditions than has China. Chinese dishes are highly prized, not only in Asia, but throughout the world. While much of this notoriety is due to excellence of food preparation which characterizes Chinese cooking, a great deal is due to the wide variety of food crops and animals grown in China, and to the centuries-old tradition of producing that food.

This book provides readable background information on China's varied plant and animal production systems. It also illustrates how modern-day China is using science and technology to increase its food production, and to improve the quality of crops and animals being grown. Likewise, it shows how China is blending in new crops and cultural practices with its time-honored traditional agricultural production systems.

I have been very much impressed and pleased with the remarkable progress I have witnessed in Chinese agricultural research and education activities since I first visited that country in 1974. I have been equally impressed and pleased with the increasing cooperation between Chinese scientists and their counterparts in other countries. Each of the eight visits I have made to China have provided increasing evidence of technological advances and of international cooperation.

This book records significant examples of technological advance and international cooperation. The research and development aspects are covered in both general and specific crop and animal terms. The authors provide up-to-date coverage of the production of major food crops and animals in China and show how science and practice have been combined to yield effective production systems. Certainly, the practical use of research fundings on Chinese research farms is well illustrated.

One also sees evidence of international cooperation in the discussions of crop improvement, cultural practices and the creation and adaption of other improved technologies. International cooperation is evident also in the list of co-authors for this book. Three senior Chinese scientists and others have joined with a senior American counterpart to produce this fine treatise. Such cooperation is a culmination of years of open and friendly interaction, not only among these authors but among Chinese and American agricultural scientist generally. It also illustrates the degree to which the Chinese have welcomed collaboration with agricultural scientists and educators throughout the world. Such international cooperation has most certainly been mutually beneficial to the Chinese and to their overseas cooperators.

The chapters of this book also remind us of the remarkable changes which have taken place in agricultural production systems in China in recent years. These changes are characterized by significant increases in "individual responsibility" making it desirable and profitable for cultivators to adopt modern technology. China's experience is being carefully examined by leaders in developing countries everywhere as they seek means of stimulating individual responsiveness to modern technology and to opportunities for increased food production.

This book is indeed a tribute to the scientists and other leaders of agricultural programs in China. Agriculturalists throughout the world are indebted to the knowledgeable authors of this book for so effectively presenting the joint attributes of technology generation and utilization, and of international cooperation. It will be widely read and should set an example for other such joint efforts.

Nyle C. Brady
Professor Emeritus, Cornell
    University and
Senior Assitant Administrator for
    Science and Technology
U. S. Agency for International
    Development

PREFACE

China is an old agricultural country with more than 7,000 years of farming history. The rich traditional and cultural experiences of the Chinese farmers are a precious inheritance for the people of the entire world. During the past more than thirty-five years since the founding of the People's Republic of China, the speed of agricultural development has exceeded that of the world average. Especially in the last eight years, great changes have taken place in rural China. It is a universally admitted great achievement that China is feeding 22% of the world's population on only 7% of the earth's arable land. Chinese agriculture currently is moving to a new stage of development and the great mass of farmers are working hard for a better and more prosperous life.

Feeding A Billion, represents a vast collection of genuine history, information, statistics and resource materials with a scientific evaluation, commentary and vivid descriptions. It presents to us the hard and creative efforts as well as the remarkable accomplishments which China has gained in developing and utilizing its agricultural and natural resources and its high yielding technologies as a result of combining traditional practices with modern science and technology and carrying out in depth rural economic reforms.

The publication of this book will help our foreign friends to have a better understanding of China. It will also provide some beneficial suggestions to countries of the world who are seeking improved ways for rapid agricultural development.

This is the first book which has been co-authored by both Chinese and American authors on Chinese agricultural development. The American author, Dr. Sylvan Wittwer, during his five visits to China has traveled through China's major agricultural regions and even into some remote areas. He has made a splendid contribution to the agricultural scientific exchange between China and the United States. Professors Yu Youtai, Sun Han, and Wang Lianzheng of China are not only outstanding researchers in the agricultural sciences, but also have had rich experiences in agricultural administration. It has been a rewarding experience for the four scholars on this joint authorship.

I am very pleased to see the publication of *Feeding A Billion* and take this opportunity to express my congratulations to the co-author's and my greetings to the broad mass of readers.

He Kang, Minister
Ministry of Agriculture, Animal
Husbandry and Fishery
People's Republic of China

CHINESE PROPER
AND
GEOGRAPHICAL NAMES

During the course of this project (1980-1987), the Chinese were in the process of converting the romanization of proper and geographical names from the old Wade-Giles system to the new Pinyin system which was officially adopted by the government in 1979. In this book, the new, revised romanized spellings, including the elimination of hyphens in the case of given names, are used. Listings in the "For Further Reading" sections following each chapter, are alphabetical and by surnames, except where original literature citations dictate otherwise.

UNITS, MEASUREMENTS AND EQUIVALENTS

Officially, and in principle, China uses the metric system of measurements. Such has been adopted throughout this volume. In Chinese practice, however, traditional units, now defined in terms of metric units, are also used. The most distinctive and widespread usage is the mu or mou, a measurement of area which consists of 667 square meters or one-fifteenth of a hectare or one sixth of an acre. Yields per unit area are often expressed as jin per mu. A table of comparative conversion units for areas and weights for the Chinese, Metric and U.S. systems follows:

CHINESE	METRIC	U.S. (ENGLISH)
1 mou (mu)	0.0667 hectare	0.1647 acre
15 mou (mu)	1.0 hectare	2.4711 acres
1 jin (catty)	0.5 kilogram	1.1023 pounds
1 dan (100 jin)	50.0 kilograms	110.23 pounds
1 dun (ton)	1,000.00 kilograms (1 metric ton)	2,204.6 pounds
1 jin/mu	7.5 kilograms/hectare	6.93 pounds/acre

CHINESE DYNASTIES AND HISTORY

DYNASTY	YEAR
Xia	About 21st - 16th Century B.C.
Shang	About 16th - 11th Century B.C.
Zhou	About 11th - 841 B.C.
Spring and Autumn	841 - 476 B.C.
Warring States	475 - 221 B.C.
Qin	221 - 206 B.C.
Han	
Western	206 B.C. - A.D. 24
Eastern	25 - 220 A.D.
Three Kingdoms	220 - 280
Jin	
Western	266 - 316
Eastern	317 - 420
Southern and Northern	420 - 589
Sui	581 - 618
Tang	618 - 907
Five Dynasties (South)	
Ten Kingdoms (North)	
Song	
Northern	960 - 1126
Southern	1127 - 1279
Yuan	1279 - 1368
Ming	1368 - 1644
Qing	1644 - 1911

Many chapters in this volume refer to events in periods designated in Chinese history. Herewith is a listing of dynasties and years covered by each.

1
INTRODUCTION

by Sylvan Wittwer

China today is feeding over a billion people, or almost one-fourth (22%) of the world's population, on 7% of the earth's arable land. This is 4.4 million hectares less land for grain production than forty years ago, when the population was one-half of what it is today. China's food production technologies, many of which are still being developed, could be valuable for meeting food needs in other parts of the world. Can these unique technologies be appropriately described, given visibility, and exchanged or transferred to agriculturally developing countries and even the Western world? Any future program designed to create a well-fed society must take China's well advanced, emerging and traditional food production technologies into account.

It may well be that the people who produce food most efficiently--as well as the meek--will inherit the earth. This could well be China's ultimate destiny. For the past three millenia, millions of Chinese have not known from where their next meal would come. Historically, famines have ravaged and floods have devastated China's food-producing systems. Untold millions have starved. Yet China, today, is the hallmark of success in food production and agricultural reform. Within an eight-year period (1978-1986), it has gone from a state-controlled economy to a market-driven one, coupled with economic incentives and personal initiatives that together have achieved over a 10% annual increase in the total agricultural output between 1981 and 1985. Never before has such a remarkable record for a nation of such size been achieved. China is a living world example that farmers respond positively to increasing production when given incentives, resource inputs and the technology to do so.

This book is not a treatise on economics and agricultural development in China. Several volumes, authored by economists, deal with analyses of the agricultural sector, regionalization of crop and livestock production, and the impacts of resource allocations on agricultural output. Interrelationships of income and per capita food consumption, the financing of Chinese agricultural development, the role of agriculture in Chinese development strategies, credit, transportation and marketing have also been covered (see *For Further Reading*).

Accounts abound in technical, semi-popular, and popular reports of the changing economics in the Chinese agricultural sector, of the incentives and mechanisms, the workings of the responsibility production contract system and the agrarian revolution, the advantages and disadvantages of their agricultural research and extension programs, and the adequacy or inadequacies of the food supply, as do vivid inside documentaries of the Chinese countryside. Not all are in agreement (see *For Further Reading*).

This book does not attempt to decipher the economic and social impacts of the historical past of the Soviet model with its emphasis on heavy industry, the Great Leap Forward (1958-1959), the ironically misnamed Cultural Revolution (now officially called the "Ten (1966 to 1976) Disastrous Years"), the smashing (purging) of the Gang of Four, or the propagandization of the Four Modernizations. References will be made, however, to private plots, free markets, sideline industries, and family, village, township and county enterprises; and to the market-driven responsibility production program in which, under the regime of Deng Xiaoping--China's *de facto* leader--and Premier Zhao Ziyang family farming, has in one sense been re-established. Today, the state owns the land but the families have the responsibility of looking after it.

To use land and people more efficiently (land is limited, people are surplus), China, with the state holding ownership, has returned the land to families and small groups to farm. The "responsibility production system" (*Zhe Renzhi*) in force since 1979 and now extended to virtually all of China, is alive and thriving. Agricultural production has risen by almost 8% per year and rural incomes have more than doubled since 1981, with exports expanding from $7 to $27 billion. The proportion of rural poverty has dropped from 31% in 1979 to 6% in 1986. Hunger has essentially been banished.

It is a simple deal between government and peasant. The peasant contracts to deliver a certain amount of an agricultural commodity that he produces at a fair price. In return, he is free to produce--by himself or with a group--as much more as he can and, to a certain extent, sell it for whatever price he can get.

One important feature of the responsibility production system is that it allows specialized households. For example, one can concentrate on raising hogs, fish, chickens or ducks; producing peaches, grapes or melons; or growing greenhouse vegetables without having to worry about producing grain. One may also engage, for a secondary income, in other profit-making enterprises or sideline industries; this profit one keeps.

As will appear in the pages of this book every aspect of food production and all agricultural commodities are being impacted by the responsibility system. Increasing agricultural output is one, but may not be the most important objective. Agriculture in China is moving steadily toward diversification, specialization, commercialization and modernization. Diversification, resulting in great production of commodities other than grain (e.g. livestock, fish and lumber) is a major objective. This leads to greater income for farmers, establishes personal property, creates industries in the countryside, and puts more emphasis on non-farm production, thereby reducing the desire to migrate to cities. While farmers remain "tenants of the state," the state is fully committed to the contract responsibility system of agricultural production which is the basis for decision priority. All of this is moving toward a mixed cooperative and private agricultural marketing system. Most everyone seems to have great enthusiasm for the system and its future. Farmers are encouraged to unite in production policies through cooperative systems on the basis of their individual enthusiasm. One may well raise the question, however, as to how long a system will survive where the peasant farmer may earn ten times more than a government official, airline pilot or factory worker. A second question arises as to whether the rapid growth in agricultural output (above 5% a year) can be maintained. Annual increases of even 3 to 4% per year are hard to maintain. Will a plateau be reached before the end of the 1980s? No country with a centrally controlled economy has tried to move so far, let alone so fast, toward a free market economy.

Again, no factor in the Chinese economy has affected food production more positively than that of the responsibility production system. It is bringing about major adjustments and transitions in Chinese agriculture. The first could be labeled *economization*. Marketing and marketing economics are assuming a dimension as never before. What to plant or produce, and when, are now issues of profit or loss. Production of rapeseed in 1985, for example, was much more profitable than growing wheat, and there was a falling-off of wheat production over the previous year. Second is the emphasis on *diversification*. Farmers are going to grow or produce that which is most profitable. A third area of transition relates to *modernization*. More scientific and enlightened farming systems will result. Farms will increase in size. Only the best farmers will survive as competition will become increasingly severe. *Mechanization* will also eventually increase. Food production, however, will remain labor intensive. Mechanization should not be equated with modernization. Farmers with secondary incomes (part-time farming), common in the U.S.A., Western Europe and Japan, are appearing. So far, tractors are used more to haul crops than to till the soil. Centers for the service of farm equipment and purchase of parts, fertilizers and other inputs will assume an increasingly important role. China is now walking a tightrope between the need to move cautiously and slowly to avoid massive unemployment and migration to the cities during this process. Finally, *private* enthusiasm, innovation and creativity will replace the *collective*. This may put a damper, at least temporarily, on mechanization but not production.

The primary focus in this volume is on agricultural, primarily food production, technologies--traditional and modern--that now enable China to feed its billion-plus people. Attention is also given to the effective management of resources--land, water, energy, wastes, byproducts, fertilizers and pesticides. Emphasis is on food-producing systems and not on the non-food components of crop production agriculture such as rubber, cotton, silk, mulberry bushes, tea and tobacco. The authors are mindful that China is the native land of tea and the first country in the world to discover and make use of this beverage. Likewise, China is the place of origin of silkworm breeding and the mulberry tree. Chinese silks are known all over the world for their elegance and craftsmanship, historically designated as the "Magnificent Rosy Clouds of Dawn from the Orient" which were exported via the "Silk Road."

The approach, herein, is nontechnical, and combines the efforts primarily of three Chinese agricultural scientists and an American who has traveled extensively and observed Chinese food production technologies firsthand.

Reliability of statistical information on Chinese agricultural production, inputs and outputs, natural resources, crops, livestock, fishery and forestry has much improved since 1978. Until recently, there has been a scarcity of data concerning Chinese agriculture. Relevant statistical information for this book was derived from various United States Department of Agriculture Economic Research Service Reports, such as the annual China Situation and Outlook Reports; reports of missions sponsored by the Committee on Scholarly Communications with the People's Republic of China; reports of the U.S. National Academy of Science, the World Bank Country Studies, and those obtained directly from the Chinese Statistical Bureau; and the extensive reports of the Ministry of Agriculture, Animal Husbandry and Fishery yearbooks. English translations of crucial information were provided by Mr. Qu Ningkang of the Division of Science and Technology Exchange Bureau of Science and Technology of the Ministry of Agriculture, Animal Husbandry and Fishery; by Mr. Zhao Weijun of the Scientific Information Institute of the Chinese Academy of Agricultural Sciences; and by the co-authors.

Attention in this book is directed to the mainland provinces of China. Only occasionally are references made to the province of Taiwan and other islands, although they are included in all maps of China found in this volume. The senior author and editor is familiar with food-producing systems in Taiwan, having served as the agricultural advisor from 1981-1986 as a member of the Science and Technology Advisory Group for the Executive Yuan.

Agricultural development, followed by industrialization proceeded at a rapid pace in Taiwan during the decades of the 1950s, 1960s and 1970s. There was no "cultural revolution" there. The current responsibility production contract system in China is not applicable to Taiwan. Mechanization has proceeded at a more rapid pace in Taiwan. Yet mainland China and Taiwan have many things in common, such as the predominance of rice and the importance of sweet potatoes, sugarcane, Beijing ducks, peanuts, litchee, pigs, aquatic resources, Chinese cabbage, tomatoes, and watermelons; and, as on the mainland, small farms predominate. Methods of food preparation have a familiar ring, as do some of those for waste recycling. Crops such as wheat, maize, rapeseed, sugar beets, cotton and even soybeans are grown only in limited areas, if at all, in Taiwan.

Chinese agriculture today is more than crop production, although the food crops still predominate. Agriculture includes the rapidly expanding sideline industries of animal husbandry (beef cattle, dairy cows, pigs, sheep and goats), poultry (chickens, ducks, geese), rabbits, forestry and fisheries (fresh and saltwater). The rise of sideline industries--often described as family, village, township and countryside enterprises--has given rise to many part-time farmers, producing secondary incomes in increasing numbers. Gone are the communes and state farms with their brigades of workers. Much of the planting, tilling and harvesting of crops is now done by individual farm families early in the morning and late in the afternoon, before and after working in the factories. Meanwhile, some farmers are getting rich.

Forestry is becoming increasingly important for the production of wood, timber and logs. Even more important is its recognized value for land and water stabilization, for its prevention of soil erosion, as "greenwalls" or windbreaks, for beautification, and for fuel. There is also a major transition now occurring in China from using crop residues for fuel to using firewood. The crop residues are being added to the soil to build up the organic matter.

China has one of the most ancient histories (over 7,000 years) of any nation and it is rural China that dominates that history. Although China has a vast land area, land use for food production holds a high priority. The nation has widely fluctuating climates and geography and is unevenly endowed with resources of soil, water and energy. The good soils are not where the water is and the hydroelectric power potentials are not in the heavily industrialized areas. Most of the countryside of China consists of mountains, plateaus, gobi, deserts and areas otherwise unsuited for agriculture (Figure 1). Hills and mountains cover 65% of the total land area. Northern and western China are too dry or too cold for intensive cultivation, except with irrigation. Few are the places in China with potentials for crop production where mountains are not in view on a clear day. There are still uncertainties as to the actual cultivated land area in China. While 100 million hectares is often designated, the actual area could be 25 to 35% higher. Even at the highest estimate, the amount of cultivated land hardly exceeds the 317 million acres (130 million hectares) planted to crops in the U.S.A. in 1985. About 11% of the land area is usually referred to as "under cultivation" and this equates to only a quarter of an acre (approximately 1/10 hectare or 1.5 mu) of tillable land for each inhabitant. The United States has eight times that amount.

Figure 1. The agricultural regions of China.

The hillsides of China are graded into millions of hectares of terraces. They have the appearance of giant steps one above the other. Terracing, however, is not new in China. It dates back at least 2,000 years and reflects generations of back-breaking labor in turning mountain slopes into tillable fields.

There are 1,300,000 hectares of land currently subject to severe wind and water erosion. Twenty percent of China consists of mountains and plateaus in excess of 3,000 meters in elevation. Eighty percent (over 800 million) of the Chinese live in the countryside, and over 90% live in a land area roughly comparable to the eastern half of the United States--a region about equal to that extending from Minnesota southward to Louisiana and eastward to the Atlantic. The Chinese population in comparable areas is six times the density of the eastern United States. Accordingly, China has, of necessity, developed clever forms of land use and food utilization.

The agriculture of China's past has been aptly described by F. H. King the author of *Farmers of Forty Centuries*. This volume as well as a much earlier one *An Agricultural Encyclopedia of the Sixth Century* or Qi Min Yao Shu and still older works describe farming techniques as they were developed, refined and passed down by peasants through the centuries (see Chapter 2, "Agricultural History Over Seven Thousand Years").

It is generally conceded that the well-defined limits of natural resources (land, water, climate and energy) for agriculture and food production, especially in China, provide a strong motivation for family planning. China has had an egalitarian food distribution policy and continually attempts to provide a healthy, albeit austere, diet for everyone. The approach has been to feed people with grains and vegetation first and then with livestock products. But Chinese people have a pent-up demand for improved diets, which means more animal products, fruits and vegetables. This book emphasizes how China is attempting to meet the demand for higher quality food and projecting its needs for more and better food for the future (see Chapter 35, "More and Better Food for the Future--Prospects to the Year 2,000"). This will be done through increased crop yields, improved management of natural resources, a leap forward in animal agriculture and fishery and improvements in the agricultural environment.

China is not an ordinary agriculturally developing country. Generalizing about any aspect of agricultural development (crop production, irrigation, plant protection, animal husbandry, forestry, fisheries or mechanization) of the Chinese subcontinent is hazardous. Its current agricultural production systems are a curious mixture of the ancient, the traditional and the ultramodern. While many practices in food production, the recycling of wastes, water management and land use date back centuries, the Chinese have developed new technologies that have astonished the world's scientific community, especially for the major food staples--rice, wheat and corn--which supply well over half of China's food.

Biological innovations in Chinese agriculture include the following. The first semi-dwarf rice varieties were released in 1959, seven years before the International Rice Research Institute released its first IR-8 variety (see Chapter 11, "Miracles of Rice"). China was the first nation, in the 1970s to develop and popularize hybrid rice. Techniques for rapidly stabilizing important varietal characteristics, which were first developed in China, are now widely adopted and studied elsewhere. The Chinese have pioneered in wheat breeding for dwarfness, cold hardiness, adaptation for the humid tropics, maximum yield trials, and identifying germplasm resistant to rust and scab (see Chapter 12, "Wheat Campaigns"). Hybrids predominate for corn and cover over 75% of the area planted (see Chapter 13, "The Rise of Corn"). Haploid culture (regeneration of new plants from pollen grains rather than embryos and having a single gene complement) for rice is the most advanced in the world. Several new varieties have recently been introduced, and very promising results are now being obtained with wheat and corn (see Chapter 32, "Test Tube Plants"). With haploid culture, new varieties with remarkable uniformity can be obtained in three generations, whereas the usual hybridization techniques require ten or more.

There has been significant research in *Azolla* culture, a field in which the Chinese now exercise world leadership. *Azolla* appears naturally as a green scum on the surface of the water in rice paddies. It is a source of biologically-fixed nitrogen for rice and is a high protein feed for pigs. This is only one example of many where the Chinese have improved nutrient availability for crops.

All of the above biological advances have been complemented by improvements in the land base (see Chapters 6, 9, "Good Crops From Salty Soils" and "Organic Farming--Growing Plants the Organic Way"), improved management and control of water resources (see Chapter 4, "Water Resources--the Lifeline of Chinese Agriculture"), and many innovations in developing rural energy resources (see Chapter 10, "Energy Resources in the Countryside"). The overall result is that China's grain production has been steadily upward and progressively less subject to annual fluctuations from weather (floods, drought). The negative direction has not exceeded 7% since the disasters of the early 1960s. This is in sharp contrast to the records of the U.S.S.R. and the U.S.A. (Figure 2).

Climate should be considered both a resource to be used wisely and a hazard to be dealt with. It is a major factor affecting land use in any country. The vicissitudes of China's climate have made crop production hazardous, perhaps more so than in any other land areas of comparable size. The variability of precipitation is repeated almost every year, with floods in the South and droughts in the North. To this end, the Chinese have pursued two technologies: one ancient, that of irrigating to lessen the hazards of drought; the other modern, using plastic covers and mulches for crops to diminish the effects of adverse temperatures, droughts and hot, drying winds.

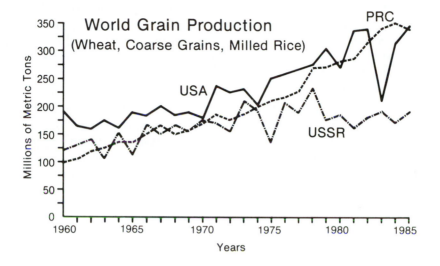

Figure 2. Comparative grain production patterns in the USA, PRC, and the USSR from 1960 to 1985.

Large-scale crop irrigation schemes date back over 2,000 years, and today approximately 50% of all crop land in China is irrigated, resulting in more cropping area that is irrigated than in any other nation. For the U.S.A. only 15% of the total crop land is irrigated. The world's oldest existing irrigation system, which is called the "Dujiangyan" and dates to about 200 B.C., may be seen today in the Chengdu Plain of Sichuan Province (see Chapter 4, "Water Resources--The Lifeline of Chinese Agriculture"). The importance of water control--the interplay between irrigated lands in the higher reaches and the flood-prone lower basins-- has remained central throughout the history of Chinese agriculture. Men who developed the capacity to control the behavior of water have become and remain cultural heroes to hundreds of millions of chinese.

The use of plastic soil mulches for agricultural production began in 1979 and has since grown almost exponentially each year through 1985. It now totals 1.3 million hectares and has become the most expansive development of protected cultivation for crop production on earth (see Chapter 31, "The Plastic Revolution"). Irrigation, organic manures, plastic covers and mulches have improved both the stability and magnitude of crop production. Chairman Mao Zedong considered water the most critical input for raising agricultural yields per unit of land area. This is now strikingly true not only for China but for the other four most populous nations on earth: India, the U.S.S.R., the U.S.A. and Indonesia.

Fertilizer usage in China is heavily skewed toward irrigated lands, resulting in stable yields of rice, wheat, corn and vegetables. Significant increases in fertilizer use, both organic and chemical, have occurred, especially since 1976. Chemical fertilizer usage increased more rapidly than organic, and was greater than that of any other country for a comparable period (1976-82). Meanwhile, China has become the world's third largest chemical fertilizer producer and user, following the U.S.A. and the U.S.S.R. The outlook is for continued expansion.

Beyond the use of commercial fertilizers and animal manures, the Chinese maintain the productivity and fertility of soils with applications of human excrement or night soil, waterlogged compost ("Caotang Sludge"), and canal and pond mud. Ashes from the combustion of plant materials supply considerable potash, and azolla culture is an important source of nitrogen for rice culture, especially in the southern provinces. Oil cakes--the residues from oil seeds of soybean, rape, cotton, and sesame--have been used as fertilizer, but recently it has been found more profitable to feed them to livestock.

Residues from animal manures, following anaerobic digestion which produces methane, are also important fertilizers for crops. Eighty percent of the fertilizers used on vegetable crops in 1977 was organic. Today it is somewhat less but still exceeds 50%. Composts are still seen everywhere in the vegetable-producing areas. China probably has the world's most efficient system of waste recycling. Great emphasis is currently being placed on pig manure, both as a fertilizer and for the generation of methane (biogas). Over 300 million pigs in China help meet the ever-expanding demands for animal protein by transforming aquatic plants and other coarse feed substances into human food and fertilizers for crop production.

China has long been recognized as the Rice Bowl of the Far East. With 24% of the world's land devoted to rice, China produces over 36% of the world's supply or about 178 million metric tons in 1984. This dropped to 169 million in 1985. The Chinese people like rice and it is nutritious. Rice yields (5.4 metric tons per hectare) in China, up from 4.0 in 1980, exceed the world's average of 3.2 metric tons per hectare and are well above the average for Southeast Asia. Cultivated in the wet paddy fields, it is among the highest yielding of the cereal grains. Rice, as distinct from other cereal grains, is almost entirely consumed directly as human food. Some rice is now used in formulated feeds for pigs. The oldest remains of cultivated rice have been found in eastern China and northern India and date back over 7,000 years.

The agricultural revolution of the 1980s in China is not confined to rice. Overall rural production grew 52.4% between 1978 and 1984, with crop production at 47% and a gain of 71% for livestock. Other rural sectors--forestry, fisheries and household sideline industries--gained 50 to 100%. China became the number one wheat and cotton producer in 1984-85, second in corn production and third in soybeans. Wheat production reached a record 88 million metric tons in 1984, an increase of 40% even though the area did not change appreciably from 1981. Rice yields during the same period rose by 30%, and cotton a phenomenal 175%. During the very writing of this volume, we have witnessed the most extensive agricultural production revolution history has thus far recorded. Included are economic incentives (the responsibility production system), influxes of advanced and traditional technologies, a generally favorable climate with no major natural disasters, and increased availability of inputs (fertilizers, pesticides, machinery and irrigation). Meanwhile, China has now become an exporter of major agricultural commodities (rice, wheat, corn, soybeans and cotton).

China, the land of fish and rice, has a 3,000 year history of fish culture. In fish breeding, China is a world leader. Fish ponds are often surrounded with mulberry bushes, and as the silkworms eat the mulberry leaves, their droppings fall into the ponds and are used for feeding the fish. Integrated farming systems can produce 2,500 ducks or 250 pigs in combination with one hectare of fish ponds. (The ducks are also used to control weeds and insects in rice paddies, where they occupy a unique ecological niche in the food system). The livestock and poultry manure, which filters or drops into the ponds, is the main food used to produce up to 6 metric tons of fish per year per hectare with little or no other feed supplement. Many other by-products, including human wastes, are recycled into integrated fish farming systems. China also has many ponds and lakes stocked with mixed cultures of many species chosen for varying water depths. Some feed on grass and other vegetation. Following the fish harvest, the ponds are often drained and the mud is used for fertilizer. Progress in fish culture in China is based, to a considerable extent, on supplementary feeding, much of which comes from agricultural wastes. Experiments are in progress to make use of fibrous vegetable matter, material which, in China and elsewhere, is available in much larger quantities than the amounts of grain produced.

The Chinese produce and consume large quantities of a great variety of succulent or green vegetables. There are "greens in the water," or aquatic vegetables as well as those produced on land. Immature vegetation used for human food assures high digestibility as well as important proteins, minerals and vitamins. Harvesting vegetation in the immature stages enables production in a shorter period of time and more harvests per year. In some of the southern provinces, as many as ten vegetable crops are grown on the same land in a single year, resulting in one of the most intensive farming systems in the world. There are hundreds of crop combinations associated with the inter-cropping of vegetables (see Chapter 21, "Vegetable Abundance--From Yardlong Cowpeas to Bitter Melons").

The following quotation is from *A Preliminary Survey of the Book, Qi Min Yao Shu, An Agricultural Encyclopedia of the Sixth Century*, by Shih Sheng-han (Science press, Beijing, 1974):

> Lucid apprehension of the natural requirements of plants does not mean passive waiting. Quite on the contrary, as the old Chinese saying ("human resolution can overcome Heaven's destiny") goes, the Chinese peasants have the unquenchable determination to wrestle with any crop under the most unfavorable conditions by their incessant labor. By observing and fulfilling the demands of the objects of cultivation, rarities can be produced in the most unpromising spot and time. This also explains why the ancient Chinese people have domesticated, and afterwards also successfully imported, so many kinds of fruits, nuts, culinary and industrial plants. Thus warmhouse greens for ritual services were on record in the Han (-2nd cent.) and alfalfa, peas, grapes, and walnuts have been imported about the same time.

Almost all fruits--tree fruits both deciduous and tropical, soft fruits (berries) and nuts--found elsewhere in the world are also found in China. They range from the exotic litchi in the South to the hardiest of apples, pears, and plums in the Northeastern provinces and the Hami melons and white seedless grapes of the Xinjiang Autonomous Region. New early-ripening varieties of watermelons have found a special spot in China. Almost five billion kilograms were harvested in 1985 and even more in 1986. During the heat of the summer, they are China's most popular thirst-quenchers, and satisfy a taste for sweetness (unlike the U.S.A., where soft drinks are the most widely used beverage exceeding even that of water). Sales of watermelons in China far exceed those of soft drinks or any other fruit. There is a wealth of other unexploited genetic resources for both fruits and vegetables (see Chapter 23, "Indigenous and Exotic Fruits").

Nuts are grown extensively as well as found in the wild in China. However, with the exception of the peanut, considered an oil crop, they are not given special attention in this book. Many nuts are consumed raw as well as roasted. They include peanuts, chestnuts, walnuts, hazelnuts (filberts), beetlenuts, almonds, pine kernels or pinenuts, melon, sunflower and pumpkin seeds, gingko and cashews.

When the outside world thinks of China, it thinks of rice and chopsticks. But the one ever-present food is Chinese cabbage. It is the common vegetable staple, with species and types regionally adapted to suit the needs and appetites of the people. Chinese cabbage is the lifeline, year-round vegetable for the Chinese. Several crops a year are produced in the southern provinces, and production in the North is supplemented by crops grown in plastic greenhouses and under plastic row covers in the late fall and early spring. Large quantities are stored for winter use in the North. For eating, it is boiled, stewed, fried and pickled (see Chapter 22, "Chinese Cabbage--Year-Round").

Soybeans originated in China, most likely in what is now the Heilongjiang Province. The native types, found alongside the cultivated varieties, constitute one of the world's richest and largely untapped food resources. Annual production of soybeans in China approximates 10 million metric tons grown on 7 to 8 million hectares of land. They are found as far south as the Vietnamese border and extend to the 50th latitude north, at elevations as high as 500 meters. Soybeans, in a variety of food preparations, are a significant source of protein in the Chinese diet. They are also important as an intercrop and for soil improvement in field rotations (see Chapter 14, "Soybeans--The Miracle Bean of China").

China's record in feeding its people is worthy of note when compared to most other agriculturally developing nations, especially those nations having more favorable land/population ratios. Visitors of today and for the past decade have seen in China a nation of people that appear to be happy, healthy, well clothed and adequately nourished. There are no beggars or drunks. The cities are generally clean, with flower- and tree-lined roadsides. This is in a country where hunger has been common for centuries and catastrophic regional famines were annual events. Memories of starvation are still live for many of the aged Chinese people.

The high consumption of vegetarian (plant) products, supplemented with still limited quantities of fish, pork and poultry, accounts in part for the high density of people per unit of cultivated land. This enables Chinese farmers to eke out a living on very small land areas. "Tofu" or bean curd, rice and vegetables make a balanced diet for the Chinese. Rice is the predominant grain in most provinces but wheat, corn, sorghum and millet are prominent in others.

The Chinese eat almost everything. It is said that they eat all things with wings except an airplane, all creatures with furs except dusters, anything with legs except a stool or a table, and everything that swims or floats. What the Chinese do not eat for pleasure they may well take for medicine. Hundreds, even thousands, of plants contribute to native or traditional Chinese medical treatments. Concoctions of several items rather than the single prescriptions typical of Western medicines are the rule (see Chapter 25, "Plants to Keep People Healthy"). Important considerations with respect to food for the Chinese are that it should be fresh and should require as little fuel as possible for cooking. Thus, stir frying with vegetable oils (see Chapter 20, "Diverse Sources of Edible Oils") which involves a continuous turning of the food and which seals in the nutrients, is the common mode of food preparation.

Nevertheless, there are problems of seasonal as well as chronic food surpluses, shortages and malnutrition. Problems of losses in post-harvest handling of food products reach enormous proportions. As much as 50% of China's harvest of fruits and vegetables in some areas never reach the consumer. Improved utilization of what is produced is the challenge for the future. This means advances in post-harvest handling, transportation, and food processing and preservation. This is true even though most of the food consumed in China has a very limited or narrow circuit in the production, marketing and consumption cycle. Local production plays a predominant role in feeding the people. While this has many advantages, it has created pockets of malnutrition, especially with some of the trace elements such as selenium and iodine, which would otherwise not occur if food commodities were derived over a wider geographical area.

Scientific achievements in food production have extended beyond the Western nations that first produced them. As agricultural science advances and new food-producing technologies are developed, the threat of famine retreats. China has a history of 150 generations of farmers, through 40 centuries, devoted to gardening. The Chinese are more like gardeners than farmers and are adept at ecological, self-sufficient, sustainable agricultural systems. Hillsides and slopes are terraced and rimmed to conserve soil and water; nightsoil and every other kind of manure is applied to the land; special composts are formulated; legumes are grown to enrich the soil and crop rotations are meticulously followed.

The environmental challenges (soil erosion, deforestation, sand encroachment, desertification, overgrazing, floods, land decline, soil salinity, dust storms and droughts) associated with either stabilized or enhanced food production in China are enormous. These are also global environmental problems. Rivers truly drain the blood of China. The Yellow River is often called "the Sorrow of China," winding its long way through the extremely vulnerable Loess Plateau of the Northwest and Inner Mongolia. It has the highest content of sediment of any river in the world, and the silt raises the riverbed by a foot a year in some areas. Yet some remarkable environmental achievements have been made in China during the past thirty years in reforestation, the establishment of windbreaks or "green walls," desert and salty soil reclamation, water management, pest and disease control and environmental improvement. These will be described in the pages which follow.

Two general types of food production technologies characterize present world agriculture. The one is highly mechanized and becoming automated, and is capital intensive. The other is labor intensive and sparing of natural resources. The first characterizes much of the current U.S.A. agricultural production system and results in an output for farm workers that is the highest in the world. Similar systems exist or are emerging in Canada, certain elements of the European community, Australia, New Zealand, Brazil and Argentina.

The second type of technology is not as productive per farm worker but is higher yielding per unit land area, often has a higher cropping index and is more sparing of natural resources. This system characterizes the current Japanese, Indonesian, Western European, Korean and Chinese systems. Because of future constraints in the costs and availability of natural resources, an inevitable shift will occur in the United States and in other nations with similar agricultural systems from less of a natural resource-based to a more scientific and biologically-based agriculture. Our world is now moving from a demand-driven economy with perceived unlimited natural resources to a natural resource-limited economy.

For the decades ahead, we may project that the agriculture of the Western world will be in juxtaposition with China and much of the Far East. Technologies that will increase outputs and reduce inputs, such as those which are traditionally Chinese, might serve as models to aid farmers--not only in agriculturally developing countries faced with soils of low fertility, limited water supplies and severe pest control problems but also in the Western world--cutting economic, energy and environmental costs. Almost all future increases in production will have to come as a result of increases in yield (output per unit land area per unit time) and from growing additional crops during a given year on the same land. Here the Chinese have been uniquely successful. There are really no other long-time viable options.

In view of current world food problems, Sino-African cooperation for agricultural development should be encouraged. Areas of focus for increasing food production could be the role of economic incentives and the blending of modern production technologies with the traditional. These would include water management, the use of organic fertilizers, biogas energy production, integrated management of grain production and pest control, protected cultivation, and the reclamation of problem soils so successfully carried out in China. China has also made major progress in flood control, construction of water diversion canals, irrigation of new lands and water conservation. Good crops are now being grown on reclaimed salty soils and the drainage of those that were waterlogged.

Agriculture in China includes crop production, animal husbandry, fishery and forestry. During the decade of the 1980s, with grain self-sufficiency having been achieved, there has been a rising interest in and remarkable expansion in oil seed production, cotton, animal husbandry, forestry and fisheries. Afforestation has proceeded beyond that of any other nation, and even beyond the expectations of the Chinese. The results are having positive impacts on land and water stabilization, on reductions in soil erosion, as protective barriers for crops and livestock against wind, desert and sand encroachments, and on the maximization of both food and tree crop production. The least heralded and most important of all has been a shift to using firewood and logs for fuel instead of crop residues, which can now be added back to the soil to build up and maintain the organic matter.

Technologies that will increase outputs and spare inputs are now as important for the agriculturally developed world as for developing nations. Many of these are now in progress in China and are described in the chapters which follow.

Similarly, the products and practices of Chinese agriculture--many of them unique and of considerable curiosity to peoples of the Western world, and all of them important for feeding over a billion people--will be described.

Agriculture in China is shaping the lives of 800 million people. That is roughly one-third of the world's farm population. Hence, the Chinese experience in food-producing systems should be of great significance and interest to the rest of the world, still struggling, as is China, to provide and deliver an adequate, nutritious and wholesome diet to its people.

FOR FURTHER READING

Buck, J. L. 1938. *Land utilization in China*. Nanjing: Commercial Press.

Hsu, R. C. 1982. *Food for one billion: China's agriculture since 1949*. Boulder, Colo.: Westview Press.

IDEALS. 1985. *Proceedings on agriculture in China*. Vol. 1, *Challenges and opportunities*. Beltsville, Md.: Institute of International Development and Education in Agriculture and Life Sciences.

Institute of the History of Natural Sciences. Chinese Academy of Sciences. 1983. *Ancient China's technology and science*. China Knowledge Series. Beijing: Foreign Language Press.

King, F. H. 1911. *Farmers of forty centuries*. Emmaus, Pa.: Rodale Press, Inc.

Lardy, N. R. 1978. *Economic growth and distribution in China*. New York: Cambridge University Press.

———. 1983. *Agriculture in China's modern economic development*. New York: Cambridge University Press.

———. 1984. Prices, markets, and the Chinese peasant. In *Agricultural development in the Third World*, ed. C. K. Eicher and J. M. Staatz, 420-35. Baltimore: Johns Hopkins University Press.

Leeming, F. 1985. *Rural China today*. New York: Longman Group, Ltd.

Mosher, S. W. 1983. *Broken earth--The rural Chinese*. New York: The Free Press.

———. 1983. *Journey to the forbidden China*. New York: The Free Press.

Nai-ruenn Chen; Chi-ming Hou; and Yi-chang Yin. 1983. Agricultural development in China: Mainland and Taiwan, 1952-1975. In *Conference on the agricultural development in China, Japan and Korea*, 893-1019. Taipei: Academia Sinica, Institute of Economics.

Opletal, H. 1983. China's agrarian revolution. *D + C. Development and Cooperation* 5 (September/October): 19-20.

Perkins, D. H. 1968. *Agricultural development in China--1368-1968*. Chicago: Aldine Publishing Company.

Plucknett, D. L., and H. L. Beemer, Jr. 1981. *Vegetable farming systems in China*. Boulder, Colo.: Westview Press, Inc.

Schell, O. 1984. A reporter at large (China). *The New Yorker*, 23 January.

———. 1984. *To get rich is glorious*. New York: Random House, Inc.

Shih Sheng-Han. 1974. *A preliminary survey of the book, "Ch'i Min Yao Shu": An agricultural encyclopedia of the 6th century*. Beijing: Science Press.

Smil, V. 1981. China's agro-ecosystem. *Agro-Ecosystems* 7:27-46.

———. 1981. China's food: Availability, composition, prospects. *Food Policy* 6(2): 67-77.

———. 1983. *The bad earth: Environmental degradation in China*. Armonk, N.Y.: M. E. Sharp, Inc.

———. 1985. China's food. *Scientific American* 253:116-24.

Stavis, B. 1978. Agricultural research and extension services in China. *World Development* 6:631-45.

———. 1985. Some initial results of China's new agricultural policies. *World Development* 13(12): 1299-1305.

Sung, M. 1985. China plans sweeping reforms in science. *Science* 228:559-60.

Tang, A. M. 1984. A critical appraisal of the Chinese model of development. In *Agricultural development in the Third World*, ed. C. K. Eicher and J. M. Staatz, 403-19. Baltimore: Johns Hopkins University Press.

Tang, A. M., and B. Stone. 1980. *Food production in the People's Republic of China*. Research Report #15. Washington, D.C.: International Food Policy Research Institute.

Tong, B. T. 1984. *Science and technology in China*. London: Longman Group, Ltd.

Trescott, P. B. 1985. Incentives versus equity: What does China's recent experience show? *World Development* 13(2): 205-17.

U.S. Department of Agriculture. Economic Research Service. 1984, 1985, 1986. *China outlook and situation report*. Washington, D.C.: Government Printing Office.

Walker, K. R. 1984. *Food grain procurement and consumption in China*. New York: Cambridge University Press.

World Bank. 1983. *China--Socialist economic development* 1: 105-71. Washington, D.C.

2

AGRICULTURAL HISTORY OVER SEVEN THOUSAND YEARS

by Yu Youtai

The story of agriculture in China is one of persistent struggles against nature, and rich experiences gained over thousands of years of productive practice. It is an account of meticulous farming, crop rotations, use of organic fertilizers, intensive cultivation, integrated farming systems, and transitions from one crop or type of livestock to another. Ancient books on agriculture have been preserved and present great detail concerning production practices from as long ago as the sixteenth century B.C.

From the beginning of Chinese history, agriculture served as the foundation of the national economy. Chinese agriculture originated in the primitive society of the early and middle New Stone Age. It then went through over 1,300 years of the Slave Society and over 2,700 years of Feudal Society, and finally entered the age of Socialist Society. Altogether, it has undergone a history of over 7,000 years (Table 1).

Mythology and Archaeology

The Chinese people collectively struggled against nature, while at the same time recognizing, mastering and utilizing objective laws of nature. Not having written records in primitive society, the people applied and cherished the memories of these struggles; but they always gave credit to deified prehistoric mythical heroes for any major achievements in agricultural production. Many beautiful mythological stories were composed by the people. Among the most famous characters were Shen Nong and Hou Ji. The tales about Shen Nong showed that the Chinese people had entered the period of agriculture from the age of fishing, hunting and gathering very early.

Shen Nong (Figure 1) was also called Emperor Yan, the spirit of the sun, and had a twofold nature as both an agricultural and a medical god. From the agricultural god came the mythical tradition of a being with a "human head and oxen body" and of "millets falling down like rain from

TABLE 1
Some Highlights of Chinese Agricultural History

Approximate Years[1]	Highlights
5000-2100 B.C. (New Stone Age in Primitive Society)	Farming villages established in the Wei and Yellow River valleys. Millet, wheat, beans, rice, hemp, cabbage and melon cultivated. Human labor followed by farming implements of stone and wood. Bareland cultivation. Stone mortar and pestle for grinding grain invented.
2100-476 B.C. (Slave Society)	
1600-1100 B.C. (Shang Dynasty)	Bronze farm tools introduced. Chinese characters inscribed on bones or tortoise shells.
770-476 B.C. (Spring and Autumn)	Use of iron plow drawn by oxen. Description of "5 grains" (millet, glutinous millet, soybeans, wheat, rice). Fallow land farming introduced. Water-lifting implements invented
475 B.C.-A.D. 1840 (Feudal Society)	
475-221 B.C. (Warring States)	Flood control and irrigation well developed. Regionalization of agriculture. Ridge farming and crop rotations introduced. Value of animal manures established. Expansion of winter wheat production. Food-processing equipment and technologies developed.
221-207 B.C. (Qin Dynasty)	Great Wall constructed.
206 B.C.-A.D. 220 (Han Dynasty)	Intensive farming, intercropping, multiple cropping, and bed culture developed. Sowing plow and dragon-bone water lift invented. Expansion of paddy rice production.
581-618 (Sui Dynasty)	Grand Canal constructed.
618-907 (Tang Dynasty)	Plow with a bend beam invented.
1127-1279 (Southern Song Dynasty)	Concept of constant renewal of soil fertility introduced.
1368-1644 (Ming Dynasty)	Corn and sweet potatoes introduced.
1644-1840 (Qing Dynasty)	Multiple cropping extended over all China.

[1]The dates given for each highlight may not always coincide with the official dynasty dates.

Shen Nong as the mythical medical god, tasting grasses for medicinal purposes.

Shen Nong as the mythical agricultural god teaching people farming.

Hou Ji, a mythical agricultural god, is said to have supplied the world with different grain seeds for planting.

Figure 1. Chinese mythological gods.

heaven." As a god of medicine, the mythical tradition recounted "knowing the nature of a hundred different kinds of grasses by whipping them with a reddish brown whip," and "encountering seventy poisonous grasses a day when he tasted the nature of a hundred kinds of grasses."

Two mythical traditions surround Hou Ji. One said that he, as the son of the Emperor of Heaven, brought to man's world a hundred different kinds of grain seeds for planting. The other said that he played games of planting hemp and beans when he was very young, became good at farming, and as an adult taught the people how to cultivate. Finally, he was assigned to be an agricultural official.

During recent decades, many ruins of primitive societies have been unearthed and large numbers of archaeological studies conducted in various areas of China. According to human fossils, materials and implements preserved in these ruins, the inference was drawn that the Old Stone Age in China started about 1,000,000 years ago and the New Stone Age about 10,000 years ago. Up to the 1970s, large numbers of agricultural implements, crop seeds and domesticated animal bones of the New Stone Age were excavated in many provinces and regions. Investigations of these materials showed that Chinese agriculture had a history of more than 7,000 years. Several kinds of New Stone Age tools are illustrated in Figure 2. Crop seeds excavated from the New Stone Age included: proso-millet, millet, rice, beans, hemp, peanut, cabbage, lotus, water chestnut, melon, peach, date and chestnut.

According to tradition, Chinese characters were created by Cang Ji in the early years of the New Stone Age, but this cannot be established with certainty. As far as we know now, the earliest Chinese characters were inscribed on bones or tortoise (land-loving turtles) shells excavated in Anyang county of Henan Province at the end of the nineteenth century (Figure 3). These inscriptions, made around the fourteenth century B.C., preserved records of the collective production of agriculture and of animal husbandry in the Chinese Slave Society.

Ancient Books on Agriculture

The earliest book which systematically recorded Chinese agricultural activities was *Xia Xiao Zheng*. It was the calendar of the Xia Dynasty, estimated to have been written around the sixteenth century B.C. Its collection of approximately 400 words recorded the knowledge of agriculture, astronomy and medicine in the early and middle period of the Chinese Slave Society. It stated that the land and people all belonged to the emperor (the Son of Heaven). "Lei" was the chief implement for turning the soil. The main crops were broom millet, grain millet, wheat, rice, bean, hemp, vegetables and melons. Problems mentioned in

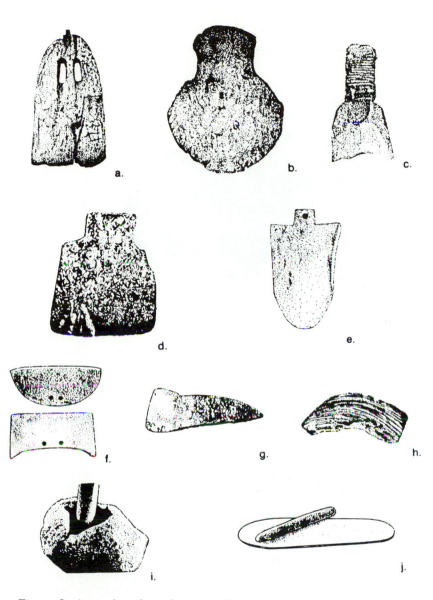

Figure 2. Agricultural implements of the New Stone Age excavated in various sites of China:

a, wooden plow	*f*, stone knife
b, stone plow	*g*, stone sickle
c, bone plow	*h*, shell sickle
d, stone spade	*i*, stone motar
e, jade spade	and pestle
	j, stone grinder

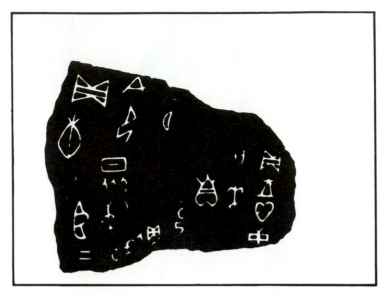

Figure 3. Chinese characters of the 14th century B.C. inscribed on a tortoise shell.

cultivation management included irrigation, flood control and drainage, making compost, transplanting and insect and mouse control. Rather good methods were given for raising sheep and chickens as were techniques for horse breeding and castration. Silkworm raising and mulberry bush pruning were also outlined.

Nearly 400 books on ancient Chinese agriculture were published prior to the middle of the nineteenth century and before the end of the Chinese Feudal Society. Many written before the fourteenth century were lost; some were incorporated into volumes of history and still others were parts of comprehensive collections on related subjects.

Some of the more important ancient books on Chinese agriculture (Table 2) described intensive land cultivation, full utilization of fields, and preservation of soil fertility. They emphasized deep plowing, timely tilling of the soil, planting times, local conditions and crops, the use of natural resources, crop rotation, intercropping and multiple cropping. Relationships between soil fertility, soil moisture and light and the growth of crops were carefully recorded. Soils were classified into categories and species with suitable crops suggested for each. Early attention was also given to forestry, animal husbandry, fisheries and related industries.

TABLE 2
Important Books on Ancient Chinese Agriculture

Century and Dynasty	Name	Author	Summary of Contents
16th B.C. (Shang)	*Xia Xiao Zheng*	------	Brief record of agriculture, astronomy and medicine in the Slave Society.
End 1st B.C. (Western Han)	*Fan Shengzhi's Book*	Fan Shengzhi's	Summary of farming experiences in the Guan Zhong Region.
6th A.D. (Southern and Northern)	*Key Skills for the People or an Agricultural Encyclopedia (Qi Min Yao Shu)*	Jia Sixie	Skills of farming, crop rotation, plowing, care of livestock, fish culture and food processing in the middle and down reaches of the Yellow River.
Early 14th A.D. (Yuan)	*Agricultural Book*	Wang Zhen	Systematic statements on farming, mulberry growing, grains and farming implements.
Early 17th A.D. (Ming)	*Complete Book on Agricultural Practices (Nong Zheng Quan Shu)*	Xu Quangqi	Summary of historical achievements in Chinese agricultural science and technology.
Middle 17th A.D. (Ming)	*Skillful Hands Create the World (Tian Gong Kai Wu)*	Song Yingxing	Details on ancient Chinese techniques for industrial (handicraft) and scientific agriculture.

Chinese Agriculture: From Uncultivated Land to Multiple Cropping

In primitive Chinese society, agriculture was started by using wood and stone tools to hack down trees and set them on fire. Seed was then put into holes made with a pointed wooden stick called a "Lei." Because setting trees and grass on fire was the beginning of agricultural production, Shen Nong, god of Agriculture, was also named "Lie Shan" which means "to burn the mountain." When the fertility of the land had declined after several continuous years of cultivation, people moved to another place to claim a new piece of land. In modern times this "slash and burn" or "shifting cultivation" method is still extensively used in some agriculturally developing nations in the tropics. This primitive system of leaving lands uncultivated has also been called bareland cultivation. According to the excavated cultural relics, this type of primitive agriculture was estimated to have continued in China 5,000 to 6,000 years before the beginning of the New Stone Age.

The people next settled down and utilized nearby lands by first cultivating and then allowing them to lie fallow in turn, instead of moving to other places to cultivate barelands. Thus began for agriculture the system of fallow land cultivation. Farm implements were also further developed from the simple "Lei" (stick) to the "Si" (plow share) or "Lei-Si" and the hoe. The invention and extension of the iron plow and plowing with oxen especially marked the high points in the development of productive forces in the eighth-seventh century B.C., when China reached the end of its Slave Society. According to ancient records, there were different schedules for allowing land to lie fallow one of two years depending upon the fertility of the soil. This was similar to the development of agriculture in ancient Western Europe, which was characterized by the two- or three-plot system of leaving land uncultivated. The difference is that it occurred almost a thousand years earlier in China.

By the third century B.C., at the beginning of the Chinese Feudal Society, techniques for agricultural production had developed to a high level. It was recognized, for example, that a piece of land should be cultivated by rotating the crops in order to avoid a decline in soil fertility. Also, to obtain more food and fiber, multiple cropping (growing more than one crop a year) was suggested as an alternative to growing single crops year by year. The advantages of multiple cropping are emphasized in literature published in the latter part of the first century B.C. At that time multiple cropping of millet and wheat was common. After the seventeenth century, it extended over all of China. Three crops, on the whole, can generally be harvested in two years within the reaches of the Yellow River, two crops a year in the reaches of the Yangzi River, and three crops a year in the reaches of the Pearl River. Thus, Chinese agriculture very early achieved worldwide fame with its high cropping index (number of crops harvested per year from the same land) and multiple-cropping technologies.

Regionalization of Agriculture

This gradual transition from leaving a plot of land fallow and uncultivated to continuous rotational and multiple cropping occurred only in the cultivated land areas. The large grassland areas in North, Northeast, and Northwest China were not included. Thus, the general concept of agriculture in China is the production of farm crops, not including animal husbandry and forestry. Historically, agriculture, forestry and animal husbandry developed in separate regions rather than through a mixture of crops and livestock grazing on the same land. This was deemed necessary to insure sufficient food and fiber by crop farming (Figure 4).

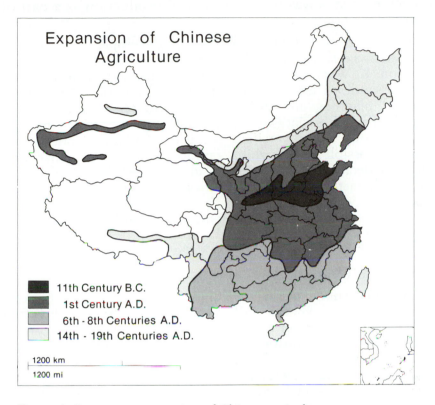

Figure 4. Progressive expansion of Chinese agriculture.

Early in the Feudal Society of the fifth to third centuries B.C., regionalization of agriculture developed with food and fiber crops emphasized in the central parts of China, animal husbandry in the west and north, fisheries in the east, and forestry in the mountainous regions. The area that produced food and fiber crops was later extended to the southern parts of China. Farmers have managed tens to scores of mu of land (15 mu of land equal one hectare) covered with crops, with "a family of five persons" as a unit, for over two thousand years.

The production of feed for livestock is not generally considered a part of farming in China. Farm animals are fed wastes and by-products which otherwise have very little value. Farmers may raise a few pigs, chickens, ducks or other livestock, but these are only a small portion of the total farm output. This pattern of agricultural development was in contrast to the transition from ancient to modern agriculture which occurred in Western Europe, where a rotation of forage and farm crops developed and much emphasis was placed on animal production as a part of the agricultural economy.

One of the reasons Chinese agriculture developed as it did was the diversified ownership policy which ultimately resulted in very little land per person. In Western Europe, land was inherited by only one son of the noble landlord and was not allowed to be sold. This permitted centralized planning and utilization of land resources. By contrast, during the Feudal Society of China, land was inherited by many sons. Land ownership was diversified and general planning and utilization became impossible. Meanwhile, rapidly increasing populations also resulted in decreasing amounts of land per person. Thus, a distinct historical characteristic of early Chinese agriculture, which persists to this day, has been one in which crop farming assured an increasingly important role to the production of more food and fiber per unit of land area and time.

Intensive Cultivation

Intensified farming began in Chinese agriculture as far back as the third century B.C., when a unified dynasty (the Han, 206 B.C.-A.D. 220) was established after a long period of war. Irrigation of crops, the improvement of animal-drawn farm implements, and new cultivation methods were emphasized. The Feudal Society generated a high level of agricultural production, which was sustained for about one and one-half centuries. A solid social and technical basis for intensive cultivation developed and has continued for over 2,000 years.

The goal of the Chinese intensive land cultivation system is to fully utilize--and at the same time protect--the land resources. This necessitates a high cropping index (involving continuous, multiple, and intercropping) which is assured by appropriate crop cultivation, rotation, fertilization, irrigation, and an increase in soil fertility. The means of optimizing these practices depend upon local conditions of climate, topography, soil types, and kinds of crops to be grown.

The origins of intensive cultivation in ancient Chinese agriculture may be characterized by three classical delineations:

1) Ridge farming developed early in the fifth century B.C. On high, dry lands crops were planted in furrows, while on low, wet lands crops were planted on ridges. Under the ridge-farming system, plants in the furrows were more drought resistant. The system was good for fallow

(resting) soil: the crops were easy to fertilize, and cultivation was convenient for animal operations. Ridge farming occupied a predominant position in Chinese agriculture. Later, it was considered on par with farming on level ground and is still acceptable.

2) During the second century B.C., Zhao Guo, of the Han Dynasty, developed a method known as "Dai" land technology. As crops planted in furrows grew, the ridges were then leveled and the furrows filled in during the summer through weeding and cultivation. "Dai" means substitution of furrows. This technique of crop cultivation required less labor for weed control and resulted in better harvests. It prevailed in the upper and middle reaches of the Yellow River.

3) Later, Fan Shengzhi, also of the Han Dynasty, proposed a method called "Qu" land, which was a further development of the "Dai" land. Here the land was divided into rectangular or square plots and crops were planted in the furrows. Deep plowing and a full stand of evenly spaced seedlings were required. This was the beginning of the gardening style of cultivation in the farmlands of the plains regions which persists to this day.

The application of large amounts of organic fertilizer or animal manure was another early tradition of Chinese agriculture. The value of manure was stressed early in the fifth century B.C.--more than a thousand years before a similar development occurred in Western Europe. In the beginning, the manure consisted only of a wet weed compost. This progressed to the use of livestock and green manures during the second century A.D. Because manure was not utilized in ancient Western European agriculture, the theory of "declination of land fertility" prevailed in that part of the world. At the same time in China, however, manure application was stressed and confidence in its use was established. Chen Fu, of the Southern Song Dynasty in the twelfth century A.D., proposed this entirely different concept of "constant renewal of land fertility." Agricultural production methods practiced over thousands of years in China have proved that the application of organic fertilizers or manure is the most effective means to improve soil structure, raise the productivity of the land, and achieve a "sustainable agriculture," even with intensive cultivation. The Chinese-based "organic agriculture" has not only won international recognition in recent years but has had a long history of confirmation in practice as well.

The "Five Grains" and "Six Animals"

The first priority in Chinese agriculture has been the production of the food crops known as the "Five Grains." Second is the production of livestock known as the "Six Animals." The most commonly used phrase in China to describe a good agricultural year is "bumper harvest of five grains" and the "flourishing of six animals." The "six animals" are horses, cattle, sheep, chickens, dogs and pigs (see Chapters 5 and 26, "Potentials of Grasslands" and "Three Hundred Million Pigs").

The expression "five grains" first appeared in the Chinese literature of the eighth-fifth centuries B.C. The grains were millet, glutinous millet, soybean, wheat and rice. First, they were defined as the five basic food crops cultivated in the reaches of the Yellow River. Later, the "five grains" concept assumed a new meaning and became a general term for all food crops. Because of differences in time, region and the characteristics of various food crops, and because of the introduction of new crops from foreign countries, references to the "five grains" continued to change. A general picture follows of the development of Chinese agriculture as reflected by changes in the meaning of "five grains."

"Shu" and "Ji," Leaders of "Five Grains." "Shu" is broomcorn millet (*Panicum miliaceum*); "Ji" is a variety of "Shu." The main difference is that "Ji" is not as glutinous when cooked as is "Shu." In the most ancient Chinese characters inscribed on bones and tortoise shells, these two words appeared most frequently of all the grain crops. Seeds of "Shu" and "Ji" were also found in excavated relics of the New Stone Age shown to have a history of six to seven thousand years. All of these remains suggest that, from the end of the Chinese Slave era to the beginning of the Feudal Society, "Shu" and "Ji" were the two most important food crops.

"Shu" and "Ji" were also comparatively drought-resistant crops with a shorter growing period than other grains and stronger tillering. Their vigorous growth enabled them to compete successfully against weeds. These plant characteristics enabled the Chinese peasants to grow "Shu" and "Ji" successfully in the marginally cold and dry areas of what is now North Central China in the middle reaches of the Yellow River, where the Chinese nation had its origin. Here the growing seasons are short, precipitation is low, and droughts are frequent. The early Chinese people had only a limited capacity to struggle against nature, as it was not until after the sixteenth century B.C. that bronze farm tools came into use. Under such environmental conditions, "Shu" and "Ji" were the most important of the "five grains." As mentioned under "Mythology and Archaeology," the name of one of the Chinese agricultural gods was "Hou Ji." Here "Hou" represents the official and "Ji" the food crops, which indicates the important position that "Ji" occupied.

Rise of Millet. As with "Shu" and "Ji," millet is one of the most ancient crops in China (see Chapter 15, "Millet and Sorghum--the Ancients of Crops"). The gradual rise in the level of agricultural technology was accompanied by increases in the productive forces. The use of the iron plow drawn by oxen had its origin in the eighth century B.C. near the end of the Chinese Slave Society. Higher-yielding millets gradually raised the level of food production. Prior to the fifth century B.C., the iron plow and plowing with oxen had been used extensively. There were also additional inputs from the agricultural technologies of manure application, proper cultivation and irrigation. Under these conditions millet became the leading food crop. "Shu" and "Ji" dropped to the level of crops for disaster relief and their cultivation was moved to the far northwestern and northeastern border regions.

Growth and Decline of Soybeans. The soybean is also one of the ancient food crops of China. It is comparatively drought resistant and can be cultivated without manure. It fertilizes itself through naturally occurring biological processes that extract nitrogen from the air. In ancient times, farmers would grow some soybeans as a part of their food production program each year. They gave equal importance to millet and the soybean as substitutes for "Shu" and "Ji." Soybeans were also called "Shu," which is pronounced the same but written differently than Shu from the Chinese word "Shu" which designates broomcorn millet. (See Chapter 14, "Soybeans--The Miracle Bean of China.")

It was not until China entered the Feudal Society that food processing technologies were developed. Then fermented and salted soybeans, thick soybean sauce, bean curd, bean sprouts and many other products became commonplace. The soybean then moved from a main food crop to the category of a nonstaple food and an oil crop.

The Rise of Wheat. As the soybean declined as a major food crop, wheat was on the increase. Prior to the eighth century B.C., spring wheat was much more important in China than winter wheat. However, because winter wheat ripened earlier and was higher yielding, it was a food source while the new spring crop was still in the blade and vegetative and the previous year's harvest had been consumed. Thus, winter wheat was welcomed by farmers, and its production was greatly expanded during the fifth century B.C. An interesting recent development has been the production of modern spring wheat varieties in the central and southern provinces. They are planted in the fall (September-October) and harvested in the spring (April-May). Having a low chilling requirement like winter wheat, they have the advantages of early harvest and high yields. From the beginning of the Chinese Feudal Society in the third century B.C. until now, wheat has remained one of the main food crops, second only to rice.

Wheat was considered to be a coarse food grain before the fifth century B.C. While it had been extensively cultivated for a long time, only the broiled and boiled whole kernel could be used as food because of the lack of grain processing equipment. The boiled whole grain wheat kernel was not tasty. Only after processing equipment was developed during the latter part of the fifth century B.C. was wheat considered to be a fine (or noble) food grain. It then gradually became the main food for people in many of the northern parts of China (see Chapter 12, "Wheat Campaigns").

Rice: the Latecomer Surpasses the Old-Timers. Rice (paddy) is China's most important crop now and one of the most ancient of all, originating in the southern part of China. At the beginning of the Chinese Feudal Society of the fifth century B.C., rice was cultivated in the reaches of the Yellow River. The area was limited, however, because of a lack of water. Later, the production of rice in that area increased somewhat with the construction of irrigation facilities. But rice became number one in Chinese food production as a result of cultivation in the reaches of the Yangzi River and what are now the southern provinces.

The southern parts of China have a warm climate with plentiful rainfall--ideally suited for rice production. This area, however, was not reclaimed for agricultural production and had only a sparse population until the first century B.C. Rice production then developed very rapidly. During the course of its development, new styles of land utilization were designed. Paddy fields surrounded with dikes were constructed in the low-lying regions. Level, terraced fields were established on mountain slopes. New growing techniques included ratooning, double cropping, continuous cropping and intercropping. All were designed to raise the index of cropping food production. Since the sixth century A.D., rice has been the leading food produced in China.

Corn and Sweet Potato. Both of these originated in America. They were introduced into China during the sixteenth century, but until the eighteenth century were planted primarily only in the mountainous regions. During the early years when these crops were first introduced, the economy of the Chinese Feudal Society gradually declined. Many poor farmers then moved to the mountain areas where corn and sweet potatoes were their primary food. Both crops were suitable to grow on the poor soils of the mountain slopes. Corn is also edible when half ripe, and the sweet potato can be eaten as soon as the tuberous roots are formed. These two crops were considered to be treasure troves of food by the mountain people. During the past century, the production of both corn and sweet potatoes in China has expanded very rapidly in the lowlands as well as on the mountain slopes. Often they are planted as companion crops on both the flatlands and on the mountain sides. The corn is harvested first, and then the sweet potatoes cover the entire soil surface. This not only reduces soil erosion but provides a valuable food resource in that both the tops and roots can be consumed by either man or beast (see Chapter 13, "The Rise of Corn" and Chapter 18, "The

Sweet Potato--A Treasure Trove from Head to Toe"). Both require much less water than rice and are now among the major food crops of China, surpassed only by rice and wheat.

FOR FURTHER READING

Chen Dunyi. 1983. *Chinese economic geography*. Beijing: Zhanwang Press. (In Chinese)

Chen Wenhua. 1978. *Brief chart of Chinese ancient agricultural science and technology*. Beijing: Agricultural Press. (In Chinese)

Chinese Academy of Sciences. 1983. *Ancient China's technology and science*. Beijing: Foreign Language Press.

Chinese ancient agricultural science and technology. 1980. Beijing: Agricultural Press. (In Chinese)

Du Shiran. 1982. *Manuscript of history of Chinese science and technology*, vol. 1. Beijing: Science Press. (In Chinese)

King F. H. 1911. *Farmers of forty centuries*. Emmaus, PA: Rodale Press, Inc.

Luo Mingdian. 1980. The understanding of the soil fertility in Chinese ancient times. *Chinese agricultural science and technology*. Beijing: Agricultural Press (In Chinese)

Research Laboratory of Agricultural History of the South China Agricultural College. 1980, 1982. *Agricultural history research*, vols. 1, 2. Beijing: Agricultural Press. (In Chinese)

Yuan Ke. 1979. *Selected explanations of ancient mythology*. Beijing: People's Press of Literature. (In Chinese)

3

9.6 MILLION SQUARE KILOMETERS OF TERRITORY

by Sun Han

Historical

"Everything comes from the soil."

So goes an old and famous Chinese saying.

China, during its long course of history, has always recognized the importance of agriculture and its land resources. It is said that during their primitive prehistoric society, the Chinese showed great reverence to She Shen, god of the Land. According to mythology, his name was Hou Tu and he was the son of Gong Gong, the chief of a primitive tribe (see Chapter 4, "Water Resources—the Lifeline of Chinese Agriculture"). Each spring and autumn, the emperors and kings of different dynasties would offer sacrifices to She Shen and thus these were called the "Days of She."

On the west side of Tiananmen Square in Beijing, the emperor of the Ming Dynasty built a temple (1421 A.D.) for the god of the Land. It was used for offering sacrifices. It is a square, three-story, white marble construction in which yellow-, blue-, red-, black- and white-colored soils are displayed. Although the place has now become Zhongshan Park in memory of Mr. Sun Zhongshan (Sun Yat-sen), the temple is still well preserved and remains an important historical site.

The soils of five colors in the temple represent China's central, eastern, southern, northern and western regions, respectively. They scientifically illustrate the five soil color types which were formed under the influences of water, temperature and other natural conditions prevailing in the different regions. The diversity and geographical variations of the agroecotypes in China may be the most unique in the world since they cover such vast ranges in latitude, longitude and altitude.

China's Land Resources

Overall, China's land resources are as diverse and contrasting as any place on earth. South China is a land of rice, lakes, canals, rivers and fish. People are everywhere who live by both water and land. In the north, the Yellow River--known as "the Sorrow of China"--gives both life and death (droughts and floods often occur in tandem). It is a land of wheat, corn, soybeans, sorghum and millet, with draft animals and dusty fields merging into the wide open spaces of deserts to the west and northwest, grasslands to the north and forests to the northeast. The west is desert, ranging from high plateaus and mountains with permanent snow fields to depressions that are below sea level and the hottest in summer of any place in China. In the northwest, there are grazing cattle, sheep and goats. Horses and cowboys may dot the landscape. There are farmers with long-handled shovels, irrigating the desert lands and growing cotton, grapes and melons. The land is sparsely populated, mostly with minority groups.

The Chinese people describe their country as "a large territory with immense resources." It is true that the absolute area of China's territory is very large, second only to the U.S.S.R. and Canada. With such a huge population, however, the arable land per person is much less than the world's average. It is an all-encompassing factor as one views the future development of China's rural economy. There is a great gap in income levels between Chinese farmers and those in advanced countries. They have only 7% of the world's total farmland, yet must feed 22% of the world's population.

Of China's 9.6 million square kilometers (3.7 million square miles) of territory, 19% is desert, perma-frost, glacier and mountains of exposed rock--none of which can be used for agriculture. Seven percent of the land is covered by cities, industries, mines and roads. The remaining 74% of the land has or can be used for agriculture, forestry, animal husbandry and fisheries.

The absolute amount of land in China is large, but the average per person is very small. In fact, the averages in amounts of total land, arable land, forest area, and grassland per capita in China are all lower than world averages. The average total land area per capita in China is less than one hectare, which is only 30% of the world's average. However, the average arable land per capita is only 0.1 hectare, which is 27% of the world's average, and the average forest area is only 0.13 hectares or 12% of the world's average. A grassland area per capita of 0.3 hectares is less than one-half the world's average.

Time Compensates for Space

What cannot be made up for in more space for agricultural expansion in China is made up in time. This has been accomplished by remarkable expansions in multiple, sequential and relay cropping systems, together with other technological innovations, to change the distribution of crops and raise agricultural production.

Multiple cropping systems were first developed in the early years of the Tang Dynasty (618-690 A.D.). It began in the arid regions of north China, where a crop of winter wheat, soybeans (or other legume), and millet were harvested within a two-year span. Thus the cropping index was increased to 1.5 compared to 1.0. In the paddy areas of South China, a crop of rice and wheat or barley were harvested in one year, making a cropping index of 2.0. With progressive expansions in population, and where climatic conditions permitted, multiple cropping systems became more widely adopted. Thus, an important reason why the Chinese have been able to feed such a large population with such limited arable land resources is that they have used "time to compensate for space."

Agricultural Climatic Zones of China

From north to south, China can be divided into eight temperature zones and the Qingzang Cold Plateau (Figure 1). First is the *cold temperate* zone, which occupies only a small area in the northernmost part of Heilongjiang. Accumulated temperatures or heat sums above 10°C are less than 1600°C and the frost-free period is less than 100 days. The short growing season allows the production of only single crops of early-maturing spring wheat and potatoes.

Second, the *temperate* zone covers most of the three northeast provinces (Heilongjiang, Jilin, Liaoning) and the most northern parts of North China. There the annual heat sum above a base of 10°C is 1,600 to 3,400°C, and there are annually 100-160 frost-free days. The major crops are spring wheat, sugar beets, potato, maize (corn), soybean, sorghum and millet. It is a one-crop-a-year system.

Third, the *cold plateau* belt covers the Qinghai-Xizang (Tibetan) Plateau of southwest China. Two-thirds of the area has an altitude in excess of 4,500 meters above sea level. Only in the most southern of the marginal valleys can maize (corn) and rice be grown. Barley, wheat, peas and potatoes can be grown in the area below 4,000 meters. Winter wheat has recently been introduced in the Yarlung Zangbo Valley of Xizang and grown at a height of 4,100 meters. This is the world's highest place for planting winter wheat, and an impressive experimental record yield of 15 tons per hectare has been achieved in Qinghai (see Chapters 7 and 12, "Agriculture in the Highlands of Tibet" and "Wheat Campaigns").

Figure 1. The eight temperature zones of China.

Above 4,500 meters the average temperature in the warmest month is less than 10°C and sometimes lower than 6°C. There is no absolute frost-free period. Hence, it is difficult for crops to reach maturity. Only a few grazing animals--Tibetan buffalo, sheep and goats--can survive (see Chapter 7, "Agriculture in the Highlands of Tibet").

The fourth climatic zone is the *warm temperate* belt which extends from the southern end of the medium temperate belt to the Qin Ling, Mountains and the Huai He River. Annual accumulated heat sums above 10°C range from 3,400 to 4,500°C, with 160 to 190 frost-free days. The cropping indices range from three harvests in two years (1.5) or two in one (2.0). Winter wheat is widely grown and often multiplanted or interplanted with maize, soybeans, peanuts, cotton or rice.

South of the Qin Ling Mountains and the Huai He river and extending southward are the *north, middle* and *south subtropical* zones, which have annual accumulated heat sums above 10°C of 4,500-5,000°C, 5,000-6,500°C and 6,500-8,000°C, respectively. Frost-free days number 210-250, 250-300 and above 300, in the same order. For the *north subtropical* zone an annual harvest each of rice and wheat is common. In the southern part of this zone, two crops of rice may be produced or two crops of rice plus a winter crop of wheat, barley or rapeseed. These are the dominant cropping systems. Two harvests of rice in one year is common in the *middle subtropical* zone. For the *south subtropical* belt, rice is harvested two to three times a year, and sweet potatoes or maize can be planted in the winter.

The *tropical* belt includes the Leizhou Peninsula, Hainan Island, Zhongsha and Xisha Archipelagoes of Guangdong Province, the border areas of Yunnan and the southern third of Taiwan. The Nansha is located in the Equator belt. Accumulated temperatures above 10°C range from 7,500 to 9,000°C and above. These areas are frost-free. Three crops of rice or four crops of sweet potatoes may be harvested in one year.

Multiple Cropping and Transplanting

The adoption of multiple cropping in China has not only been favored by climatic endowments, but is a product of the accumulated wisdom of the people extending back thousands of years. Early maturation and cultivars of crops with high and stable yields have been a continuing priority. Varieties with short growing periods which are tolerant to either early spring or late autumn cold injury have been selected. Appropriate varietal combinations and crop rotation patterns have been developed, suitable for local seasons and natural conditions. Ingenious methods of interplanting have been devised, such as leaving spaces between rows of wheat or rapeseed where cotton, maize or even watermelons may be planted before the wheat or rapeseed matures and is harvested. While the growth of young plants for the second crop may be suppressed for a short time, the benefits derived from the mother crop--as a windbreak--may outweigh the temporary competition for water, nutrients and sunlight (Figure 2).

Both interplanting and transplanting are labor intensive, and are rational approaches in substituting time for space where land resources are limited and the labor force is immense. Transplanting is an important technology for gaining time in crop production. It is widely, almost universally, used for rice, sweet potatoes and many vegetables. Up to 25 percent of the cotton in some areas is also transplanted. A limited amount (less than one percent) of maize (corn) is also transplanted. Here deep furrows are prepared, into which water is admitted and the corn transplanted, sometimes when the plants are a foot high. For crops that are transplanted, a small area is used for a seed bed which will provide enough transplants for an entire field. The time gained to harvest will vary from two to six weeks.

Figure 2. Young watermelon plants tranplanted between wheat rows in Jiangsu Province.

How to mechanize or automate these labor-intensive cultural practices still stands as an important innovative challenge to Chinese science and technology.

People and Agriculture--Concentrated in The East

China has only one ocean coastline. The U.S.A. has two. The western border of China goes deep into the heart of the world's largest continent --Eurasia. That border is one of deserts and mountains. Southeastern China is strongly influenced by a monsoon climate, while in the Northwest a continental climate prevails. Differences in precipitation between regions is largely a function of distance from the sea. For most parts of China, moisture-laden air for precipitation comes from the Pacific Ocean. Thus, there is a decrease from the seashore inland, from southeast to northwest. From the western part of the Yunnan Autonomous Region to southwestern Tibet, moisture-laden air comes from the Indian Ocean. Here, precipitation decreases from west to east or from south to north. For the northern Xinjiang Autonomous Region, the moisture comes from the Arctic Ocean. There, precipitation decreases from west to east.

Most of the moisture-laden air from the Pacific reaches only the southeastern half of China. The 400-millimeter isohyet (a line depicting equal rainfall) extends from the Da Xingan Ling Mountains of

Heilongjiang in the northeast, diagonally to Lhasa of Tibet in the southwest, thus dividing the country into two major parts. The east, with its wet climate, is agriculturally the most important. The west is dry and made up mostly of deserts and grasslands. In the east, the annual 800-millimeter isohyet extends along a line from the Huai He River to the Qin Ling Mountains. The area to the south is mainly paddy field agriculture. To the north is the main rain-fed cropping region. Far to the west, the annual 250-millimeter isohyet goes from the western part of Hulunber League to Gangdis Shan of northwest Tibet. This isohyet represents the most western marginal line for rain-fed agriculture in China. The vast area west and north of this line, except for some hills and mountains in north Xinjiang, is dry semi-desert or desert where there is no agriculture without irrigation.

Meteorologists use an aridity index (ratio of the possible evaporation and precipitation when average daily temperatures are greater than 10°C) to classify regions as wet or dry. Accordingly, China can be divided into four regions. First is the *wet* region, which covers 32.2% of the 9.6 million square kilometers of territory. Here the aridity index is less than 1.0. Irrigation is used only on rice and is not needed for dry-land crops.

Second is the *semi-wet* region. It covers 17.8% of the total territory, and the aridity index ranges from 1.0 to 1.49. Dryland crops can be grown without irrigation but there are often seasonal deficiencies of water.

Third is the *semi-dry* region. This covers 19.2% of the total land territory and has an aridity index between 1.5 to 1.9. Here, crop yields are low and lack stability if there is no irrigation.

Last is the *dry* region, which extends over 30.8% of the total territory. The area is semi-desert with an aridity index ranging from 2.0 to 3.99. The harvest of dryland crops is very unpredictable. In desert areas exceeding an aridity index of 4.0, there is no agriculture without irrigation.

The wet and semi-wet regions comprise just about half of the country's territory and the dry and semi-dry the other half. These differences in moisture between the east and the west have determined the nature of China's agriculture. They, more than any other factor, have also accounted for the significant regional differences in social and economic development. The effects of the east-west moisture differences on both agricultural and economic development have been far greater than any created between North and South China arising from gradients of temperature.

Of China's more than one billion people, 90% are concentrated east of a line running from Aihui County in Heilongjiang Province southwest to Tengchong County of Yunnan Province. People are scarce in West

China. Most of them are in regions where those of minority nationalities live in compact communities. Meanwhile, along with 90% of the people, 90% of the arable land, the forested areas and inland waters are all in the eastern part of China. Thus, it can be truthfully stated that of China's 9.6 million square kilometers of territory, only the eastern half is truly functional in feeding almost one billion people. As was true of the U.S.A. one-hundred years ago, the West has great potential for China's economic and agricultural development in the decades ahead. The most critical issue and limited resource will be water.

Mountains, Terraces and Land Reclamation

China is now a land of few forests, but mountains are almost everywhere. Two-thirds of all of China is covered by mountains, hills, basins and plateaus of high elevation, and with undulating landscapes. All of these are a serious constraint for agricultural production. This is particularly true for 25% of China's territories, mostly in the west, where mountains and plateaus are in excess of 3,000 meters in elevation. It is the remaining territories, mostly in the east, where plains of low elevation--usually less than 500 meters--predominate. Here, there are only a few mountains exceeding elevations of 1,000 meters.

Hence the eastern parts of China are the most favorable for agricultural development. Yet few are the sites, even in eastern China, where on clear days mountains are not in view. There is no combined land-water-climate resource for agricultural productivity that even approaches, in magnitude, that of the Central and Midwest U.S.A. corn and grain belt.

There are special landscapes in the mountainous regions of southwestern China known as "vertical agriculture." This describes changes wrought on agricultural production with increases in elevation. For each rise of 100 meters, annual mean temperatures drop by 0.5 to 0.6°C. Similarly, heat sums decrease with elevations and growing seasons are shortened.

Seven vertical climate zones or belts have been identified for the mountainous regions of Yunnan, Guizhou and Sichuan provinces, moving upward from the valleys of 1,000 meters elevation to the high plateaus of 4,500 meters above sea level. They are the *lower valley subtropical*, the *upper valley subtropical*, the *mountain warm temperate*, the *mountain cool temperature*, the *mountain cold temperate*, the *high mountains subfrigid* and the *high mountain frigid* belts. For the lower valley subtropical belt, double crops of rice and cotton and single crops of sugarcane, sisal hemp and coffee can be harvested. By starting in the valleys below and proceeding upward to the tops of the mountains, the cropping systems and kinds of crops change, and cropping indices are reduced. In the high mountain subfrigid belt, there are no crops or trees and only a few cold-tolerant cattle and goats can survive. On the high mountain frigid belt, there is snow cover the year around.

More than half of China's arable lands are on mountain slopes. It was common during the middle of the Tang Dynasty of the eighth century to build farm land on slopes to solve the problem of shortages of arable land. It was done, however, without dykes, and soil and water erosion were catastrophic. Dufu, a poet of the Tang Dynasty, described the problem as follows: "In the third year soil fertility became exhausted because of water and soil erosion, and the land cannot be used anymore."

During the Song Dynasty of the tenth century, terraced fields with dykes were built along many mountain slopes. Today, they can be seen everywhere in the hilly and mountainous areas. Some terraced fields are more than one-hundred tiers high. Most, built with local stones, are truly magnificent to view (Figure 3). Many generations of back-breaking

Figure 3. Terraced fields of paddy rice.

toil have gone into their construction. Some terraced fields grow dryland (rain-fed) crops, others paddy rice; the harvests are unpredictable. Except for terraced fields irrigated by mechanical pumping or from reservoirs, most are rain-fed. They are called "lands looking for rain." Terraced fields are usually small and scattered. Transportation between fields is limited and cultural practices almost impossible to mechanize. For some of the steeper terraces, it is even difficult for cattle to maneuver in the fields. There is a complete reliance on human labor.

Land reclamation on steep mountain slopes in China is often accompanied by widespread water erosion and an upsetting of the ecological balance. The most serious has been on the Loess (wind-blown soil) Plateau (Figure 4) which extends across China's eight northern provinces and autonomous regions. At 540,000 square kilometers, it's the world's largest and is located in the upper reaches of the Yellow River. Serious erosion is prevalent on about 430,000 square kilometers, with an annual flow down the river of about 1.6 billion tons. This makes the river turbid and muddy, hence the name Yellow River. Its silt load is the heaviest of any river in the world. A result is that the riverbed is often much higher than the land alongside. In ages past, high banks were built on both sides to prevent flooding and to control the flow to the sea. These banks over the long history of China, were broken down countless times, resulting in the flooding of vast areas.

This eternal flooding of the Yellow River has been a result not only of natural conditions associated with the loose soil structure on the Loess Plateau, sharp changes in topography and landforms, and heavy summer rains, but even more from human activities. Irrational land use, deforestation, farming of the grasslands and overgrazing have all contributed.

Soil erosion in the mountainous areas of South China is also becoming serious. The amounts of sands and silts carried by both the Yangzi and the Pearl rivers are increasing. This is not only resulting in soils of lowered fertility but is increasing the threats from floods and droughts in the lower river basins.

Land Resources for the Future

The 100 million hectares of arable land constitutes but a small part (10.4%) of China's total. Reserve land resources, yet to be reclaimed, for growing crops or grasses are only 33 million hectares. Most of the barren lands yet to be converted to farmland are now natural grasslands or sparse woodlands. Some are along the seashores or marsh lands which are used for propagating fish, shellfish and shrimp. Most small areas can be classified as really unused barren lands. Hence, future land

Figure 4. Devastations resulting from soil erosion in the Loess (wind blown soil) Plateau.

reclamation schemes will likely lead to conflicts in land use among the interests of farming, forestry, animal husbandry and fisheries. Careful programming will be necessary.

It is conservatively estimated that, in China, only 13 million hectares of new land remain for crop production. They are in the more remote areas of Heilongjiang Province and the Xinjiang Autonomous Region. If all these lands are reclaimed, the maximum for effective cropping will not likely exceed 10 million hectares (see Chapter 8, "From Bare Lands to Bread Baskets"). This constraint to horizontal expansion of land resources must be recognized for any strategic planning in the future for agricultural development in China.

Historically, the exploitation of natural resources essential for agricultural production in China has been a serious problem. After the founding of the new China, great achievements were made in water and land conservation and low yield land improvement. However, an exploding population, coupled with a weak material and technical base for agricultural production, and improper use of natural resources through the 1950s, 1960s and even through the 1970s, resulted in further deteriorations of the agricultural production base. Extending areas for crop cultivation were at the costs of destroying forests and grazing lands and the draining of lakes. Terraced fields were built in southern mountain areas and on the northwestern Loess Plateau on 30- and even 40-degree slopes. The results were catastrophic. Little grain was harvested, vegetation was destroyed, and there were serious losses from water and wind erosion. Desertification spread with an increase of wind blowing in semi-desert areas. Fish habitats and propagation sites were destroyed and the storage capacity for irrigation reduced by drainage of lakes. Overcutting of forests was rampant, and the amounts removed greatly surpassed the rates of new growth. As a result, forestry resources not only degenerated but approached exhaustion. Grasslands were overgrazed by blindly increasing the number of livestock. This resulted in a serious reduction in carrying capacities.

Currently, the total highly erodible soil area in China is about 1.2 million square kilometers. Since the mid 1960s, desertification (encroachment of desert lands) has increased by 3 million hectares, and degenerated grasslands occupy 23% of the total grassland areas.

Coupled with these are increasing problems of air pollution throughout the eastern coastal areas, the major cities and industrialized areas, and the Yangzi River basin. These are also the most intensive food-producing regions. Acid rainfall is also becoming more prevalent with the increasing combustion of coal as an energy resource for countryside enterprises.

These dire circumstances of resource degeneration have recently drawn the attention of academia, the press, and the central government. The improper use of land resources has been termed by Chinese scientists as "plundering-like management." With direction from the central government, it is now national policy to protect and rationally use the agricultural resources of the nation. Traditional approaches have been the widespread use of biomass and composts as natural fertilizers, nonchemical approaches to pest control, preventative action against desertification, and a massive reforestation program. Recent progress in grain production, with several successive years of good harvests, is resulting in a restructuring of agricultural production according to local conditions and needs. Improperly opened and operated slopes, grasslands and lakes are being returned to forestry, animal husbandry and fish production. The Chinese people, especially in the arid and mountainous regions, are mobilized and carrying out grass-planting and reforestation on a large scale and using genetically improved species to do it. While there has been a positive improvement in the country's ecological environment, much remains to be done to preserve, protect, manage and utilize China's resource base for future food production.

FOR FURTHER READING

Academia Sinica. 1980. Natural geography of China. Beijing: Science Press. (In Chinese)

Anonymous. 1985. Xinjiang: Vistas for development. *Beijing Review* 28(40): 13-16.

Crop Science Society of China. 1981. *Treatises on tillage systems*. Beijing: Agricultural Press. (In Chinese)

Hsuing Wen-Yue, and F. D. Johnson. 1981. Forests and forestry in China. *Journal of Forestry* 79 (February): 76-79.

Huang Ping-wei. 1981. Environmental factors and the potential agricultural productivity of China: An analysis of sunlight, temperature and soil moisture. In *The environment: Chinese and American views*, ed. L. J. C. Ma and A. G. Noble, 45-71. London: Methuen and Co., Ltd.

Institute of Geography. Academia Sinica. 1980. *A general review of agricultural geography of China*. Beijing: Science Press. (In Chinese)

Leeming, F. 1985. *Rural China today*. New York: Longman Group, Ltd.

Liu Chenlie. 1985. Modernizing the great northern wilderness. *China Reconstructs* 34(2): 50-53.

National Agricultural Regionalization Committee. 1981. *Integrated agricultural regionalization of China*. Beijing: Agricultural Press. (In Chinese)

Ren Mei'e. 1980. *Essentials of natural geography of China*. Beijing: Commercial Press. (In Chinese)

Smil, V. 1983. *The bad earth: Environmental degradation in China*. Armonk, N.Y.: M. E. Sharp, Inc.

Stopler, T. E. 1985. *China, Taiwan and the offshore islands*. Armonk, N.Y.: M. E. Sharp, Inc.

Sun Han. 1980. Agricultural resources must be reasonably utilized. *Journal of Dialectics of Nature*, no. 1. (In Chinese)

———. 1980. Reasonable utilization of natural resources in agriculture. *Nongye Jingji Luntang* [*Collected Essays on Agricultural Economics*], no. 1. (In Chinese)

———. 1984. Agricultural natural resources of China and their reasonable utilization. *Soil and Water Conservation in China*, no. 11. (In Chinese)

———. 1984. Regional differentiation rules with respect to agriculture and agricultural regionalization in China. *Soil and Water Conservation in China*, no. 12. (In Chinese)

Wu Chuan-chun. 1981. The transformation of agricultural landscapes in China. In *The environment: Chinese and American views*, ed. L. J. C. Ma and A. G. Noble, 35-44. London: Methuen and Co., Ltd.

Zhu Shi-Song. 1981. China's great greenwall. *American Forests* 87(5): 24, 58-59.

4

WATER RESOURCES--THE LIFELINE OF CHINESE AGRICULTURE

by Sun Han

The dragon is a symbol of the Chinese nation. According to ancient legends this supernatural animal lived in both the sky and the sea, and the Chinese called themselves descendants of it. It is said that the dragon was accompanied by wind and clouds when it roamed the sky. It drank water from the seas, rivers and lakes and poured it out on the earth as rainfall. Thus, the dragon was worshipped as the god of Water by the Chinese people, and Dragon King Temples have been built everywhere since olden times. In ancient times, when droughts or floods occurred, frightened peasants--believing they had infuriated the Dragon King god--swarmed in great throngs to the Dragon King Temples to pray for forgiveness and blessings.

Not all, however, believed these myths. In past dynasties some politicians and intellectuals with foresight and sagacity, and even some wise tribal leaders in primitive societies, led the people to build water conservation projects to protect themselves from natural disasters and bring benefits to later generations as well.

The achievements in flood control in China during the past several thousand years are now praiseworthy to the entire world. Moreover, as construction of water conservation projects has been emphatically stressed since the founding of the new China, significant financial investments have been made by the state, and major human resources have been allocated. Improvements in water management constitute the single most important development in Chinese agriculture in the past thirty years. The result has been epoch-making progress. Water conservation projects in China from 1950 to 1985 have proven to be the single most important natural resource base for a steady increase in agricultural output, both horizontally (extensively) and vertically (intensively). No one goes now to pay homage to the Dragon King Temples. They have all been abandoned except as tourist attractions.

China's Water Resources--An Overview

Water conservation holds top priority for China because water resources per capita are very limited. Water for crop irrigation remains the most important factor in achieving dependability and increasing the magnitude of food production. Thus, water resources and their management are the key to feeding a billion people, and water will be China's most critical natural resource for the future.

First, the total amount of water resources is great, but is relatively small per capita. The total annual precipitation approximates 6,000 billion cubic meters, an average rainfall of only 630 millimeters or 5% of the world total. The annual river flow is 2,600 billion cubic meters, or only 2,700 cubic meters per person compared with an average of 10,930 for the entire world. In this regard, China--though number one in population--is sixth among the world's nations in water resources following Brazil, the U.S.S.R., Canada, the U.S.A. and Indonesia.

Secondly, China's water and land resources are very unevenly distributed among regions. Combinations of good soil and water resources are the exception rather than the rule. They are seldom balanced, nor do they usually occur together in the same place or at the same time. The total annual flow or run-off of the Yangzi, the Pearl and other rivers in the southeastern coastal areas and southwestern China constitute 82% of the total. The arable land in these watersheds (drainage areas), however, constitutes only 38% of the country's total. By contrast, the run-off of the Huai He, the Hai He, the Yellow rivers in northeastern and northwestern China constitutes only 18% of the total, while 62% of the nation's arable land is in their drainage areas. For the amounts of surface water per hectare of arable land, the range is from 58,980 cubic meters in the Pearl River valley of the far southern to only 2,820 cubic meters per hectare for the Hai He River valley in the north.

River Valley	Cubic Meters/Hectare
Zhu Jiang (Pearl)	58,980
Chang Jiang (Yangzi)	39,645
Songhua Jiang	6,480
Huang He (Yellow)	4,290
Huai He	4,215
Liao He	3,210
Hai He	2,820

The situation is further complicated by frequent floods in the south, where water is abundant but land is scarce, and the droughts in the north, where good land is plentiful but water is limited.

A third water resource constraint is the great variations in rainfall from year to year, and season to season. Rainfall for most parts of the country is generally scarce in the winter and spring and abundant during summer and autumn. It is often heavily concentrated in the rainy season with frequent flooding accompanied by heavy damage. Precipitation during the flooding seasons in the north constitute 70-80% of the total. Also, annual precipitation may vary several-fold from year to year. The interannual variations of North China are immense. In 1959, the annual precipitation for the Beijing area was 1,405 millimeters compared with only 250 millimeters in 1921. This was more than a fivefold difference between the two years.

Floods and droughts are common in China. During the 2,155 years between 206 B.C. and 1949 A.D., an estimated 1,092 heavy floods and 1,056 major droughts were recorded. That is an average of one severe climatic hazard a year.

Exceptional calamities have occurred in recent history. A nationwide drought in 1928 resulted in 120 million refugees. In that year, newspapers described China as a barren land stretching thousands of miles in every direction. Roads were thronged everywhere with roaming and starving refugees. By contrast, catastrophic floods literally inundated the Yangzi, Han Shui, Huai He, Yellow and Hai He river valleys from 1931 to 1939. Vivid accounts of the destruction caused by these floods shocked the entire world (Figure 1).

Soon after the new China was founded and was experiencing economic recovery, Party Chairman Mao Zedong decided that the Hai He River must be brought under permanent control. His clarion call was that it had to be harnessed to eliminate floods and drought in the Hai He River valley.

Chairman Mao next inspected the Yellow River and declared, "Work on the Yellow River must be done well." In 1963, following an exceptionally destructive flood in the Hai He River valley, he again stated that the Hai He River should be brought under permanent control. He also made many strategic decisions concerning the construction of water reclamation schemes and projects for the Yangzi River. His proposals, declarations and decisions were a mighty force in pushing forward the construction of water conservation projects. They were among his greatest contributions to the new China.

Flood Control and Agricultural Output

The Yellow River or Huang He is appropriately named as both "China's Mother" and "China's Sorrow." Down through the ages, the lives of China's people have been bound up with the river both as a life-giving benefactor and a raging natural force which had to be tamed. The

Yellow River valley is the cradle of the Chinese nation. It is where primitive tribes first settled and lived mainly from agricultural production in the Shen Nong Age (2,737 B.C.). The soft, friable soil that enabled it to become the cradle of Chinese civilization was also its doom. The Yellow River, which carries the world's heaviest load of silt (1.6 billion tons a year), has repeatedly filled up the river beds in the lower reaches of the North China plain and sent the water cascading over the countryside. While the Yellow River valley has a moderate climate and fertile soils favorable to agricultural production, floods have occurred

Figure 1. Calamities of drought and floods.

repeatedly, seriously threatening the survival and development of the Chinese nation. Waging battles against the floods of the Yellow River has been a perpetual task since antiquity, with more people living and dying in the effort than in any other place of comparable size on earth. It has been said that the Yellow River brings one-hundred damages to China with only benefit: irrigation.

The history of flood control in China begins with the story of Dayu in the twenty-first century B.C. This is so believed because of the many relics left as evidence. According to ancient records, tribal leaders in the Yellow River Valley held meetings and elected Gong Gong and Gun (Kun) in succession to be in charge of flood control. They both failed after many years' efforts to build earthen dykes to ward off the water. Gun was finally sentenced to death by the Emperor Shun, the leader of the tribal union. He then appointed Yu, the son of Gun, to continue. Yu, a wise and industrious man, directed his people and engaged with them in physical labor. Many times he passed by his home without stopping during a thirteen-year period of living in the open. He learned lessons well from his ancestors. Finally, he succeeded in bringing the flood waters of the Yellow River under control. By dredging, he deepened the channel. Then he dug diversion canals for rivers and lakes eventually leading to the sea. This relieved the heavy flow of blocked water in the mainstream.

After a fantastic effort, Yu conquered the river. For his success as a hydrological engineer, Yu was given sovereign authority as leader of the tribal union by Shun. Thus, Yu became a hero of the Chinese nation, venerated as "Yu the Great" and respected by all generations which followed.

Every stable dynasty in China's history, in the absence of a major war, built some water conservation projects for flood control. Many were started in very early times and later repaired and reinforced by the efforts of subsequent generations. Even now they play a significant role. To avoid inundation by breaching, the great dykes along the lower reaches of the Yellow River--1,800 kilometers in length--were started in the Spring and Autumn Period. To provide transportation, flood water diversion, drainage of waterlogged soils and irrigation, construction of the Grand Canal extending from Beijing to Hangzhou began in the late Warring States period. Finally, for protection against tidal waves in the Jiangsu and Zhejiang provinces, a seawall of several hundred kilometers was started during the Eastern Han Dynasty in the first century. All of these great and ancient water conservation projects can be proudly matched with that attraction which visiting tourists know best--The Great Wall.

The accomplishments in flood control after the new China was founded are exceeded by those of any ancient dynasty. A total of

170,000 kilometers of dykes have been repaired and newly built on rivers, lakes and seawalls during the past 35 years, as well as 86,000 new reservoirs with a total water reserve capacity of 421 billion cubic meters.

The Yellow River, twice flooded in three years of history and historically called "The Sorrow of China," has not caused one serious disaster for more than thirty years. It successfully withstood the tests of two heavy floods, one in 1958, the other in 1982. This was accomplished with an elaborate system of flood control projects consisting of reservoirs and dykes along the main waterways and tributaries, coupled with many retention basins and a realignment of rivers and newly built watercourses leading to the Yellow Sea and the Yangzi River. The 3,500 kilometer-long dykes along the Yangzi held firm during the high water in 1954 and again in 1983 because new flood control projects had been built in the lower reaches of the Yangzi, the dykes were reinforced, and the largest tributary--the Han Jiang River-- had been harnessed. The flood discharge volume of the Hai He River valley was greatly increased by digging and dredging more than 30 major watercourses, and the flood storage capacity was greatly increased by enlarging the number of reservoirs in the mountainous areas of the upper reaches of the Hai He River. Similar progress has been made in harnessing the Huai He, the Pearl, the Liao He and the Song Hua Jiang rivers.

There is no time, however, for relaxation. The flood losses were heavy in Henan Province in 1975 and in Sichuan Province in 1981 from torrential rains over wide areas. The battle against devastating floods must continue, perhaps for several generations. Efforts in reforestation must gain momentum, coupled with soil stabilization and water conservation projects in the upper reaches of rivers and in the mountainous areas. The only viable long-term answer to the problems of silting and flooding of the Yellow River will be to prevent soil erosion in the middle and upper reaches. With soil erosion in the Loess Plateau still rampant, strategies for permanently harnessing the river are still problematical. The Loess Plateau remains the weakest (most fragile and erosive) region of China.

Irrigation and Agricultural Productivity

China abounds with ancient water works for irrigation. One of the greatest irrigation projects in the world is the Du Jiang Weir in Guanxian County about 40 kilometers south of Chengdu in Sichuan Province (Figure 2). Water was channeled from the Min Jiang River, a tributary of the Yangzi, to irrigate 200,000 hectares of rich farmland in the Chengdu Plain.

Figure 2. The Du Jiang Weir in Guanxian County is the oldest and most famous water works in China.

Until the water was harnessed, the rapid flow in the upper reaches of the Min Jiang, at over 3,000 meters above sea level, often caused inundations in the middle and lower reaches of the Chengdu Plain. To combat this, the Du Jiang Weir was built in the middle of the Min Jiang River bed, separating it into an inner and outer river to channel the water and divert floods. An opening, named Treasury Bottle Mouth, was dug through the Yulei Hill near the Guanxian County town. The ravages of the Min Jiang River were thus abolished by excavating these two great canals on the plain of Chengdu. This transformed otherwise disastrous floods into beneficial water resources. Under normal conditions, the water is diverted into the inner river or channel for irrigating the Chengdu Plain. During times of flooding, the surplus water overflows into the outer river, thus assuring water control without building a dam. This great irrigation system was originally constructed in 256 B.C. and provided water for over 200,000 hectares of rich farmland without modern engineering technologies and in the absence of the modern science of water conservation. It was built by Li Bing, a local official in Sichuan, and his son. The components were gravel, bamboo and wood. There was no cement or steel. Because there were no explosives, rock hills were removed by sprinkling cold water on rocks heated with charcoal to make them crack so they could be stripped off layer by layer. The entire project, with its channels and subchannels, was laid out on the spot only by visual survey of water flow and topographical conditions; there were no surveying instruments. An inscription carved by Li Bing at the site remains to this day: "Dig the sand-beach deep, so there will be enough water for agriculture. Make the overfill spillway low, so that surplus water can run off and not cause floods." For more than 2,200 years, the Du Jiang Weir has made the Chengdu Plain a fertile, richly endowed agricultural area. Two great Men Temples were built in 497 A.D. at the Du Jiang Weir for offering sacrifices to the spirits of Li Bing and his son, Li Erlong, who completed the project, in recognition of their great contributions. The temples are well preserved to this day. The Du Jiang Weir still remains functional, and the irrigated areas have been expanded severalfold.

The Du Jiang Weir is only one of several great irrigation schemes built in ancient China. Among the others are the vast irrigated expanses in the Great Bend of the Yellow River valley of Inner Mongolia and Ningxia; the Shaope Irrigation Project in Anhui Province; the twelve canals channeling water from the Zhang He River in Hebei Province; the Zhengguo Canal of Shaanxi Province; the Lingqu Canal of Guangxi Province; and the Taihu Lake Water Conservation Projects.

A rapidly expanding population has caused irrigated agriculture and new irrigation projects to assume an ever more important dimension for agricultural development since the founding of the new China. Vast areas previously devoted to dryland cropping have been converted to irrigated farmlands and paddy fields. Expansions of irrigated cropland have been the most important means of achieving a greater dependability of production as well as significantly increasing the magnitude of output. Since the early 1950s, 5,300 large-to intermediate-sized irrigation areas have been developed; 150 major irrigation districts each serving 20,000 or more hectares have been established; 80 million electric horsepower irrigation facilities have been constructed; and 2.5 million motor pump wells have been dug. Irrigated areas of farmland increased from 14 million hectares in 1949 to today's 47 million or nearly 50% of the arable land (Figure 3). The area sown to paddy rice has expanded from 22.7 to 33.3 million hectares, and irrigated dryland crops from 3.2 to 22.7 million hectares. These developments in irrigation are beyond those achieved during the same period by any other nation. Currently, only one-half of the total cropped area is irrigated, but the food grain output is two-thirds of the total. Irrigation has been applied to an extent unequalled elsewhere on earth. Agriculture in China consumes 88% of the total fresh water with industries and urban households accounting for the balance. The vast expanses of irrigated farmland now constitute the most important natural resource base for food grain production in China.

Many different irrigation technologies are used in irrigating crops (Figure 4). The large irrigated flatlands where water is abundant may

Figure 3. Irrigation of rice in Xinjiang (top), and furrow irrigation in Guangdong Province (bottom).

not be unusually attractive, but the water channeling projects for irrigating arid and mountainous areas are something to behold! The Red Flag Canal in Linxian County, Henan Province is a good example (Figure 5). It begins in Pingshun County of Shanxi Province and carries 25 cubic meters of water per second to Linxian County. Construction began in 1960 and was completed nine years later. It runs a total of 2,000 kilometers with the trunk canal, other canals and all the branches, and cuts through 1,250 mountain peaks. The canal includes 180 tunnels totalling 31 kilometers in length and 150 aqueduct bridges with a total length of 6.5 kilometers. There are 338 reservoirs, 250 water pump stations and 52 hydropower stations alongside. It irrigates 40,000 hectares of farmland and provides water for daily use and electricity for the industrial and agricultural production of the area.

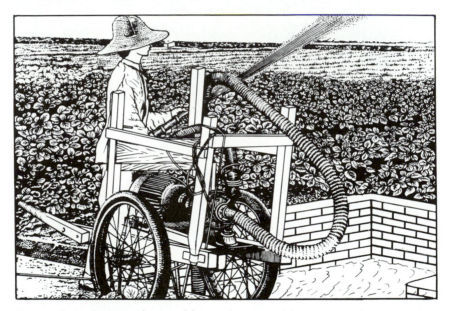

Figure 4. Irrigation of vegetables with a portable pump and nozzle in Guangdong Province.

The "Kan-Er-Jin" is another unique approach to water conservation and management dating back 2,000 years (Figure 6). These underground tunnels created by the Uygur people in Turpan and Hami channel water from the Tianshan Mountains in China's far northwest Xinjiang Autonomous Region to the desert areas of Turpan and Hami. Most of the water would otherwise be lost through surface evaporation from open canals during transfer through the long distance in the desert from the melt of the mountain snowfields. Vertical wells were dug at 25-meter intervals along the underground tunnels. The well depths decrease gradually in accordance with the downward slopes. The water eventually

Figure 5. The Red Flag Canal in Henan Province.

comes to open ditches near the desert farmlands where it is used for irrigation. A description of the "Kan-Er-Jin" was recorded as *jingqu* (welled ditch) in classical historical records more than 2,000 years ago, when they were adopted in some arid areas in Central and Southwest Asia.

Interregional Water Transfer

A characteristic and major constraint on future agricultural development in China, both vertically and horizontally, is the uneven distribution of water resources. The mismatch of abundant, good land with water deficits in the North and the restriction of good land in the South, where water is most abundant, is a cruel disparity of food-producing resources in a nation of over one billion people. For the strategic development of agriculture, there has been much discussion in recent years of diverting water from the abundant regions of the south to the water-deficient areas of the north. Chairman Mao Zedong proposed such a project as early as 1952.

Figure 6. The "Kan-Er-Jin" under ground water system in Xinjiang.

A project is now underway, the first stage having been approved in February, 1983, to channel water from South to North China by pumping from the Yangzi River through the Grand Canal. This would supplement the water supply in the valleys of the Yellow River, the Huai He and the Hai He. They are important agricultural areas for the production of food grains, cotton, edible oils and other cash crops. Water resources, however, are inadequate; and the drought-stricken area has approximated 20 million hectares during the past three decades. This is over half the drought-afflicted acreage in China. Moreover, as droughts occur successively, reservoirs dry up, water transportation is disrupted because of drops in water levels, underground water tables recede, and soil subsidence is rampant because of overutilization of groundwater. A lack of water has put a damper on future agricultural production, transportation and industrial expansion and is affecting the daily life of the people. Beijing currently (1987) has a serious water shortage from overdraft of groundwater.

The first stage of this project was started in the mid-1960s in the Jiangsu Province, where four large pumping stations were installed to channel an average of 4.1 billion cubic meters of water per year from the south to the northern part of that province (Figure 7). The result has been a change in the cropping system from the traditional three dryland

Figure 7. A large pumping station for water transfer.

crops in two years to two crops of rice and wheat in one year. An annual increase in food grain output of 1.25 million tons has been realized. The project has also insured bumper harvests in Jiangsu during drought years as well as a relief from inundations by flooding during periods of heavy rain.

This interregional water transfer project will be conducted step by steps in the decades ahead. The water channel capacity will be 700 to 1000 cubic meters per second starting with the Yangzi River, 200 to 600 cubic meters per second in the North at the Yellow River, and terminate in Tianjin, a major industrial city in North China. Thus the water shortages in Beijing and Tianjin--two of China's largest cities--will be overcome.

This project will involve crossing the southern part of Shandong Province and then the Yellow River. The Jiangsu pumping station will be enlarged and others installed with the necessary transmission lines. A major task will be the construction of an underground siphon culvert passing through the Yellow River bed.

There will be costs (estimated at $5.2 billion but this could easily be doubled), risks and hazards with this project. Salinization, already a problem in the north plain's farmland, could worsen. Careful consideration, however, will be given to prevent undesirable ecological side effects and secondary salinization, with which the Chinese have had considerable experience (see Chapter 6, "Good Crops from Salty Soils"). The potential benefits reside in both vertical and horizontal enhancement of agricultural production, greater industrialization, and meeting the challenge of feeding over a billion people.

FOR FURTHER READING

Biwas, A. K.; Zuo Dakang; J. E. Nickum; and Liue Changming, eds. 1984. *Long distance water transfer: A Chinese case study and international experience*. Dublin: Tycooly International Publishing Ltd.

Clayre, A. 1985. *The heart of the dragon*. Boston: Houghton Mifflin Co.

Editorial Board of China Water Conservancy. 1981. Water conservancy in China. *Almanac of China's Economy* 4:144-48. (In Chinese)

Han Baocheng. 1986. Three gorges project: Is it feasible? *Beijing Review* 29: 16-20.

———. 1986. The benefits of the three gorges project. *Beijing Review* 30: 22-23.

Ma Zongshen. 1982. Floodwater in ancient China and deeds of Hsia Yu in water control. *Agricultural Archaeology*, no. 2. (In Chinese)

Nickum, J. E. 1983. *Irrigation management in China: A review of the critical literature*. World Bank Staff Working Paper No. 545. Washington, D.C.: The World Bank.

Pierres, S. 1984. *Water: Rethinking management in an age of scarcity*. Worldwatch Paper 62. Washington, D.C.: Worldwatch Institute.

Qian Zhengying. 1983. The problems of river control in China. *Proceedings of the Second International Symposium on River Sedimentation*. Beijing: Water Resources and Electric Power Press. (In Chinese)

Stone, B. 1983. The Chang Jiang Diversion project: An overview of economic and environmental issues. In *Long-distance water transfer: A Chinese case study and international experience*, ed. A. K. Biswas, Zuo Dakang, J. E. Nickum and Liu Changming. Water Resources Series, vol. 3. Dublin: Tycooly International Publishers Ltd.

Wang Huayun. 1984. Taming the Yellow River. *China Reconstructs* 33(7): 37-40.

Wang Zhibin. 1985. A brief history of farmland water conservancy in Yellow River valley. *Agricultural Archaeology*, no. 2. (In Chinese)

Wu Minliang. 1983. Scientific value of Dujiang Weir and great profits of the past serving the present. *Agricultural Archaeology*, no. 2. (In Chinese)

Zhang Yue. 1984. Exploitation and utilization of water resources in China. *Almanac of China's Economy* 5: 77-82. (In Chinese)

FOR FURTHER READING

5

THE POTENTIALS
OF GRASSLANDS

by Yu Youtai

China's grasslands are rich, picturesque and colorful. An Inner Mongolian folk song of 1,500 years ago describes the landscape, the thriving and luxuriant grasses and the grazing of cattle and sheep:

Blue and bright the sky shines,
Far and wide the steppe runs;
Softly and gently blows a breeze
Over the exuberant wilderness,
Revealing sheep and cattle from among the bending grasses.

Distribution

Almost 40% (353 million hectares) of China is grassland--about three times the amount of cultivated area. China's grasslands compare in magnitude to those of Australia, the U.S.S.R. and the U.S.A.--the other large countries with vast grassland areas.

Four-fifths of China's grasslands stretch extensively and continuously in ten pastoral regions and agricultural-pastoral areas, from the most northeastern sections to those of the far northwest. Some are called steppes, which are the easternmost parts of the European-Asian belt and comprise an area of 287 million hectares. Less than one-fifth of China's grasslands (about 47 million hectares) are scattered in the hillside pastures and mountainous regions of the southern and middle provinces. In addition to these two grassland areas, there are other widely dispersed areas amounting to about 20 million (Figure 1).

China's grasslands are used as range, hay pastures and artificial pastures. Administrative divisions and the natural conditions of topography, elevation, climate and vegetation divide the grasslands roughly into the following regions.

Figure 1. The grasslands of China.

The Northeastern and Inner Mongolian Meadow Steppes. These include grassland areas in the northeastern three provinces and the eastern parts of Inner Mongolia, where the terrain slopes gently and the mountains are low. The winters are cold and long, the summers humid and short, and the climate ranges from semi-arid to semi-humid. Precipitation occurs mostly during the summer and ranges from 350 to 750 mm. The soil is fertile and the herbages grow luxuriantly. The potential for hay production here is rich, and improved man-made or artificial pastures are easily established for the support of beef cattle, dairy cows and fine-wool sheep. Although the Northeastern steppe occupies only 2% of China's total grassland area, it is one of the best.

Inner Mongolian Steppes. This region includes the dry and desert steppes in the middle parts of Inner Mongolia and the northern parts of Hebei Province. It has a gently sloping terrain, and a semi-arid and comparatively dry climate. Annual precipitation varies from 200 to 350 mm, most of which occurs in summer and autumn. Rainfall and pasture productivity decrease from east to west. Within the steppes of the eastern parts of this region there are many hay pastures, but the western parts are semi-desert and the grasses are short and sparse with only a few improved hay pastures.

Within the Inner Mongolian steppes there is an abundance of grasses suitable for raising sheep and lambs for fine wool (Figure 2). These steppes are one of the most important natural resources supporting China's animal industries.

Figure 2. Fine wool sheep of Inner Mongolia.

The Northwestern Deserts. This region extends from the western parts of Inner Mongolia through the Ningxia and Gansu provinces and on to the extensive Gobi Desert regions of the far northwest Xinjiang Autonomous Region. It is the territory of the Bactrian "two-humped" camel. Mean annual precipitation ranges from 100 to 200 mm. The climate is dry, sunlight is intense, evaporation is high, and summers are warm to hot. The melting alpine snow converges into numerous rivers and brooks which flow toward the steppes. There are many highly productive mountainous and alpine pastures for the grazing of sheep and cattle during the summer months. This area is also famous for producing fine-wool sheep and lambs.

The Xinjiang grasslands or pastures, which are divided into the southern and northern parts by the Tianshan Mountains constitute the major portion of the grasslands in this region. Those south of the Tianshan Mountains, in the Xinjiang are dry, desert steppes which are hot in summer. The annual precipitation is less than 100 mm. In the Xinjiang north of the Tianshan Mountains the climate is semi-humid because of airflow from the Arctic Ocean. The annual precipitation is 100 to 200 mm, possibly as high as 500 mm in some of the meadow steppes of the alpine valleys. Grass production here per unit land area is the highest in all of China's grasslands. Here there are mountains, snowfields, pastures (some improved), fields, streams, forests, yurts, flowers and birds--the music of nature. The pastures are of especially high quality in the Yili region of the Northwest, where the ranging cattle and sheep and the "cow-boys" and sheep-herders that look after them are often reminiscent of the "Old West" in the U.S.A. (Figure 3). Xinjiang is big in area but small in population, hot by day and cold by night, rich in tradition but new in spirit. It is a "Home on the Range" for China.

Figure 3. A herd of horses in Northwest China.

Qinghai-Xizang Cold Alpine Range. This area is made up of the high, cold, mountainous regions of the Qinghai and Xizang (Tibet) provinces and the western extremities of the Sichuan Province--the unique plateau known as the "Roof of the World," where most of the mountain ranges have elevations of over 3,000 meters. This region is one of the oldest for the development of animal husbandry in China. The Xizang Range comprises the major part of this region. It has a cold and dry climate and annual precipitation of less than 200 mm. In northern Xizang there are vast herds of economically valuable wild animals such as donkeys, yaks and Tibetan antelopes. Grasses no higher than 50 millimeters (known as alpine meadow grasses) spread over more than 90% of the land area of southern Xizang. This carpet-like grassland cover in the alpine meadows is considered an economic treasure for animal husbandry.

The Qinghai Range is a desert and semi-desert steppe fit only for pasturing camels and Mongolian sheep. The range around Qinghai Lake in the northeastern Qinghai Province is especially suited for developing semi-fine wool sheep of the wool- and meat-type. In the Yushu Range of the southeastern section of Qinghai Province, rainfall is high and vegetation is good. This is an ideal pasture for sheep. "Xining Wool," well known in China, is produced there. All of southeast Qinghai is an alpine meadow and is the main production area for yaks.

The Qinghai-Xizang Range which extends from Tibet eastward to Sichuan Province is referred to as the Sichuan Range. For the most part it is a vast and luxuriant swamp meadow abounding in the short Kobresia. The "Songpan grassland" where the Chinese Red Army passed through on its long march is in the eastern part of this region (Figure 1).

The Middle and Southern Mountainous and Hillside Grasslands. This region is made up of the vast hilly lands from the warm temperate zone of mid-China to the subtropical and tropical zones of South China, and includes the grasslands of the Yunnan-Guizhou Plateau.

The lowlands, river valleys and plains in the mountains of this part of China are mostly farmlands. Forests are commonly found on the highest elevations of the mountains. Secondary grasslands are found only where the slopes are steep, the soil layers thin and the forest destroyed. Consequently, in this region of mountainous and hillside grasslands, the farmlands and forests are distributed in staggered, scattered patterns and growing conditions for grassland vegetation and grasses vary greatly. The region is generally characterized by warm weather, sufficient moisture and favorable temperatures. Many varieties of grasses and herbage thrive in this area. Alternatively, however, there are areas where the herbage is of poor quality and cannot endure treading. This region's greatest potential is for beef cattle production.

Throughout China's vast territories there are also scattered grasslands in front of hamlets, surrounding houses and at brooksides. Such grasslands cannot be ignored as forage resources in the development of animal husbandry, and they are especially important for individual households with only one or two animals.

The Composition of China's Natural Grasslands

China's richly endowed grasslands abound in a great variety of native herbages for livestock. They may be grouped according to five main families of forage plants.

Palatable Grasses. Grasses are the principle herbages of China's grasslands. They constitute 90% of the vegetation in the meadow steppes and 70% in the other steppes. Only in the desert steppes are they inferior to the non-grass Compositae (daisy family) and Chenopodiaceae (goosefoot family) herbages. Although the nutritive value of the grasses may not be as high as some other herbaceous species, grasses have soft stems and leaves, with the edible parts greatly exceeding those of other herbages. Both as green forages and as hay, grasses are highly palatable to all kinds of livestock (Figure 4). Some of the major species include the following.

Figure 4. Dual-purpose (milk and meat) red cattle in the grasslands.

Chinese wild rye (*Aneurolepedium chinense* [Trin.] [Kitagawa]) is widespread in the northeast steppes and is one of China's best grasses. Harvested as hay, it develops a special flavor and can be stored for long periods. It is good not only for fattening beef cattle but is also excellent as a forage for dairy cattle. It is called "The Concentrate Among Herbages."

Brome grass or awnless brome (*Bromus inermis* [Leyss]) is widely distributed in China. This grass is highly resistant to alkalinity and grows in almost all soils with reasonably good drainage. It is not only one of the most widely adaptive of all grasses but is palatable for all kinds of livestock.

Sheep fescue (*Festuca ovina* [L.]) is widely distributed in both the northwest and southwestern regions of China. It is drought resistant and winter hardy and grows mainly on the steppes. Because of its high nutritional value, it is used for fattening. It is especially valuable, as the name implies, for the fattening of sheep and thus has enjoyed the laudatory title of "Sheep-Fattening Grass."

High Protein Legumes. Legumes, along with grasses, comprise the principal forages of grassland vegetation. The proportion of legumes in a grassland or pasture usually runs from 5 to 10% and seldom more than 10 to 25%. Legumes are sparse on desert and semi-desert steppes. China's principal grassland legumes follow.

Alfalfa (*Medicago sativa* [L.]) is a highly nutritious perennial legume for all kinds of livestock. One kilogram of high quality alfalfa hay corresponds to one kilogram of bran or half a kilogram of grain sorghum. In China, it is called "King of the Herbages."

Red Clover (*Trifolium pratense* [L.]) is one of the world-famous legumes grown in China. It is rich in nutrients and has a sweet flavor. The hay is good for the finishing (fattening) of both cattle and sheep. Red clover grows like a biennial rather than a perennial and requires frequent reseeding.

Astragatus adsurgens is a perennial which is widely distributed in China. It is among the most drought-, wind-, and blowing sand-resistant of all the herbages. The Chinese call this legume "Sadawang," which means that it grows luxuriantly in both wind and sandstorms. The herdsmen of the Xinjiang Autonomous Region of Northwest China call it "King of the Sand." It is, in addition to its resistance to adverse climates, one of the best legumes available for a green forage, green forage paste or hay meal.

Composite Herbages. Of the total native grassland vegetation, composites are slightly more than 10%. From the eastern meadows to the western desert steppes, the proportion of composite herbages gradually increases and the feeding value rises proportionally. The palatability for different animals varies. Camels, as compared with other grazing animals, relish composite plants.

Wormwood or wild sage (*Artemisia frigida* [Wild]) is the most important of the composite plants. It is a small perennial subshrub characterized by both drought resistance and winter hardiness. It can endure severe treading and has remarkable regenerative ability. Wild sage, rich in mineral nutrients, effectively fattens all kinds of livestock and promotes lactation for milk animals. In the winter and spring when the range is short of herbages, it is regarded as the "Rescue Grass."

Alkali- or Saline- and Drought-Resistant Plants of the Chenopodiaceae (goosefoot family). These are found on both desert and semi-desert steppes. They are succulent, fleshy, saline (salt) resistant and rich in nutrients. The most abundant and nutritious are winterfat (*Eurotia ceratoides* [L.] [Mey]), prostrate summer cypress (*Kochia prostrata* [L.] [Schrad.]) and Russian thistle (*Salsola colina* [Pall]). Camels are the best foragers for such plants, followed by sheep, goats and finally horses; cattle do not find them palatable. Winterfat is known as the "Camel's Wormwood." Dead Russian thistle plants are shaped like a bulb and form a ball in the winter and spring. They are the "tumbling tumbleweeds" of rangelands. They roll across the grasslands and desert landscapes with the wind. Hence, they are called "herbage rolling with the wind," or the "vagrant" of the range. It is the herbage that camels like best, but in other parts of the world it is considered an undesirable weed.

Sedges. Sedges are widely spread over bogs and low wet grasslands. The sedge (*Carex desertorum* [L.]) is short and small. If harvested before heading or seeding, it rivals grasses for pasturage, silage-making or hay-making.

One sedge variety, (*Corbresia bellardi* [All.] [Degl.]), is distributed chiefly over the alpine meadows. It is characterized by its soft texture, high nutrient value and palatability. In the Qinghai-Xizang Plateau of Tibet, the crude protein content of Corbresia may be 15 to 20% and the crude fat 6 to 8%. It is also high in a number of vitamins and thus is praised as the "Herbage Rich in the Three Nutrients."

The Precious "Live Wealth" of China

The animals pastured on China's grasslands now account for approximately 35% (excluding pigs) of the population of different livestock. Of this total, 80% of the sheep, 75% of the camels, 50% of the horses and 20% of the cattle come from the grasslands. Some world-famous breeds of animals have had their origins in the grasslands of China.

Horses. In China they are known as "light vehicles on the range." They have long been used both for warfare and for agriculture. An old Chinese saying declares, "Boats in the South and horses in the North." Horses are an important means of transportation in North China. They can be classified as follows.

The Mongolian pony is native to the Inner Mongolian steppe and is now distributed over the entire northern region of China. Mongolian ponies were first introduced into the Western world in the thirteenth century during an expedition by King Cheng Jisihan. It has been reported that the ancestors of all the famous horse breeds in the world can be traced to the Mongolian and Arabian ponies. Although the Mongolian pony is relatively small, it has great adaptability, endures coarse fodder and hard work, has a long life, and is able to travel long distances.

The "Sanhe" horse (Figure 5) is big and tall by contrast, with a beautiful body conformation and a purplish red color. It is good at fast and long-distance running, and has outstanding drafting ability. The Sanhe horses were bred from the Mongolian pony and are the champion horses of China.

Figure 5. The "Sanhe" horse -- China's champion breed.

The "Kazak" horse is found throughout the steppes of the North Xinjiang Autonomous Region. Its body conformation resembles that of the Mongolian pony but is slightly taller. It is used both as a draft animal and for its milk, but is mainly for riding. Its milk ("Koumiss") is the favorite among beverages for the nomadic minorities of Northwest China. The "Yili" horse, an improved breed of the Kazak, is an excellent light horse. It is called "Heaven Horse" in Chinese history.

The "Hequ" horse is also found in the northwestern extremes of China. It is taller and more powerful than the Mongolian pony and can be used for both riding and drafting, but is more suitable for draft purposes. The Hequ horse has long been considered a contribution from the border area to the central government because of its excellent riding and drafting abilities.

The "South-West" horse has been popularized in the southwest provinces of China. It has a relatively short body and is strong and nimble, adept at traversing rugged mountain paths, and is most suitable as a pack animal. Its packed weight may surpass one-third of its body weight, making it superior to all other small-sized horses of the world.

Sheep. In the grasslands of China, sheep are known as "pearls in the green sea." During their long history, they have spread widely throughout the country. There are many breeds, which can be roughly divided into three groups.

"Mongolian" sheep are the most common breed throughout the country and comprise about one-half of the total sheep in China. The meat or mutton is delicious, having delicate fiber mixed with fat. The instant boiled mutton of the Dong Lai Shun Restaurant in Beijing is renowned both in China and abroad.

The two best known breeds developed from Mongolian sheep are the "Tan" and the "San Bei." The former abound in the Ningxia Province. They have pure white, shining fur or wool, which is warm, light and rich in appearance. The Tan sheep with its beautiful light fur is found only in China. The San Bei sheep are most famous for the wool of the lamb, which is a shining, dark purple color, while the wool ends are black and curved, resulting in a beautiful pattern. The San Bei lamb fur and that of the marten (a weasel-like carnivorous mammal with a long tail and a coat of fine fur) are among the most valuable furs in the world.

The "Kazak" sheep are found mainly in the Xinjiang Autonomous Region. The famous "Xinjiang Fine-Wool Sheep" (Figure 6) is a cross or hybrid of the famous Kazak and the male Caucasus sheep from the U.S.S.R. It is the first of the fine-wool breeds and had its origin in China in 1954.

The "Xizang" (Tibetan) sheep is the characteristic breed of the cold alpine meadow. In numbers, it is second only to Mongolian sheep. The Tibetan is a kind of coarse-wool sheep and provides excellent material for carpets known to the world as "Xizang Wool."

Goats. One of the earliest of domesticated herbivorous farm animals, goats range from agricultural to pastoral areas. They are gregarious animals, obey orders and are desirable bellwethers (leaders of the flock) for sheep-grazing. Goats are very tolerant of coarse fodders, like to eat branches and leaves of bushes, and do not vie with other animals for forages. Well-known goat breeds in China include the following:

The "Kahmiri" is distributed in southwestern Xizang and is a down-bearing breed. The down hair is well known in international markets as cashmere, a name now being used as a general term for all kinds of down hairs. The world's annual output of goat down hair is 6,000 tons, half of which is produced in China.

The "Albas White" goat is found most widely in Inner Mongolia. This is true also of the "White Down Goat." These goats can be used both for their down and meat. The down hair output is high. A famous breed found in southern China is the "Riverside Big White" goat, which is raised in the Guizhou Province.

Camels. In China, camels are called "boats in the desert" because of the way a camel train moves or floats across the vast expanse of a desert. Camel raising was recorded in China as early as the third century B.C. There are two species of camels: one-humped and two-humped. Chinese camels are two-humped (Figure 7) and are distributed mainly in the desert steppe, where they easily traverse desert and sand dunes. Camels have great stamina and vitality and adapt to the harshest environments. They relish the Russian thistle or the tumbleweed and the bitter astringent grasses which other animals will not touch. Camels are of major importance on China's arid desert steppes. Their numbers approximated 500,000 in 1985.

It can well be said that every part of the camel is useful. The wool provides a high quality raw material for textiles, while camel meat and milk are the favorite foods of local herdsmen. "Camel's hump" is regarded as one of "The Eight Rare Delicacies" at a Chinese banquet (other delicacies include the camel's hoof, the monkey-head mushroom, bear's paw and edible bird's nest). The camel's skin, bones, blood and afterbirth are used as raw materials for light industries and are often used for medicine.

Figure 6. "Xinjiang Fine-Wool" sheep.

Figure 7. The two-humped Chinese camel.

Yaks. Yaks (Figure 8) are the distinctive breed of cattle on the Qinghai-Xizang Plateau. The animal feeds on rough grasses, and its ability to go without food approaches that of the camel. The yak has great stamina and high resistance to disease and cold. Its hairy winter coat reaches to the ground to form an apron-like protective barrier against the wind and snow. The yak's large hooves are sharp-edged like mountain-climbing shoes, so they can easily travel the snow-covered mountains. This makes them an invaluable means in Tibet for transporting both humans and produce and has earned them the name of "Vehicles on the Highlands." Furthermore, the yaks also provide the Tibetans with butter, meat, fuel, hides and wool, from which carpets, tents, bags, saddles and even ropes are made. There are currently four million yaks in China (mostly in Tibet). There could be a great future market for this hard, frizzy-haired cousin of the American buffalo and the many products it furnishes despite the most extreme of environments.

Figure 8. The yaks of the Qinghai-Xizang Plateau.

The Grasslands--Nature's Zoological and Botanical Gardens of China

Rare birds, wild animals and valuable medicinal herbs are a treasure trove of China's grasslands. Mongolian gazelles (Figure 9) and wild horses, donkeys and camels on the Qinghai-Xizang Plateau are noted for their remarkable speed and endurance. Tibetan gazelles, white-lipped deer (*Cervus albirostris* [Przewalski]) and wild yaks native to the "Roof of World" are seldom seen in foreign zoos, and are among the national treasures of China. The *Rucervus eldi*, exotic deer in Guangdong Province, are beautiful in posture and praised as world rarities.

The vast grasslands are also a natural habitat for wild rats, with over 170 species now identified. The species vary with the types of grasslands.

While they dig holes, gnaw grasses and are generally destructive of grasslands, they provide a large number of pelts. The Himalayan coarse-furred marmots (Figure 10), for example, produce pelts that compare favorably with those of otters and martens.

The grasslands have many bird varieties. Among them are the skylarks and larks noted for their soaring flight and beautiful songs. The long-eared and feathered bustard (*Otis tarda*) (Figure 11) is among the largest birds of the grasslands. Bustards can neither fly high nor sing, but they like to gather in the haunts of skylarks as if they were their faithful audience. Alpine snowcocks are found year-round in the Xinjiang Autonomous Region, where they perch on grasslands at sea levels above 3,500 meters. The northern and northwestern steppes in China are called "Land of Fish beyond the Great Wall" because they are criss-crossed by many rivers and streams, with a scattering of lakes and ponds. These regions have a rich fishery resource potential. The predominant species are crucian carp and the salmon-like *Hucho*.

Optimal Utilization of Grasslands and Looking to the Future

The grasslands are the most important resource base in China for the further development of an expanding livestock industry. They also impact on the climate of North China, conserve soil and moisture, resist winds, fix the sand and maintain an agro-ecological equilibrium. Overgrazing of grasslands in the North and West has resulted in serious soil erosion, deterioration of plant resources, desertification and salinization.

Excessive cultivation, lumbering and removal of valuable medicinal herbs in many areas and over long periods are additional problems. According to 1976 statistics, there were approximately 47 million hectares of deteriorated range where water conditions were comparatively good and population density was high. Range deterioration is accompanied by a gradual decrease in grass of good quality, a great increase in poisonous and harmful plants, serious soil erosion and a conspicuous decline in grass yields. All these factors lead to a decrease in the quantity and quality of animal products. Rare birds and animals and medicinal herbs also tend to disappear. The result is an ecological imbalance. Alternatively, almost one-third of the outlying desert steppes, which lack transport capabilities and water resources, have neither been developed nor utilized. Most grasslands of the mountainous and hillside regions in South and Central China have not yet been put to good use.

It is estimated that until now the livestock population on China's rangelands (grasslands) is equivalent to only 46% of the potential

Figure 9. Mongolian gazelles are native to the "Roof
of the World."

Figure 10. Himalayan
coarse-furred marmots
have pelts comparable to
otters and martens.

Figure 11. The largest
bird of the grasslands
(*Otis tarda*).

carrying capacity. The production potential of China's grasslands is also far greater than the current output. To better utilize the grasslands, the Chinese have recently seeded pastures, planted trees, returned the reclaimed grassland and forests to pastures and woodlands, and improved and established the rangelands. New approaches for reclamation include combinations of agriculture and forestry (agriforestry) and animal husbandry, according to ecological balance. Government actions intended to promote future ecological equilibria for grasslands include the following actions.

There is an intensification of efforts to establish and utilize the vast arid and semi-arid western rangelands. The principal measures include sound scientific grazing systems; paddock grazing; rotation of hay harvests with pasture to allow for herbage restoration; fencing the paddocks; building livestock sheds; providing access to paddocks and water sites; developing mechanization of animal husbandry; improving the control of rats and other pests; overdrilling with quality grass and fertilizers; establishing wells as a source of irrigation; and controlling the carrying capacity and livestock population.

Stock should be fattened for slaughter the same year they are born. The frequent natural calamities of drought, high winds, cold and snow in the northern and western pastoral areas make it difficult to protect livestock and to establish improved pastures. There is the Chinese adage that livestock are "well-fed in summer, fat in autumn, thin in winter and dead in spring." Livestock losses are often of such magnitude that the country's demand is far in excess of the supply. The "white calamity" caused by heavy winter snows often results in more than a million dead animals in some years. This is precisely what happened in the winter of 1985-86, when more than 1.7 million head of livestock died of starvation due to a snow storm that hit Qinghai Province. It is urgent that lambs and beef cattle be fattened for slaughter the year of their birth.

Sufficient utilization of existing hay pastures and the establishment of artificial pastures according to local conditions is important. Improved hay production, harvesting and storage would alleviate the shortage of forages in winter and spring. Only regions with comparatively good water supplies, moderate temperatures and productive soil should be selected for establishing artificial or managed pastures. To serve a modern livestock industry in China, managed pastures covering up to 3 to 5% of the total grassland area must be developed. Stable high yields per unit land area must be achieved through intensive cropping systems in the same way that land and water are managed for the production of staple food crops in the farming areas. The mode of pasture feeding must be changed, using a feeding regime of overwintering with supplementary feeding for finishing or fattening. Cooperation with the nearby semi-pastoral unit and farming districts must be sought, whereby the pastoral area supplies the pasturages for summer ranges and fattening of stock and the farming or semi-pastoral area supplies partial forages for winter and spring.

The southern and middle grasslands of the mountainous and hillside regions must be increasingly utilized. These areas are characterized by a warm, wet climate and a long growing season. Most of the vegetation is secondary, having been formed after the destruction of forests. It is scattered over the steep alpine slopes where the soil is thin, fragile and easily eroded. Transportation is difficult and water resources are often insufficient. Although these mountains and hillside grasslands are often rich in herbage yields, the herbages are of low quality and contain few legumes. More importantly, most mountainous grasslands cannot endure the trampling or treading of the grazing animals. Thus, it is easy to cause deterioration of the pastures--soil erosion often becomes rampant, especially in the northern pastoral area. The relationship between agriculture, forestry and animal husbandry in mountainous regions must be handled cautiously and wisely.

FOR FURTHER READING

Chinese Academy of Agricultural Science. Institute of Rangeland. 1980. *Grasslands.* Beijing: Science Press. (In Chinese)

DeBoer, A. J., ed. 1984. *Ruminant livestock in intensive agricultural areas of Sichuan Province, China: Current status and development research.* Report of a joint study team on Livestock Development Prospects in Sichuan Province, China. Morrilton, Ark.: Winrock International.

Dewey, D. R. 1983. *Exploration for forages in central and northwestern China, July 12-August 20.* Administrative Report. Washington, D.C.: United States Department of Agriculture/Agricultural Research Service.

Hoefer, J. A., and P. J. Tsuchitami. 1980. *Animal agriculture in China.* People's Republic of China, Committee on Scholarly Communication. Washington, D.C.: National Academy Press.

Stewart, B. A. ed. 1983. Range livestock production in the People's Republic of China. *Proceedings of the International Symposium.* Consortium for International Development, Winrock International Livestock Research and Training Center, Society for Range Mangement, New Mexico State University, 9-10 March.

Zhang Minghua. 1982. *China's grasslands.* Beijing: Commercial Press. (In Chinese)

Zhaorigebatu. 1985. The changing grasslands. *China Reconstructs* 34(5): 25-26.

6

GOOD CROPS
FROM SALTY SOILS

by Sun Han

> You have only your methods of cultivation and utilization of
> soil to blame if you fail to reap good crops from it.

Such are the brave words coming from Chinese farmers. These words
describe the tremendous efforts of Chinese farmers, in a country of
enormous populations and limited natural resources. They have sought
every possible way to improve harvests on small pieces of land, with
many obstructing factors. Productivity of otherwise arable land is
constrained by saline-alkali (salty) conditions, water and wind erosion,
sandy soils in dry and windy deserts, waterlogged lowland areas, and the
red soils of the hills. These "problem soils" account for one-third of the
cultivated lands in China (Figure 1).

Largest among these are the 7.2 million hectares of saline-alkali or
salty soils. They may be classified according to three regional types,
based on natural conditions and the distinguishing features of their
formation and amelioration. First are the inland arid and semi-arid
saline-alkali soils, enclosed or semi-enclosed in the basins of the
Northwest, primarily in the Xinjiang. Here, the underground run-off
and dissolved salts have no outlet. With the arid climate, scanty rainfall
and high evaporation rates, salt accumulation at the soil surface is
intense. Second are the saline-alkali soils in the eastern semi-arid and
semi-moist monsoon areas. Here, spring droughts followed by summer
waterlogging are frequent. The result is a significant seasonal alteration
of salt accumulation and desalinization and frequent exchange of the salt
between the soil and the groundwater, resulting in the salinization of soil
and mineralization of groundwaters. Third are the salt-loaded tidal soils
along the seacoasts, where drainage is poor and the land is soaked with
seawater. Here, high salt levels occur in the soil as well as the
groundwater.

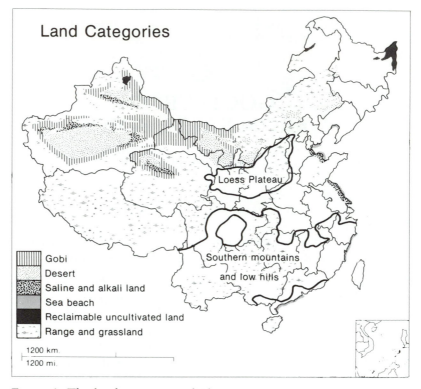

Figure 1. The land catagories of China.

Historical

Chinese farmers have been struggling for ages to ameliorate salty soils and make them productive. According to ancient agricultural records, such soils were made productive through rice culture before 600 B.C. Irrigation with the muddy waters of the Yellow River began in 360 B.C. By 246 B.C., salts were being washed away with water from irrigation channels. During 125-144 A.D., excess salts in the waterlogged lowlands were washed out through rice culture combined with channel drainage. Regrettably, effective wide-scale soil improvement programs were not possible during the long years of small farm economy. Since the founding of the People's Republic of China and the establishment of collectives, however, soil improvement programs for salty soils have been vigorously pursued as a part of agricultural development. Masses of farmers have been engaged in large-scale water conservation projects. Sixty percent of the otherwise unproductive saline-alkali or salty soils have now been improved for crop production. Yields have doubled, and doubled again, on such soils. Harvests of 7.5 tons of cereals or 750 kilograms of ginned cotton per hectare have been achieved. Such programs have contributed greatly to the overriding task of feeding the billion-plus people of China.

The Chinese have learned how to make salty soils productive by combining their own distinctive traditional ways with blends of modern technology. Essential for the amelioration of such soils is the ability to control drought, flooding and waterlogging as well as salinization and alkalization. Water conservation programs must be combined with agro-biological measures, and the elimination of salt combined with improvement of soil fertility.

Water Removal of Salt

"Salt comes and withdraws along with water."

This is a pointed declaration of Chinese farmers as to the interactions of water and salt in regions with saline-alkali soils. There is no concentration or convergence of salt in soils without the horizontal flow of water from areas of high concentration to those that are low. Similarly, there is no upward accumulation or downward leaching of salt in soil without perpendicular movement of water. Water movement, in turn, is determined by run-off on and below the soil surface. Thus, control and regulation of water-salt movement--through irrigation and drainage, in a basin or a region--is essential for improving the productivity of saline-alkali soils. Salinization can be either aggravated by inappropriate, or ameliorated by appropriate, water management technologies.

Some case histories may be drawn from relatively recent events. During the 1950s to the early 1960s, drainage was seriously neglected in the Jinmen Canal and Suiyue Temple Irrigation Networks of Hebei Province. The result was secondary salinization and eventual abandonment. Also, in Hebei, Shandong and Henan provinces, there was a large-scale diversion of water from the Yellow River for direct irrigation and to storage reservoirs built on the plains. There were no drainage outlets, and groundwater tables rose. The result was an increase to 3.24 million hectares of saline-alkali soils, up from a previous area of only 1.87 million hectares. Similar problems were encountered on some of the state farms in the reclaimed areas of the Xinjiang Autonomous Region of Northwest China. Excessive irrigation, coupled with poor drainage and aggravated salinization, reduced yields so greatly that farms were abandoned and the people had to move away.

Figure 2. A small-sized, fresh water reservoir.

These calamities set in action a comprehensive program to control aridity, flooding, waterlogging, salinization and alkalization. Water conservation projects for saline-alkali soils should include control of main river courses and all irrigation and drainage networks (Figure 2). While an overall systems approach must be taken for drainage, irrigation, water storage and water supply, drainage must be the focal point. It is primarily for drainage that canals have been constructed to direct the Huai He into the sea. Similarly, for the Hai He and other major river courses, the aim must be the opening of broader outlets for region-wide drainage. This is in addition to the use of water for irrigation. An ideal field drainage system requires an elaborate channel network with main outlets 1.2 to 1.5 meters deep and 200-300 meters between outlets. To do this, Chinese farmers have been digging innumerable channels for more than thirty years, chiefly by manual labor. Where gravity drainage is not possible or outlets are obstructed, pumping stations should be installed, thus combining the power-induced drainage with that of gravity.

Ideally, a drainage system should serve many purposes. It removes flood waters, irrigation wastewaters and leakage waters from channel outlets, and lowers the groundwater level. It will also expel from the soil the strongly mineralized water formed from salt leaching by rain or irrigation water and drain off saline waters, thus insuring steady desalinization. All these water conservation or removal programs are needed for the amelioration of salty soils near the sea. Dykes are also constructed along the seashores and floodgates installed at the mouths of rivers to protect against tidal soaking with salt and brackish waters. The Chinese rejoice that such projects have been comprehensively constructed along the entire coastline of China. These projects have contributed greatly to the enhancement of crop production and the feeding of a billion.

Crop irrigation from well water is of special importance in the amelioration of the saline-alkali soils in the highly populated monsoon areas of eastern China. Fresh groundwater resources occur in many areas where saline-alkali soils prevail. Shallow-level water is pumped from vertical wells, dug at such locations, and used for irrigation. This provides drought relief while salt is leached off and desalinization promoted. The lowering of groundwater levels from pumping also reduces resalinization. Underground space is also vacated, which increases the "storage capacity" for downward drainage and alleviates surface flooding.

A region that has traditionally suffered from severe droughts, waterlogging and soil salinization is Fengqiu County of Henan Province. During the 1970s more than 4,800 wells were dug, and crops were irrigated with the water. The results were phenomenal! Droughts were largely eliminated, waterlogging was alleviated, and groundwater tables were lowered two to four meters. The saline-alkalized areas were reduced by 80 percent, and the yields of cereal crops increased fourfold.

Growing Rice--Making Salty Soils Productive

A remarkably successful traditional practice in China has been the improvement of productivity of salty soils by rice culture. Such problem soils may be improved by rice production as long as freshwater resources are available, whether it be in the South, North, East or in West China. Growing rice accelerates the desalinization of salty soils as well as the ground water. Paddy-grown rice, of all major food crops, has the most intensive water requirement. During growth, the paddy fields are flooded, drained and renewed periodically (Figure 3). There is a continuous washing away of the salts. Such dissolved salts may percolate either downward by gravity or horizontally into drainage channels and canals. Data assembled from many areas show that rice production for

Figure 3. Paddy rice cultivation is a means of improving the productivity of saline-alkali soils.

one year reduces the salt content in the upper meter of the soil horizon, especially in the upper 20 centimeters, from levels of 0.6 to 1.0% salt to levels of 0.1 to 0.3%. Flooding, draining and renewing water in rice paddies through descending freshwater greatly dilutes the mineralized groundwater, and a surface layer of desalinated water is formed. In the coastal salt-impregnated soils, the mineralized levels of groundwater decreased from 30-35 grams/liter to 3.0-9.8 grams/liter following one year of rice cropping.

The effectiveness of soil and groundwater desalinization is increased with the duration of rice production. Rainfall in the Huang-Huai-Hai region is most concentrated during July and August. This renders the land prone to waterlogging, and dryland crops are difficult to grow. Rice, however, grows vigorously during this warm rainy period. The requirement for water is high and the rainfall can be fully utilized. The rice paddy fields also aid in water conservation. They reduce run-off and alleviate waterlogging in neighboring fields of dryland crops. Rice growing in such a region provides a double environmental return, and at the same time adds to the food supply. It minimizes waterlogging during the wet summer and improves the productivity of saline-alkali soils. Yields of rice exceeding 7.5 tons per hectare have been obtained from many fields reclaimed from these problem salty soils.

The effects of planting paddy rice on amelioration of salty soils depends not only on the duration of rice culture but even more so on unimpeded drainage outlets and whether the drainage system washes away the salts and controls the groundwater table. Observations at the Xinyang Experimental Station in Jiangsu Province showed that under good drainage, and with only one rice crop, the rate of desalinization in the 0-50 centimeter soil horizon was 74%. Mineralization of the groundwater dropped to 5 grams/liter after three crops of rice. With poor drainage, the desalinization rate for one year was only 49% while the mineralization of groundwater still remained high (7.5 grams/liter) after growing rice for seven years.

Rotation of rice with green manure crops combines improved land utilization with maintenance of soil fertility. This practice has been successfully pursued in the Huaibei region (north to the Huai He River) of Jiangsu, where vetch (*Vicia spp.*) is adapted for growing as a winter legume. Here farmers say, "Grow vetch first if you want to eat rice," and "Don't grow rice without vetch."

During the initial years of growing rice on salty soils, green manure crops are planted each winter. With progress in soil desalinization and improvement in soil fertility, the rotation system could be rice-green manure-rice-wheat. Such a system combines the results obtained in the amelioration of salty soils through planting rice and improving soil fertility from green manuring. This insures high yields of rice. Thus, the Huaibei region of the Jiangsu Province, formerly subjected to many natural disasters and characterized by low crop yields on salty soils, has been transformed into an important high-yielding site for commodity grains. This is a result of many years of water management, planting of rice, soil amelioration and fertility improvement.

Establishment of Farmland Ecological Systems

To transform saline-alkali soils into high-yielding farmlands in China requires more than desalinization of salty soils. There must be other improvements, including capital. They include the development of forest (including windbreaks) networks, land leveling, improvement of soil fertility, suitable cropping systems, green manuring and other acceptable ecological farming systems.

Forest Networks. The massive root systems of forest networks on farmlands remove water from underground and transpire it through the leaves into the atmosphere. This lowers the groundwater table. The Chinese farmers call this "biological drainage." It has proven effective. For example, the groundwater level on one block of black or honey locust (*Robinia pseudoacacia*) was lowered from 1.0 meters when the trees were planted to 1.2 to 1.5 meters five year later. A forest network also improves the microclimate around farmland. As a natural windbreak, it slows the wind speed over the ground surface, retards the exchange of air and alters the pattern of airflow (Figure 4). As a result, ground surface evaporation under the shelter of a forest network may decline by 10%. Thus the accumulation of salts from soil surface evaporation is slowed. Forests also provide firewood for relief of fuel shortages. Crop stalks and residues may then be plowed under for soil enrichment rather than used as fuel for cooking and home heating. The leaves that fall from certain trees and shrubs--such as false indigo (*Amorpha fruticosa*)--also improve soil texture and crop productivity.

Forest productivity has also been improved. Some salt-tolerant and rapidly growing shrubs and tree species have recently been identified. Others are under testing. Measures have also been taken, in recent years, to insure survival of a high percentage of transplanted trees and shrubs so that they will grow into forests. Complementary measures employed in

Figure 4. A forest network improves the microclimate around farmland.

reforestation include digging trenches to wash away soluble salts, filling depressions, and excavating and replacing problem soils.

Land Leveling. The horizontal distribution of salts in the soils of arid and semi-arid regions is affected by the undulatory microrelief of the surface. Salts tend to converge on the highest or most elevated parts. In monsoon areas this phenomenon is even more pronounced, as it is influenced by irrigation during dry periods. The saline patches cannot be eliminated if the land remains unlevel and is not evenly irrigated. Accordingly, farmers in salty soil areas expend vast labor resources to level their lands, plot by plot and year by year.

Green Manuring. Salty soils lack fertility and infertile lands are prone to salinization. Salinity and infertility go hand in hand. The application of adequate amounts of organic manures improves soil fertility, salt tolerance and crop yields. For the long term, any improvement in soil fertility and other chemical and physical characteristics will improve the movement of both water and salts in the soil, especially in the tilled layers.

The value of green manure crops for the amelioration and enrichment of saline-alkali soils has been demonstrated on large areas in many regions of China. Reference is made not only to paddy fields but also to drylands. In addition to adding organic matter and mineral nutrients, green manures--when microbiologically decomposed--produce various organic acids which help neutralize soil alkalinity. On one occasion, alfalfa (*Medicago sativa*) was planted in Fengqiu County, Henan Province to improve a "tile-like alkali soil" (a highly alkaline soil composed mostly of Na^+ and HCO_3^-). The result was a lowering of the pH by 0.5 to 1.4 points, and mineralization was reduced 7 to 23% with little detection of sodium bicarbonate ($NaHCO_3$). Moreover, under the protection of the dense foliage of a green manure crop, evaporation from the ground surface is reduced and resalinization prevented. Also, since a large amount of groundwater is absorbed by the deep roots of the green manure crop and transpired by the leaves, the water table is lowered and convergence of the salts to the ground surface is reversed. The use of green manure crops also diminishes the volume weight of the soils, improves soil structure, reduces the evaporation of soil moisture and inhibits resalinization. There are thus many benefits derived from green manuring in its amelioration of salty soils.

Land Utilization and Cropping Systems. Finally, an important aspect of the integrated approach to the management of salty soils is rational land utilization and cropping systems to fit local conditions. Chinese scientists have now designed regional programs for the integrated management of salty (saline-alkali) soils. Included are suggestions for the most reasonable use of land resources. Rice, dryland food crops (wheat, maize, sweet potatoes) and industrial crops (cotton, sugar beets, sunflowers) are recommended, respectively, for the most suitable soils and reeds. Other areas are designated for fruit crops, forest crops and forages. For the future, various patterns of land utilization will be developed for saline-alkali areas coupled with acceptable ecological systems for such farmlands.

FOR FURTHER READING

Editorial Board of the Book. 1982. *A survey of agricultural soils in China*. Beijing: Agricultural Press. (In Chinese)

Farmland Irrigation Institute. Chinese Academy of Agricultural Sciences. 1977. *Amelioration of saline-alkali soils in Huang-Huai-Hian Plain*. Beijing: Agricultural Press. (In Chinese)

Institute of Soils. Academia Sinica. 1978. *Soils in China*. Beijing: Science Press. (In Chinese)

Li Tianjie, et al. 1979. *Soil geography*. Beijing: People's Education Press. (In Chinese)

Shi Yuanchun. 1983. *Water-salt movement in Huang-Huai-Hai Plain and integrated control of drought, water and salts*. Shijiazhuang: Hebei People's Press. (In Chinese)

7

AGRICULTURE IN THE HIGHLANDS OF TIBET

by Li Ansheng and Shao Qiquan

Tibet is the highest and thus one of the most exotic and inaccessible places on earth. It encompasses the Qilian, the Kunlun, the Tanggula, the Gangdis and the Himalayas mountain ranges, all lying from north to south at 5,000-6,000 meters above sea level. The Qinghai-Xizang plateau, which includes Tibet, is commonly called "The Roof of the World" because of its average elevation of 4,000 meters. It is the youngest and widest plateau on earth and still rising. Almost twice as big as Texas, it comprises one-fourth of the total land of China (Figure 1).

Most of Tibet, then, is a plateau, ranging in elevation from 12,000 feet to Mount Everest, the highest point on earth at 29,028 feet. All forms of life are sparse here. The sky is a blinding blue, the air chilly. But with 3,000 hours of sunlight a year, it is the sunniest spot on earth.

Only 270,000 hectares of land are cultivated in all of Tibet, comprising just .22 percent of the total area. Agriculture in the highlands is strictly limited by the severe geomorphology and accompanying climatic patterns, which are completely different from lands nearby. Differences are great even within the highlands, resulting in crop types specific for highland adaptation evolving through natural selection.

Uniqueness of Crop Ecology in the Highlands of Tibet

Cropping systems in Tibet may be classified according to three regions: the relatively warm and humid lower valleys; the temperate and chilly upland valleys; and the high, cold areas. The warm and humid areas range between 1,000 and 3,000 meters above sea level and have an average annual precipitation of 1000 millimeters and annual mean temperatures of 10-16°C. The cropping system is one per year and in some places two. The main crops are naked seeded spring barley, spring

Figure 1. The Qinghai-Xizang Plateau or "Roof of the World."

wheat, winter wheat, naked seeded winter barley, peas, rape and corn. Rice, soybeans and peanuts are cultivated in some of the lowest valleys.

The temperate and chilly areas range in elevation from 2,700 to 4,200 meters. These areas could be subdivided into two regions: the semi-humid and the semi-dry. The semi-humid region receives precipitation of 500-800 millimeters per year and has average annual temperatures of 7° to 10°C. One crop per year is the norm. However, two crops per year are possible in some of the lowest and warmest places, where winter wheat, naked seeded spring barley, spring wheat, peas, rape and early maturing cold resistant corn are prevalent. Only crops with a growing season of 200 days or less can be produced here. The semi-dry areas, 3,400-4,200 meters above sea level, have an average annual precipitation of 200-500 millimeters and mean annual temperatures of 5°-9°C. Only one crop per year is produced here. This may include winter wheat, naked seeded spring barley, spring wheat, peas and rape.

The high, cold area may also be classified into two regions: the semi-dry and the semi-humid. The lands in these areas range between 4,000 and 4,500 meters above sea level, with precipitation ranging from 300 to 700 millimeters and mean annual temperatures of between 0° and -3°C.

With a growing season of only 130 to 150 days, only one crop per year is possible. Only crop varieties that are resistant to low temperatures and dry, poor soils can be grown. These are naked seeded spring barley, some spring wheat, rapeseed and turnips. Potatoes have also been produced up to 4,500 meters above sea level. Generally, the growing season is very short and temperatures are low. But while temperatures are low, the amplitudes between night and day are very high, sunlight is intense and solar radiation is strong. These conditions greatly contribute to the development of certain crops. The filling of seeds may be extended, respiratory losses made minimal and senescence of leaves delayed, thereby allowing the products of photosynthesis to accumulate over a very long period. The development of storage organs such as seeds, tubers, bulbs, roots and fleshy stems is therefore highly favored. For example, the weight of 1,000 grains of wheat or barley produced here may be 40 to 50 grams. This is considerably above that of about 35 grams for other parts of China. Similarly, single potato tubers may weigh 1-1.5 kilograms each, and turnip roots of 5-10 kilograms may be produced. Because of the high incidence of sunlight--the highest in the world in some areas--the seeds and fruits of Tibet are sometimes brightly colored. There are black and violet seeds of barley; in fact, naked seeds of barley may be classified as to white, blue and violet. Moreover, the color of seeds can change quickly with different ecological conditions.

Because the temperatures during seed set are low, cereals such as wheat and barley usually have long awns. The grains also exhibit other highland features. They are long, the starch is high and they are well filled. Seeds grown here usually have a long dormancy period. Hence, the oil content of rapeseed reaches 46.0-51.6% and the sugar content for sugar beets is 18-22%. All of these features are specifically associated with the low temperatures and high light intensities of the highlands. Seed storage is especially favored because of the dry air, low temperatures and low oxygen content in the atmosphere. Thus, Tibet can be viewed as a "germplasm bank" where a great diversity of cereals is concentrated and where there is natural preservation.

Classification and Distribution of Crops in the Tibetan Highlands

Thermal conditions, which vary widely with differences in elevation, are the main determining factors for crop distribution and classification. Spring temperatures ease upward very slowly in Tibet's agricultural areas. Summers are cool and mean annual temperatures are low. Mean average temperatures for the northern highlands will range from 11° to -5°C, but for the south will hover around 10°C. For the most southern agricultural areas, the average temperatures reach 18-23°C during the vegetative period, with mean annual temperatures of 10-16°C. As a result of this wide variance, geographical limits for the growth of crops in Tibet have been established. Naked-seeded spring barley can be cultivated at a maximum elevation of 4,700 to 4,750 meters. Only in the lower valleys of the south can corn and rice be produced and this is only on one percent of the total cultivated area.

Unique Features of Crops in the Tibetan Highlands

The agricultural areas are located primarily in the southern and southeastern parts, in the Yarlung Zangbo River Valley and those of the Nu, Lancang, and Jinsha Rivers. The elevation here ranges between 2,700 and 4,200 meters above sea level. Here is found 75% of the cultivated land of Tibet and 80% of total crop production. The soils are fertile. Rainfall is usually adequate and sunlight is good. Barley and wheat are the leading crops, covering 75% of the cultivated land area and providing 82% of the total production. Productivity can be very high, with winter wheat approaching an average yield of 3 metric tons per hectare in some of the valleys. The average yield for spring wheat and barley is about 2.25 metric tons per hectare. A world record of 15 tons per hectare for the yield of winter wheat was achieved on the Qinghai plateau at the Institute of Botany in 1977. This surpassed an earlier world record of 14.1 tons per hectare produced in the Puget Sound area of the State of Washington in the U.S.A. in 1965.

Yield of cereals is a function of three factors. These are the number of spikes (seeds) per unit of land, the average number of grains per spike, and the weight of the grain. High cereal yields in Tibet result from the large spikes, the large number of grains per spike, the high percentage of fertile grains and a high weight for 1,000 grains (Figure 2).

Winter wheat in the river valleys averages 40 to 50 grains per spike, while spring wheat and spring barley average 30 to 45 grains. The weight of 1,000 grains is usually 40 to 50 grams. The number of spikes averages 13,300 to 20,000 per hectare. For the top yield, however, the number of spikes was 53,300 per hectare.

Record grain yields are very specific to Tibet and are the result of its unique ecology and climate. Tibet is the only place on earth where winter wheat is sown in the autumn of one year and harvested in the autumn of the next year. It is truly a "year-around crop". Spring wheat and naked seeded spring barley will mature in 200 to 280 days. The extended periods of low temperature accompanied by high intensity sunlight during both the seedling stage and during grain filling increases the number of spikelets per spike as well as the size of the grains. Meanwhile, the low temperatures and dry air limit the proliferation of insects and diseases, thus encouraging optimal development.

Figure 2. Naked-seeded barley in highlands of Tibet.

Another feature of highland agriculture is an even greater potential for crops where vegetative organs are used for food. Turnips and cabbage may be planted at an elevation of 4,800 meters and the potato at 4,500 meters. In such an environment enormous yields of very large heads, roots and tubers are the result.

Conclusions

The highlands of Tibet are unique among the agricultural landscapes and food producing systems of China. Located in an area that receives more sunlight than any other place on earth, with great amplitudes between day and night temperatures and a remarkably hostile climate except for the hardiest of crops, they offer a treasure trove not only for studies of crop ecology, but also for the discovery and preservation of genetic materials that can survive such extremes, and in an essentially pest free environment. The highlands are also an area that can be conducive not only to high yields of climatically adapted crops, but also to the development of unusual vegetative size, color and diversity.

FOR FURTHER READING

Shao Qiquan, et al. 1984. *Crops in Tibet*. Beijing: Science Press. (In Chinese)

8

FROM BARE LANDS TO BREAD BASKETS

by Yu Youtai

The Rise and Development of State Farms

Throughout the long history of agricultural development in China, most of the land suitable for cultivation has been utilized for crop production. Accordingly, reserve resources for cultivated land in China are now small in quantity or poor in quality. Moreover, they are for the most part found only in the distant (outer) provinces and autonomous regions (Inner Mongolia, Xinjiang, Tibet, Guangxi) and require large investments to reclaim. This limitation in land resources has made it necessary for future agricultural development in China to stress improvement of yields per unit of cultivated land. An added alternative to greater efficiency in the use of cultivated land has been the vigorous reclamation of what were bare lands to make them equally suitable for cultivation and crop production.

Since the establishment of the New China in 1949, 32.7 million hectares (or 490 million Chinese mu) of bare land have been reclaimed for agriculture. This has not only contributed significantly to agricultural development and food production for the Chinese but has also greatly improved the strategically important border areas. The reclamation of lands suitable for agriculture is continuing under unified government programs. New water management schemes using improved irrigation and drainage are generally necessary, and these require large investments in labor and materials. Most large land reclamation projects are now being carried out by the government, whereas small, bare land areas may be reclaimed by individual farmers living nearby.

Shortly before 1949, there were a few farms, established for experiments in the old liberated areas of the northeastern region. After that, the establishment of state farms was greatly accelerated. They differed greatly in size and were progressively established in the

Heilongjiang Province, the Xinjiang Autonomous Region and through-out the interior and southern provinces. The overall historical development (1949 through 1983) of Chinese state farms, their numbers, areas and the commodities produced by them, are summarized in Table 1.

TABLE 1
Development of State Farms and Commodities Produced

Time	Farms (No.)	Area Cultivated (1000 HA)	Grain (M MT)	Cotton (1000 MT)	Rubber (1000 HA)	Livestock Numbers (Millions)
1949-The New China	26	30	---	---	---	---
1957-Last Year of First 5-Year Plan	804	1,050	0.729	18	69	2.04
1966-Eve of the Cultural Revolution	1,940	3,089	4.04	77.5	158	10.14
1979-After Rectification	2,047	4,357	7.037	80.4	9.9**	12.0
1983-After the Responsibility System	2,070	3,428*	8.146	145.0	15.8**	13.6

*Grain and Soybean Hectares
**Production (1,000 MT)

As with other enterprises and programs in China, the developmental progress of state farms was seriously abused during the inappropriately named Cultural Revolution (1966-1976). The tragedy was that all state farms which had previously been under good management were left without direction. Profits rapidly changed to deficits. Beginning in 1977 with the end of the Cultural Revolution, steps were taken to rectify these mistakes. All state farms were reconstructed and given clearly defined missions such as the production of commodity grains, industrial raw materials, livestock and animal products, nonstaple foodstuffs for cities, or products for export. Their roles as experimental sites for the demonstration of new technologies and agricultural modernizations for farmers were reestablished. The result has been that, with greatly improved management, the agricultural production capacities of state farms recovered rapidly. Deficits were made up, surpluses were increased and, beginning in 1977, four large reclamation regions (Heilongjiang, Xinjiang, Guangdong and Yunnan) were established.

Thus state farms have witnessed a degree of success since the Cultural Revolution. While there were many natural disasters (droughts and floods) in 1980 and 1981, good harvests were wrested from the land, and large quantities of commodity grains were turned over to the state. As a result, state farms contributed to both an agricultural and an industrial output value each of which exceeded the highest in history. Since 1980, with the extension to state farms of the responsibility production contract system, a new enthusiasm of all members and workers has been created. State farms in China are once again on the road to favorable development (Figures 1 & 2).

Distribution of Bare Lands and State Farms

According to the latest estimates, China still has 33 million hectares (500 million Chinese mu) of bare lands which are suitable for agricultural development. Of these, 10 million hectares have productive soils, while the balance of 23 million hectares are of less value. Some of the provinces and autonomous regions still richly endowed with bare lands and having great potential for increased agricultural productivity are in the far northern parts of China, inlcuding the Xinjiang, the eastern parts of Inner Mongolia Autonomous Region and the Heilongjiang, Gansu, and Ningxia provinces. In South China they include the Yunnan, Guangdong and Jiangxi provinces. State farms are found in almost all provinces and autonomous regions of China. According to natural conditions and the location of bare lands, the distribution can be divided into the following six regions.

Northeastern. This includes parts of the Heilongjiang, Jilin and Liaoning provinces and Inner Mongolia. Yearly accumulated temperatures range from 1,600-3,200°C, with a growing season of 90-180 days. The yearly precipitation is normally from 500 to 700 millimeters. The soils are fertile and are suitable for growing wheat, soybeans, corn, rice, sunflowers, potatoes, and sugar beets. There are now 390 state farms in this region covering 2.3 million hectares of cultivated land. This is over 50% of the total cultivated land in all the Chinese state farms.

The potential for reclamation is greatest in the Sanjiang (Three River) Plain of the Heilongjiang Province, the largest plain in China. There, yearly accumulated temperatures are 2,300 to 2,500°C. The growing season is 120 to 140 days and the yearly precipitation 500 to 700 millimeters. An abundance of organic matter has created a deep, black, fertile soil. The land in this region is made up of large open areas which are flat and suitable for mechanized farming. The Sanjiang Plain now has 52 large-sized state farms. It is the largest single reclamation region in China and a model for future reclamation projects.

Northwestern. This region is comprised of the Xinjiang and Ningxia Autonomous Regions and the Gansu Province. It boasts the hottest and driest spot in China--the Turpan Depression. Yearly precipitation in this

Figure 1. The output value of state farms are the highest in history.

Figure 2. A poultry slaughterhouse.

region is less than 250 millimeters, hence irrigation is essential for cultivated agriculture. The "Kan-Er-Jin" underground water system in Xinjiang matches the scale of the Great Wall in human creation. Sunlight intensity is high and the days are long in summer. Being a desert area, the temperature varies greatly from day to night. Yearly accumulated temperatures range from 2,000-4,500°C. Nevertheless, there are now 353 state farms in this region with about one million hectares of cultivated land or approximately 25% of the total cultivated land of all Chinese state farms. Xinjiang alone has the largest pasture area and the greatest expanse of improved pastures in all of China. Wheat, corn, long staple cotton, rice, potatoes, the Hami melons and seedless grapes are grown here.

Southern China. This includes parts of the Guangdong and Yunnan provinces and is the main region for the production of natural rubber in China. The yearly precipitation is from 1,250 to 2,400 millimeters. There is no frost or freezing temperatures, the yearly accumulated temperature being 8,500 to 8,800°C. There are now 160 state farms in this region--covering an area of about 270,000 hectares or 4 million Chinese mu--devoted to the production of rubber.

Coastal. This region encompasses part of Liaoning, Hebei and Jiangsu provinces. The region has rich sea coast resources, excellent natural conditions and a yearly precipitation of 650 to 1,100 millimeters. There is a yearly accumulated temperature of 3,200 to 4,500°C, and a growing season of 175 to 230 days. The soil in this region has a salt content of 2 to 3% and, after reclamation and drainage, is suitable for growing many crops such as cotton, cereal grains and oil crops (see Chapter 6, "Good Crops from Salty Soils").

Low-lying Lake Region. This area is south of the Yangzi River. State farms in this region include parts of Hunan, Hubei and Jiangxi provinces. There is a total of 270,000 hectares of cultivated lands which, like the coastal region, are suitable for the production of cotton, grains and oil crops.

The Livestock Areas. This region includes parts of Inner Mongolia, the Xinjiang Autonomous Regions and the Heilongjiang Province. Here are vast expanses of grasslands with many livestock (cattle, sheep, goats) farms. The areas are ideal for an expanding livestock industry but conditional upon improved management of land and water resources and the introduction of improved pasture grasses and legumes.

General Picture of State Farms

According to statistics for 1983, there were 2,070 state farms in China (Table 1). Of those, 48% were primarily for the production of grains and beans and some cotton, 21% for livestock, 14% for fruit and tea, 8% for rubber and 9% for ginseng, pilose antler and other export items. The primary focus of state farms is food production. More than 80% were established for growing grain (grain in China includes all cereals, soybeans, potatoes and sweet potatoes) and other basic foodstuffs. The establishment of state farms has truly been a key factor in transforming bare lands to "bread baskets" in China.

Size. The sizes of Chinese state farms differ greatly depending upon location, commodities produced, condition of the land and type of management. For example, in the Heilongjiang Reclamation Area of the northeastern region, the average area of cultivated land for a state farm is about 20,000 hectares. Eleven farms have more than 30,000 hectares and the largest over 100,000 hectares. In the Xinjiang Reclamation Area of the northwestern region, the average area of cultivated land for state farms is 5,000 hectares the largest having 20,000 hectares. State farms that produce rubber in the South China region generally have a cultivated area of 2,000 to 3,000 hectares, with a few reaching 4,000 to 5,000 hectares. The size of state farms used mainly for the production of rice or export crops in South China is only 500 to 2,000 hectares of cultivated land. There are some very small state farms with less than 500 hectares (a few less than 100 hectares) of cultivated land.

Productivity. The average productivity of the total staff (members and workers) in all state farms in 1979 was 1,692 yuan for the total output value. For the commodities, it was 1,463 kilograms for grain, 22 kilograms for oil products, 233 kilograms for sugar, 16.5 for cotton, 41.5 for pork, 67.5 for milk, 3 kilograms for tea, and 20.5 for rubber.

The average productivity for grains per laborer in all state farms for 1979 was 1,917 kilograms. This was about 70% higher than the 1,142 kilograms for the commune workers. The average productivity of grains for the Heilongjiang state farms of 9,000 kilograms per worker was the highest in all of China.

Demonstration. The level of mechanization of state farms is also far greater than that in household and countryside enterprises. For grain, it was 85% for tillage, 50% for harvest and 74% for threshing. Additionally, state farms, as experiments, have made many contributions as demonstration sites for advanced agricultural techniques for farmers. These include improvements in tillage systems, plant breeding, new fertilizer technologies, protection of plants from insects and diseases, irrigation and farm mechanization. State farms have truly served as a vanguard in accomplishing the modernization of Chinese agriculture (Figure 3).

Development of the Friendship Farm: A Case History in Heilongjiang

The Friendship Farm was established for grain production in 1954 with aid from the U.S.S.R. and was so named in memory of that

Figure 3. Mechanical harvesting of soybeans in Heilongjiang.

assistance. The first year five branch farms were established on a total of 33,000 hectares, of which 25,000 were cultivated. Final development of the farm provided a total land area of 187,000 hectares, 98,670 of these being cultivated. Meanwhile, ten branch farms have been established. The total population is 110,000 while laborers number 53,000. The average cultivated land is 0.89 hectares per person, 1.97 hectares per laborer, and 4.09 hectares per farming laborer.

The farm is located in the center of the Sanjiang Plain of the Heilongjiang province. It is 53 kilometers from east to west and 46 kilometers from south to north--the largest state farm in China. It is in the frigid-temperate zone with a continental climate. There are wide differences between summer and winter temperatures, and a short frost-free period of 120-130 days extending from approximately May 20 to September 20. An effective accumulated temperature of 2,600°C produces one crop per year. The approximate percentages of crops include wheat at 50%, soybean at 35%, and maize, millet and sorghum combining for a total of 15%. Average yields approximate 2.75, 4.13 and 1.35 tons per hectare, respectively, for wheat, maize and soybeans. Grain and soybeans account for 90% or more of the total productive capacity of the farm.

The farm owns a large amount of machinery. Most of it is domestically manufactured with minor components imported from the U.S.S.R., Eastern Europe and the U.S.A. The extent of basic agricultural mechanization is estimated at 91% for the entire farm. Broken into categories it is 100% for tillage, 97% for sowing, 79% for cultivation and management, 75% for harvest and 72% for all other operations. This state farm has one of the largest degrees of mechanization in China.

A history of the development of the Friendship Farm, typcial of the development of other state farms from 1955 to 1985, is given in Table 2. The Friendship Farm has served as a model for the development of other Chinese state farms.

A *Production Test Using U.S. Farm Machinery.* In 1978, a production team of the fifth branch farm of the Friendship Farm introduced

TABLE 2
Highlights in The Development of The
Friendship Farm in Heilongjiang

Year	1955	1960	1965	1970	1975	1980	1985
Total land (1000 ha)	33	180	206	206	206	185	183
Cultivated land (1000 ha)	25	58	66	76	69	106	92
Employees (1000)	1.4	21.8	21.3	38.4	45.6	43.2	45.0
Farming teams (crops)	13	83	78	91	96	97	108
Animal husbandry teams	1	20	8	8	6	6	3
Forestry teams	-	-	-	-	-	5	7
Industry teams	3	65	18	26	41	44	48
Tractors	106	202	396	455	527	922	1109
Combines	100	97	213	234	240	390	458
Trucks	38	63	106	114	148	198	356
Total Value Agri. Production (Millions of yuan)	1.4	16.8	9.9	14.6	29.8	33.5	35.0

machinery supplied by the John Deere and other U.S. companies which included tractors and equipment for tillage, sowing, cultivating, plant protection, center pivot irrigation, and drying and food processing. The new equipment was characterized by large horsepower, extensive width, high operating speeds and a multiple-operations design. It was compact and had good maneuverability. After a few modifications to meet local agronomical requirements, the equipment, served well the needs of the production team where it was assigned. Significant increases in grain yield, labor productivity and profit were achieved from 1978 to 1983 (Table 3).

TABLE 3
The Agricultural Status Prior to and after
Introduction of U.S. Farm Machinery to a Production Team

Year	Cultivated Land (Ha)	Employees	Farming Laborers	Grain Yield t/ha	Productivity per farming laborer (t)	Profit per farming laborer (1000 yuan)
1977	1,000	326	242	1.9	7.0	deficit
1978-1983	1,518 (average)	55	20	2.54	19.6	19.1
1983	1,518	55	20	3.89	29.6	35.7

Only 55 of a total of 326 employees were retained in the production team for grain and soybean production. Of these 55, only 20 were agricultural laborers, the remainder (271 employees) were then available for setting up additional teams for reclamation of new lands as well as for the production of sideline industries. A new team (the tenth) for sideline production was created for raising pigs, rabbits, black wood ears and other mushrooms, watermelons and some processing industries for farm products. They became even wealthier than the original team members.

Positive results obtained from the use of farm machinery over a six-year period included the following:

1) Three-year rotations for wheat-corn-soybeans and four-year rotations for wheat-corn-corn-soybeans were established.

2) New agricultural technologies that replaced human labor were developed.

3) A method for irrigation of drylands by center pivot systems was demonstrated.

4) Improvement of soil fertility by plowing under crop residues was shown.

5) A diversified economy was created.

The above practices proved successful and will have a positive, long-time effect on the development of both agricultural production and modernization at state farms in the northeast and other areas yet to be reclaimed for agricultural purposes.

There are problems, however, yet to be solved. These include the management and profitable employment of the surplus workers when released as farm laborers, the availability of spare parts, and access to suitable fuel and other operating essentials for the new equipment.

FOR FURTHER READING

Chinese Agricultural Reorganization Committee. 1981. *Comprehensive regionalization of Chinese agriculture.* Beijing: Agricultural Press. (In Chinese)

He Kang, ed. 1980, 1981, 1982, 1983, 1984, 1985. *Chinese agricultural yearbook.* Beijing: Agricultural Press. (In Chinese)

History of the Friendship Farm Committee. 1985. *History of the friendship farm.* You Yi County: You Yi County Press. (In Chinese)

9

ORGANIC FARMING--GROWING PLANTS THE ORGANIC WAY

by Sun Han

"Pig farming earns no money, but be rewarded from the land." So spoke Chen Yongkang, the famous model farmer from the Tai Lake area, as a young man (see Chapter 11, "Miracles of Rice").

And former Chairman Mao Zhedong once said, "A pig can be regarded as a small fertilizer plant."

Thus, from the lowly level of a farmer to China's top leaders, the importance of pig manure has been reaffirmed for agricultural production. It is used both as a source of fertilizer and for improving the productivity of land.

Historical

Organic manures have been used in Chinese agriculture for over three thousand years. In ancient times, farmers observed that weeds left in the fields after weeding, as well as the ash remaining after burning stubble and other plant litter, caused plants to thrive and increased production. Gradually farmers learned that manuring was one of the most effective means of increasing farm output, and this led to a consciousness of the importance of the practice. Chinese agricultural documentaries, *Xunzhi* and *Liji*, written over 2,000 years ago, provide descriptions of the use of human and animal wastes, plant ashes and grasses, and how they benefited crop production and improved soil fertility. In ancient times Chinese agriculture relied heavily on organic manuring for sustaining production and maintaining soil fertility.

Manuring remains of prime importance today for optimizing agricultural production on the limited land resources now available to feed one billion and more. Even after the founding of the People's Republic of China and the development of a commercial fertilizer industry, farmers were still encouraged to exploit all sources of organic manures. Accordingly, their use was continued on a large scale. During the early 1950s, the total annual consumption of chemical fertilizer was only 80,000 tons. The level in 1985 had reached 75 million tons (17.4 million tons of net ingredients). This was up from 5.4 million tons in 1975. This is truly remarkable when compared with the growth in other countries using large amounts of fertilizer. China is now second only to the U.S.A. and the U.S.S.R. in commercial fertilizer usage. Fertilizers dominate the agricultural chemical sector of China, with nitrogen fertilizer principally in the forms of ammonium bicarbonate (16%N), ammonium sulfate (21%N) and ammonium chloride (25%N). While chemical fertilizer usage has greatly increased, the Chinese policy is still one of "walking on two legs." It is "principally the organic and combine the manure with the fertilizer." About half the nutrients applied to crops are from organic sources. The significance of the "organic way" is not limited to plant nutrition. It includes soil improvement by increasing the organic matter content, quality enhancement of farm products, a reduction in energy consumption in fertilizer production, and the establishment of a balanced agricultural ecosystem.

The Huge Manure Resources of China

The manure resources used in China are of four groups. First are the farmyard manures of the Chinese countryside. They are the most important. They are collected and prepared on the farm from local materials. Included are human and animal wastes, byproducts of biogas fermentation, straws and crop residues, oil cakes, plant ash, composts and waterlogged composts, sludge, pond mud and butchery wastes. Near coastal areas, farmers use "sea manures"--inedible marine animals, wastes from seafood processing plants, seaweeds and other plant materials. Second are the green plant manures, which include wild and cultivated, annual and perennial, terrestrial and aquatic plants. All of these can be buried in the ground in fresh or green condition as manure. Third are the peats and the humic manures. The peats are the decaying residues of plants found in marshes and former lake bottoms. The humic manures are a kind of processed manure using peat and minerals as raw materials. Finally, there is the domestic sewage and industrial wastes that contain organic matter. In summary, every bit of organic material that can be decomposed in the soil and converted into available soil nutrients has been used for manuring the soils of China.

The use of organic manures, according to the long-standing practice of farming the organic way in China, has many benefits. They are complete fertilizers which contain nitrogen, phosphorus, potassium and other nutrients to meet the requirements for plant growth. They decompose slowly in the soil, producing an enduring or lasting effect, and are not easily leached away. Organic manures add to the humus content of the soil. This, in turn, improves the soil's physical and chemical properties, including soil structure. Additional benefits derived from organic manures are improvements in aeration, percolation, absorption and buffering capacities, and desirable soil microbiological effects (Figure 1).

Figure 1. Fertilizing leafy vegetables with night soil.

Scientific research, coupled with traditional farmers' experiences, has now demonstrated that the integration of organic and inorganic crop fertilization is more beneficial than the use of one of them alone. In other words, it's "walking on two legs," integrating the traditional with the modern. The strategy is to use organic manures as the basal fertilizer and the inorganic as a top dressing. The appropriate ratio of the two and level of application depends on the fertilizers used, the soil types, season of the year and the crops. The best combinations of the organic and inorganic, for mutually benefiting crop productivity and having the greatest fertilizer use efficiency, are constantly sought after. The result is that both crop yields and soil fertility are enhanced and production costs reduced.

Human and Animal Wastes--Turning Wastes into Valuables

Of great surprise and concern to the Chinese when they visit the U.S.A. or other Western countries is the failure to use human and animal excretions and to consider them as troublesome wastes. This to the Chinese is an extreme extravagancy.

Human and animal wastes for China are both huge and valuable resources for good manure. The mean annual excreta per person is 90 kilograms of feces and 350 kilograms (liters) of urine. These amounts contain 39 kilograms of organic matter, 2.65 kilograms of N, 0.93 kilograms of P_2O_5 and 1.0 kilograms of K_2O. These amounts Chinese people annual provide 39 to 40 million metric tons of organic matter and 4.6 million metric tons of N, P_2O_5 and K_2O nutrients from their excreta.

Pigs annually contribute more than twice as much manure as do the people (Figure 2). One pig, during eight months of feeding, excretes 950 kilograms of feces and 1,250 kilograms of urine, which in total contains 173 kilograms of organic matter, 8.5 kilograms of N, 4.8 kilograms of P_2O_5, and 9.8 kilograms of K_2O. All this equals the production of 87 million metric tons of organic matter and 11.6 million metric tons of N, P_2O_5 and K_2O, produced from the equivalent of 500 million pigs fed in China each year with an average feeding period of eight months. Other farm animals--cattle, sheep, goats, horses, mules, donkeys, rabbits, ducks, geese and chickens--provide additional manure. All, however, cannot be collected and used as fertilizer, particularly the excreta from grazing livestock. There are also losses from volatilization and leaching.

Figure 2. Pigs are by far the most important source of manure in China.

Even so, the available nutrients are no less than those now derived in China from all chemical fertilizers. From the standpoint of quality, they are considered far superior.

Chinese farmers, through long experience, have a deep appreciation of the merits of using human and animal wastes in crop production. Some are classified as readily available, others as moderately or slowly released. Some are considered "hot" and others as "cold." Use relates to these and other characteristics and has been vindicated by modern day research. Human waste, for example, is rich in nitrogen, 70 to 80% of which is readily available. The carbon/nitrogen ratio is narrow. It is readily decomposed in the soil and is generally used to supply nitrogen as a top-dressing or as a top-basal treatment. Pig wastes are also rich in nitrogen. The carbon/nitrogen ratio is narrower than for other livestock and thus more easily decomposed. With pig manure, litters are added such as straw, grass or mud. This controls the rate of decomposition. Pig manure is generally used as a basal application. Well-decomposed manure is used for early-maturing, short-season crops. For late-maturing or winter crops, less decomposed manure is used, thus releasing nutrients gradually into the soil to fit plant requirements. Horse manure is considered "hot." It is rich in cellulose, Hemi-cellulose and thermophilic bacteria, but loose in texture. It is commonly used as a fermenting material to catalyze the heating of a hotbed for growing plants or as a component of compost to accelerate decomposition. The manure of ruminant cattle, by contrast, is considered "cold." It is dense, wet and more difficult to decompose and generally is used as a basal application.

There are problems in the handling and preservation of human and animal manures. Preventing the loss of nitrogen is one; killing pathogenic organisms is another. Human waste or night soil is generally collected and stored in leach-proof pits close to its point of use (Figure 3). This reduces the loss of nitrogen and is more sanitary.

Litter is added to absorb liquid wastes for penned livestock. As the animals tread on the accumulated manure, a slow anaerobic rotting occurs. After several months the manure is removed. This is good for the collection and preservation of manure but is adverse to the health of the animals. Taking all factors into account, a modified approach is to use the wet sty (or flush sty) during the summer. The excreta is flushed with water into pits outside the pig sty. This reduces the nitrogen loss while it is stored in the pits. During winter, spring and autumn litter is added to and removed daily from the sty to prepare compost. The compost piles are sealed with mud to reduce losses from volatilization. The disadvantages of these two methods are the vast expenditures for labor and transportation. Adequate storage and decomposition are the most important factors for sanitary purposes and the control of pathogenic parasites and diseases. It is believed that the ammonium (NH_3) produced

Figure 3. Night soil is collected and stored in leach-proof pits.

during the storage of compost serves as a powerful disinfectant. The sanitary affect may further be improved by adding calcium cyanamide along with some pesticides or germicides.

Green Manure Crops from Intercropping

The area devoted to the cultivation of green manure crops in China peaked in the 1970s. There was then a total of 13 million hectares comprising 13% of the arable land or 8% of that tilled. In addition, wild plants and aquatic weeds growing elsewhere were used as green manures. The growing of green manure crops has been more popular in South than in North China, in the lowlands rather than the uplands, and with legumes rather than nonlegumes. Green manure crops not only provide large quantities of organic biomass but can also be used as fodder for livestock. They reduce soil erosion, and improve the productivity of salty and alkaline soils and those that are sandy and heavily eroded.

China has an abundance of genetic resources for green manure crops. There have also been new introductions from abroad. Various types of green manure crops have been selected and conditions developed to fit local ecological conditions, soil types and cropping patterns. Some of the most popular species are the following.

Chinese milk vetch (*Astragalus sinicus* L.) is resistant to warm weather and excess moisture, but less tolerant to cold and drought. It is produced primarily in paddy fields south of the Huai He River. Widely grown in the southern wetland areas, it will produce up to 60 tons of green material per hectare. This corresponds to the equivalent of about 6 tons of dry matter, 1440 kilograms of ammonia sulphate, 300 kilograms of superphosphate and 440 kilograms of potassium sulphate.

Vetch species (*Vicia cracca*, L., *V. villosa*, Roth., *V. sativa*, L.) have moderate tolerances to cold and drought but not to heat. They are usually grown in the wet lands and upland areas of the Yellow and Huai He river districts.

Sweet clover (*Melilotus officinalis*, L., *M. albus*, Desr.) and alfalfa *Medicao sativa*, L.) are cold and drought tolerant and tolerate soils of low productivity. They are grown along areas of the Great Wall and in northeastern and northwestern China.

Sesbania (*Sesbania cannabina*, Retz.) is tolerant of salty soils. It is a good pioneering crop for amelioration of salty and alkali soils.

Astragalus huangheensis, Fu.-L. is resistant to cold, drought, and salty and poor soils. It can grow on sandy and/or salty soils in the Xinjiang Autonomous Region, fix itself to sand dunes and ameliorate poor land. Because of such characteristics, it has been given the exaggerated nickname *Shadawang* meaning "thriving by the sand raid."

In the single-cropping northern agricultural regions, green manure crops are planted before the main crop each year or once every two or three years. But for most multiple-cropped areas, various intercropping systems are practiced. The intercropping may be simultaneous and row by row with the main crop, mixed together or relay intercropped. This means sowing the green manure crop before harvest of the main crop and burying it on site immediately or several weeks later. These methods of "intercropping" neither reduce the sowing area of the main crops nor interfere with regular plantings.

The arrangements for intercropping are interesting, diversified and ingenious. A typical one involves the growing of vetch in a cotton-wheat double-cropping pattern. In the late autumn, after the last weeding in a cotton field, vetch seeds are sown between the cotton rows. When the cotton is harvested and the stalks removed, wheat is sown in the rows where cotton plants grew. The wheat and vetch crops grow simultaneously until spring. In May, the vetch is buried in place and the cotton seeds are planted on the tops of the rows. The wheat and cotton then grow together until harvest. Accordingly, the vetch--a soil-improving crop--does not interfere with the growth of either wheat or cotton, but many contribute substantially to an improved fertility of the soil for both crops.

Aquatic Plants as Sources of Organic Manures

The cultivation of aquatic plants has expanded rapidly since the 1960s. They are becoming increasingly important as sources for organic manures, especially along the Yangzi River basin where the climate is warm and water plentiful. Major aquatic species are the water peanut (*Alternanthera philoxeroides*, Griseb.), water hyacinth (*Eichhornia crassipes*, Solmns.) (Figure 4), water lettuce (*Pistia stratiotes*, L.) and azolla (*Azolla imbricata*, Roxb.). These aquatic plants and others are cultivated in ponds, irrigation canals and small lakes. The nutrient content of the fresh material averages 0.2% N, 0.07% P_2O_5 and 0.1% K_2O for water hyacinth and water lettuce; for the water peanut it is 0.6% K_2O. These aquatic plants may be used as a feed for pigs, goats or sheep, or as a basal manure for midseason or late rice or fall season wheat or rape. Disadvantages include the large amounts of water in the fresh materials; the high labor requirement for management and transportation; material needs for driving poles and drawing ropes; difficulties in maintaining and over wintering the seedlings; and a lagging production interest in recent years.

Figure 4. Water hyacinth is a feed for pigs as well as an important source of organic manure.

Azolla

Azolla is uniquely different from other cultivated aquatic plants. It has a symbiotic relationship or partnership with a blue-green algae called *Anabaena*, which has the power to fix atmospheric nitrogen (N) and make it available for crop production (Figure 5). Thus, the N content is

Figure 5. Azolla, a miniature fern and its nitrogen fixing partner; the blue green algae Anabaena, are an important source of nitrogen and green manure in crop production and as a high protein feed for pigs.

much higher than in other aquatic plants. Its effects on soil amelioration are also greater, and it has a higher nutritional value as a feed for livestock. Azolla is propagated in early spring by covering the beds in the paddy fields with plastic covers, which causes an earlier warming. The azolla is taken out of the propagation beds in May or June and spread into paddy fields. It reproduces over the whole field very rapidly among the paddy rows and is buried into the soil manually. That which remains develops or reproduces again and again, and may be turned over up to three times a year with appropriate management. Temperatures of 35°C or higher will kill azolla. Thus, special measures such as shading must be taken to enable seedlings to survive hot summers. In the autumn, the azolla is transferred into ponds and small canals for propagation and then to protected nursery beds to pass the cold winter and provide the necessary seedlings for the next year.

The native Chinese species, *Azolla imbricata*, is moderately cold resistant. However, it is difficult to maintain and to over winter, and it reproduces very slowly in the spring. These constraints have limited its further development and uses. In 1977 the Wenzhou Prefectural Institute of Agriculture of the Zhejiang Province introduced 1.8 grams of *Azolla filiculoides* from North America. It was superior in its cold tolerance, reproduced rapidly, was high-yielding, had salt tolerance and was of edible quality. Use of this species and others extended rapidly into the thirteen southern and three northeastern provinces. A total area of 370,000 hectares was devoted to its culture in 1980.

Since 1983 many wild species of azolla have been found and named. Mechanisms of both photosynthesis and biological N_2 fixation have been studied at the Zhejiang Academy of Agricultural Sciences and elsewhere, where at least seven different species of azolla have been under extensive trials for their comparative feeding and fertilizer values and for biological nitrogen fixation. Not only has azolla proven a useful experimental material during the past 200 years, but it is also used as a fertilizer in rice production, applied as a manure or by cocultivation. It is also a high protein feed source for pigs. Its use in some areas is termed a "Second Green Revolution."

Waterlogged Compost ("Caotang Sludge")

A unique manure widely used in the wetlands of the middle and lower reaches of the Yangzi River is waterlogged compost ("Caotang Sludge"). It consists of canal and river sludge mixed with organic materials that are decomposed under water.

Some traditional but unique technologies are employed in the preparation of waterlogged compost (manure). During late winter and early spring, farmers collect sludge from canal and river bottoms using a specially designed tool--a piece of cloth attached to the ends of two bamboo poles (Figure 6). The collected sludge is stored temporarily in shallow pits along the river banks and mixed with chopped rice straw. In early May, after the milk vetch (*Astragalus sinicus*, L.) has "grown up," the prepared sludge is transferred into circular pits at the corners of rice paddy fields and mixed with cuttings of milk vetch and pig manure. (These circular pits have a diameter of two meters and a depth of 1.6 to 1.7 meters, and are dug in early spring). A layer of water several centimeters deep is then maintained over the entire mixture. After two weeks, the contents in the pit are turned over and more water--along with animal and human wastes--may be added. After another two weeks, the waterlogged compost is ready to use as a basal manure for rice plants. The following materials are needed to supply a waterlogged compost for a 17 cubic meter pit: 16 tons of river or canal sludge, 0.8 tons of rice straw, 0.35 tons of milk vetch and 1.5 tons of pig manure. The processed compost is then sufficient for basal manuring 0.5 hectares of paddy crops.

Decomposition in waterlogged compost occurs anaerobically and under the usual outdoor spring temperatures. During the processing of the compost, the released nutrients are readily absorbed by the sludge and little is lost. These include both readily available and slowly or moderately available nutrients, which are very suitable--almost ideal-- for rice culture.

The collection and preparation of the compost and the digging of pits, however, is very labor intensive (Figure 7). About 180 person days per hectare are required. The procedures are extremely arduous and difficult to automate or mechanize. Thus, while the production of Caotang Sludge has traditionally been an important process in many of the most intensive agricultural districts in the rice basket of China, it is becoming less and less attractive to farmers who, under the new production responsibility contract system, are moving rapidly to a commodity economy in which rural labor is migrating to other industries.

Biogas Production-Household Units

The use of small-scale biogas units has been vigorously popularized over the past decade in rural China. They provide both an energy resource and a means of improving organic manures for fertilizing crops (see Chapter 10, "Energy Resources in the Countryside"). Such units are usually constructed underground in an open space near the house. The usual household-sized pit ranges in volume from 6 to 10 cubic meters and is usually of brick and cement. Straw, grass, and human and animal wastes are the usual raw materials. A carbon/nitrogen ratio of 25 is preferable. Water is added after loading of the raw materials, such that the dry matter content is about 10% by weight. Biogas, the basic

Figure 6. Collecting sludge from a river bottom.

ingredient of which is methane, is then anaerobically produced. Under climatic conditions which are not too cold, the basic energy require-requirements for cooking and lighting may be provided for a 4- to 6-person family.

During anaerobic digestion in the production of biogas, 40 to 50% of the organic carbon is transferred into gases. The other elements (nutrients), for the most part, remain in the sludge and slurry except for a small loss of nitrogen. The carbon/nitrogen ratio becomes significantly narrower. The remaining sludge or slurry becomes a complex manure, richer in nutrients than most composts. The mineral nutrients (N,P,K) therein are valuable fertilizers for top dressing.

Fuel is critical in China's countryside. One-half to three-fourths of the straw is usually burned as fuel with a heating efficiency of only 10 to 15%. When these same organic materials are transformed into biogas and used as fuel, the heating efficiency may reach 50 to 60%. A 10-cubic

Figure 7. The preparation of "Caotang Sludge" is very labor intensive.

meter biogas unit operational for eight months a year may save 1,200 kilograms of straw. Thus, with effective biogas production, more organic matter can be recycled on the land for crop production. This means less destruction of woods, forests, shrubs and grasslands and an accompanying improvement in the environment of the countryside. The extension of small-scale biogas technologies in the Yangzi River basin areas and particularly in Sichuan Province has contributed to a reasonable utilization and recycling of organic materials, provided some protection to agricultural ecosystems, and improved the living environment in the countrysides of China.

Conclusions and Projections

One of the most admirable features of Chinese agriculture is that, altogether, organic sources furnish about half of all nutrients applied to crops. These sources are a combination of animal manures, human excreta (night soil), "sea manures," crop residues, products of biogas fermentation, oil cakes, dredgings (mud) from ponds and waterways, green manure crops and waterlogged compost or "Caotang Sludge." There are no social constraints to their use in China, nor are there philosophical constraints to using a combination of organic and nonorganic or chemical fertilizers. In this regard, the Chinese have no peers when it comes to sheer ingenuity and sophistication in the recycling of organic materials and the maintenance of soil quality through organic manipulation. This is another example of making the best of two worlds or "walking on two legs." Intricately integrated farming systems are involved, utilizing resources derived from animal husbandry, fisheries, people and the land. Almost all are labor intensive but are natural resource-conserving and result in sustainable food production at high levels. Survival of these systems under the new production responsibility contract program will be followed with interest as labor becomes more critical and the use of chemical fertilizers expands. The gathering, composition, distribution and application of organic materials is much more time-consuming than the use of chemical or inorganic fertilizers, which is accompanied by higher costs and seasonal labor shortages. Perhaps a model will survive which is both adaptable and acceptable to the Western world.

FOR FURTHER READING

Chinese Academy of Agricultural Sciences. Institute of Soils and Fertilizers. 1985. *Regionalization of green manure crops in China*. Guiyang: Guizhou People's Press. (In Chinese)

Hsu, R. C. 1982. *Food for one billion*. Boulder, Colo.: Westview Press.

International Food Policy Research Institute. 1984. Agriculture in China. In *Annual Report*, 19-20. Washington, D.C.: International Food Policy Research Institute.

King, F. H. 1911. *Farmers of forty centuries*. Emmaus, Pa.: Rodale Press, Inc.

Li Shiye. 1984. Azolla in the paddy fields of East China. In *Organic matter and rice*, 169-78. Las Banos, Philippines: International Rice Research Institute. (In Chinese)

Lumpkin, T. A., and D. L. Plucknett. 1982. *Azolla as a green manure: Use and management in crop production*. Boulder, Colo.: Westview Press.

McCalla, T. M., and D. L. Plucknett. 1981. Collecting, transporting and processing organic fertilizers. In *Vegetable farming systems in China*, ed. D. L. Plucknett and H. L. Beemer, Jr., 19-44. Boulder, Colo.: Westview Press.

Stone, B. 1986. Chinese fertilizer application in the 1980s and 1990s: Issues of growth, balance, allocation, efficiency and response. In *China's economy looks toward the year 2000*. Vol. 1, *The Four Modernizations*, ed. U.S. Congress Joint Economic Committee, 453-96. Washington D.C.: U.S. Government Printing Office.

Wen Dazhong, and D. Pimentel. 1984. Energy inputs in agricultural systems in China. In *Agricultural, ecosystems and environment*, 11:29-35. Amsterdam: Elsevier science Publishers.

Wen Qixiao. 1984. Utilization of organic materials in rice production in China. In *Organic matter and rice*, 45-46. Las Banos, Philippines: International Rice Research Institute. (In Chinese)

Xie Jian-Chang, and M. Hasegawa. 1985. Organic and inorganic sources of potassium in intensive cropping systems: Experiences in the People's Republic of China and Japan. In *Potassium in agriculture*, 1177-99. Madison, Wisc.: American Society of Agronomy, Crop Science Society of America, and Soils Science Society of America.

Yuan Congyi. 1984. The utilization of animal and human wastes in rice production in China. In *Organic matter and rice*, 179-92. Las Banos, Philippines: International Rice Research Institute. (In Chinese)

10
ENERGY RESOURCES IN THE COUNTRYSIDE

by Sylvan Wittwer

China is a country built upon agriculture. Its agriculture provides 85% of the people's subsistence, 70% of the raw materials for light industries, 40% of all industry, and a considerable amount of the total revenue. Agricultural development is providing the resource base for industrial progress. Aside from food, shelter and clothing, one of the most important concerns is the need for energy in the farm household for heating, cooking, lighting and agricultural production.

Rural China, where 80% of the people live, can be likened unto a great laboratory for evaluating the potential of diverse, decentralized and renewable energy resources with self-reliance as the guiding principle. Included are small scale hydropower and solar energy innovations as well as biomass alternatives such as wood, crop residues, animal dung and biogas digesters.

The muscle of toiling masses has traditionally been and remained up to the early part of the twentieth century the chief source of energy for rural China. This expenditure of muscle power by man and beast may still be seen in the pulling, pushing and carrying of enormous loads of produce, bricks, night soil and other cargo over land and along waterways, through the countryside and along city streets. Human beings and animals sometimes hitched together or in tandem were and remain a means of energy for transport (Figure 1).

Chinese agriculture is very intensive and requires a high energy input on a unit basis. It has become increasingly so because there has been virtually no expansion of cultivated land area since 1949, even though the population has doubled. The recent phenomenal growth in agricultural productivity has been achieved through an intensification which has required increased inputs of both traditional and modern energy resources. The limiting factor has been fuel availability rather than the capacity of the land to produce food. Much of the energy used in

Figure 1. Human muscle is a source of energy for transport.

Chinese agriculture still comes from animal sources and extensive recycling of biomass. Primary energy sources for cooking are crop residues and firewood. The contributions of animal dung are negligible.

Like other components of rural development in China, energy policy has required "walking on two legs," being big and small at the same time. The energy policy has led to the simultaneous development of rural and diversified small scale industries with centrally located large scale units. Furthermore, it has emphasized a mixture of modern energy sources (fossil fuels, electricity, geothermal, biogas) and traditional ones (animal draft power, human labor, crop stalks and residues, solar power, and firewood). A truly comprehensive approach has been taken to solve China's rural energy problems.

Increasing energy inputs into ever more intensified food producing systems are reflected in the production of nitrogen fertilizer, power irrigation, tractors and electricity. All of these modern energy-intensive uses have increased by over 100-fold since 1949.

Electricity

Demands for electricity to power pumps for irrigation, for increased rural production, and for expansion of rural industries (countryside enterprises) are increasing rapidly. There is often only enough electricity to run 80% of the industry at one time, and power outages are common. Thousands of factories may be shut down for many hours each week. It has been reported that the food processing industry in Guangzhou (Canton) as late as 1985 was operating at less than half capacity because of shortages of electricity. Forty percent of China's rural population, as of 1984, was still without electricity, and domestic fuel supplies were short for at least two months of each year. Increasing numbers of air conditioning units, television sets, electric fans, refrigerators, sewing machines and washing machines have added to the energy demands. Electricity remains an almost universal constraint for further industrialization and the development of countryside enterprises. Frequent power failures, interruptions of supplies, and unstable voltages are also very disruptive to the satisfactory operation of laboratory instruments, computer circuits, and programming of research efforts.

Coal and Oil

Coal and oil still play a relatively minor role in the total energy budget of rural China, even though Marco Polo noted in the thirteenth century the burning of black stones (coal?) by the Chinese, and the world's first oil well was alleged to have been drilled in the Chinese countryside in the year 1521 A.D.

China ranks as number one in world coal consumption and has enormous reserves. It is followed closely by the U.S.S.R. and the U.S.A. Coal provides 70 to 80% of the energy consumed in China for the production of heat and electric power. China is more dependent upon its coal for commercial energy than is any other major country. Hence, coal, as an energy resource, continues to be the priority for development. For rural areas, however, where energy deficits continue to be acute, coal still provides less than 10% of what is needed.

While coal remains the overall key to China's energy future, its use engenders and portends severe environmental problems. These have only recently been given the attention they deserve. Acid rainfall and air pollution have become serious. This is particularly true in the highly industrialized area of the Yangzi River basin, which is also China's bread (rice) basket. No accurate assessment of damage to crop production from air pollution has yet been made, but it must approach the $2 billion loss experienced annually in the U.S.A. Environmental pollution hangs as a dark cloud as coal resources continue to be developed.

China is basically self-sufficient in oil as well as in coal. The oil embargo and energy crisis of the 1970s had little direct impact. Likewise, China is the only developing country that has created an oil industry without relying heavily on other nations for the technology. Oil consumption, however, is low in comparison with other major countries, reaching only 114 million tons in 1984, the highest level to that date.

Sources of Energy in the Countryside

Biogas. Here, China is the world's pioneer and continues as the pacesetter. While firewood (logs, branches, twigs, brush, roots and leaves) and crop residues and byproducts (straw, stalks, grasses, reeds, charcoal, vegetable oils) still remain as the two primary sources of energy for cooking, heating and lighting, biogas is becoming a close third. China is, by all odds, the world's leader in methane generation from organic residues and farm wastes. Crop residues, when removed from the land for use as an alternative fuel to biogas, increase soil erosion 5- to 40-fold and intensify water runoff and the removal of soil nutrients.

Accurate figures on the number of biogas generators in China are hard to come by. They began with a few thousand in 1973 and rose to between 7-8 million by 1978. Five million or nearly 70% of the total were in Sichuan Province, which also has an abundance of manure from one hundred million pigs, each of which, when mature, produces about two tons of waste per year. While 20 million generators were projected by 1980 and 70 million by 1982, such figures are no longer realistic. The number in 1980 was only marginally higher than in 1978. It has been reported, however, that 600,000 additional units (biogas-generating pits) were built each year from 1982 to 1984 and that the number is expected to double by 1990. Biogas generators are now located all over China except in the far northern parts. They are concentrated in the middle and southern provinces. In the countryside they are estimated to meet the energy needs of from 35 to 50 million people.

Biogas consists of 60 to 70% methane, 30 to 40% carbon dioxide and trace amounts of hydrogen sulfide and nitrous oxide. Being a convenient fuel for cooking, heating and lighting homes, it is used very much like natural gas in the U.S. It may also be used to warm little pigs in farrowing ("maternity") units, heat greenhouses, generate electricity, pump water, run irrigation pumps and sprayers (Figure 2), and power motorized vehicles (cars, buses, trucks, mowers and tractors). Additionally, it may be used to improve the fermentation of more methane by inducing higher temperatures in the generators that produce the biogas. Other applications are as an energy source for grain drying and to power food-processing machinery. Sources of raw material to generate biogas are all products of the countryside: night soil and animal manures, grasses, aquatic plants, crop byproducts and water. These are all mixed together. Anaerobic decomposition is then encouraged in airtight containers. A storage receptacle for the generated gas permits withdrawal as needed.

Figure 2. Biogas as a source of energy for spraying crops.

The availability of plastic liners, tubes and storage containers has also encouraged the recent adoption and use of biogas generators (Figure 3).

Aside from the production of a renewable fuel--an energy resource that will conserve firewood and substitute for fossil fuels--additional benefits of biogas generation are derived from the upgrading of some farm wastes, manures and vegetable refuse for crop fertilization, thereby reducing sanitary threats and contributing to a cleaner environment. These values are considered even more important than the generation of methane, hence Chinese farmers welcome biogas generators (see Chapter 9, "Organic Farming--Growing Plants the Organic Way"). No social constraints are placed on their use in a nation long accustomed to the collection of night soil for crop fertilization. Today in China, besides the millions of family unit generators, over 150 small-scale electrical generating plants use biogas as a fuel; and many small factories run their internal combustion engines with it.

Many active biogas research stations study such factors as: differences in microbiological fermentations; the nature, design and structure of generators; the merits of different sources and combinations of raw materials; the effects of pressure within the generators on fermentation; the means for improving the production of stable and constant supplies;

Figure 3. Biogas used for heating water in a tea kettle.

the effects of fermentation temperatures; and the utilization and field testing of residues and their composition as compared to the original composts.

Biogas generators, along with windmills, solar cookers, and small hydropower units, provide sources of decentralized energy. They can be constructed of locally available materials by off-season workers who otherwise would be idle. These are some of the secrets of China's success in developing rural energy resources.

Hydropower. China has the largest hydroelectric power potential in the world, with an estimated one-tenth of the planet's potential. It far exceeds any other country including the U.S.S.R. and the U.S.A. Less than 5% of that potential, however, has thus far been tapped, and that mostly since 1965. While the bulk of hydropower resources is located in some of the most remote, mountainous areas of western and southwestern China, much of it could be transported or transmitted to major industrial centers in the east and south with existing technology.

China is now investing heavily in both large and small hydropower projects ("walking on two legs"). In 1984, an additional 1,421 small hydroelectric generating plants were installed, bringing the total of such operating units to 78,000 (Figure 4). Nearly 90,000 small-scale hydro systems have been built in the countryside during the past three decades. They account for 35 to 40% of the nation's hydroelectric capacity and supply a large share of rural electrical needs. Consumption of rural electric power in 1984 rose 6.2% above 1983.

Figure 4. A small hydroelectric power station.

As to the future, the light at the end of the tunnel for China and much of the developing world may well be generated by hydroelectric power. The Chinese model will involve both "mini" and "macro" units. Dams, turbines and generators are developing power from 1,600 large rivers and tens of thousands of small rivers and streams. By the turn of the century the plans call for hydro facilities to provide two to three times as much energy as they do now.

Small hydropower stations have many advantages over large ones for China. They can be completed in a short time with participation from the masses, and despite the mountainous terrain can be constructed in all parts of the country. Small stations also promote the development of local irrigation and construction projects and increase local financial holdings. They are an essential part of totally integrated water management systems and rural development. The large hydroelectric stations, however, will remain the backbone of power supply for large industries.

Solar Energy. Solar energy, with its solar cells, flat type and porous bed collectors, suggests geographical areas that abound in year-round sunlight. Two thousand hours per year of bright sunshine cover two-thirds of China, with considerably more in the high and dry northwest. Tibet, with its 3,000 hours of sunshine per year, is the world's sunniest clime. In China solar energy operates railway signals, black light lamps for trapping insects, water distillation units, hot water heaters and solar-powered cookers, boats and welding machines. Portable solar cookers numbered 100,000 in 1985, and even in some of the more remote areas are the most visible impact of this alternative energy resource, although examples of the practical utilization of the sun's energy abounds in China. For instance, ancient homes were built on the north side of courtyards facing south to admit as much sunlight as possible. The practice persists to this day. Many research institutes and hundreds of scientists are seeking different uses of solar energy and to increase the efficiency of its conversion. Solar energy is secure, clean, safe, nonpolluting, abundant, renewable and decentralized. On the other hand, solar energy must be collected and concentrated to be usable for large scale applications, and some solar energy technologies require large amounts of materials and land. Hydropower, a form of solar energy, can cover up extensive productive agricultural lands with its associated reservoirs and have detrimental effects on natural biota. These constraints are now becoming a major concern in China.

Drying in the Sun. Another and probably the most important yet least advertised use for solar energy in the Chinese countryside (because of the primitive approach) is "drying in the sun." Most of the harvested grain--wheat, rice, barley, flax, buckwheat and rapeseed--is harvested and dried in the sunlight both prior to and after threshing in drying yards especially designed for this purpose at the farmstead (Figure 5). Only a few grain-drying stations using coal or oil as fuel have been built on state farms and practically none in the countryside. This often results in high losses from rotting and decay in almost all parts of China. Artificial grain drying will not likely be extended to the countryside until fuel becomes available at reasonable prices.

One of the most visible yet minor aspects of drying in the sun can be observed beginning in late May with the first harvest of barley, wheat and rapeseed in the south and central provinces, and continuing through to September and October with rice, flax and buckwheat in the Yellow River valley of the North. The harvested but as yet unthreshed grain crops--straw and all--are spread out to cover the black-topped highways and other surfaced thoroughfares. The grain is positioned so that another but nonrenewable energy resource--the moving cargo of trucks, buses and cars with their rubber tires--grinds and threshes out the grain from the straw and chaff. These motorized vehicles disperse the peasants as they thunder down the highways but perform a unique energy-

Figure 5a. Solar drying of rice near Xi'an.

5b. Solar drying of corn on a roof in Shaanxi Province.

conserving threshing operation (Figure 6). The finished product looks remarkably good. It is clean and has few cracked grains.

The practice of grain drying on the highways is considered to be illegal by the Ministry of Transportation, but the farmers do it anyway. The government tries not to antagonize the farmers because there are so many of them. Moreover, agricultural development is vital to the nation's economy; and the government, under the present system, cannot financially penalize farmers by withholding their pay. Grain drying on the highways blends modern and traditional technologies. It's another example of Chinese ingenuity, a crude example of "walking on two legs," using solar energy to dry grain spread over thoroughfares in combination with fossil fuel-powered traffic to thresh the grain and separate it from the chaff.

Conclusions

Many unique characteristics of energy sources and their uses are demonstrated in the Chinese countryside. However, the ingenuity of the people in providing energy for rural needs will continue to be taxed as food production intensifies and becomes more energy dependent. The prominent feature of "walking on two legs" to provide needed energy resources blends traditional and modern, renewable and non-renewable,

Figure 6. Drying grain on a black top highway in Jiangsu Province.

large and small. Decentralized programs, small hydropower units, household biogas generators, windmills, small coal mines and solar heaters are intended to ease rural household fuel problems where centralized systems are not a practical option.

China is a world leader in decentralized rural energy development, and China's experience could well be a model for other developing countries. Without question, this nation leads in biogas generation with its approximate 10 million farm level digesters which upgrade many agricultural wastes and byproducts for crop fertilization, eliminate sanitation threats, and establish a cleaner environment. They also provide fuel for heating, cooking and lighting, for internal combustion engines, motorized vehicles, irrigation pumps and a variety of other purposes. The Chinese technology for large as well as nearly 100,000 small hydropower units is now utilizing scarcely 5% of the potential hydroelectric power resources of the nation.

FOR FURTHER READING

Deudney, D., and C. Flavin. 1983. *Renewable energy.* New York: W. W. Norton and Co.

Edelmann, W. 1986. Biogas Production. *World Farmers' Times* 1(2):11-14.

Hong, C. M.; M. T. Koh; and T. Y. Chow. 1980. Production and utilization of biogas in Taiwan. *Proceedings of the International Symposium on Biogas, Microalgae and Livestock Wastes,* 15-17 September, Taipei.

Miller, A. S.; I. M. Mintzer; and S. H. Hogland. 1986. *Growing power, bioenergy for development and industry.* Washington, D.C.: World Resource Institute.

Pimentel, D.; L. Levitan; J. Heinze; M. Loehr; W. Naegeli; J. Bakker; J. Eder; B. Modelski; and M. Morrow. 1984. Solar energy, land and biota. *Sunworld* 8(3): 70-73.

Smil, V. 1976. *China's energy achievements, problems, prospects.* New York: Praeger Publishers.

Taylor, R. P. 1981. *Rural energy development in China.* Washington, D.C.: Resources for the Future.

Tong, B. Tang. 1984. *Science and technology in China.* London: Longman, Inc.

U.S. Department of Agriculture. Economic Research Service. 1985. *China outlook and situation report.* Washington, D.C.: Government Printing Office.

Wen Dazhong, and D. Pimentel. 1984. Energy inputs in agricultural systems in China. In *Agricultural, ecosystems and environment,* 11:29-35. Amsterdam: Elsevier science Publishers.

———. 1984. Energy flow through an organic agroecosystems in China. In *Agricultural, ecosystems and environment,* 11:145-60. Amsterdam: Elsevier Science Publishers.

Woodward, K. 1980. *The international energy relations of China.* Stanford, Calif.: Stanford University Press.

World Bank. 1985. *China: Long-term development issues and options.* A World Bank Country Economic Report. Washington, D.C.

Wo-Yen Lee. 1980. China's new and renewable energy resources. *Mazingira* 4(3/4): 68-75.

Zhang Jigao, ed. 1986. *International seminar on rural energy technology proceedings.* Beijing: China Machine Press.

Zhu Xiaozhang. 1983. Small hydropower stations. *China Reconstructs* 32:44, 47.

11

MIRACLES OF RICE

by Sun Han

Rice is the world's single most important food. It is the most important food crop for the developing world and the main staple in the diets of the vast populations of South and Southeast Asia, where 91 percent of the world's rice is grown. It has always been the Asian staff of life.

Among the cereal grains of the earth, rice is unique on at least three counts. It is used almost exclusively as human food, having little value for livestock feeding or for industrial uses. It is the only one that is cooked and eaten as a whole, usually polished, grain; and, as a semi-aquatic cereal, it's the only one that is most commonly grown in standing water. It flourishes from the 53rd degree latitude north along the borders between China and the U.S.S.R. to 40 degrees south in central Argentina, making it one of the world's most widely adapted crops.

In China, rice has acquired many uses. The modern practice of throwing handfuls of rice on newlyweds as a token of good luck probably originated in China as a symbolic gesture to grant fertility and prosperity to young couples. Rice also has its therapeutic values. In bygone days, the Chinese treated wounds with rice stalk ash. Rice is also used to produce the famous yellow wine of the Zhejiang province. produce the famous yellow wine of the Zhejiang province.

Of the eight most populated countries on earth having more than 100 million people, rice for five of them--China, India, Indonesia, Japan, and Bangladesh--is indispensable (the U.S.S.R., Brazil and the U.S.A. being the only exceptions). Seventy to 80% of all their calories come from rice.

Rice provides almost half of the food for the Chinese people and is produced in every province, municipality and autonomous region. India and China are the two largest rice-growing countries of the world, with a combined rice acreage exceeding half of the world's total. India has 16%

more rice area than China, but China produces 87% more rice grain and over 36% of the world's total, having set a whopping new record of 178 million metric tons in 1984. Production from 1979 to 1984 increased 24%, entirely from yield increases. There are many ways in which the Chinese have improved the yields of rice, since there is little opportunity for expanding the rice area (Figure 1).

Origin of Cultivated Rice

The origin of cultivated rice has long been a fascinating and controversial subject for agronomists, botanists, and archaeologists.

Figure 1. Rice paddy fields in the lower reaches of the Yangzi River.

Disagreements cannot be resolved through a study of ancient literature, because rice growing preceded man's earliest recorded history. A more reliable approach is to investigate the geographical distribution, in the hope of unearthing archaeological traces of wild rice, the ancestor of the cultivated rice.

The common cultivated rice (*Oryza sativa* L.), grown worldwide, can be traced to the work of Watt in 1892. Until the 1950s, most scholars favored India as the place of origin. In 1928 Shigekane Kato, a Japanese scholar, identified for the first time the two subspecies of cultivated rice. He named hsien rice *Oryza sativa* L. subsp. *indica* Kato, because he believed it originated from India. He likewise believed that keng rice evolved in Japan and thus designated it as *Oryza sativa* L. *subsp. japonica* Kato.

Other scholars took the position that cultivated rice originated from China. Among the earliest was de Candolle in 1886, who based his views on some legends from a prehistoric era recorded in ancient books. It was said that in 2,700 B.C., the epoch of "Shen Nong" (the god of farming), rice had alreayd been the first of the "Wu Gu" or five cereals, viz. rice, two kinds of millet, wheat and soybeans. But it is not likely there will be any convincing evidence to explain one's stand on the basis of legendary records.

There is, however, little doubt that cultivated rice originated from wild rice. Geneticists at present usually agree that the wild perennial rice (*Oryza rufipogon*), from which the common annual wild rice (*Oryza nivara*) evolved, is the earliest ancestor of cultivated rice. Through a long period of cultivation, the *Oryza nivara* was domesticated as *Oryza sativa*.

Investigations of wild rice in China occurred at a late date. For this reason foreign workers recognized only the regions along India and Thailand as the centers of diversity for wild rice. Ting Ying (1888 - 1964), a distinguished geneticist and breeder of rice, was China's earliest worker on rice evolution and the first president of the Chinese Academy of Agricultural Sciences. His studies on the distribution and evolution of wild rice and its evolutionary relationship with cultivated species began in 1926. Today, the majority of scientists have acknowledged that the genetic distribution of the common cultivated rice ranges from southwest China through the northern parts of Indochina, Thailand and Burma, and along the foothills of the Himalayas to northeastern India.

China has recently devoted much attention to the investigation of rice germplasm resources. It is believed that during the New Stone Age, the climate of the Yangzi River valley was warmer than today. Accordingly, one can infer that the northern border of wild rice distribution was in the Yangzi River valley regions. Ting Ying suggested many years ago that China's germplasm of rice was not derived from India or any other foreign country. He also noted that Kato's two subspecies, O. *sativa* L. *subsp. indica* and O. *sativa* L. *subsp. japonica*, should be renamed as subspecies hsien (O. *sativa* L. *subsp. hsien* Ting) and subspecies keng (O. *sativa* L. *subsp. keng* Ting), respectively. Subsequent scientific research has made clear that Ting's opinion is correct.

Archaeologists have attempted to designate the exact location of the earliest domestication of wild rice. Allchin reported in 1969 that eleven samples of carbonized rice grains had been excavated from different places in India. Most of these samples were identified as remains of 2,000 to 3,000 years ago, but two samples with an age of 3,700 to 4,200 years were believed to be the oldest. Chang reported in 1976 that India initiated rice growing 4,000 years ago in what are now the Maharashtra and Rajastan states. Remains of rice unearthed from other Southeast Asian countries are all later than those from India. Traces of carbonized rice grains recently unearthed in Sulawesi of Indonesia are believed to be 6,000 years old but were considered collections of wild species by the natives instead of cultivated ones.*

China has carried out extensive archaeological excavations since the middle of the twentieth century. Some 2,000 sites of New Stone Age relics have been found in the Yangzi River valley and regions south of it. Archaeologists obtained remains of cultivated rice from more than thirty of these sites, ranging from the middle and lower reaches of the Yangzi River of the south and southwest of China, and to the southeast coastal regions. Among these sites, the earliest is the Lujiajiao Relic in Tongxiang County of Zhejiang Province. Here carbonized rice grains were identified as 7,040 years old. The second earliest, 6,960 years old, is from the Hemudu Relic in Yuyao County, Zhejiang Province. Numerous rice-farming tools were found coexisting with a stack of carbonized mass corresponding to 120 or more tons of rice grains. This is convincing evidence of prehistoric rice farming on a large scale. Moreover, both hsien rice and keng rice were identified in these remains. Rice growing in China, as found in Chinese archaeological excavations, precedes by almost 3,000 years that of other countries.

Plentiful and Manifold Types of Cultivars

In China, wherever rainfall is abundant or irrigation water is available there is rice production. It extends from the southern border of Hainan Island near 18° north latitude to Mohe County of Heilongjiang Province at 53° north latitude. The rice belts in China include the southern,

---

*See paper by T. T. Chang. 1976. The origin, evolution, cultivation, dissemination and diversification of Asian and African rice. *Euphytica* 25(2):425-441 in "FOR FURTHER READING" for additional details of the history, origin and distribution of rice.

central, southwestern, north, northeastern and northwestern areas (Figure 2). It can be observed on the plains and coastal areas of Jiangsu province to the terraced fields of Yunnan-Guizhou plateau 2,000 meters above sea level, to the irrigated high-yielding desert areas near Urumqi and Shihezi of the Xinjiang Autonomous Region. Rice growing in China exceeds that of all countries in elevation and degrees north latitude. The most important rice-producing areas (accounting for 90% of the country's total) are the regions south to the Huai He River and Qin Ling Mountains. Varied and plentiful types of cultivars have evolved through thousands of years' cultivation under diverse environmental conditions. It is estimated that in China there are more than 40,000 rice cultivars of native origin.

It is unique to China that both the hsien and the keng rice subspecies are grown, while tropical and subtropical rice countries produce only the hsien. Moreover, temperate zone countries such as Japan and Korea grow only keng rice. Starch grains of hsien rice are less glutinous and more expansive after cooking, while those of keng rice are more glutinous, less expansive and sticky. Accordingly, people in different rice-producing areas and nations have formed different preferences for rice in the diet. Hsien rice is characterized by its tolerance to dampness, high temperatures and strong illumination. Thus, it is mainly cultivated in China's southern tropical regions and the plains of subtropical regions south to the Huai He River. Keng rice, by contrast, is tolerant to drought, low temperatures and weak sunlight. Hence, it is found in districts around Tai Lake, the regions with low temperatures north the Huai He River, and in the high elevations of South and Southwest China.

Varying degrees of glutinous rice exist within both the keng and hsien subspecies. Glutinous types may derive from the nonglutinous ones. Glutinous rice, especially of the keng type, is very sticky, because its amyloid structure is composed chiefly of amylopectin, which constitutes more than 80% of the starch grain. In the starch grains of the nonglutinous rice, amylose predominates and little amylopectin is present.

The Chinese people are very fond of glutinous rice. With it they make various delicious foods and light refreshments, including seasonsed sweet meals and porridges, dumplings with meat, sweetened stuffings and rice cakes.

Since ancient times, saccharifying yeast has been ingeniously used to make a very sweet and wine-flavored dessert, "jiuniang" (fermented glutinous rice). China was probably the first country to master wine brewing. Glutinous rice is used as the chief raw material. Sorghum has been used for several thousand years to make strong wines and glutinous rice the mild ones. The yellow glutinous rice wine has a good flavor with both a slightly sweet and sour taste. The most famous place of yellow wine production is the Shaoxing district of Zhejiang Province. Here the

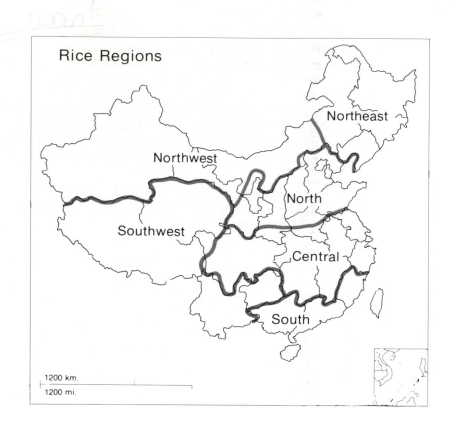

Figure 2. The six rice regions of China.

rich and mellow taste of aged Shaoxing Wine is not in the least inferior to the best grape wine of the Western world.

Rice varieties responsive to various daylengths have evolved owing to latitudinal differences. These include both the long day- and short day-sensitive varieties as well as intermediate types. Cultivars of various maturities can thus meet the needs of different regions and farming systems.

Rice cultivars grown in China are mainly of the paddy irrigated type. However, there are numerous upland cultivars suitable for places where there is insufficient water. The aerenchyma (spongy-corky air tubes extending from the roots to the tops which facilitate gaseous exchange) in upland rice are somewhat degenerated but more water can be retained in the plant. This results in more tolerance to water deficiency. There are also some peculiar rice cultivars that can endure total submergence. Deepwater rice can grow in water as deep as 1.5 meters, while floating rice with stem lengths of more than five meters can spread its leaves above the water surface and adapt to prevailing flooding patterns and water depths.

Transplanting of paddy rice is almost universal (Figure 3). This allows two to three weeks earlier maturity where seedlings are grown in protected plastic-covered beds. It is also much more efficient than direct seeding in utilizing limited land and water resources.

Among the more than 40,000 local Chinese rice cultivars, there are many significant and varied types. The longest seed panicle is up to 40 centimeters and there may be as many as 500 seed grains in a single panicle. Some seed grains are so large that 1,000 will weigh up to 60 grams. Certain cultivars are resistant to most diseases and insects, while some are tolerant to alkaline and others to acid soils. In the mountainous districts of the southwest, and low temperature areas in the northeast, and northwest of China, there are cultivars that are tolerant to low temperatures. Some can grow and flower normally at temperatures as

Figure 3. Hand transplanting of rice.

low as 15°C. There are aromatic types (both glutinous and nonglutinous) and rices with purple color grains. In feudal times aromatic rices were enjoyed only by emperors and their kinsfolk. Purple rice with its purplish-red milled grains is considered a blood tonic according to traditional Chinese medicine. It is usually made into desserts and offered as a delicacy at only the most prestigious banquets.

A Prelude to The Green Revolution of Dwarf Rice

People the world over, agriculturists or not, know of the "Green Revolution." It is usually associated with achievements of the international Maize and Wheat Improvement Center (CIMMYT, Mexico) and the International Rice Research Institute (IRRI, the Philippines). Some respectfully call Dr. Norman Borlaug of CIMMYT the father of the "Green Revolution."

During the 1950s and 1960s, with the continuous increase in the use of fertilizers and irrigation, the traditional rice cultivars with their elongated and weak stems often toppled over and lodged so that production was frequently impeded by these additional inputs rather than enhanced. For this reason CIMMYT and the IRRI initiated breeding programs, in which dwarf types of wheat and rice were selected. The result was that groups of dwarf, fertilizer-responsive and high-yielding cultivars of "Mexican Wheat" and "Philippine Rice" were introduced. These new cultivars quickly gained popularity in many countries and led to bumper harvests and self-sufficiency in grain production.

However, the breeding of short and sturdy rice culms (stems) was first initiated in China. This has not been generally known to the Western world because of the lack of communication with China for almost thirty years. Breeding for dwarfism in China dates to the sixth century's Jia Sixie, an agronomist during the Northern Wei Dynasty, who wrote in his classic work *Qi Min Yao Shu* (*Essentials in Agricultural Production or Key Skills for the People*) that "rice plants with dwarf culms ripen earlier and yield more, while those with tall culms ripen late and yield less." For many centuries, Chinese farmers have selected rice cultivars and types with desirable morphological characteristics of stems and leaves. By the mid-1950s, dwarfism had become a primary objective of Chinese plant breeders.

Hong Chunli, an experienced farmer and plant breeder of Chaoyang County in Guangdong Province, was the first to achieve, through breeding, high-yielding dwarf rice cultivars adaptable to heavy fertilization. By successive selection, he bred a new early cultivar of hsien rice named "Ai Jio Nan Te." It was only 65 to 70 centimeters high, responsive to heavy fertilization, highly resistant to lodging, and yielded

30% more than the original cultivar "Nante 16." It quickly became popular in many areas of South China.

By the late 1950s and early 1960s, China already had dwarf high-yielding varieties of rice. This was before the International Rice Research Institute was even established. Breeding of dwarf rice by means of crossing was first initiated by the Guangdong Academy of Agricultural Sciences (GAAS). Dwarf germplasm was introduced in 1955. A new dwarf source-- the "Guangxi Ai Zi Zhan"--was also discovered about this time and was crossed with some tall culm (stemmed) cultivars. In 1959 a new high-yielding dwarf cultivar named "Guang Chang Ai" was released and its rapid acceptance in Guangdong Province increased yields from about 3.4 to 5.6 metric tons per hectare. The area under production with this cultivar in Guangdong and other provinces peaked at 700,000 hectares. A continuous line of dwarf introductions from the GAAS followed. The Academies of Agricultural Sciences of Jiangsu, Zhejiang, Hunan and other provinces also made use of the "Guangxi Ai Zai Zhan" as well as other dwarf sources in their rice breeding programs. New dwarf cultivars led to even larger production records. In Taiwan Province, native dwarf sources of rice were also used. In 1962 a new dwarf cultivar, "Taichung Native 1," derived from the dwarf rice "Dee-geo-woo-gen," was introduced at the Taichung District Agricultural Improvement Station by Lin Kehming.

The International Rice Research Institute (IRRI) was founded in 1960 in the Philippines and obtained the dwarf "Dee-geo-woo-gen" of Taiwan in 1962. In 1966 the high-yielding dwarf rice "IR-8" was released and evaluated as the first of a series of the "Miracle Rices." China had, however, already released more than ten dwarf rice cultivars, each with its own merits and adaptability. This was confirmed by the U.S. National Academy of Sciences Plant Studies Delegation to China in 1974. All regions for hsien rice production in South China realized the benefits of these newly improved rice cultivars with dwarf culms. This review of the development of dwarf rice cultivars in China is not intended to depreciate the accomplishments of IRRI or its valuable contributions to the development of world agriculture, but rather to provide a factual account of the historical development of dwarf rice breeding. This background may also help to explain why China has proceeded so rapidly in other rice improvement programs.

Hybrid Rice--A Significant Breakthrough for Rice Improvement

The Chinese have long recognized and utilized heterosis, or what is called hybrid vigor. The previously mentioned *Qi Min Yao Shu* recorded that the mule--the F_1 hybrid of the horse and ass--was much stronger than either parent and could be adapted to hard labor and rough feeds. *Tian Gong Kai Wu* (*Objective Reality of Things in Nature*), published in 1637, also described the utilization of heterosis in silkworm husbandry. For reasons not fully understood, such crossing usually produces superior offspring (Figure 4). Until now, with the exception of rice, research and application of heterosis in many crops such as corn, sorghum, and tobacco has lagged behind in China.

Figure 4. Hybrid rice.

Hybridization in corn is relatively simple. The male (tassel) and female (silk) flowers are on different parts of the same plant. To produce the hybrid, the tassel is mechanically removed from what is to be the female or seed parent. The silk is then cross-pollinated by wind-distributed pollen of the male plant growing nearby. Thus, seed is easily produced for the hybrid which is to be planted the following year.

The production of hybrid rice seed is much more difficult as rice is a self-pollinated crop. The flowers are small and monoclinous, (having both the male (stamens) and female (pistil) parts in the same flower). To obtain F_1 hybrids by hand removal of the anthers from each rice flower is extremely time consuming and difficult and thus impractical for field application. Accordingly, the "Three Line System" was developed. In this method, the first line is the cytoplasmic male sterile maternal or A-line plant. The second is the maintainer or B-line. Plants of the maintainer line pollinate the male sterile line and make it productive but the progeny or offspring are still male-sterile. The third is the fertility-restorer line, which is the paternal line or rice plant, which pollinates the male sterile line and restores the ability to produce seeds having strong hybrid vigor. Thus F_1 seeds having heterosis or hybrid vigor are produced for practical sowing to produce hybrid seed. Since the late 1950s, scientists in Japan, the U.S.A. and the IRRI have attempted to develop breeding technologies for the utilization of heterosis in rice but all have failed. The Chinese initiated research on hybrid rice production somewhat later.

In 1964 Yuan Loungping, a 40-year-old plant breeder in the Qianyang Agricultural School of Hunan Province began his experimentation and by 1973 had achieved satisfactory results. China now leads all nations in hybrid rice research and the production of hybrid rice. After successful multi-site tests in 1975, hybrid rice production rapidly extended both north and south of the Yangzi River basins. Hybrid rice acreage in 1983 was 6.66 million hectares, over 20% above the previous year, with yield increases of 750 kilograms per hectare above regular rice varieties. Many different hybrids adapted specifically to location and human preference have now been developed, thus providing another option for improved rice production in China.

The development of male sterile rice selections in China is a fascinating story. Yuan Loungping discovered a male sterile plant in 1964 from which he and his coworkers, using more than 1,000 cultivars, made more than 3,000 crosses. However, after six years of research, he failed to maintain the male sterility trait because of closeness in heredity backgrounds of the breeding lines. He then turned his studies to wild rice. In 1970 Yuan Loungping and his assistant Li Bihu found, on Hainan Island off the coast of South China, a peculiar plant of wild rice (*Oryza spontamin*) with creeping culms, shriveled anthers and abortive pollen. It was precisely the male-abortive type they had been looking for. By artificial (hand) pollination, a few precious seeds were reaped.

In 1971 this discovery attracted great attention from the Chinese Ministry of Agriculture. Supportive scientists from more than twenty research institutes in ten provinces and municipalities became part of a research program for breeding "three lines" using the male-abortive common wild rice as the principal genetic material. Ten thousand cross combinations were made using thousands of cultivars to backcross with the wild-pollen abortive type. The Pingxiang Agricultural Institute of Hunan Province introduced the first batch of male-sterile and maintainer lines in 1972. Through the coordinated research efforts of many scientists, thousands of cultivars from China, Southeast Asia, Africa, America and Europe were test-crossed and screened. More than 100 lines which possessed restoring ability were identified. Meanwhile, scientists in Guangxi and Hunan provinces identified restorer lines from Southeast Asia cultivars which had vigorous growth, well developed anthers, and numerous pollen grains with restoring rates of more than 90%.

With sets of "three lines" assembled came the problem of producing hybrid seeds in bulk. Interrelations between leaf age and flowering date were identified and the flowering dates of paternal and maternal plants were then synchronized by adjusting sowing dates to optimize pollination. Relying upon these and other supplementary measures, seed multiplication techniques were designed to produce high seed yields that were labor and cost efficient. Hybrid rice seed yields of over 750 kilograms per hectare were now achieved (Figure 5), providing the necessary base for expansion of hybrid rice culture on a wide scale. Meanwhile, scientists at different locations studied the growth and development characteristics of hybrid rice, and developed high-yielding cultural techniques to offset the highly technical and labor intensive aspects of hybrid rice production. Single crop yields using hybrid rice seed from paddy fields in the Xuzhou district of Jiangsu Province have exceeded 13.5 metric tons per hectare.

Figure 5. Hybrid rice seed production: one pollen row is alternated with four seed rows.

Hybrid rice cultivars, of which there are now many in China, have strong root systems with high absorptive capacities and high tillering ability, are vigorously vegetative, and have large panicles of grain. During later growth the dry matter accumulation far exceeds respiratory losses. Hybrid rice yields are higher than conventional varieties under the same environmental conditions and with the same resource inputs. Thus for rice, China's number one crop both in area and volume, the productive capacity of the limited land resources is significantly increased. In summary, hybrid rice in China today is the product of a marvelous chain of events. First, an outcross in a wild abortive type occurred. Second, a

Mr. Li Bihu saw it and recognized its significance. Third, the offspring from the cross were male-sterile; and fourth, they had viable pistils.

Hybrid rice technology was first transferred from China to the United States in 1980. Five different hybrid rice combinations grown in California yielded 11.1-11.7 metric tons per hectare which was 166-180% more than the improved American cultivar Starbonnet. The International Rice Research Institute in the Philippines today recognizes China as the world's leader in hybrid rice production technology. This technical achievement of Chinese scientists in hybrid rice culture is now exerting a significant influence not only in China where land productivity has a very high priority but in other rice-producing countries as well.

The most recent (1985) development for furthering rice improvement in China was the establishment of the China National Rice Research Institute (CNRRI) in Hangzhou of Zhejiang Province, with Zhu Zuxiang as Director General. This institute has the responsibility of coordinating nationwide research on rice with close linkages to the International Rice Research Institute (IRRI) in the Philippines.

A Model of Traditional Intensive Farming--
Chen Yongkang

The Chinese have a tradition of intensive farming, especially in rice culture. The experiences with rice cultivation are numerous and many have been recorded in old agricultural books and local chronicles written during different dynasties. In *Qi Min Yao Shu*, a chapter on rice describes in detail cultural techniques which include soaking seeds to accelerate emergence and special approaches to weeding, irrigation, short-term drainage for muddy fields, harvesting and storage. Transplanting of nursery-grown rice seedlings was also first mentioned in this book. In *Shen's Agriculture Book* (17th century), top dressing with manure in accordance with the growth of the plants was recorded. Many traditional and practical experiences may be related to now recognized scientific principles.

Farmers in the Tai Lake area of Jiangsu Province have inherited a tradition for intensive rice culture. Rice is grown at a very high plant density which reduces the requirement for cropland. The Tai Lake area is the most famous of the high-yielding rice areas.

In a village of Songjiang County in this area lived a peasant, Chen Yongkang. His father and forefathers were all experienced in rice growing. He worked on the farm as a child and vigorously studied rice growing techniques. He bred a new late keng rice cultivar called Laolaiqing (green when old). He also had a good command of cultivation techniques for single-cropped late keng rice which consistently produced from a single crop yields of 7.5 metric tons per hectare. He applied these techniques freely according to different soil fertility regimes and plant performance. He managed each stage of field work skillfully and strictly and described clearly each key step that should be followed. His set of cultural technologies resulted in a yield of 10.5 metric tons per hectare for a measured plot harvested in the autumn of 1951. The government and research institutes took notice of this achievement.

In 1952, the Jiangsu Academy of Agricultural Sciences and other research institutes assembled scientists from multiple disciplines and went to Chen's village. They systematically studied his cultural practices from sowing to harvesting. His experiences were recorded and summarized (Figure 6). They included the careful preparation of nursery seed beds, choosing appropriate seeding rates, raising vigorous seedlings, determining reasonable planting densities, applying alternative irrigation procedures using shallow water layers, and top dressing with fertilizer at different developmental stages. These high-yielding cultural techniques combined with the cultivar Laolaiqing bred by Chen had been adopted in the Tai Lake area and had played a dominant role in increasing rice production. Laolaiqing became the major cultivar of the local late keng rice until dwarf types replaced it. For his contribution, the central government gave Chen Yongkang the honorable title of "National Model Worker."

Figure 6. Preparation of rice nursery seed beds in the Tai Lake area of Jiangsu Province.

At a 1958 National Rice Conference, Chen reported his experiences of visual diagnosis popularly known as "three yellows and three blacks" (in the rice-growing period, the leaf colors should be managed to shift three times from dark green to greenish yellow) to manipulate the growth and development of the rice plant for higher yields. Chen was next invited to become a research fellow at the Jiangsu Academy of Agricultural Sciences in 1959. The academy then organized a research team composed of scientists from six disciplines to study Chen's experiences. Scientists from two other institutes of the Chinese Academy of Sciences and from four colleges also participated in the cooperative research program. After three years' study, they summarized Chen's experiences. The "three yellows and three blacks" coincided with the physiological needs of the rice plant at various stages of growth, as reflected by optimal tiller number, growth rate, and plant form to maximize yield through proper fertilization and irrigation practices. At a symposium in Beijing in 1964, Chen and his coworkers presented a paper entitled "Studies on the Visual Diagnosis and Cultural Measures for Higher Yield of Late-maturing Keng Rice," which was highly acclaimed by the participants.

In 1964-1966, there was a surge for popularizing Chen's experiences. The Jiangsu Academy of Agricultural Sciences established a demonstration center at Wangting in the Tai Lake area with many associated demonstration plots in the counties. Some provinces and municipalities in East and Central China with comparable environmental conditions adopted similar programs. Chen and his colleagues were in great demand for lectures and demonstrations. The center managed by Chen attracted thousands of peasant emulators from various locations, and his comprehensive high-yielding techniques were quickly mastered by large numbers, with the result that rice production was greatly advanced.

Chen Yongkang (Figure 7) is a man who was never satisfied with present accomplishments. He was always looking for new programs and opportunities. When triple-cropping systems were introduced in the Tai Lake area, he studied the cultivation techniques for high-yielding triple cropping. In 1978 the total yearly output of one crop of barley and two crops of rice on his high-yielding experimental plots reached 24.43 tons per hectare. This compares favorably with the highest annual yield per unit area of grain crops ever recorded.

More recently, Chen and his colleagues modified some technical practices in rice production. These included raising rice seedlings in a nursery workshop, minimum tillage for improvement of soil physical properties, mechanized transplanting of rice seedlings, conservative fertilizing techniques to reduce costs and integrated pest management. These innovations have led to the modernization of rice production, based on traditional experiences combined with the latest technologies for higher yield.

Figure 7. Chen Yongkang in his high-yielding rice field.

Chen Yongkang was born in 1907. Until his death in 1985 he worked in the field and participated in demonstrations and extension activities throughout the countryside. He was a classic example of how traditional intensive rice cultivation can be developed by a Chinese peasant, but he also remained a representative of Chinese peasantry diligence and simplicity. In 1983, Chen was elected a member of the Standing Committee of the sixth National People's Congress. He represented over 800 million Chinese peasants in the highest organization of state power.

FOR FURTHER READING

Chang, T. T. 1976. The origin, evolution, cultivating, dissemination and diversification of Asian and African rices. *Euphytica* 25(2): 425-41.

————. 1984. Conservation of rice genetic resources: Luxury or necessity. *Science* 224:251-56.

Chinese Agricultural Heritage Research Institute. 1984. *History of Chinese agricultural science.* Beijing: Science Press. (In Chinese)

Ting Ying. 1961. *Rice cultivation in China.* Beijing: Agricultural Press. (In Chinese)

————. 1985. *Selected papers of Ding Ying on rice.* Beijing: Agricultural Press. (In Chinese)

International Rice Research Institute. 1978. *Rice research and production in China.* Las Banos, Philippines.

————. 1980. *Rice improvement in China and other Asian countries.* Las Banos, Philippines.

————. 1982. *Rice research strategies for the future.* Las Banos, Philippines.

Jiangsu Academy of Agricultural Sciences, ed. 1963. *Chen Yongkang's experiences in high-yielding cultivation of rice.* Shanghai: Shanghai Science and Technology Press. (In Chinese)

King, F. H. 1911. *Farmers of forty centuries.* Emmaus, Pa.: Rodale Press, Inc.

Lin Shih-Cheng, and Yuan Loung-Ping. 1979. Hybrid rice breeding in China. In *Innovative approaches to rice breeding. Selected papers from the International Rice Research Conference,* 35-51. Los Banos, Philippines: International Rice Research Institute.

National Academy of Science. 1975. *Plant studies in the People's Republic of China.* A trip report of the American Plant Studies Delegation. Washington, D.C.: National Academy of Sciences.

Raskin, I., and H. Kende. 1985. Mechanism of aeration in rice. *Science* 228:327-28.

Scientia Agricultura Sinica. 1977. *Development of hybrid rice in China outlined.* Sixth International Conference on Coordination in Hybrid Rice Research, 12-21 December, Nan-Ch'ang. (In Chinese)

Shih Sheng-Han. 1974. *A preliminary survey of the book, "Ch'i Min Yao Shu":* An *agricultural encyclopedia of the 6th century.* Beijing: Science Press.

Swaminathan, M. S. 1986. Rice, the most important crop of the developing world. *World Farmer's Times* 1(1): 8-10.

Wortman, S. 1975. Agriculture in China. *Scientific American* 232:13-21.

Yan Wenming. 1982. The origin of rice growing in China. *Agricultural Archaeology,* nos. 1, 2. (In Chinese)

FOR FURTHER READING

12
WHEAT CAMPAIGNS

by Wang Lianzheng

Wheat, in cultivated area and production output, is the largest single food crop on earth. None other occupies as much arable land surface as does wheat. Almost 250 million hectares are devoted to wheat production with an annual output of over 440 million metric tons. As a direct food for people, wheat is second only to rice. But unlike rice, used almost exclusively and directly for human food, wheat is often fed to livestock, especially in Western Europe. It is also used in bread making, as a cereal grain, for pasta and for producing alcoholic beverages. In the developing world, wheat and rice are considered "noble" grains in contrast to corn, barley, sorghum and millet, often referred to as "coarse" grains.

As cereals dominate all other crops for human food (they provide 50% of the world's protein and 60% of the calories), so wheat dominates the cereals. Bread from wheat or "bread for man" has long been considered the "staff of life." To be a "breadwinner," in the broad sense, is to earn one's food or bread (usually from wheat). As standards of living rise, wheat becomes a more important part of the human diet, replacing corn, barley, sorghum, millet, rye and even rice. This is true today in all the major populated countries--China, India, the U.S.S.R., Indonesia and Japan, and now including the Philippines, the European community and Mexico. For some time wheat has been the staple food of the Soviet Union, the United States, Canada, France, Australia, New Zealand, Argentina and many other countries.

While rice is still by far the most important crop in China, wheat is closing the gap. It is produced in every province, autonomous region and municipality. Wheat flour, a staple food in all of northern China, is used in making steamed bread, noodles, dumplings, pancakes, and fried doughtwist. Only in recent years has steamed bread become a staple food of the Chinese people. From 1949 to 1978 the total output of wheat in China increased 290% and the average yearly increase in yield was

4.8%--a more rapid expansion than in the U.S.A., Japan, Western Germany, the U.K. and Yugoslavia during the same interval, but slightly slower than in Brazil, India, Turkey, and Mexico. The gains in wheat production in China since the 1980s have been equally phenomenal as a result of rising living standards, technology inputs, and economic incentives for farmers to produce. In 1980 the total cultivated area for wheat was nearly 29 million hectares with a total output of 55 million metric tons, placing China behind only the U.S.S.R. and the U.S.A. in wheat production. Since 1980, there has been a 50% increase in wheat production with no expansion of area cropped. In fact, Chinese wheat production grew from 41 million metric tons in 1977 to 88 million metric tons in 1984, and yields more than doubled from 1.46 metric tons per hectare to nearly 3.0 tons. This is well above the 2.6 metric tons per hectare in the U.S. recorded for 1984 and 1985. China may soon reach the 100 million ton per year mark in wheat production. It is obvious that wheat scientists and producers in China and the Western world could learn much from each other.

In 1984 and 1985, China became the world's largest wheat producer, surpassing both the U.S.S.R. and the U.S.A. and thus becoming the new "breadbasket of the world." This is one of the most outstanding records in food production the world has ever seen. It is a success story by every measure. The new responsibility production system with its economic incentives has contributed, but only because other essential inputs and infrastructures were available along with the blessings of a generally good climate and favorable weather.

Wheat--An Ancient Crop of China

Wheat is one of the most ancient crops of the world. It was the cereal crop of the early civilizations in the Middle East and there are numerous references to it in Biblical records. The "corn" of the Old Testament in the Bible was really wheat. Some scholars have suggested that wheat originated from Southeast and Middle Asia. According to Vavilov (see, For Further Reading) wheat was introduced into China from the west and north (Turkey, Pakistan, the Xinjiang Autonomous Region and Mongolia) and from the south (through Yunnan from India). It was a major commodity for trade along the Silk Road of ancient times. Carbonized wheat seeds have been found among the historical remains left from the New Stone Age, according to Diao Yutai of Anhui Province. Wheat has been cultivated since the Xia Dynasty 4,000 years ago in the Huai Bei Plain.

The words "Lai" and "Mai," meaning wheat and barley, were inscribed on bones of the Shang Dynasty unearthed in the Henan Province. "Bin Feng" ("July") in the Book of Songs reads, "He (Rice)

Ma (Hemp) Shu (Soybean) Mai (Wheat)." After the Chungiu (Spring and Autumn) period of the sixth century B.C., the area of wheat production extended to Gansu, Shanxi, Hebei, Shandong and other provinces of the middle and lower reaches of the Yellow River. During the Warring States period of the third century B.C., wheat was sown south of the Inner Mongolia Autonomous Region and the southern parts of the Yangzi River and eventually in all provinces, and was second in production only to rice (see "Ben Cao Gang Mu," a compendium of *Materia Medica* written by Li Shizhen in the sixteenth century A.D.). Thus, the Chinese have accumulated a wealth of traditional experiences in wheat production over the centuries.

Cultivation Practices

To prepare the soil in rain-fed areas, fields must, according to Chinese tradition, be plowed deeply and harrowed twice to hold the moisture. During the Warring States period (403-221 B.C.), the areas for rice and wheat production were greatly enlarged by alternately constructing deep trenches and ridges for draining off flood waters. Also, during the Tang Dynasty rotations of wheat and cotton were practiced.

In ancient China, wheat was irrigated to supplement the rainfall and fertilizer was applied prior to the onset of cold weather. Wheat was sown by broadcasting, drilling or hilling using animal-drawn plows invented during the Western Han Dynasty which have been used for over 2,000 years. During the fourteenth century A.D., an effective method of sowing combined with fertilizing was developed. According to the book *Agricultural Silkworm Classic* (1334 A.D.), the rate for sowing wheat was calculated according to soil fertility, rainfall, and the onset and length of the growing season.

Both hoeing and irrigation are important in the management of wheat fields. Hoeing in combination with harrowing loosens the soil and preserves soil moisture. Hilling the soil around the wheat roots reduces injury from cold and freezing temperatures.

Regions of Production

Wheat is produced now in all provinces, municipalities and autonomous regions of China. Winter wheat production predominates (85%) and extends from the 30th latitude in the south to the 40th north latitude. As a result of the varying climate and natural conditions in China, different types of wheat culture have evolved.

Three large areas dominate China's wheat production: the northern winter wheat region, the southern winter wheat region, and the spring wheat regions. Spring wheat is grown at both the most southern and northern geographical extremities of China (Figure 1).

Northern Winter Wheat. This includes 60% of China's total wheat area and covers most of Henan, Shandong, Hebei and the Hubei Plain, plus the northern parts of Jiangsu, Anhui and Shanghai. Other winter wheat areas in eastern China include the eastern part of Liaoning and the area

Figure 1. The three wheat regions of China.

south of the Tianshan Mountains in the Xinjiang Autonomous Region. Both in area planted and in total production the Henan, Shandong and Hebei provinces make up 40% of the country's total output. The most intensive cultivation of winter wheat is in Henan Province, which ranks first in the country and where approximately five million hectares are produced for a total annual output of 16 million metric tons. Here the weather is temperate with a yearly average temperature of 12.5 to 14°C and an average of -3 to -0.5°C in January, so that freezing is not a serious problem. Rainfall averages 500 to 700 millimeters per year, three-fourths of which falls during the summer. Hot winds in May and June in some areas may interfere with harvest. The growing season for common winter wheat varieties is 230 to 250 days. The cropping system or index is two crops in a year or three crops in two years. Crop rotations with wheat consist of spring corn (i.e. planted in the spring), summer corn, sorghum, millet and soybeans. For the northernmost parts of the winter wheat belt, the hardiest varieties are selected. The entire growing season for these varieties exceeds 260 to 290 days. The most common varieties are "Nongda 183," "139," "311," "Xinong 6028," "Jinnong 3," "17," "Jinan 2," "9," "Youbaomai," "Boai 7023," and "Fen Chang 3."

The South and West. This area of production accounts for over 20% of the total wheat output. It is grown most extensively in the Yangzi River valley, Alluvial Plains and middle and lower reaches, the Huainan Plain, the Hanshui Valley, the Jiangxi hill area, and the middle and northern parts of the Yungui Plateau. Here the climate is warm and mean annual temperatures average 15 to 17°C. The rainfall is heavy with an average of 1,000 to 1,500 millimeters per year. Temperatures do not drop below freezing during the wheat-growing season. Wheat is interplanted or intercropped with cotton, soybeans or sesame in arid land areas. Along the Yangzi River and the Yangzi Delta areas, wheat crops are mainly subwinter or spring varieties. In fact, in provinces of South and Central China, spring wheat is sown after rice in the autumn as winter wheat and harvested in the spring. Special drainage systems installed in the wheat fields make this possible. What are observed to be rice paddies from mid-June to September may be seen as amber fields of wheat in late May and early June from spring wheat planted as winter wheat in the previous September and October. This is true for parts of Sichuan Province and the Jinsha River areas of Yunnan and Guangdong provinces and in Jiangsu, Guangxi, Fujian.

Southern Winter Wheat. In South China spring wheat has been a successful venture and has become an integral part of the triple-cropping system in areas concentrating on the rotation of wheat and rice. Most of the arid lands are double cropped with wheat or other cereals. Wheat is usually sown after rice, cotton, corn, millet or barley. There is also some limited transplanting of such crops as corn, soybeans, cotton and wheat from nursery beds, similar to the procedures used for transplanting rice and certain vegetables. Cotton, as a cash crop, is often interplanted, or transplanted in some instances as a relay crop, in fields of wheat before the wheat is harvested. Wheat may also be interplanted in cotton fields. Because rice fields usually have heavy clay soil, land preparation must be such as to prepare a fine and smooth seed bed for the wheat crop that follows. In some years, the winter climate may be unduly warm, which results in excessive vegetative growth of wheat if sown too early. This may result in some winter injury from the potential cold waves of late winter and early spring.

No suitable varieties of wheat are yet available for early fall planting or for the lowland tropics. With late fall plantings, where harvesting is delayed, yields may be seriously reduced by the high temperatures and heavy rains of spring and early summer. Excessive vegetative growth of wheat should be avoided and controlled during the winter months. Early maturity is a prerequisite for all wheat varieties, irrespective of time of planting.

Spring Wheat. About 5 million hectares of spring wheat are grown in China, which is 16 to 17% of the total wheat area planted. The output is 12 to 13% of the total wheat produced. Yields of spring wheat are usually less than winter wheat. Spring wheat, other than that grown as winter wheat in the south, is found in the northeast areas including Heilongjiang, Jilin, central and northern parts of Liaoning, and the north and northeast parts of Inner Mongolia. Here are found the lowest temperatures in China. The average January temperature ranges from -12 to -20°C and the average annual rainfall from 450 to 700 millimeters. This is the most abundant rainfall among the areas devoted to spring wheat-production. During the summer, the days are long and the temperatures vary greatly between day and night--conditions which are suitable for spring wheat cultivation. The Heilongjiang Province is one of the largest spring wheat producing areas in China. Here, in 1984, about 2 million hectares were devoted to spring wheat production with a total output of 4.5 million metric tons. Production is more highly mechanized (Figure 2) in this area for this crop than elsewhere in Chinese agriculture, mainly because of large areas of virgin land recently reclaimed (see Chapter 8, "From Bare Lands to Bread Baskets"). Wheat production has also increased in the northern and northwestern areas which include Hebei, The Great Wall, the Yanbei areas of Shanxi Province, most parts of Gansu, Ningxia, and Inner Mongolia, the northern part of Qinghai, and the Xinjiang Autonomous regions between the Tianshan and Altay Mountains. There is a pronounced continental climate in these areas and a shortage of rainfall. Precipitation ranges between 100 to 400 millimeters per year. Rainfall decreases progressively from east to west, with most of it occurring from June to August. The Hetao Plain of Inner Mongolia, the Hexi Corridor of Gansu, the Yinchuan Plain of Ningxia and the Huangshui Valley of Qinghai are famous as the Granary of Saibei. Water is available for irrigation and the soil is fertile. The largest of the wheat-producing areas is the Gansu Province with 1.4 million hectares, followed by Xinjiang with 1.35 million hectares (including some winter wheat), Inner Mongolia with 0.95 million hectares, and Shaanxi Province with 0.93 million hectares (which also includes some winter wheat). Spring wheat is now also planted on the southwest plateau and in south China but on a small scale. Barley prevails in Xizang (Tibet), where the mean annual temperature is low because of the high elevation, the growing season is short and the time required for spring wheat maturation is rather long.

Keys to High Output

China's wheat output has increased greatly in recent years because of the support of government policies. The total area devoted to wheat production grew from 21 million hectares in 1949 to 29 million hectares in 1979, at which level it has stabilized through 1985. Yields of wheat increased by 50% from 1980 to 1985. The recent introduction of the responsibility production contract system has also pushed research and the rapid adoption of new technologies for the improvement of wheat production. What then have been the main technological inputs for raising the yields of wheat?

Improved Disease-Resistant Varieties. A number of greatly improved disease-resistant varieties have been developed and introduced by agricultural colleges and research institutes. During the 1950s, wheat varieties were not disease-resistant. The spring varieties were highly susceptible to stem rust and the winter varieties to stripe rust. The solution has been the development of varieties resistant to all types of rust (leaf, stem and stripe) and common bunt. Stem rust on spring wheat is now controlled by the use of disease-resistant varieties such as "Hezuo Hao," "Qingchun," the "Keshan Series" and "Gannong." Meanwhile, a

Figure 2. Wheat fields of Heilongjiang.

number of winter varieties have been developed which are resistant to stinking bunt. Some of the more important of these are varieties of the Northwest Agricultural University series--"Bima 1" and "4," and "Xinong 6028." The only wheat disease for which genetic resistance has not been fully achieved is scab (*Fusarium*), but good progress is now being made. Primary reliance for control is the application of a fungicide during flowering.

Associated with improved wheat production are varieties that have superior tillering (branching) ability and are of the dwarf or semi-dwarf ("green revolution") types that are highly disease-resistant. The varieties "Fengchang 3" and "Aifeng 3" have been selected for the northeast. Varieties of the "Jinan Series" have produced yields of 7.5 metric tons/hectare. Disease-resistant varieties have also been selected for the winter wheat areas in South China. These include "Yangmai 1" from the "Jiangsu," Mengfeng 8" from "Anhui," and "Yanzhao Youyi" and "Emei 6" from the Sichuan provinces. Other new varieties for north China include "Kefeng 1," "2," "3," "Liaochun 5," "Doudi 1," "Qingchung 5," "Ganmai 8" and "Jinghong 4." Anther culture (culture of pollen grains) is used extensively in breeding new wheat varieties. Those developed from anther culture have been planted on 50,000 hectares. Anther culture of wheat, however, has not been as successful as with rice. Likewise, hybrid wheat development in China has not proceeded as rapidly as that for rice. Many outstanding scientists and research institutions throughout China have contributed to wheat variety improvement and greater pest resistance.

Irrigation. This has been a key factor for rationally improving both the stability and the yield of wheat, as irrigation is required for half of the sown wheat areas (Figure 3). There are many types of irrigation, including electrically powered pumps for wells, ancient irrigation works such as in the Sichuan Plain, and special equipment for irrigating from springs. During winter in the South, most of the wheat fields are rotated with rice and can be irrigated or drained by the same systems used for rice. The water and soil management technologies for winter wheat (acutally spring wheat planted as winter wheat) following rice in the Jiangsu and neighboring provinces and the Tai Lake area are highly developed. In the northeast spring wheat area, most of the fields are rain fed and nonirrigated areas predominate. For the northwest, however, the proportion of spring wheat is less than in the northeast. In 1979, the winter wheat yield throughout the country was 2.3 metric tons/hectare; and spring wheat yielded only 1.6 metric tons/hectare. Yields in 1984 and again in 1985, for all wheat throughout China, were approximately 3.0 metric tons per hectare. There is a close relationship between yields of wheat and irrigation. Irrigation not only controls soil moisture but can be combined with fertilization, thus increasing the benefits. The correct timing and amount of watering at different stages of growth can increase yields. The old adage, "keeping warm with freezing water, and resisting frost with spring water," gives good results. If spring wheat is irrigated but twice, its yield may be increased 30 to 40%.

Figure 3. Rice follows wheat using the same irrigation system.

Fertilizer. According to practical experience, field application of fertilizer is a key factor for increasing the wheat harvest. Application, however, must be in accordance with climatic and soil conditions and stages of growth. Basal manure applications are more important than top dressings.

For winter wheat, most of the fertilizer should be applied in the late winter season and more attention given to fertilizing seedlings, especially in the tillering (branching) and booting stages. A key factor is the simultaneous application of fertilizer with irrigation. In fact, in China fertilizer applications are heavily skewed toward irrigated lands where yields are high and stable, such as for wheat.

Organic fertilizer is a byproduct of animal agriculture, particularly pig production, and is applied at a rate of 37.5 to 45 metric tons/hectare. In addition to the use of organic fertilizer, mineral fertilizers have played an important role in increasing wheat yields in China. In the 1950s, the average rate of application of mineral fertilizer was about 15 kilograms/hectare. However, in 1979 the use of fertilizer had increased over thirty times to 525 kilograms/hectare, and doubled again by 1984. China has had the fastest growth in fertilizer application for cereal grains of any country for a comparable period. The growth in fertilizer use, however, has been primarily with nitrogen and some phosphorus with very little potassium. Total use of potassium for all of China in 1984 was only 700,000 tons or about the equivalent of that annually used in the state of Illinois of the U.S.A. for corn and soybean production.

Planting green manure crops increases the organic matter in the soil and improves wheat yields. Farmers in the Yangzi River valley and all the South China provinces use green (plant) manure crops such as Chinese milk vetch, which is one of the reasons why they have been able to cultivate their lands for forty centuries and still maintain a high level of fertility (see Chapter 9, "Organic Farming--Growing Plants the Organic Way"). The application of compost returns straw and crop residues to the fields and also increases wheat yields.

Cultural Practices

An old Chinese saying, "30% of them are sowing, and 70% are cultural practices," emphasizes that good results in wheat production cannot be realized without management. It is important to control water, weeds and nutrient levels between crops and especially to reduce the evaporation of soil moisture. Cultural practices should be timed according to the growth of the seedlings. Excessive vegetative growth of seedlings should be avoided. Higher yields can be obtained by controlling growth through fertilizer top dressing, irrigation, cultivation, weeding and appropriate adjustments of fertilizer.

Pest Control. The forecasting of insect invasions (such as armyworms) is carried out by the Central Plant Protection Station with branches and networks in all provinces, municipalities and autonomous regions. Good insect control has been accomplished by these timely predictions through a study of life cycles. Control of wheat insects, thus far, has been mostly by insecticides. In some main wheat-growing regions, aerial spraying of insecticides is practiced. The ultimate solutions for pest control are genetically disease-and insect-resistant varieties for which considerable research is ongoing.

FOR FURTHER READING

Guo Shao-Zheng, and Chang Ying-Ziang. 1983. High yielding techniques of wheat following rice in double and triple cropping systems. Paper presented at the 14th Symposium of Asian Farming Systems, 25-29 October, Nanjing.

Hanson, H.; N. E. Borlaug; and R. G. Anderson. 1982. *Wheat in the Third World.* Boulder, Colo.: Westview Press.

He Kang, ed. 1980, 1981, 1982, 1983, 1984. *Chinese agricultural yearbook.* Beijing: Agricultural Press. (In Chinese)

Huang, R. 1981. The advances of wheat cultivar research in our country. In *Investigations of the information of agriculture and husbandry crop cultivation,* 22: 1-12. Science Discussion Meeting. (In Chinese)

Insel, B. 1985. A world awash in grain. *Foreign Affairs* 63(4): 892-911.

International Maize and Wheat Improvement Center. 1985. *World wheat facts and trends.* Mexico, D.F.

———. 1985. Wheats for more tropical environments. In *Proceedings of the International Symposium.* Mexico, D.F.

Jin Shanbao, ed. 1961. *Wheat culture in China.* Beijing: Agricultural Press. (In Chinese)

Kahn, E. J., Jr. 1985. *The staffs of life.* Boston: Little, Brown, and Co.

Laiyang Agricultural School of Shandong Province, ed. 1975. *Wheat.* Beijing: Science Press. (In Chinese)

National Academy of Sciences. 1977. *Wheat in the People's Republic of China,* ed. V. A. Johnson and H. L. Beemer. Committee on Scholarly Communication with the People's Republic of China Report no. 6. Washington, D.C.: National Academy of Sciences.

Nu Ruofeng. 1985. Grain for a billion people. *China Reconstructs* 34(11): 4-6.

Paulson, G. M. 1985. Technology for wheat production in China. In *Proceedings on agriculture in China.* Vol. 1, *Challenges and opportunities,* 164-86. Beltsville, Md.: Institute of International Development and Education in Agriculture and Life Sciences.

Yu Song Le, ed. *Agricultural practices of crops in the north regions of China* 1:22-168. Beijing: Agricultural Press. (In Chinese)

Vavilov, N. E. 1951. The origin, variation, immunity and breeding of cultivated plants. In *Chronica Botanica* 15, trans. K. S. Chester. New York: Ronald Press.

13

THE RISE OF CORN

by Wang Lianzheng

Corn is the highest yielding of the cereal grains. To the world it is known as maize; in the United States it is corn. It ranks with wheat and rice as one of the world's three most important food and feed crops. It is used for livestock feed, human consumption, industrial purposes and seed.

Unlike rice and to a lesser extent wheat, most corn is not used directly for human food; much of the grain, along with the fodder, is fed directly to livestock. Large quantities are also used for industrial purposes (e.g. corn starch and high fructose syrup). Corn is still, however, among the big three, along with wheat and rice, when it comes to feeding people. Total annual corn production for the world exceeds 400 million metric tons, with the U.S.A. providing about half of it.

Recent significant genetic improvements have resulted in increased yields and the introduction of hybrids, which in the past 45 years have extended the range of corn production 500 miles further north in the U.S.A., throughout the tropics, and into the most northern of the Western European countries. During the past 25 years, it has become a new and leading crop in northwestern Europe. Tropical hybrid corn is beginning to assume considerable importance, with great potential as a food crop in Indonesia and the African countries of Kenya, Tanzania, Zimbabwe, Zambia, Nigeria and Cameroon. Water requirements are much less for corn than for paddy rice, and among the major food crops of the earth, corn is one of the most efficient in capturing energy from the sun and converting it into plant products useful for human food, animal feed, and industrial feedstocks. As water increasingly becomes a limiting resource for agricultural production, it can be expected that corn and wheat, in relation to rice, will continue to increase in importance. This may have some adverse human nutrition effects since both the content and biological value of corn protein are less than those for either rice or wheat.

Corn in China

China is second only to the U.S.A., the world's largest producer, in corn production. Annual production, which is about one-fourth that of the U.S.A., was approximately 68 million metric tons in 1983 and rose to over 72 million metric tons in 1984. Until recently, corn in China ranked from year to year with wheat as the second most important grain crop. It is now number three, being outstripped by both rice and wheat. Since 1952 corn production in China has increased by over 230% with an annual growth rate of about 5%. During 1970-72 to 1981-83, China reported the most rapid growth in yields among major producers, with an annual 4% rate of gain. It registered a spectacular increase of 15% from 1982 to 1984 but both the producing area as well as yields fell off in 1985. Corn is used not only as a staple food for people in China, but increasingly for feeding chickens, ducks, pigs and cattle as well. China is estimated to account for almost one-third of all human consumption of corn in the developing world, yet it supplies only 12% of its cereal calories. Today, corn is grown so extensively in some Chinese provinces (Heilongjiang, Jilin, and Shandong) that to view the countryside is reminiscent of the Corn Belt scenes of the United States.

Introduction of Corn to China

The native land of corn is America. Most scholars attribute the origin of corn to be Mexico or Guatemala, the Peru Plateau in South America and the Western Amazon River Valley. As with rice, the history of corn production goes back to ancient times. Fossilized remains of pollen grains of corn have been found 45 meters below the soil surface in Mexico City.

Mexico is considered by most scholars as the home of corn. Corn in that region dates back about 4,500 years. Columbus introduced corn to Spain in 1494 and from there it spread rapidly to other countries in Europe, Africa and Asia. Within twenty to fifty years it had invaded every country on earth, including China, that was adapted for its culture.

In Li Shizhen's book *Ben Cao Gang Mu* (meaning an outline of medical plants) written in 1578 (see Chapter 2, "Agricultural History Over Seven Thousand Years") is a monograph which gives a record of corn production in China. One sentence reads: "Corn was derived from the West and it was seldom grown in our country."

Recently the Division of Chinese Agricultural Legacy found a record of corn in the monograph *Liuqing Rizha* written by Tian Yihen. It reads: "Corn was derived from the west, the old name of which was foreign wheat. It was cooked for the Emperor and his relatives, and it was called royal wheat." This record was five years earlier than that of Li Shizhen. It is evident that corn was grown in China before 1573 A.D. It was first produced in Hangzhou in the Zhejiang province. Tian Yihen further states that "this crop was introduced here and farmers like to grow it."

Therefore, as recorded in the annals of provinces, prefectures and counties, it is suggested that corn was introduced into China in the middle of the sixteenth century. Wan Goding, working in the Division of Chinese Agricultural Legacy, found a record of corn dating back to 1511 in the Yinchow Annals of the Anhui Province. Thus, corn must have been introduced into China before the year 1511 A.D.--only twenty years after Columbus discovered the new world. Since travel and communication by land were both slow and difficult, at that time, corn was probably first introduced into China from the sea. Records show that China had a strong fleet in those early days. Accordingly, corn production in China began in the coastal provinces and gradually moved inland to the most inward of the provinces. For instance, corn was grown in Sichuan Province 175 years later than in Anhui, a province near the coast, and 205 years later in the Guizhou Province. Of crops introduced into China from America, corn was preceded only by peanuts. Potatoes came to China a century later.

A global perspective of corn and its relationship to peoples and history and to other cereal grains has been put to verse:

"Wheat is the corn of history,
Poverty's corn is rye,
Rice is the corn of the Orient,
But the New World's hunger cry
Was stilled by maize, the Indian corn,
The Redman's gift to man.

Oats is the corn of hardy men,
And barley the brewer's corn,
Sorghum the corn of Africa,
But nations, westward born
Fed man and beast on Indian corn,
The Redman's gift to man.

J.C. Cunningham
(from *the Corn is Ripe*,
copyright 1944)

The cereals of nations were in ancient times referred to as corn. Only in the U.S.A. is maize referred to as corn.

The Corn Belts of China

Corn production in China is mainly distributed in an area on two sides of a line extending from Harbin in the Heilongjiang Province in the northeast to Kunming in Yunnan Province of the southwest. Within this area, there are three main regions for corn production (Figure 1).

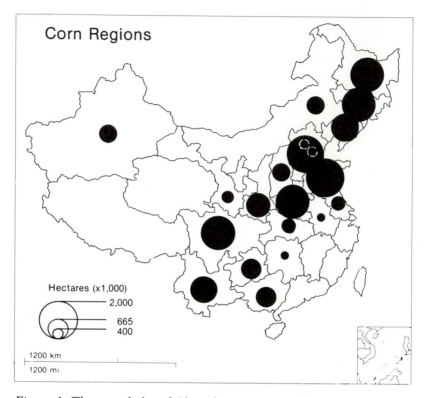

Figure 1. The corn belts of China by province and municipality.

The Northern and Northwest. This is concentrated in the Heilongjiang, Jilin and Liaoning provinces, the Inner Mongolia Autonomous Region and the Ningxia, Shaanxi, and Shanxi provinces. This region accounts for 30% of China's total corn-producing area. Yields of corn here are the highest, particularly in the Liaoning Province which leads with 4.6 metric tons per hectare. The average for all of China in 1984 was 3.96 metric tons per hectare, up from 3.0 in 1980. Northeast China is a region for spring corn production. The climate is cool and humid. The frost-free period is short, temperatures in winter are low, and evapotranspiration in the spring is high, which often results in drought. However, precipitation during the growing season is generally abundant, and corn is one of the staple and high-yielding crops for this area. Only a single crop per year is produced, making it comparable to the northern parts of the U.S.A. Corn Belt.

The Huanghuai Plain. This region is concentrated in Hebei, Shandong, Henan, the central parts of Shanxi, the southern parts of Shanxi and Shaanxi, and the northern parts of Jiangsu and Anhui provinces. It is China's largest producing area, accounting for 40% of the total corn production acreage. Total corn production for this region in 1979-1981 was the highest in China. The climate of the region is temperate and semi-humid, and the frost-free period is considerably longer than for the northern region. Both sunlight and precipitation are generally adequate, with over 2,000 hours of sunlight and a precipitation of 500-600 millimeters recorded annually. The climate is suitable for corn production. The area is adaptable to double cropping or two crops a year, one of winter wheat and the other of summer corn, or for three crops in two years which would include spring corn, winter wheat and summer corn. Corn may be sown either in the spring or summer. This region is comparable to the southern parts of the U.S.A. Corn Belt. It is not uncommon to see large plantings of both corn and cotton in the same areas.

The Southwest. This region is concentrated mainly in Yunnan, Guizhou and Sichuan provinces, the western part of Hubei Province, the southern parts of Hubei and Hunan, the most southern part of Shaanxi and a part of the Gansu Province. While this is an important region for corn production, the area planted represents only 22% of the total. The climate of this region is subtropical, temperate humid, or subhumid. The topography and relief have very complex effects on weather variability. Except for some high mountains, the average temperature from April to October is about 15°C. The growing season generally exceeds 200 days, with approximately 300 days in the southern parts of the region and the Lao Valley, and with no more than 150 days in the alpine areas. The annual average precipitation is about 1,000 millimeters. Rainfall is heaviest from April to October but is well distributed during the growing season and generally beneficial for corn production. The most infavorable factor for corn production in this region is a lack of sunlight. Cloudy days are usually in excess of 200 per year. This corn belt is where production has responded so dramatically to plastic covering of the soil (see Chapter 31, "The Plastic Revolution").

Three cropping systems characterize the region. For the alpine areas, a single crop of spring corn predominates. For the hilly regions, there are mostly five crops in two years with spring-planted corn, or two crops a year with summer-planted corn.

In addition to the hilly areas of the southwest region, some corn is also produced in the hilly regions of the most southern areas of China. It is grown most extensively in the Guangxi Autonomous Region, less so in other southern provinces.

For the far northwest, the acreage of corn in the Xinjiang Autonomous Region is approximately 600 thousand hectares. This region is suitable only for spring-planted corn. The plateaus of Qinghai and Xizang constitute a new region for corn production, where it is grown in the most protected low elevations and warm areas.

The Rise of Corn

Corn provides a large supply of both grain and forage (fodder) per unit of land area, especially where rice or wheat production is low. Large quantities of feed are used as animal husbandry expands, required particularly for the pig, cattle and poultry industries. Pig production has expanded rapidly since the early 1950s (see Chapter 26, "Three Hundred Million Pigs"). Recent increases in pig production in China are directly related to the enlargement of areas planted to corn and the increased production of feed grains and processed feeds.

In the early 1950s, China's corn production area was about 13 million hectares. Thirty years later (the early 1980s), that area reached 18 to 20 million hectares for a gain of nearly 7 million hectares. In addition to an expansion in area, yields were doubled in the same time interval, essentially going from 1.5 metric tons per hectare to over 3 tons per hectare. Yields for 1984 approximated 4.0 metric tons per hectare compared with 7.2 tons per hectare for the U.S.A.

Consequently, overall corn production increased from less than 17 million metric tons in 1956 to over 68 in 1983 (nearly 400%) with a further increase to over 73 million metric tons in 1984. These large increases in both yields and total production may be accounted for as follows.

New and Improved F_1 Hybrids. These new and improved F_1 hybrids have been the principal reasons for the increase in corn yields. Beginning in the early 1950s, an extensive collection, selection, and evaluation of corn genetic resources was carried out. Over 14,000 local varieties were collected, and the growing areas for the better ones greatly expanded. For example, the area for the superior "Gold Queen" (Jin Huan Hao) selection was expanded to 65% of the total area devoted to corn production in the Shanxi Province. The acreage of the "White Horse Dent" (Baimaya) was also greatly increased in the Liaoning and Shanxi provinces. Many improved selections of good local varieties such as Baitoushuang, Changbatang, Yinglitze, and Yejihong were also grown in much larger areas. These varieties provided excellent original material for the development of inbred lines for hybrid seed production.

From 1950 to 1959 a series of F_1 hybrids was released by some of the plant breeding institutions. However, the work was actually begun in 1923, so while the records and statistics are not complete, there were more than 100 different hybrids of leading varieties introduced. But these proved to be low yielding in comparison with F_1 hybrids derived from inbred lines.

During the late 1950s and 1960s, Chinese crop-breeding institutes gave more attention to the breeding of hybrids from the crossing of inbred lines. Double cross F_1 hybrids (a cross between first generation hybrids of four separate inbred lines) were first released in Sichuan Province from 1943 to 1945, but the work was not then extended. In the 1960s, many double cross corn hybrids were released and grown in large areas. The result of regional trials showed that the yield of double cross hybrids was increased by 23 to 27% compared with the leading inter-varietal hybrids. These double cross hybrids played an important role in increasing total corn production in China.

In the late 1960s and 1970s, however, the crop breeding institutions directed their attention toward the breeding of single cross F_1 corn hybrids (a first generation hybrid between two selected inbred lines). Many single cross corn hybrids were released and have become, as they have in the U.S.A., even more significant than double cross hybrids for increasing corn yields.

Prefectural research institutes, provincial academies of sciences in Heilongjiang, Jilin, Henan, Shanxi, Liaoning, and Shandong provinces, and the Chinese Academy of Agricultural Sciences in Beijing have, from 1966 through the 1970s and 1980s, introduced many outstanding single cross corn hybrids. Many of these are high yielding. They range in maturities from the early (105 days) (Figure 2) to late (140 days), with some adapted to early spring and others to late summer plantings. Some are leaf blight-resistant, others are lodging-resistant and flood-tolerant. All are responsive to high fertilizer levels and to irrigation. Adaptabilities range from growing at latitudes in the most northern to the most southern provinces. The new single cross F_1 hybrids are often designated by their sites of Chinese origin with such names as Danyu 6, (Dandong Agricultural Institute in Liaoning Province), Zongdan 2 (Chinese Academy of Agricultural Sciences), Nondang 1 (Nonjiang Research Institute of the Heilongjiang Academy of Agricultural Sciences), Long-dan 3 (Crop Breeding Research Institute of the Heilongjiang Academy of Agricultural Sciences), Jidan 101 (Jilin Academy of Agricultural Sciences), Yiansan 6 (Yiantai Prefecture Institute of the Academy of Agricultural Sciences in Shandong Province), and Sidan 8 (Siping Agricultural Research Institute).

Increased Use of Fertilizers. More fertilizer is another important reason for the rising corn yields in China. Chinese farmers have historically

Figure 2. A high-yielding and early, single cross corn hybrid.

used fertilizer applications and the results have shown a continuous increase in crop yields, with soil fertility being maintained and even improved.

Organic manures in combination with mineral fertilizer are the principal fertilization procedure for corn. Recently there has been a marked increase in the use of organic fertilizers as a result of expansions in pig production and the development of other types of animal industry. Increased amounts of organic fertilizers have played an important role in increasing corn production. As a general rule, organic fertilizer is first applied or spread broadcast on the surface of the soil and then plowed under. In some instances, organic fertilizers are applied alongside the seeds at the time of planting.

Chinese farmers have also had good results in growing green manure crops. Leguminous green manure crops have significantly improved corn yields. They not only add nitrogen, phosphorus, potassium and other nutrients and organic matter to the soil but also greatly improve the soil structure. The nitrogen, phosphorus and potassium provided by green manuring with legume crops help meet the nutrient requirements of corn. Therefore, green manure crops grown either for fallowing or interplanting in corn fields play an important role in increasing yields. Trials conducted by the Hanzhong Research Institute of the Shaanxi Province have shown that corn yields may be increased 40 - 48% by the use of green manuring (see Chapter 9, "Organic Farming--Growing Plants the Organic Way").

Along with the increased use of organic fertilizers, applications of inorganic or mineral fertilizers have risen from 35 to 100 kilograms/hectare in the early 1950s to 525 kilograms/hectare in the early 1980s. From 1976 to 1982, China had the fastest growth rate in fertilizer application (6 to 13 million metric tons per year) of any country for the same period. Much of this was nitrogen used on corn. For the regions with the highest yields of corn, such as Changtu County in the Liaoning Province and Huaide County in the Jilin Province, commercial fertilizer applications now reach 1.12 metric tons/hectare. Corn is particularly responsive to nitrogen. With nitrogen deficiency, the corn plant is dwarf, develops yellowish leaves and does not produce dense grain. When phosphorus is in short supply, corn seedlings appear red or purple in color. With potassium deficiency there is slow growth and marginal burning of the leaves. Under such conditions, remarkable yield increases may be obtained by applying nitrogen, phosphate and potash fertilizers. Corn is also used as an index for assessing soil moisture levels. Single stalks are often observed among other crops to signal the need for irrigation, which is evidenced by the curling of the leaves (Figure 3). leaves (Figure 3).

Optimum Planting Densities in Combination with Other Cultural Practices. Increased planting densities played a significant role for enhancing

Figure 3. Occasional corn plants in fields of other crops signal the need for irrigation.

corn yields. Relationships between numbersof ears, size of ears and weights of grain with photosynthetically active leaf surfaces, root-absorbing surfaces, the full utilization of sunlight, temperature, water, mineral nutrients and accumulation of photosynthates have been established. All regulate corn yields. Planting density or plant populations per unit land area in China increased from 22,500 to 30,000 plants per hectare in the 1950s to 45,000 to 60,000 plants per hectare in the 1980s. These planting densities compare favorably with those currently practiced in the U.S.A. Combinations of optimum planting density with adequate amounts of fertilizer and water from irrigation will produce the best yields. Irrigation of corn in combination with top-dressing of fertilizers has been found effective in some areas. Planting densities should be increased under conditions of (a) high soil fertility, (b) irrigation use, (c) high rates of fertilizer application, (d) corn plants with dwarf strong stalks, and (e) optimal cultural practices. Under opposite conditions planting densities should be decreased.

Corn is seldom grown as a single crop or as monoculture in China as it is in the U.S.A., except in the north and northeast regions. It is usually intercropped with sweet potatoes, cotton, soybeans, squash, or other low growing plants. Intercrops of sweet potato with corn may be observed in the hilly and mountainous regions of Sichuan and adjacent provinces. Low growing intercrops help stabilize the soil, provide a needed groundcover, reduce soil erosion and may, as a green manure crop, improve the soil and add to the food supplies (Figure 4).

Figure 4. Intercropping of corn with sweet potatoes.

Changes in Cultural Practices. Hand thinning of seedlings at the three-to four-leaf stage is a common practice because planting machines are not available in the majority of the corn-producing regions. Seedlings are transplanted into the unseeded areas. Improved techniques for transplanting corn seedlings have been developed in recent years. This is done with late maturing varieties which have a high accumulated temperature requirement. Deep furrows are prepared and irrigated and the corn seedlings are transplanted, sometimes when the plants are a foot high. Transplanting of corn seedlings in China is limited, however, and accounts for no more than one percent of the total crop. But it does represent a unique means of extending the northern boundaries for production of a staple food crop and achieving a more perfect stand of plants. An additional modern innovation to increase yields and extend the margins of productivity for corn in China is the use of plastic soil covers or mulches (see Chapter 31, "The Plastic Revolution").

Weed control for corn in China, unlike the widespread use of herbicides in the Western world, is achieved through timely tillage and cultivation. Chemical herbicides are not widely used for corn production. There is a commitment to remove weeds by hand in exchange for reducing chemical pollution to fields.

Insect and Disease Control. Here there have been some important developments. Many insects and diseases may depress corn yields. The most severe diseases are common smut (*Ustilago maydis*), turcicum leaf blight (*Helminthosporium turcicum*), Maydis leaf blight (*Helminthosporium maydis*)--also known as the Southern Corn Leaf Blight which caused devastation to the crops in the U.S.A. Corn Belt in 1970, stalk rot (*Diplodia maydis*), and downey mildew (*Sclerospora spp.*). Corn diseases may be controlled by breeding resistant hybrids for use in combination with crop rotation, chemical treatments, removal of crop residues and other good management practices.

The most devastating insect on corn production in China and throughout the world is the corn borer, (*Pyrausta nubilalis* (Hubner). It produces one to six generations a year, the numbers of generations increasing from north to south. Generally there are one to two, two to three, three to four, or five to six generations a year in the Northeast, the North, the East and the most southern regions of China (Guangdong and Guangxi provinces), respectively. Recently, Trichogrammatid egg parasites [*Trichogramma ostriniae* (Pang and Chen)], have been successfully used to control corn borers in all of China. They are called "living insecticides." Underground insects such as the Mongolian mole cricket, [*Gryllotalpa unispina*, (Saussure)], the grooved circle beetle, [*Pleonomus canaliculatus* [Foldermann]], the northeast ginat black chafer, [*Holotrichia diomphalia*, (Bates)], and the armyworm, [*Leucania separata*, (Walker)] also cause severe damage. They must be controlled in a timely manner for full establishment of corn seedlings. This control is accomplished primarily through chemical treatments.

Each of the above mentioned techniques of tillage, cultivation, transplanting, crop rotation, soil preparation, fertilization and pest control plays an important role in increasing corn production and improving crop yields.

Future Outlook

Chinese farmers are continuously endeavoring to increase corn production. Plant scientists have made great strides by improving corn varieties, developing high-yielding hybrids, adopting new cultural practices, increasing the use of fertilizers, the introduction of plastic soil mulching and integrating systems for pest control. By such means, corn yields have increased dramatically and thousands of local varieties and new hybrids have been released since corn was introduced into China over 400 years ago.

The rise of corn production in China has been phenomenal, but not accidental. It constitutes a dramatic response to a need for its development, a greatly expanded animal industry and the encouragement of food processing. Corn is now not only a basic food commodity but also an important source of fodder and grain for ever expanding livestock, pig, poultry and fish industries. Current per capita consumption of corn as a livestock feed in China is only 3 kilograms compared to 591 for Hungary, 476 for the U.S.A. and 76 for the U.S.S.R. According to recommendations of an advisory group of hybrid corn specialists from the Chinese Ministry of Agriculture, a policy should be adopted to stabilize the planting area, increase yields, improve quality, and develop a processing industry. Corn production could be greatly expanded in South China. Special attention must be given to improving both the quality and availability of good hybrid seed. The future will see more corn produced in China as a cereal grain for people and as a feed crop for livestock because of the continued development of adaptive hybrids, a water requirement much less than that of paddy rice, and a capacity under many climatic conditions to produce more total digestible nutrients per unit time and per unit resource input than for any other crop.

FOR FURTHER READING

He Kang, ed. 1980, 1981, 1982, 1983. *Chinese agricultural yearbook*. Beijing: Agricultural Press. (In Chinese)

International Maize and Wheat Improvement Center. 1984. *Maize facts and trends. Report 2. An analysis of changes in third world food and feed uses of maize*. Mexico, D.F.

Li Jingxong, ed. 1958. *Cultural practices of crop production*. Beijing: Press of Higher Education. (In Chinese)

Mangelsdorf, P. C. 1986. The origin of corn. *Scientific American* 255(2): 80-86.

Ministry of Agriculture, Animal Husbandry and Fishery. 1985. *Statistics of Chinese agriculture*. Beijing. (In Chinese)

Shandong Academy of Agricultural Sciences, ed. 1962. *The cultural practices of corn in China*. Shanghai: Shanghai Press of Science and Technology. (In Chinese)

U.S. Dpeartment of Agriculture. Economic Research Service. 1984, 1985, 1986. *China outlook and situation reports*. Washington, D.C.: Government Printing Office.

Wang Lianzheng. 1966. Studies of the physiological causes of "red seedlings" of corn and their control. *The News of Plant Physiology* 4:14-16. (In Chinese)

14

SOYBEANS--THE MIRACLE BEAN OF CHINA

by Wang Lianzheng

The soybean--known in the United States as the "gold that grows," the "Cinderella Crop," the "balance of payments champion," the "market's miracle legume," and the "queen of the commodity exchanges"--is called the "miracle bean" by the Chinese. Today, soybeans supply one-fourth of the world's fats and oils, about two-thirds of the world's protein concentrate for animal feeds, and three-fourths of the world trade in high protein meals. The soybean is the world's most important grain legume, both in total production and for international trade. In China it is regarded as a major food and grain crop.

Soybeans play an important role in feeding the Chinese. They are to some degree what milk and dairy products are in the U.S. diet. Soybeans are high in nutrient values, containing approximately 40% protein and 20% oil. About 60% of their value comes from the meal, which is high in protein, and 40% from the oil. Compared with most other staple foods, soybeans have two distinct advantages. They have about three times the protein of cereal grains, and they capture (fix) their own nitrogen from the atmosphere through the *Rhizobium* bacteria found in the root nodules. They are widely known as a soil-improving crop. They fertilize themselves as far as nitrogen is concerned, but need adequate phosphorous and potassium and other nutrients from the soil or fertilizer to fix the nitrogen.

World soybean acreage has doubled during the past twenty years. This represents a greater expansion than for any other major crop. Of the 80 to 100 million metric tons of soybeans produced annually worldwide, the largest contributors are the U.S.A., with 50 to 60 million, and Brazil with about 15 million; China is number three with an annual production of about 10 million metric tons.

The cultivated soybean is native to China, where it has been grown for over 5,000 years. From China, soybean culture expanded east to Korea and then southward to Japan. Europeans were first introduced to soybeans in the early nineteenth century, probably by Jesuit missionaries who had been stationed in China. In Europe, soybeans remained a horticultural curiosity in the Jardin des Plantes in Paris and the Kew Gardens in London for many years.

The first recorded introduction of soybeans into the United States is credited to Samuel Bowen, who planted them near Savannah, Georgia in 1765. Soybeans were initially regarded as more of a botanical curiosity than an economically significant plant. The first U.S. Department of Agriculture bulletin devoted to soybeans was published in 1899 and concentrated on the soybean as a forage and green manure crop for soil improvement. They were of initial interest only as a hay crop and highly regarded as "soil building" because they "fixed" nitrogen. No more than eight varieties of soybeans were then grown in the U.S.A. Beginning in 1898, however, the U.S. Department of Agriculture introduced hundreds of varieties from Asian countries. Since 1941, soybeans have ascended from an insignificant soil-building and forage crop in the U.S.A. to become one of the world's most important economic commodities.

China--The Place of Origin for the Cultivated Soybean

Scientists of the world have concluded that China is the place of origin for the cultivated soybean. They do not agree, however, as to the exact location within China or the date of origin. A review of ancient Chinese literature shows that the soybean was extensively cultivated and valued as a food centuries before written records were kept. Records prior to 2,000 B.C. state that the crop was considered the most important cultivated legume and, according to the mythical Shen Nong (see Chapter 2, "Agricultural History over Seven Thousand Years), one of the five sacred grains essential to Chinese civilization. The others were rice, wheat and two kinds of millet. The latter two are sometimes designated as a barley and a millet.

W. J. Morse (referred to as the Father of American Soybeans), after reviewing the ancient history of the soybean, states, "The first written record of the plant is contained in the books by Ben Cao Gang Mu (*Materia Medica*), describing the plants of China by Emperor Shen Nong in 2,838 B.C." The soybean is repeatedly mentioned in later records as the most important cultivated legume.

Hymowitz, however, has challenged Morse's conclusions. He states, "In the earliest record of man's use of the soybean, dating back to the herbalist Ben Cao Gang Mu of the legendary Emperor Shen Nong, is an often-repeated statement in soybean literature. No fewer than six different years have been acclaimed as the publication date for Shen Nong's book." Published statements, such as "The soybean is one of the oldest of cultivated crops," and "The soybean has been known to man for over 5,000 years," are repeated from one agronomic publication to another without citation or explanation. On the basis of historical, geographical, and taxonomic evidence, Hymowitz concluded that the soybean, as we know it now, first emerged in northeastern China around the eleventh century B.C., and the Manchuria was most likely a center for diversifying the soybean, as this area provided the greatest opportunity for the overlapping and intercrossing of various species.

Fukuda, in 1933, also favored Manchuria as the center of origin on the basis that 1) soybeans are distributed widely in Manchuria and less frequently in other parts of China; 2) numerous soybean varieties are grown in Manchuria; and 3) many of these varieties apparently have primitive characteristics. Nagata suggests that the soybean originated in China proper, probably in the northern and central regions. He based his conclusions partially on the distribution of *Glycine ussuriensis*, which is considered the progenitor of the cultivated form, *Glycine max*.

Chinese authors also differ as to the place of origin of the soybean. Lui Shilin mentioned that during the Shang Dynasty, Chinese farmers began to grow soybeans. Ma Rhuhwa and Zhang Kan stated that "Soybeans originated in China and were domesticated there."

Wang Jinling of the Northeastern Agricultural College at Harbin and others have studied the photoperiodic responses of wild soybeans from the northern part of the Heilongjiang Province to the southern part of Hunan Province. They found that, among the wild soybeans of the Yangzi River valley, there are typical short-day types of primitive characteristics. It was concluded that the Yangzi River valley of South China was the site of origin for the cultivated soybean. Soybeans with moderate short-day behavior, when moved from that region, were found suitable for North China. But the Yellow River valley also has a large number of wild and semi-wild soybeans of many types and cultivars. Here the cultivated soybeans may have originated from the wild soybeans through selection.

Lui Shilin has suggested that the cultivated soybean may have originated from many different places in China. In the southern and northern parts of China there are many regions, each with its early developing civilizations and ancient records of soybean cultivation. Also, wild soybeans as well as the cultivated are widely distributed and of many different day-lengths and ecotypes.

We must conclude that China is without question the original home or native land of the cultivated soybean as we know it today and from which all current varieties have their origin. We must also conlude that there are many sites within China from which they may have sprung forth. Finally, there is still much wild genetic material in China from which improved varieties could yet be developed.

Ancient Literature

Soybeans were first called "Shu," and the word "Shu" appears repeatedly in *Shijing* [the Book of Songs], which is one of the five Chinese classics dating from 1,100-771 B.C. The Chinese name of "soybean-dadou" first appeared in the book of Shen Nong from the third to fifth centuries B.C. (See Chapter 2, "Agricultural History Over Seven Thousand Years.) The soybean was described as a crop flowering in 90 days and maturing in another 60 days, with a growing season of 150 days.

In "Xiao Ya" from *Shijing* [the Book of Songs] it is mentioned that "...in Central China there was the soybean and farmers collected it." Another song, "Guofen" (1,000 B.C.), states that "...in October rice and soybeans are collected." A book by Zuo Zhuan (351 B.C.) reports that "the King of Zhou has a brother who wa unable to tell soybeans from wheat." In *Mo Zi* (400 B.C.) it is stated that, "relating to farming and forestry, if soybeans and millet were plentiful, the people had enough to eat."

Archaeological Findings. In 1959, in Houma County, Shanxi Province, archaeologists unearthed soybean grains now found in the Natural Museum in Beijing. According to C^{14} determinations, they are 2,300 years old. The seed coats have a yellow color, and the weight of a hundred grains is abut 20 grams. These are the earliest and oldest of archaeological soybean seed relics in the world (Figure 1).

Figure 1. The earliest and oldest soybean seed relics in the world.

Distribution of the Wild Soybeans. Many Chinese scientists have recently collected and studied wild soybeans found in Isikeng, Tahe County, Heilongjiang Province of the north, Fuyuang County, Heilongjiang Province in the east, Gansu and Ningxia in the west, and Guangdong Province in the south. The characteristics of wild soybeans vary according to area, including those in the Henan, Shanxi, Shaanxi and other provinces of Central China. Because of the many different intermediate types between the cultivated and the wild soybean, it is concluded that the cultivated soybean evolved from the wild.

Distribution of the Cultivated Soybean. During the Zhou Dynasty, the soybean was grown mainly in the Yellow River valley as a main food staple. Ancient Chinese literature simultaneously referred to the soybean and to millet. It was reported that "people eat soybean grain and soybean leaf soup." During the Han Dynasty, in Central China, the people suffered one calamity after another. It was then that large numbers of peasants migrated to the northeast and carried soybeans with them, (see *Book of Fan Senzhi*, 100 B.C.). At that time, the area for soybean culture was forty percent of all crops.

About 1,000 B.C., China had close cultural and economic relations with Korea. During the period of Zhanguo (400 B.C.), China and Korea exchanged agricultural experiences. In the Qin and Han dynasties, in China, there were also close connections with Japan, who sent embassies to the Han Dynasty. The soybean was probably introduced to Korea and then to Japan during these periods.

Nagata suggested that the cultivated soybean was introduced into Korea from North China and then disseminated to Japan sometime between 200 B.C. and the third century A.D. A second route of entry may have been from Central China to southern Japan, especially to the island of Kyushu, since Japan had frequent dealings with China from the sixth to eighteenth centuries.

Soybean Germplasm Resources in China

China has an extraordinarily rich and varied soybean germplasm collection (more than 7,000 selections). The soybean's adaptability is a result of its unusual variability. Each climatic pattern, crop rotation system and use for soybeans has its own adapted cultivars. These cultivars include different ecotypes adapted for spring, summer and winter sowing at different locations and with wild and semi-wild types. The cultivars vary greatly according to maturity, seed size, chemical composition of the seed, pod-bearing characteristics, and disease and insect resistance. They are literally treasure troves, which have accumulated from practice and scientific inputs over many centuries.

The current cultivars have played an important role historically in world soybean production, and will continue to do so in the future as they attract the attention of soybean scientists worldwide.

Versatile Uses for Soybeans in China

The soybean, with its many products, is one of the most versatile plants known to people, science and industry. In China, it is grown primarily for its seed, which is widely used in the preparation of hundreds of food items (Figure 2). Meanwhile, China is expanding its use of soybeans. Soybean food technology has progressed in China to a remarkable degree. No other country has developed, from a single crop, such a wide variety of products for direct human consumption. Soybean preparations not only give flavor to the diet but supply to a considerable extent the necessary protein and other essential nutrients. Nutritionally, the protein of the soybean is similar to animal protein, with remarkable similarities in the patterns of amino acid distribution.

The protein content of soybeans, weight for weight and based on essential amino acids, is about twice that of meat and of most beans and nuts, four times that of eggs and cereals, and twelve times that of milk. On a dry weight basis, the seed is composed principally of protein (about 40%), oil (20%), carbohydrates (22-30%), fiber (3-6%) and minerals (3-6%), although these amounts vary considerably.

Figure 2. Soybeans are widely used in the preparation of many food items.

Soybeans as a Food Staple. In the Shandong, Henan and Hebei provinces, soybeans are used primarily as a staple food. Soybean flour (10-20%) is added to wheat flour and the flour of miscellaneous other crops for noodles, steamed bread and buns. In North China and the Liaoning Province, soybean flour is added to milk to produce a milk powder substitute. Cereal protein is low in the amino acid lysine and soybean protein corrects that deficiency. The addition of 5-10% soybean protein to wheat flour results in a remarkable improvement in nutritive value.

Soybeans as a Foodstuff. Soybeans play a conspicuous role in the Chinese diet. The most commonly used soybean food products are fresh or dried bean curd, bean milk, soy sauce, soy sprouts, fermented bean curd, jellied bean curd and thin sheets of bean curd. Soybeans are also used extensively and directly as sprouted beans, boiled beans and as green vegetable beans. They provide a healthy snack for Chinese school children who, in some areas, carry paper bags of them--pods and all--to eat at school.

Blanched sprouts of soybeans and, to a lesser extent, mung beans and peas provide a tender, crisp, nutritious and tasty fresh vegetable product. They are widely popular in China, representing a unique culinary contribution which is only now receiving deserved popularity in the salad bars of the Western world.

There is also an expanding use of processed soybean proteins for human consumption. They are a partial or complete substitute for meat in processed food items, and also serve as meat analogues. They are also being consumed increasingly in the guises of cheese analogues and more simply as cooked sprouts and soy milk (which has been served in China for ages). The Heilongjiang and Jilin provinces are taking the initiative in transforming the soybeans into a variety of meat analogues.

The Soybean as a Main Oil Crop. Soybean, rape, peanut, sunflower, sesame and cotton seed are the main oil crops of China. In northeast and northern China, soybean oil is the most important cooking oil. Soybean oil contains from 80 to 85% unsaturated fatty acids, which tend to keep blood cholesterol levels at a healthy low. The oil is classified as semi-drying and is intermediate between the rapidly drying oils, such as linseed and tung, and the nondrying peanut oil.

Soybeans for Industrial Uses. The soybean has many industrial uses in China. One of the most important is in the production of high grade industrial enamels. It is also used extensively in the manufacture of varnishes and alkyl resin paints, and in inks and stains, pharmaceuticals, oilcloth, linoleum and synthetic rubber. Soybean protein is used in adhesives, paper coatings, water-thinned paints, plastics, printing inks and textile fibers. It is widely used in the production of lecithin, hormones, vitamins, furfural, bakelite and monosodium glutamate. The latter is extensively used in Chinese cooking. Research is resulting in an ever-widening range of industrial and food uses for the soybean and its products.

Soybeans as Feed for Livestock and Poultry. The soybean cake, or the meal that remains after the oil has been extracted, is a valuable high-protein product for feeding livestock and poultry. It increases milk and egg production as well as the output of other livestock products. In addition to soybean cake, the leaf, stem and pod residues of the soybean are also good feedstuffs. With the current remarkable expansion of dairy cattle, pig, poultry and rabbit industries in China, the expectation is that soybeans will increase in importance.

Soybeans Fertilize and Enrich the Soil. The root system of the soybean is deep and extensive. There are numerous nodules on both the main and branch roots. The bacterium (*Bradyrhizobium japonicum*) in these nodules may fix nitrogen from the air. The average amount fixed is about 100 kg/ha, which is 35 to 50% of the total nitrogen recovered by the plant. Leaves, branches and root residues in the soil increase the organic matter and enrich the soil. Thus soybeans provide a "biofertilizer" by providing nitrogen for themselves as well as for crops which follow. Chinese peasants call the soybean a "soil fertilizing crop." (Figure 3).

Figure 3. Soybeans are a self-fertilizing crop.

Export Importance. Chinese soybeans became an important product for export at an early date. By 1918 over 600,000 tons of whole beans and hundreds of tons of soybean oil and soy cake were exported annually. Historically, soybeans, tea and silk have been China's three largest agricultural exports. In recent years, however, the domestic demand for soybeans has increased, with a decrease in the quantity shipped abroad. A moderate percentage (10-20%) of the soybeans produced in China are used directly as human food in the form of sprouts or immature beans in the pod and as many products derived directly from the beans. There has been a surplus of soybeans in recent years in China, and exports to the U.S.S.R. and Japan have been increasing. Utilization of soybeans in China will vary with the province. In Heilongjiang, the leading producer with 30% of China's soybeans for 1984, 40% were exported to the U.S.S.R. and Japan, 35% went for human consumption, 10% went for seed purposes, and 15% were exported to other provinces in China. In the Jiangsu Province, 80% of the soybeans produced go directly for human consumption.

There has been a steadily growing demand for soybeans in China accompanied by steady increases in production. Despite the growing domestic demand, some 925,000 metric tons of the approximately 10 million tons produced in 1984/85 were exported. Soybean meal exports rose from 170,000 tons in 1981 to more than 600,000 tons in 1984 and are expected to continue expanding into 1985/86 (Figure 4). In the future, however, the combined domestic demand for edible oil and the increased demand in China for livestock feed will result in a slower pace of increase in efforts.

Characteristics of Soybeans in China

Growth Period. Chinese soybeans have been classified into thirteen maturity groups. They range from 000, which is very early, to X, which is very late. These maturing groups are correlated as to both latitude and elevation. In the northeast and northern parts of China, there is only one crop per year. Soybean cultivars in the extreme northern part of the region belong to maturity group 00, an example of which is Beihoodo. In the southern part of the Heilongjiang Province the varieties "Heinong 26" and "Dongnong No. 4" belong to Group I. Those in the middle, such as "Jilin 3," belong to Group II and those in the south, such as "Tefeng-18," to Group III. On the plains between the Yellow River and the Huai He, soybeans are planted after winter wheat. The soybean cultivars in that area are represented by Groups V and VI. Some spring-sown cultivars belonging to maturity groups III and IV are also planted in this region. In the broad Yangzi River valley, most soybeans sown after winter crops belong to maturity groups VI and VII, and most autumn-maturing soybeans sown after early rice belong to Groups VIII and IX. In the extreme southern provinces of China, soybeans sown in late July belong to Groups IX and X.

Figure 4. Soybeans have been and remain a major export crop for China.

Disease and Insect Resistance. Increasing the disease and insect resistance of soybeans is an important challenge which is being addressed by many research institutes and agricultural colleges. Over 2,000 cultivars were recently evaluated in an effort to find a strain which is resistant to pod borers (*Leguminivora glycinivorella, Lepidoptera tortricidal*). The cultivar "Teziasilihuang" (Iron Pod) was found to be a source of resistance and further resistant cultivars have since been developed and released ("Jilin 3," for example). Several cultivars have been found resistant to the cyst nematode and many to frog-eye leaf spot. Scientists from the Northeast Agricultural College, the Nanjing Agricultural College, the Keshan Agricultural Institute and the Institute of Genetics of Academia Sinica have found several cultivars, including "Heihe No. 3," which are moderately resistant to soybean mosaic.

Seed Size. Seed size varies greatly with where soybeans are grown in China. The large-seeded *Glycine max* (the cultivated soybean) was derived from the small-seeded *Glycine soja* through long-term selection under intensive cultivation. Large-seeded soybeans are much more desirable and adaptable to intensive farming than are the small-seeded types. Soybeans produced in the eastern part of the Northeast have 100-seed weights ranging from 16 to 22 grams. In the western part of the Northeast, where annual rainfall is much less and the soil is alkaline, 100-seed weights range from 13 to 16 grams. The loess plateaus of the Shaanxi and Shanxi provinces have an annual rainfall of 400-500 mm and soil fertility is low. Here small (13 grams per 100 seeds) black-seeded soybeans are the dominant type. On the plains between the Yellow River and Huai He the seed size ranges from 13 to 16 grams per 100 seeds.

Soybean seed size also varies according to usage and cropping systems, especially in the Yangzi River valley. Here seed size of some vegetable-type soybeans may be 38-40 grams per 100 seeds. An example is "Dashachindo," with 100 seeds weighing 40 grams. The seeds used for bean sprouts may weigh only 4 to 5 grams per 100 seeds. Seeds from soybeans sown after winter crops of wheat, barley or rapeseed range from 10 to 15 grams per 100 seeds. Since the inheritance of seed size of soybeans is quantitative, the potential for selection among progenies of crosses is great.

Chemical Composition and Nutritional Value of Soybean Cultivars. Varieties of soybeans differ in chemical composition and nutritional value. Those collected from the main soybean-producing area of the Northeast have a high oil (20-23%) and a moderate protein (38-42%) content. Soybeans with protein higher than 43% are rare.

Long-term selection for specific usage has played an important role in the ultimate composition of Chinese soybeans. Soybeans produced in the Northeast are used for both oil and protein, those in the Yangzi

Valley as a human foodstuff, and those in the Yellow River and Huai He valleys for both oil and human consumption. The protein of the "Biloxi" soybean may be as high as 48%, and the oil content of "Hei-nong 8" up to 23.4%.

Pod-Bearing Vine Characteristics. Soybeans are divided into indeterminate, determinate and semi-determinate pod-bearing vine types. Indeterminate types (vine types) perform better than the determinate (bush types) when exposed to water stress, low fertility, or a short growing season. Indeterminate types are more prolific. Determinate soybeans, on the other hand, produce greater yields under intensive cultivation and with low plant population per unit land area, because the plants do not lodge (topple over) from excessive growth. Cultivars with tall and stiff main stems of moderate branching, with many nodes on the main stem, and which are suitable for mechanical harvesting, are most promising for Northeast China.

Production Regions and Cropping Systems

Historically, soybean production in China reached a record high of 11.3 million metric tons in 1936. By 1985, however, the total soybean area under cultivation in China was approximately 7.8 million hectares, with a total production of over 10.5 million metric tons and an average yield of about 1.35 metric tons per hectare. These yields are considerably less than those of 1.90 metric tons per hectare for the U.S.A. and 1.65 for Brazil. Soybeans are cultivated mainly in eight provinces: Heilongjiang, Henan, Shandong, Anhui, Jilin, Liaoning, Jiangsu and Hubei. These represent territories with highly variable soil and climatic conditions and different cropping systems. Accordingly, soybean production in China may be characterized by five cultural regions (Figure 5).

Spring-Sown. This region includes the three northeast provinces (Heilongjiang, Jilin and Liaoning) and a part of North and Northwest China. The Northeat is the number one soybean-growing region encompassing about 40% of the area China devotes to soybean production. One crop a year is produced.

The cultivars are early, with maturity groups ranging from 00 to III. The growing season is from 100 to 150 days. "Tiefeng 18," a new high-yielding spring type soybean which is disease resistant and grows well in both cold and warm climates, has been grown extensively in the northern and north central provinces. In the eastern and northern parts of the Heilongjiang Province, there are many large farms. A typical crop rotation is spring wheat-spring wheat-soybean, or spring wheat-corn-soybean. Other crop rotations are corn-soybean-millet or sorghum, or wheat-corn-soybean. Mechanical planters are used for seeding and

Figure 5. Soybean production regions in China.

cultivation is mechanized. In recent years, chemical insecticides have been used for insect control. Chemical herbicides may also be used for weed control. Phosphorus fertilizer is usually applied with the planter at the time of seeding, and nitrogen fertilizer during cultivation. Techniques are being pursued for fertilization that will not inhibit symbiotic nitrogen fixation. On the large farms, the harvest is by combine (Figure 6). For smaller units, soybeans are usually hand harvested.

Northern Summer-Sown. This region, which includes the Shandong, Henan, and the northern parts of Jiangsu and Anhui provinces, is also a major soybean production area. Planting is usually in June or July following the harvest of winter wheat. The cultivars are generally determinate. A rotational system of two crops a year on the same land is usually practiced with winter wheat, soybeans, maize or sweet potatoes. A system of three crops in two years is also common.

Figure 6. Cleaning and Storage of soybean.

Southern Summer-Sown. This region includes the Yangzi River Valley, which is made up of the southern parts of Hubei and Jiangsu provinces and the northern parts of Zhejiang, Jiangxi and Hunan provinces. Summer soybeans are planted as a mono-culture or intercropped with maize in June following the harvest of winter wheat, barley or rapeseed. Harvest is in October. In this region soybeans can also be sown in the spring or autumn.

Autumn-Sown. This region includes the southern parts of Zhejiang, Jiangxi and Hunan provinces and the northern parts of Guangdong and the Fujian provinces. Most autumn soybeans in these provinces are sown in late July after the harvest of an early rice crop. They are small-seeded and belong to the VIII and IX maturity groups. These cultivars are extremely late-maturing. Autumn-sown soybeans are harvested from early to mid-November.

Winter-Sown. This region includes the frost-free southern parts of Guangdong and Guangxi provinces. Soybeans are sown in winter, usually in November, and harvested in March and April. The soybean cultivars for this region are extremely late-maturing (Group X). There can be three crops in a year. The rotation is early rice, mid-season rice and then soybeans.

In addition to solid field production, soybeans throughout China are often grown on small patches of land not suitable for regular farming. These include the spaces between rice paddies and on the ridges that separate them, on the banks of drainage ditches and in the spaces between greenhouses and among trees in an orchard.

Potentials in Anther Culture and Genetic Engineering

China has made significant advances in anther culture of soybeans and other crops (see Chapter 32, "Test Tube Plants"). Soybean haploids (pollen plants) were obtained in 1979-1980 at both the Heilongjiang Academy of Agricultural Sciences (HAAS) and Jilin Academy of Agricultural Sciences. Cytological observations showed that these plants developed from haploid pollen. Anthers from stable varieties or second generation hybrids were used containing immature pollen grains. The potential of haploid culture will be for the development of extremely uniform new soybean varieties derived from the spontaneous or colchicine-induced conversion back to diploids.

China, with its rich genetic resources of both the wild and semi-wild soybeans, also has a great potential for soybean improvement through innovative approaches in genetic engineering. One approach would be to screen for tumor-forming types and forms of infection with *Agrobacterium tumefaciens* (crown gall) as a vector for gene transfer, and then follow the fate of foreign genes after they are introduced into the soybean genome by means of the Ti plasmid of *A. tumefaciens*.

Important Chinese Scientists in Soybean Improvement

No people from any nation have contributed more to soybean improvement than the Chinese. Numerous soybean cultivars have been created and preserved that now play an important role in soybean production and the continued improvement of soybeans in China and throughout the world.

Among the oldest of Chinese contributors to soybean variety improvement were Wang Shou, Jin Shanbao and Din Zhenlin. They conducted thorough studies on genetic and variety improvement, morphology, seeding, fertilization, irrigation and cultivation. Likewise, there are many contemporary scientists, representing many institutions of higher learning and research centers, who continue to contribute to soybean genetics (particularly the genetics of quantitative characters), breeding for insect and disease resistance, classification, cultivation and the identification of the soybean regions according to cultivation, soybean germplasm, and soybean cropping systems. Many leading Chinese scientists, especially those specializing in genetic improvement, have been active participants in the joint U.S.A./China Soybean Symposia initiated in 1982.

China now has two famed soybean research sites. One is at Gongzhuling of the Jilin Academy of Agricultural Sciences, and the other is the recently dedicated Soybean Research Institute at Harbin in the Heilongjiang Province. Scientists at these two sites, along with those in other institutions, are actively engaged in soybean improvement and exploring new frontiers for the "Miracle Bean of China."

FOR FURTHER READING

Dovring, F. 1974. Soybeans. *Scientific American* 230(2): 14-21.

Fukuda, Y. 1933. Cytogenetical studies on the wild and cultivated Manchurian soybeans (Glycine L.). *Japanese Journal of Botany* 6:489-506.

Hymowitz, T. 1970. On the domestication of the soybean. *Economic Botany* 23:408-21.

Ling Yi-lu, and Gai Jun-yi, 1985. *Soybean production and research in Jiangsu Province and South China*. Nanjing: Jiangsu Academy of Agricultural Science and Nanjing Agricultural University.

Lui Shilin. 1982. Origin and evolution of the cultivated soybean. In *Soybeans*, ed. Wang Shou and Lui Shilin, 1-14. Beijing: Shanxi People's Press. (In Chinese)

Ma Rhuhwa, and Zhang Kan. 1983. Historical development of soybean production in China. *Proceedings of the 1st China/USA Soybean Symposium and Working Group Meeting*. Series no. 25. Urbana, Ill.

Morse, W. J. 1950. History of soybean production. In *Soybean and soybean products*, ed. K. S. Markley, 3-59. New York: Interscience Publishers Inc.

Nagata, T. 1959. Studies on the differentiation of soybeans in the world with special regard to that of Southeast Asia. *Proceedings of Crop Science Society of Japan* 28:79-82.

Wang Jinling. 1982. *The soybean*. Harbin: Heilongjiang Press of Science and Technology. (In Chinese)

Wang Jinling. 1982. *The soybean*. Harbin: Heilongjiang Press of Science and Technology. (In Chinese)

———. 1983. Ecological distribution of soybean cultivars in China. *Proceedings of the 1st China/USA Soybean Symposium and Working Group Meeting*. INTSOY Series no. 25. Urbana, Ill.

Wang Lianzheng, and Shao Qiquan, et al. 1984. Tumor induction of Glycine Sp by *Agrobacterium tumefaciens* and gene transfer. *Scientia Sinica*, no. 11. (In Chinese)

Xiaoya, and Guofen. *From B.C. 11 century to B.C. 711. Shijing [The book of songs]*. (In Chinese)

FOR FURTHER READING

15

MILLET AND SORGHUM--THE ANCIENTS OF CROPS

by Yu Youtai

Millet

> There are many treasures with millet
> Nobody and no animals can get along without it.
> People like the millet meal,
> Animals may be fed by the straw of millet,
> Brans of millet are good feed for pigs,
> And the millet stubble can be used as a good fuel.

So goes an ancient proverb showing the importance of millet in North China. Millet is one of the most ancient of crops (see Chapter 2, "Agricultural History Over Seven Thousand Years"). It is still one of China's most important food crops. Although millet occupies only 6-7% of the total cultivated land on earth devoted to the production of food crops, the total area as well as production holds a high place among some South Saharan African countries and in India.

Millet is especially renowned in the northern part of China for it was from the bases in the north that the war with Japan and the war for liberation were first won. With millet and the rifle, the Chinese overcame the enemy, even though there was a shortage of both food and weapons. Thus, high praise was given to millet.

Distribution of Millet

Millet and sorghum are very widely produced in China, stretching from 32 to 50 degrees north latitude and from 108 to 130 degrees east longitude (Figure 1). The four production regions for millet can be divided as follows.

Spring Millet of the Northeast. Included are the three northeastern provinces and the eastern part of the Inner Mongolia Autonomous Region. Here the temperatures are low and the growing seasons are short.

Spring Millet of the North Plateau. This region includes the western portions of Inner Mongolia; the Gansu, Ningxia, and parts of Shanxi, Shaanxi and Hebei provinces; and the Xinjiang Autonomous Region. The climate is dry, there is little rainfall, and the growing season is short.

Spring and Summer Millet of the North China Plain. This area includes the Beijing municipality, most of Hebei, and parts of Shandong, Shanxi and Henan provinces. Temperatures are moderate. There is a medium-to-long growing season with moderate rainfall. Millet is sown both in spring and in summer.

Summer Millet of the Yellow River and Huai River Reaches. Parts of Shaanxi, Shanxi, Shandong, Henan, Hebei, Jiangsu and Anhui provinces are included in this production region. These areas constitute a temperate zone agriculture and have a long growing season. Millet is sown in June or July after the harvest of winter wheat, barley and rapeseed.

Figure 1. Sorghum and millet production is widely dispersed in China, but is concentrated in the northeast.

North China has the largest acreage of millet--35% of the total for China. The second most important area is the Northeast, which occupies 26%, followed by the Northwest and East China, both with approximately 13%, the mid-South with nearly 10%, and Inner Mongolia with about 3%. Millet is produced most extensively in the Shandong, Shanxi, Shaanxi, Hebei, Henan, Liaoning, Jilin, Gansu and Heilongjiang provinces and Inner Mongolia (Figure 1).

The Merits of Millet

Millet has prevailed as a main food crop in the northern part of China for thousands of years, resistant to the many prevailing harsh environments there. The grain is easy to handle and store and is highly nutritious. Millet is the most drought resistant of all cereal grains, surpassing even grain sorghum. It requires less water for the seed to germinate and to synthesize dry matter as edible grain than either maize or wheat. Along with sorghum, it can be grown on barren lands where other crops will not survive. In China, there are also rich genetic resources, with many indigenous varieties having very high adaptability to diverse climatic regions, different growing seasons and varying levels of soil fertility. These combined characteristics enable millet to survive many natural hazards to which other cereal grains will succumb.

The millet grain is covered with a hard shell. This makes it easy to harvest, thresh, sun-dry and store. The air-dried millet can be stored under airtight conditions for ten to twenty years without deterioration of the food value. No other food grain has a comparable storage capability.

Finally, millet is highly nutritious as a cereal grain. The average protein content of the grain (9+%) is higher than that of either rice or maize. The oil and fat content (3+%) exceeds that of both rice and wheat. Millet is also rich in vitamin B_1, contains some vitamin A, and has higher levels of both tryptophane and methionine amino acids than either rice, wheat, maize or sorghum. These two amino acids are indispensable and are often deficient in plant products. They cannot be synthesized by the human body. This may be the reason why millet meal, as an important and nutritious food, is usually taken by Chinese women during the "lying-in" (after-childbirth) period.

Millet straw is an attractive forage for livestock. The digestibility of the straw is higher (by 10%) than for either rice or wheat straw. The coarse protein content approaches that of legume forages and is 50-100% higher than that of the average for grass. It is palatable for large animals and is an indispensable roughage for horses and mules. Thus, the value of millet straw may even exceed that of the grain. It is estimated that a mature horse will annually consume the amount of millet straw produced on one hectare of land. Hence, the area for millet production in a farming enterprise in North China is often determined by the number of horses and mules owned by a particular farmer (Figure 2).

Figure 2. Sorghum and millet production in Inner Mongolia.

Sorghum

Sorghum, like millet, is a worldwide commodity, grown especially in Asia, Africa and North America. Countries important in its production include the U.S.A., China, India, the Sudan, Yemen and Ethiopia.

Sorghum has been cultivated for thousands of years in China. It is believed, based on archaeological studies, that sorghum was one of the important food crops widely grown during the Zhou and Western Han Dynasties (eleventh to third century B.C.), in what are now the Jiangsu, Shaanxi, Shanxi, Hebei and Liaoning provinces.

The area in China devoted to sorghum production in 1984 was 2.45 million hectares, with an average grain yield of 3.15 tons/hectare. Both yields and the areas of productivity were smaller in 1985. During the past five years, yields have gone up substantially more than the area planted has gone down. The net result has been a significant increase (6.8 to 8.3 million metric tons per year) in total production. This has also been true of millet. Sorghum occupies slightly more than two percent of the total arable land in China. Provinces that lead in sorghum production are Liaoning, Hebei, Shandong, Henan, Jilin, Heilongjiang and Inner Mongolia (Figure 1).

Geographical Distribution of Sorghum

Like millet, sorghum is highly resilient against drought, floods, and salty, alkaline and barren soils. It is cultivated in almost all provinces (Figure 1). Four regions of production may be identified according to climate, tillage and cultivation systems.

Spring Sowing and Early Maturation. Included in this region are the Heilongjiang and Jilin provinces and Inner Mongolia. The area sown to sorghum occupies 22% of the total for China. The climate is described as frigid. Temperatures are low, growing seasons are short (120-130 days), the effective accumulated temperature is about 2,000°C, and annual precipitation is around 400 millimeters. Only one crop a year is produced here.

Spring Sowing and Late Maturation. This is the main sorghum-producing area. It includes the provinces of Liaoning, Hebei, Shanxi, Shaanxi, Gansu and Ningxia, the municipality of Beijing and the Xinjiang Autonomous Region. Fifty-five percent of the total land area devoted to sorghum in China is found in this region. Production is concentrated in Hebei, Ningxia, Liaoning, Shanxi and Xinjiang. The climate is temperate. Effective accumulated temperatures range from 2,700-4,100°C, the growing season is 150-207 days, and there is an annual precipitation of 500-700 millimeters. The region supports one crop for each year, but in some restricted areas three crops may be produced for every two years.

Spring and Summer Sowing. This region, which produces 20 percent of the nation's total, includes the Shandong and Henan provinces and parts of Hebei, Shaanxi, Shanxi, Jiangsu and Anhui provinces. The climatic zone is semi-humid temperate, with an effective annual accumulated temperature of about 4,700°C. The growing season ranges from 220-230 days and annual precipitation is 400-800 millimeters. Two crops per year may be produced here, or three crops for every two years.

The Southern Region. This includes the Jiangsu, Fujian, Guangdong, Sichuan and Zhejiang provinces. Rice predominates in this region. Sorghum production here occupies only 3% or less of the total cultivated area but is gradually increasing as a result of the expanded use of hybrids. The climate is humid subtropical, characterized by high temperatures, a long growing season and two crops per year.

Varietal Improvement and Hybrid Vigor

The development of improved varieties of sorghum in China has progressed through the stages of sorting out indigenous varieties and systematic selection to the breeding of hybrids and their utilization. The introduction of hybrid vigor has had a positive impact on the production of both sorghum and millet in China. F_1 hybrids now comprise about 90% of the total sorghum acreage. They are higher yielding, of improved quality, and more resistant to many biological and environmental constraints and to lodging (plants topple over and fall to the ground as the grain matures.)

Industrial Uses

A sorting out of the indigenous sorghum varieties of China shows 1,048 varieties listed in *"The Flora of Chinese Sorghum Varieties,"* of which 980 are for food, 50 are for industrial use, and 14 are for sugar. Sorghum in China is produced primarily for human food and to a lesser extent for feeding livestock and poultry.

There are also industrial purposes for which sorghum is produced in China. The grain is used for making liquor. It is the raw material for spirits of the highest grade, of which the world-famous Chinese "Maotai" has its origin. Since sorghum is cultivated in almost all provinces, each has its own famous liquor, the flavor of which may or may not approximate the "Maotai." After fermentation, the distiller's grains are fed to livestock.

Sugar or sweet sorghum is produced both in the South and the North for the manufacturing of sugar and syrup. It is especially prominent in the Jiangsu and Zhejiang provinces. Sugar varieties also produce grain. The sugar sorghum usually contains 10-14% sucrose and 3-5% fructose. Both the coarse sugar and the syrup produced are important raw materials for China's food processing industries. With adequate water for irrigation and soils of high fertility, yields of sorghum stalks may reach 75 tons/hectare, from which 7.5 tons of syrup or 3.5 tons of coarse sugar may be produced. At the same time, the yield of sorghum grain will be 1.5-3.8 tons/hectare. A new hybrid of sugarcane and sorghum has been developed which contains a higher sugar content and produces a higher yield--both of the stalk and of the grain--than conventional varieties of either sugarcane or sorghum.

Sorghum stalks are tall and tough and are commonly used in rural areas to build cottages, vegetable trellises and wind screens (windbreaks). The stalks can also be used as fuel and for manufacturing paper. Some varieties are especially useful as raw materials in handicraft industries.

Conclusions

Millet and Sorghum, two of the most ancient of Chinese crops, function as food security when other crops (wheat, corn, soybeans and rice) in China fail. They are among the most adaptive of all food crops to hot-dry conditions. Significant achievements have been made during the past decade in the development of new high-yielding, disease-resistant, first generation F_1 hybrids and interspecific hybrids. No crops will more effectively withstand the rigors of hot-dry weather. Yields of grain, forage and the total productive capacities for these two crops have increased appreciably during the past five years with no change in the area cropped. The multiple uses of each for both grain and straw, augur well for their continued expansion in otherwise marginal food-producing areas.

FOR FURTHER READING

Agricultural Institute of Xin County, Region of Shanxi Province. 1976. *Sorgum*. Beijing: Science Press. (In Chinese)

Bureau of Science and Technology of the Southeast Region of Shanxi. 1976. *Millet*. Beijing: Science Press. (In Chinese)

Liaoning Provincial Academy of Agriculture. 1980. *Flora of Chinese sorghum varieties*. Beijing: Agricultural Press. (In Chinese)

Shanxi Provincial Academy of Agricultural Sciences. 1979. *Cultivation techniques of millet*. Beijing: Agricultural Press. (In Chinese)

U.S. Department of Agriculture. Economic Research Service. 1984, 1985, 1986. *China outlook and situation reports*. Washington, D.C.: Government Printing Office.

Sheep Herding in the Highlands

A Poultry Farm

Beijing Ducks

Terraced Fields of Paddy Rice

Watermelons Intercropped with Wheat
in Jiangsu Province

The A-Frame Trellising
of Cucumbers

Irrigation of Rice in Xinjiang

The "Kan-Er-Jin" Underground
Water System near Turpan
in Xinjiang

Terraced Fields of
Paddy Rice Interlaced
with Corn

Fish Ponds in the Tai Lake Area
Interlaced with Mulberry Bushes
and Grass for the Carp

Freshly Baked Sweet Potato

Terraces in Sichuan with a
Variety of Aquatic and Terrestrial
Plants

Yurts in the Foothills of Xinjiang

A Family and A Yurt   Rice Cleaning and Winnowing

Chinese Cabbage for Winter Storage
in Heilongjiang

The Grand Canal

The Water Sweet Potato

Going to Market
Moving Chinese Cabbage by Barge
Chinese Fast Food

The Famous Hami Melons of Xinjiang

Irrigation and Evaporative Cooling of Vine Crops

A City Produce Market

An Abundant Harvest of Oranges

A Fresh Vegetable City Market

Private Plot Melons for Sale
Near Ürümqi

实行计划生育是我国的一项基本国

妈妈生 一个

我

朝阳区双井地区计划生育

Drying and Threshing in the Sun

The Great Wall

Promoting the One Child Family

A Small Tractor Factory   Field Threshing of Rice

Ponds of Grass Eating Carp Interplanted with Mulberry
Bushes in the Tai Lake Area

Cave Dwellings in Shaanxi Province

Rapeseed, Windrowed and Drying in the Field

Hand Transplanting of Rice

A Cave House in Shaanxi

Hand Weeding of Vegetables

Plastic Greenhouses Abound near Large Cities

Fertilizing Green Leafy Vegetables
with Nightsoil near Guangzhou

A Yangxi River Gorge

Rice Seedling Beds Covered
with Sheets of Plastic

A Yangxi River Gorge

A River Boat near Guilin

Rapeseed in Full Flower

The Angora Fur Rabbit

Marketing Soybean Sprouts in the
Streets of Shanghai

16

BARLEY--AN ANCIENT CROP MADE MODERN

by Shao Qiquan, Lu Wei, Li Ansheng and Wei Rongxuan

Worldwide the production of barley may be as much for drink (beer, malt, whiskey) as for feeding livestock, poultry and people. Its use in China has been no exception. The widely grown naked or hulless types called "Qingke" by Tibetans are admirably adapted for brewing, as well as for the milling of flour to produce the widely acclaimed baked product "Zanba," the chief agricultural product of the Xizang and Qinghai plateaus. China's barleys will rank well with Robert Burn's barleycorn of Scotland as grains highly prized for many purposes.

Barley is one of the oldest crops in China and follows rice, wheat, maize, and soybeans in importance. It has been cultivated for 5,000 years and is recorded in ancient Chinese literature as one of the five main cereals used for food. Carbonized seeds, glumes, naked grains and scales have been discovered in excavations from tombs of the Qin and Han dynasties, indicating that over 2,000 years ago barley became one of the main food crops in China. It was distributed and cultivated widely in valleys of the Yellow and Yangzi rivers, the highlands of Tibet, and the drylands of northwest China.

Barley Production in China

As one of the oldest of crops, barley is cultivated almost everywhere in China. With time, however, both the demand and uses of barley have changed. Before the 1950s, the Chinese used barley mostly for food. Because of its short vegetative period and early maturity barley was used as a catch crop between main crops. During the years of natural disasters (e.g. drought) the plantings of barley were substantially increased. Following the stagnating food production of the 1950s and 1960s, conditions in China improved and the area planted to barley decreased except in Tibet, where it remained as the main food crop. During the early 1980s, however, barley production increased tremendously along with that of rice, wheat, corn and soybeans. The demands and preferences of the people also changed. This was especially true for the increased consumption of beer, dairy products and meat. There is now a renewed interest in barley production. The growing area in China is about 3.7 million hectares, at present, with an annual output of about 6.8 million metric tons.

Origin and History of Cultivated Barley in China

Both Chinese and foreign scientists have expressed great interest in the origin of barley in China. In 1938 Aberg from Sweden obtained samples of six-rowed wild barley from Taofu County and identified it as *Hordeum agriocrithon.* He developed a hypothesis that cultivated barley originated from the highlands of Tibet. During the 1970s many Chinese scientists joined in expeditions to Tibet, Sichuan, and Qinghai provinces and collected large samples of wild barley both as grains and plants, following which distribution and genetic, cytogenetic and biochemical studies were conducted. The results showed a very close relationship between Tibetan wild barley and the cultivated grain.

Another expedition followed in 1981-84. Over 3,000 samples from 67 counties and cities were gathered. These accessions showed great diversity and polymorphism among both the cultivated selections and their wild relatives. The number of varieties exceeded that of any other place in the world. It was verified that Tibet is one of the centers of origin and diversity of cultivated barley.

Regions of Barley Production

Three types of barley are cultivated in China relating to specific geographical regions (Figure 1).

The North Spring Barley Area. This is the leading area for the production of barley in China. Included in this region are the northeastern provinces of Heilongjiang, Jilin, Liaoning, Inner Mongolia, Shaanxi, Ningxia, Gansu and Xinjiang. Climatic conditions here are ideal for the growth of barley, especially during seed filling. The days are sunny with no rain, and both the temperature and relative humidity are low. Production is mostly confined to cultivated, hulled barley with some naked-seeded. Beer production for 1984 was 2.19 million tons, two-thirds of which was processed in northern and northeast China. All the famous brands of beer are produced here, hence there has been a very rapid increase in the production of malting barley.

The South Winter Barley Area. This area may be divided into five subregions. They include the middle and lower valleys of the Yangzi River; the middle and lower valleys of the Yellow River; South China;

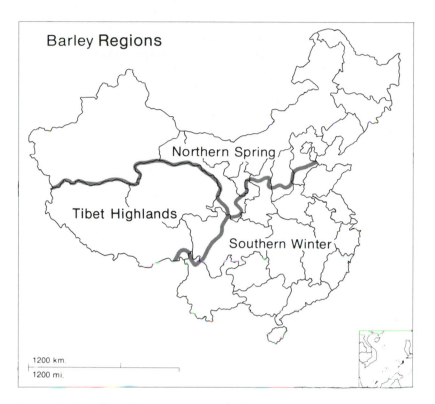

Figure 1. The three barley regions of China.

the Sichuan Valley; and the highlands of Yunnan and Guizhou provinces. The middle and lower valleys of the Yangzi River cover the provinces of Jiangsu and Zhejiang and the Shanghai municipality. The total area planted to barley is about 1.2 million hectares. This is almost one-third of the total area devoted to barley production in China. The total production in this area approximates 4.5 million metric tons, which is over half of the total production of the country. Yields in some areas of the Jiangsu Province approach the level of that in Western European countries. The main varieties are the two-rowed, hulled barley grains with a few naked-seeded types. The lower valley of the Jiangsu Province remains the main base for malting barley in China.

The Highlands of Tibet. This is the main growing region for naked-seeded spring barley. The highlands comprise a leading pasture area in China, and barley is used as the forage base.

Yields of barley vary greatly in the different regions of China. The highest for hulled barley are in the Jiangsu Province and the municipality of Shanghai. Hulled barley will, in general, outyield the naked-seeded types. But there are some exceptions. The highest recorded yield for barley was achieved in the highlands of Tibet for naked-seeded barley in 1978--in the field of the Institute of Agricultural Sciences in the Xigaze region. Here the variety Hymalai, a six-rowed barley, yielded 12 metric tons/hectare. This remains as the world record. The ample sunlight and cool night temperatures are partly responsible. Another high-yield record was set at 10 metric tons/hectare for the variety Fu 8 near Xining City in Liejiazhai County of the Qinghai Province. This was also a naked-seeded type.

Uses of Barley

In China, as throughout the world, uses of barley have developed progressively from food to forage to brewing. From the Qin Dynasty (over 2,000 years ago) up through the 1950s barley was used mostly for food, especially during years of drought. Barley thus contributed greatly to the development of China.

For several thousands of years, China has extensively cultivated the naked-seeded barley types. Chinese catalogues for barley record 5,173 varieties, of which there are 2,586 naked-seeded types or 50% of the total. Since the decade of the 1950s, the total production of barley in China has increased substantially with the transition from its being used as a food, then as a forage, and finally for brewing. The rapid development of the beer industry coupled with the expansion of animal husbandry has greatly increased the demands for both the hulled and the naked or hulless barley.

Most of the barley, about 5.5 million metric tons of a total of over 8 million, is used as feed for livestock and poultry, while the remainder is used for flour, for brewing and for other industries. This structure, however, is undergoing a rapid change in accordance with the developmental trends which follow.

There is an increasing demand for barley as a raw product for both the food industry and the feeding of livestock. Barley production, as with other agricultural commodities, has been released from centralized government control to contracts between producers and users. This production responsibility contract system has greatly stimulated the interest of farmers in the production of barley. This has been accompanied by an increasing demand for science and technology in the production and utilization of barley. Many plant breeders have recently turned their attention from wheat to barley improvement. Cropping systems in many parts of China are admirably adapted to barley production. It is the earliest maturing of all the major cereal grains, is resistant to hostile environments, and in many parts of China may be planted in the autumn and harvested the following spring or even the following autumn (as in Tibet). A national conference on barley was held in Beijing in 1984 and a Chinese Barley Science Society was established.

Barley Germplasm Resources in China

China is rich in barley germplasm resources. The recorded, systematized collection of barley consists of 11,000 samples of which 5,173 are listed in catalogues, and there are approximately 4,000 accessions from abroad. The majority (95%) have heads with six rows of grain, with the balance of varieties having only two rows (Figure 2). Barley head types, however, are changing rapidly in the middle and lower reaches of the Yangzi River basin producing area, China's chief barley basket. Two-rowed barley is gradually replacing the six, and hulled barley, naked-seeded, and spring types are replacing the winter varieties.

Unique Features of Chinese Barley

The emphasis in barley production is on early maturing. An analysis of the 5,173 native varieties shows that 32% are very early, 47% are intermediate, 18% are late and only 1% are extremely late. The earliest varieties are found in the highlands of Tibet, where they are resistant to low temperatures and mature in a very short vegetative period. Tibet is thus important for early maturing sources. Likewise, early maturing varieties are important in river valleys at low altitudes, and for intensive cropping systems where farmers may produce several crops per year on the same land. As with all other cereals there is an increasing demand for earlier maturing barley varieties of all grain types.

Most of the Chinese varieties are characterized as spring or weak winter (weak winter barley varieties are those that require a minimum of cold temperatures for flowering). Of the 2,605 varieties cultivated in the spring cropping areas, spring varieties comprise 97% of the total, leaving only 1% weak winter types and 2% of the winter types. Of the 2,139 varieties cultivated in winter barley cropping areas, 21% are spring varieties, 54% are weak winter varieties and only 25% are winter varieties. Thus, spring types of barley are grown not only in the traditional northeastern, northern, and northwestern areas, but are increasingly being planted in autumn as winter barley and harvested in May and June of the following year.

Chinese barley is generally tall to medium tall rather than dwarf. There are only a few dwarf selections. Of the many varieties grown, 37% have

Figure 2. Six-rowed barley (top); two-rowed barley (bottom).

stem heights exceeding 110 centimeters, 46% have stems of 90-110 centimeters, only 14% have stems of 70-90 centimeters, and a mere 3% have stems shorter than 70 centimeters.

Chinese barley varieties are highly tolerant to environmental stresses. Genetic resources from Tibet are especially tolerant to low temperatures. Salt tolerant varieties are found in the seaside lands, while Hubei Province provides varieties resistant to leaf yellow mosaic virus.

There are many high quality varieties including the traditional ones. In ancient societies they were a prized food for feeding the most renowned religious leaders of Tibet.

Tibetan Barley

The ancient Tibetan book, *Tui Mi Song Bu Zha*, refers to Tibet as "Ze Da Yu," which in Tibetan means "Wild Barley Area." It was recorded that, during the seventh century A.D. of the Tang Dynasty, the Emperor Tang Taizhong awarded his beautiful princess Wencheng as wife to the Tibetan Chief, Song Zan Gan Bu. This was to strengthen the unity of the Hans and the Tibetans. Tui Mi Song Bu Zha, a minister of local government in Tibet, was sent to the city of Changan to meet the princess, who brought with her much of the Han culture in the form of arts and crafts, medicines and some crop seeds--including domesticated naked or hulless barley. By such means the economic welfare of Tibet was greatly improved and a friendly unity of Han and Tibetan people established. The people of Tibet expressed their thanks and appreciation by placing a statue of Wencheng in the temple Xiao Zhou in Lhasa.

The Xizang (Tibetan) Autonomous Region, located on the frontier of southwest China, has the youngest, largest and highest elevation plateau on the earth. It is called "the roof of the world." Most elevations here are above 4,000 meters. The world's highest mountains, including Mount Everest, are located on the Nepal boundary area. Xizang covers an area of about 1,200,000 Km² and has a population of 1.7 million. Most of the people are Tibetan with Han, Mongolian, Menba and Luba minorities.

Although the Tibet latitude does not extend beyond 36°N, the climate varies significantly from south to north because of the steep topography of the Gangdis and other mountains. Not only are the overall topography, climate and flora significantly different from other inland areas of China, but the plateau itself varies from the north to the south tablelands. A prominent feature of the plateau is its agriculture and crop distribution. Tibetan hulless (naked) barley is one of these features and is not only uniquely adapted to the area but is a key staple for feeding the people.

Hulless barley, called "Qingke" by the Tibetans, is the main crop on the Xizang Plateau. There are large growing areas in a variety of regions extending to the upper-limit of growth as constrained by elevation. Barley is the most important crop in Tibetan agriculture. Both in production and in growing areas, barley constitutes more than half the total crop output for Tibet. For areas exceeding an elevation of 4,500 meters, hulless or naked barley is almost the sole crop. A long adaptation to plateau climate has conferred both cold and drought resistance on the barley, which can be grown from 1,000 meters to over 4,000 meters above sea level. The upper limit for Tibetan barley in China has been established at 4,750 meters above sea level, making it by far the most widely grown crop in Tibet.

There are diverse Tibetan barley species all fully characteristic of plateau ecology. Based on grain color, they can be divided into three types: 1) white-green with yellow, yellow-white or brown-yellow grains; 2) purplish green or dark green with purple, purplish black or black grains; and 3) bluish green with blue, greenish grey or greyish green grains. Among the three types, the white-green barley is the most desirable for its eating quality, stable yield and wide distribution. Purplish green barley is the least edible, but the most suitable for growth in droughty and cold hilly areas. Bluish green barley is intermediate between white-green and purplish green both in quality and adaptability.

According to the growing seasons, Tibetan barley can be divided into two types--spring and winter. Spring barley, historically the more prevalent one, is sown in the spring and harvested in the fall. Recently, barley has also been sown in the fall at elevations below 3,400 meters. This is known as winter barley. For a given barley variety, fall sowing gives a higher yield and matures earlier than the spring sown. For early varieties of spring barley such as the "Sixty-Day Green" and "Langkaze Green," the time for maturity is less than 100 days, while for late maturing spring varieties it may be 130 to 150 days. The time necessary for maturity increases with elevation and at the lower temperatures. For example, winter barley may mature in less than 200 days at elevations of less than 2,500 meters but will require more than 250 days to ripen above 3,000 meters elevation. Other traits such as plant heights also vary with variety and elevation.

The climate of the Tibetan Plateau favors the production of barley. The low night temperatures, the wide fluctuation between day and night temperatures, the sunny days with rain at night, and the long growing season favor photosynthesis and the accumulation of dry matter, all of which is reflected in high yields of grain. These special climatic conditions confer on Tibetan barley the prominent advantages of more heads (ears) and grains, and a high thousand-grain weight value. The low temperatures during the differentiation of young ears greatly increase their number. For the Lhasa and Xigaze varieties, the number of heads (ears) is more than 60 grams. A large head can easily be formed if, during floret differentiation, there are suitable temperatures, moisture from either rainfall or irrigation, a high light intensity, and appropriate cultural practices. The thousand-grain weight may then be as high as 40 to 50 grams, which results from the prolonged development of the milk stage in grain formation. The result is a significant increase in dry mass. Under optimal conditions during grain development, there can be an increase of one gram per day in the thousand-grain weight value. The yield of barley will commonly reach 7.5 metric tons per hectare, and as high as 10 to 12 tons if one utilizes all advantages of the plateau climate, suitable varieties, and some good cultural practices.

Atmospheric pressure on the Tibetan Plateau is so low that the boiling point of water is only about 80°C. At such a temperature food cannot be quickly cooked. The grains of naked barley, however, are very soft, of high quality, and easily baked and milled. The milled flour of the baked barley, Zanba, not only tastes good but, more importantly, is very convenient for eating, storing, and handling and saves fuel as well. These many advantages make the Zanba highly adapted for the work and lives of Tibetan peasants and herdsmen. During herding or farming they can, at will, have some Zanba. At the same time it is considered a delicacy. A grand Tibetan family dinner (comparable to roast turkey in the U.S.A.) consists of Zanba and barley wine.

Tibetan people are very familiar with the habits and morphology of their native wild barley and the many cultivated selections derived from it. Almost all possible diversity of wild barley is concentrated in Tibet, and it is well preserved. Since 1938 these different types of wild barley have attracted the interest of scientists throughout the world. These wild barley types are important for understanding the origin and evolution of cultivated barley. Tibetan people make full use of their barleys for brewing, milling, making foods, and for feeding livestock. As a result of continued progress in its culture and patient artificial selection and cultivation, the cultivated naked barley called "Qingke" by Tibetans is the most widely grown crop on the Tibetan Plateau.

FOR FURTHER READING

Agricultural Institute, Seashore Region, Jiangsu Province. 1984. *Barley Newsletter* 1:1-71. (In Chinese)

———. 1985. *Barley Newsletter* 2(1): 1-52. (In Chinese)

———. 1985. *Barley Newsletter* 2(2): 1-53. (In Chinese)

Shao Qiquan. 1982. *Wild barley from Tibet.* Beijing: Science Press. (In Chinese)

17

SUGAR ON THE TABLE

by Yu Youtai

The Origin of Sugarcane and Crystalline Sugar in China

Sugarcane, one of the most ancient of crops, had its origin in China. As far back as the eighth century B.C. (in the Western Zhou Dynasty) there were records of sugarcane cultivation, and reference to it is found in the famous poem "Zhuo Hun Fu," written by the Chinese poet Qu Yuan in the fourth century B.C. (Warring States). Sugarcane cultivation first became popular in Guangzhou and surrounding areas. It preceded the manufacture of crystalline sugar by more than ten centuries.

According to Chinese records, there were three distinct periods or stages of usage (Table 1). During the first period, which continued until about the third century, the cane was chewed for its sweetness. Later during this period, pressing cane for its refreshing juice, which relieved fatigue, became popular. The second period saw the introduction of suryp production.

The third period encompassed the manufacture of solid crystalline sugar. The sugar-manufacturing technique was first recorded in the fifth century and became popular by the seventh century. The technique for producing crystalline sugar was developed in the eighth century and over the next two hundred years became very much refined. Following sugarcane development in China, its production spread first to the Philippines and then to India, in the seventh century to Japan, and then to other parts of the world during the twelfth century. Marco Polo, the great Italian explorer of the thirteenth century, marveled in his travel notes at the Yuan Dynasty's great achievement in crystalline sugar production.

Geographical Distribution of Sugar Crops in China

Sugar for the table in China comes mostly from sugarcane (75-85%) and the balance from sugar beets. Sugarcane has traditionally been

TABLE 1
The Three Progressive Stages of Sugarcane
Usage in Chinese History

Steps	Usage	Time	Dynasty
	Ancient record of sugarcane cultivation	8th century B.C.	Western Zhou
I	Chewing and pressing for juice	up to 3rd century	Eastern Han
II	Syrup production	4th century	Jin, Southern and Northern
III	Manufacturing solid sugar	5th-7th century	Sui and Tang
	Refinement of crystalline sugar	8th century	Tang
	A well developed sugar industry	10th century	Song
	Marco Polo travel notes written describing crystalline sugar in China	13th century	Yuan

grown only in the southern parts of China and is concentrated particularly in the Guangdong, Guangxi, Sichuan, Yunnan, and Fujian provinces. Both the acreage and production in these five provinces constitute about 90% of the nation's total, with about 40% of this amount in the Guangdong Province alone. Sugar beets, on the other hand, have traditionally been grown in the northern parts of China, primarily the Heilongjiang and Jilin provinces and Inner Mongolia and Xinjiang autonomous regions. Again, sugar beet acreage and production in these four areas is about 90% of the nation's total, of which 50% is produced in Heilongjiang (Figure 1).

In 1980 the cultivated land area for these two sugar crops in China was a small part, comprising only 1.4% of the total. In the Guangdong Province, where sugarcane is grown the most extensively, it occupies only 2.6% of the total cropped area, while sugar beets in the Heilongjiang Province cover only 1.7% of the land under cultivation.

Figure 1. The sugar beet and sugarcane producing areas in China, indicating the most southern and northern boundaries, respectively.

Sugarcane production in China for 1980 occupied 473,000 hectares, with a total output of 22.8 million tons of sugarcane. Some 446,000 hectares produced 6.3 million tons of sugar beets. Since 1949 the nation's sugar production increased 4.4 times in area and 8.6 times in sugar output. The increase was 28-fold in acreage and 33 times in amount for sugar beets--a much larger increase than for sugarcane during this 30-year period (1949-1980). Yields of these two sugar crops vary greatly among the provinces, with the yields per unit land area differing by more than threefold.

Equally remarkable increases in sugar crop production have occurred since 1980. There was a total output of 48 million tons in 1984, comprised of over 40 million tons of sugarcane and over 8 million tons of sugar beets. Even more striking was the jump in sugar crop production to over 60 million tons in 1985. Sugarcane output rose by 30% to almost 51.5 million tons, and sugar beets by 7.6% over the previous year.

Actual sugar production rose from 3.470 million tons in 1984 to 4.450 in 1985. Total sugar consumption in China for 1985 was 5.5 million tons with imports making up the balance. Increases accrued from both expanded areas of production as well as yield enhancements. The annual increase in sugar products has been about 320,000 tons since 1981. This has made China the world's fourth largest sugar producer surpassed only by Brazil, India and Cuba. The outlook for the future is for expanded acreage and yield increases.

There is still further potential for increasing both the area for production as well as the yields of these two sugar crops and ultimately for intercropping the two. The greater potential for land area increase is for sugar beets. This is also true of many other parts of the world. While increases of acreage for sugarcane and sugar beets in China are restrained by climate, expansion is also restrained by the need to produce staple food crops (cereals, legumes, oil crops and roots and tubers). The future emphasis for sugar crops, as for many other crops in China, should be on increasing yields per unit land area and intercropping rather than expanding cropping areas. Yields of sugarcane and sugar beets are still below those of many other nations, leaving a tremendous potential for improvement.

Sugarcane Production--Techniques and Requirements

Sugarcane responds favorably to both high light intensities and high temperatures. It grows best under long days and is widely distributed in the tropical and subtropical areas of China, Cuba, Brazil, India, Australia, the Philippines, the United States, and Africa at latitudes extending from 30 degrees north to 30 degrees south. Production of sugar from sugarcane in Latin America now approaches 40% of the world's total while about 20% comes from Asia.

Growth requirements for a crop of sugarcane will vary from 8 to 24 months. In South China a crop will mature in 10 to 12 months, while 22 to 24 months are needed in the Hawaiian Islands of the U.S.A. Yields also differ, accordingly. The sugarcane is ripe when the sugar content in the cane juice reaches its highest level. The sugar content of sugarcane will vary with variety, region, and cultural techniques but is usually from 11 to 13%. Levels as high as 15% are possible.

Sugar production in China competes seriously with the staple food crops of rice, wheat, corn and sweet potato. It is essential, therefore, that both sugar crops and food crops be produced on the same land by appropriate cropping and intercropping systems. For the paddy rice-sugarcane producing regions, rice is the focal food crop in any sugarcane rotation production system. In dry land sugarcane regions, sugarcane, sweet potatoes, beans and other short season crops are rotated and intercropped so that all crops--tall or short, or grown for stem, root or grain--can provide a good harvest. This is achieved by utilizing most effectively the prevailing growing season, available land area, soil moisture and available sunlight. Comparative plant heights, times for maturity and harvest and pest control possibilities are also considered.

The Growing Importance of Sugar Beets

Unlike sugarcane, which has its origin in China, sugar beets originated in the Mediterranean and the Middle East. Wild sugar beets were collected for food prior to the years 3,500 to 4,000 B.C. During domestication, different varieties of sugar beets were selected for their leaves, cattle feed potential, roots and sugar content. During the mid eighteenth century, analysis of the beet roots revealed that the composition of the juice from sugar beets was comparable in sugar content to that from sugarcane. Beet sugar workshops established in Russia, Germany, and France during the nineteenth century resulted in the development of a beet sugar industry. Initially the sugar content of the sugar beet was only 6%. This was increased to 14% in the 1970s-1980s and may now exceed 20%.

Sugar beets were not introduced into China until the beginning of the twentieth century, and initially progress was slow for the development of the industry. They were first cultivated in the Heilongjiang and Jilin provinces, then extended to Inner Mongolia and Xinjiang autonomous regions and finally to other parts of China. Sugar beets are an up-and-coming crop with good prospects for the future and are becoming very profitable for farmers. They are referred to as the crop of the "golden pimple." Since sugar beet plants absorb two to three times more soil nutrients than those of cereal grains, they should be rotated in culture with other crops, otherwise the yield and sugar content of sugar beets will drop significantly with continuous cropping, and disease may increase to epidemic proportions. Sugar beets in China are generally grown only once in four to five years and in rotation with wheat, millet, soybeans, corn and potatoes.

The Future

The sugar beet, in contrast to sugarcane, is a crop adapted to a cool climate and is usually produced between the north latitudes of 42 and 54 degrees. A common belief is that sugar beets cannot be produced south of the 37 degree latitude in the Northern Hemisphere. In recent years, however, Chinese scientists have, through cultural treatments and genetic improvements, extended sugar beet production into the sugarcane territories of Fujian, Guangdong, Zhejiang, Hunan and Sichuan provinces at latitudes ranging between 22 to 25 degrees north.

The successful intercropping of sugar beets with sugarcane has now been achieved in these provinces. This extends the time for sugar extraction from raw products by two to three months. Doubling of the use of equipment in sugar factories makes such operations more efficient.

Another potential for enhancing yields and extending the boundaries of production--for sugar beets in the north and sugarcane in the south--may reside in the use of plastic soil mulches, which have thus far proven effective on field plantings of cotton and peanuts. The introduction and successful use of "sugarcane ripeners"--chemical growth regulators that enhance sugar production--offers a further opportunity for enhancing sugar yields where land is limited. Currently, either one or both of the two sugar crops are produced in most all provinces and autonomous regions. This joint culture of the sugarcane and sugar beets, uniquely characteristic of China, will likely expand in the decades ahead. High fructose corn syrup however, could offer, as it has in the U.S.A., an interesting alternative to further expansions in the production of sugarcane and sugar beets.

FOR FURTHER READING

Chen Dunyi. 1983. *Chinese economic geography*. Beijing: China Zhanwang Press. (In Chinese)

Heilongjiang Institute of Beet Sugar Industry. 1973. *Sugar beet cultivation in middle parts (of China)*. Beijing: Light Industry Press. (In Chinese)

Liang Jiamian. 1980. The history of sugarcane cultivation in China. *Chinese ancient agricultural science and technology*. Beijing: Agricultural Press. (In Chinese)

Nie Xuchang, and Tian Fengyu. 1982. *Sugar beet breeding and propagation of good varieties*. Harbin: Heilongjiang Press of Science and Technology. (In Chinese)

U.S. Department of Agriculture. Economic Research Service. 1984, 1985, 1986. *China outlook and situation reports*. Washington, D.C.: Government Printing Office.

18

THE SWEET POTATO--A TREASURE TROVE FROM HEAD TO TOE

by Yu Youtai

The Name According to Origin

Many crops now grown in China were introduced from foreign countries. A famous tradition was that names appended to them often corresponded to the time of their introduction. From the second century B.C. to the fifth century A.D. (from the Han to the Southern and Northern dynasties), plant introductions came primarily from foreign countries via the Silk Road between China and Western Asia. They were therefore designated by the prefix "hu" meaning "foreign country." Thus it was "hudou" for the broad bean, "hujiao" for pepper, "huma" for flax and "huchai" for rape.

During the fifth and six centuries (from the Southern and Northern to the Sui dynasties), plants were introduced from overseas by way of the ocean and so were prefixed by "hai" meaning "sea." Hence it was "haitung" for the crabapple, "haizao" for the date palm, and "haisen" for the sea cucumber. Names of plants introduced after the tenth century were preceded by "fan," another word for "foreign country." Accordingly, "fanqie" named the tomato, "fanlizhi" the litchi, "fanshiliu" the pomegranate and "fanshu" the sweet potato. After the seventeenth century (the Ming and Qing dynasties), plants introduced into China were prefixed by "yang" because all foreign countries were then called yang. Thus "yangchong" was the name for onion, "yangbaicai" for cabbage, "yanghuai" for locust, and "yangjiang" for Jerusalem artichoke.

Introduction to China

The true sweet potato, as it is grown extensively today in China, was imported from abroad. It originated in Central and South America and was first brought to Spain by Columbus at the end of the fifteenth century. The route to China at the end of the sixteenth century was either through India and Burma to the Yunnan Province or by way of the Philippines to Fujian Province. During the following century the introduction of the sweet potato spread over the Yangzi and Yellow River valleys and finally throughout China.

Today in China, the sweet potato is called "fanshu" or "ganshu." It also has many other local names, including the sweet potato, mountain taro, golden potato, red potato, white potato and ground melon. This proliferation of names is not surprising since China is the world's most extensive and productive grower of the sweet potato. Ninety to 100 million tons are produced annually. It is found in the hilly regions and the plains of the Yellow and Hwai rivers, the Sichuan Basin and the southeastern seashore provinces (Figure 1). While the area in China planted to sweet potatoes has declined in recent years, as it has in many other countries, yields have increased at a long-term rate of over 3% per

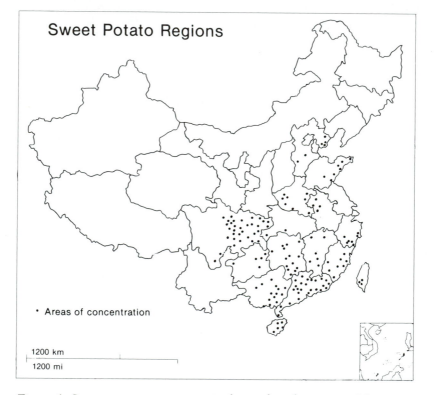

Figure 1. Sweet potatoes are extensively produced in some of the most populated areas--the Sichuan Basin, the plains of the Yellow and Huai rivers, and the southeastern seashore provinces.

year. As a principal food crop and food security storage item, its acreage ranks behind only rice, wheat and corn. Again, the sweet potato is a hardy, fast growing staple food crop which the Chinese don't always like to eat but which has saved millions from starvation when wheat and rice crops failed. The planting area occupies about 70% of that devoted to the production of all tuber and root crops. Cassava, as a root crop, has been a weak second to the sweet potato with a peak in annual output in the early 1980's of six million tons.

The Many Uses of Fanshu (Sweet Potato)

The fanshu is a farm crop which has many diverse uses. It is highly adaptable and resilient to environmental stresses including drought, and will grow in both acid and alkaline soils. The stems and leaves that creep along the ground have a strong regenerating ability and are resistant to winds, hailstorms and insects. Fanshu is planted as an intercrop with corn on the slopelands and hilly regions of Central and South China, where the creeping vines provide ground cover and reduce soil erosion. It is easier to cultivate and gives much higher yields than grain crops, and can be harvested and used as food as soon as the root enlarges. It may be eaten raw or cooked and is, therefore, an excellent crop for helping tide people over natural disasters. For good reason, then, the Chinese call the fanshu the "golden potato."

There was a common ancient saying in producing areas: "Sweet potato half year food." Since the rapid development of grain production in China, however, regions where the sweet potato is still the main food are gradually disappearing. But it remains an important supplementary food because of its popularity with the Chinese people.

Today, in the streets and lanes of both small and large Chinese cities, street vendors sell freshly baked sweet potatoes--a favorite with children and adults. The baked sweet potato ("kaobaishu" in Chinese) of Beijing is especially well known. Dried sweet potato slices can be easily stored for year round use. Many Chinese eat sweet potato slices as they would fruit. Noodles made from sweet potato starch are one of the most popular processed foods. Moreover, sweet potato starch is an important raw material for many light industries, for food processing, and for the pharmaceutical industries. In China, sweet potatoes are used in the manufacture of liquor, vinegar, gourmet powder, glucose, alcohol, plastics, synthetic rubber, artificial fiber, color film, citric acid, and erythromycin. Roots, stems, leaves and starch residues from the sweet potato plant are good feedstuffs for livestock. Sweet potato stems and leaves are used for silage and are as nutritious as alfalfa when fed to cattle. It is said that fanshu is a treasure trove "from head to toe." It is indeed a valuable crop, both because of its wide and comprehensive use and because of the way in which it diversifies the economy of the Chinese countryside.

Ganshu--The Native Sweet Potato

In addition to the introduced fanshu, there is another kind of sweet potato, named "ganshu" in Chinese, which is one of the most ancient of crops originally grown in China. Historical records, dating back to the first century B.C., reveal that the South China people used the native ganshu for food just as they did rice. In Chinese, "gan" means sweet, "shu" means potato. If we translate "ganshu" into English it will be the same as that of the introduced sweet potato. Thus, there is as much confusion in China as there is in the United States as to the naming of these two crops. The same confusion that comes in distinguishing between the sweet potato and what are called yams in China exists throughout the western world.

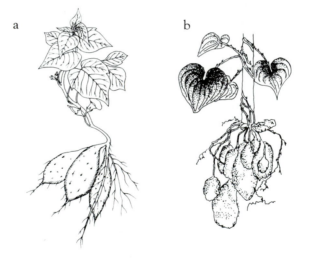

Figure 2. *a* The true sweet potato or "fanshu" which originated in Central and South America; *b*, the native Chinese sweet potato or "ganshu" referred to as the yam in Africa and elsewhere.

The ganshu plant consists of slender climbing vines, two to three meters high, with hairy stems and leaves. They produce one large tuberous root and an abundance of secondary ones for harvest. The sweet taste of tuberous roots becomes diluted after drying. The ganshu plants do not flower, but are propagated by root cuttings. They are found mainly on Hainan Island and the tropical regions of Guangdong

Province. Fanshu, the introduced sweet potato, in many ways is very similar to ganshu, the Chinese sweet potato. Yet there are obvious differences. Fanshu plants creep on the ground rather than climb. They have no hairs and the stems and leaves have smooth surfaces. There is no obvious big root on the fanshu, and the sweetness becomes more concentrated upon drying. It flowers and bears aerial fruit in tropical regions.

Thus, the introduced sweet potato, (the fanshu) and the Chinese sweet potato (the ganshu) are very similar but are also distinctly different. Botanically, they belong to different families. The introduced sweet potato belongs to the family *Convolvulaceae* with the Latin names of *Ipomoea batatas* (L.) (*Poir*); the Chinese sweet potato belongs to the family *Dioscoreaceae* with the Latin name of *Dioscorea esculenta* (L.) (*Burk*). Differences in the plant types and growing habits between the introduced sweet potato and the Chinese sweet potato or yam are illustrated in the accompanying line drawings of Figure 2. Common reference to the sweet potato in China today is usually to the introduced fanshu rather than the native ganshu.

FOR FURTHER READING

Research Laboratory of Agricultural History of the South China Agricultural College. 1980, 1982. *Research on Agricultural History*, vols. 1, 2. Beijing: Agricultural Press. (In Chinese)

Sheng Jialian, and Yuan Baozhong. 1980. *The cultivating techniques for sweet potato.* Beijing: Agricultural Press. (In Chinese)

Stone, B. 1984. An analysis of Chinese data on root and tuber crop production. *China Quarterly* 99:594-630.

Zhia Qianqiang. 1980. History of the introduction of sweet potato and potato into the North China Plain. *Chinese ancient agricultural science and technology.* Beijing: Agricultural Press. (In Chinese)

19

THE IRISH POTATO--A NEWCOMER

by Yu Youtai

Origin and Distribution

No crop has been more praised or maligned than the potato, nor have more names been ascribed to it.

> We praise all the flowers that we fancy
> Sip the nectar of the fruit ere they're peeled,
> Ignoring the common old tater
> When, in fact, he's King of the Field.
> Let us show the old boy we esteem him,
> Sort of dig him out of the mud;
> Let us show him to share our affections
> And crown him with glory--King Spud.[1]

The potato was called "baba" in Spain according to the original South American Indian word *batata* for sweet potato. The Indians also called it *papa*, by which it is still known at the International Potato Center or "CIP" near Lima, Peru. It is called the "ground apple" or the "ground pear" in France and Germany, the "Holland potato" in the U.S.S.R., the "Irish potato" in the U.S.A. and the "spud" in the State of Idaho.

As with the sweet potato, in China there are also many local names for the potato. These translate as the "ground egg," "mountain medicine egg" and "yam egg" in the northern and northwestern provinces, the *yangyu* or literally the "dirt bean" and "foreign taro" in southwestern and northwestern areas, the "soil bean" in the northeast, and the "ground bean" in Hebei, Tianjin and Beijing. The most popular name used in Chinese textbooks for the potato is *malingshu*, which translates to mean the "horse-ring" or "horse-bell" potato. The potato differs

---

[1]From the title page, "An Anthology of the Potato", author unknown. Robert McKay, editor. 1961. Allen Figgis and Co., Ltd. for Irish Potato Marketing Co., Dublin.

from the sweet potato in that the edible portion originates from an underground stem or tuber. The sweet potato is an enlarged root. The sweet potato is also naturally adapted to hot, humid climates, while the potato thrives under temperate zone conditions.

The potato had its origin in the highlands of Peru and Chile. It was first introduced to Spain and England in the sixteenth century as a medicinal and ornamental plant and from there to other European countries. Near the end of the eighteenth century, when it was supposed to cure gout, lumbago, black eyes, rheumatism, sore throat, toothaches, sprains, broken bones and impotence, it moved from pharmacists' gardens to farmers' fields with the development of suitable varieties. Gradually the potato became one of the main food crops of the world. During the middle of the nineteenth century, one nation--Ireland--became so dependent on it as a staple food that when blight (*Phytophthora infestans*) hit in 1846, one of the world's greatest famines resulted. More than a million and a half Irish died and another million and a quarter emigrated.

The potato is now produced on approximately 50 million hectares of crop land worldwide, about 9 million of which are in China. It accounts for about 300 million metric tons of food produced annually and with rice, wheat, corn and sorghum, is one of the five main food crops of the world. It is found most prominently in Western and Eastern Europe, particularly in the Soviet Bloc countries including the U.S.S.R., Poland, East Germany, Bulgaria and Romania, and in West Germany, Belgium, France and the United Kingdom. In many countries potatoes have come to rival cereals as a staff of life.

Introduction to China

The potato was introduced to China from Europe at the beginning of the seventeenth century (during the Ming dynasty). It was first grown in the Shaanxi Province in the northwestern part of China and then propagated in the northern and northeastern parts. Extensive cultivation came only after the end of the nineteenth and beginning of the twentieth centuries. The most important areas for potato production in China are the Heilongjiang Province and Inner Mongolia. The so-called Irish potato has risen to prominence as a major food crop in China, where almost 10% (30 million metric tons) of the world's total output is now found. There has been a rapid expansion in plantings as well as modest increases in yield that have aggregated a 6% per annum increase in production during the past two decades.

Regions and Cultural Systems

Potatoes are widely adaptive and have a multiple range of planting seasons. An edible food crop can be produced in as few as 70 to 80 days, some varieties in much less time. It is a good crop for insurance against natural disasters and has served China admirably when grain crops have failed. It is widely distributed throughout China, where its cultivation extends north to the Heilongjiang River, south to Hainan Island, to the eastern shore and beyond to Taiwan and west to the Xizang-Qinghai (Tibetan Plateau). It is grown in all provinces, municipalities and autonomous regions of China. Cultural conditions, systems and varieties vary greatly owing to China's dramatic climatic differences. While the potato has been adapted to almost all of them, there are four distinct regions for potato production in China (Figure 1).

Spring Crop. The short growing season, long winters and moderate summer temperatures, plus the large spread between day and night temperatures and adequate precipitation during tuber formation, make

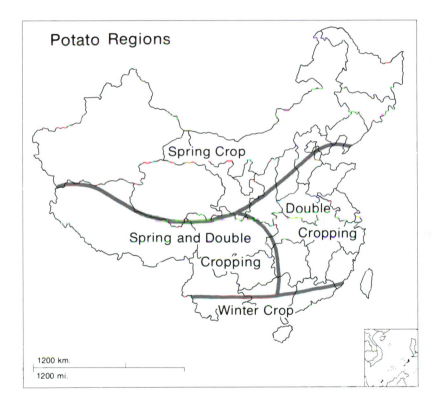

Figure 1. The potato regions of China according to the season of the year and the type of cropping.

ideal conditions for the growth of the potato in the northeastern, northern and northwestern regions of China. Here also are the production areas and sites for raising virus-and disease-free seed tubers. The area devoted to potato production in these regions is about half of China's total potato acreage. The growing season is 90 to 130 days, so only one crop planted in the spring can be grown. Potato varieties are mid-season to late in maturity with a few early-maturing varieties.

Double Cropping. In the region south to the Yangzi River and north to the Yellow River, the growing season is 120 to 170 days. Here potato cultivation is shifting from a one-crop to a two-crop per year system. Thus, two cultural systems for potato production prevail in this region. The one-crop system requires planting in the spring and harvesting in the autumn. The two-crop system requires planting in the early spring and harvesting in the summer for the first crop, and then planting in the summer and harvesting in the late autumn for the second crop. Tubers from the fall or autumn crop are used as seed tubers for the following year. Late-maturing varieties for the second crop and early-maturing varieties for the first crop are required for this region.

Distribution of potato production in the Yangzi River basin is dispersed. They are grown mainly as vegetables in the city suburbs. Owing to the long and hot summers, there are generally two crops each year--one planted in the early spring, the other in the late summer or early autumn.

Intercropping of potatoes with corn and cotton has developed in recent years. Farmers report that there is no decrease in the grain or cotton harvest with this system and that an extra crop of potatoes is obtained. Accordingly, potato production has increased significantly in the regions where corn and cotton are produced.

Winter Crops. In the southern parts of Guangdong, Guangxi and Fujian provinces, off or leisure time in winter is utilized by growing potatoes according to the two-rice, two-potato crop system. This means that for a single year there is both an early and late crop of rice and an autumn and winter potato crop. This multiple cropping system has created new opportunities for increasing food production.

Spring and Double Cropping. A single crop of potatoes is planted in the spring for the mountainous southwestern Yunnan, Guizhou and Sichuan provinces, at elevations of 2,000 or more meters above sea level. There may be two crops per year at lower elevations. Single crops of potatoes can also be grown on the Xizang-Qinghai-Plateau at 3,000 to 4,000 meters above sea level and where annual precipitation is low. With irrigation, the one crop a year of medium-maturing potato varieties is greatly facilitated.

The Increasing Importance of Potatoes in China

As a nongrain food crop, the importance of the potato is exceeded only by the sweet potato. One hundred grams of potato can produce 85 calories of heat. According to the ratio of 5 to 1 used in China to convert potato to grain by weight, the energy generated is higher than for any of the other grain crops. The potato contains from 8 to 29% starch, depending on variety, cultural conditions and climate. It is rich in protein, minerals and vitamin C. It is easy to store and has become one of the preferred vegetables for winter storage and use by people in the northern parts of China (Figure 2).

Figure 2. A potato market in Beijing.

Potatoes in China are also processed as dry slices and as noodles. Large scale processing for french fries and other fast food items could quickly change production patterns and market demands. Potato starch is an important raw product for light industries. The tubers are a good feed for livestock and the stems and leaves can be used for silage and as fodder.

The potato is still a relatively new crop for China, but yields and total production are increasing rapidly. The extensive domestic uses which have been found for the potato and its rising value in foreign trade augur well for continued increased production. As fast food establishments continue to flourish in China, the demand for potatoes will grow.

Potato Variety Development

Since the establishment of the new China in 1949, many new potato varieties have been bred from crosses involving wild species. This has opened a new era for potato development with the introduction of many popular varieties. These include the mid-late "Tiger Head" and "Ke Xin 1," the early "Ke Xin 4" and the extra early variety "NEAC 303."

Of special note is "NEAC 303," developed and introduced at the Northest Agricultural College. It can be harvested as early as July 20 in Harbin, Heilongjiang Province, with yields of 15-18 tons/hectare compared with only 6-7.5 tons per hectare for other early varieties harvested at the same time. The required growing season at Harbin is 40-45 days from sprouting to maturation. This variety is now being grown on more than 14,000 hectares in northeast China.

Potato Production from True Potato Seed and Virus-Free Plants

Here the true seeds and not the traditional tuber seed pieces are used for commercial propagation. It's an exciting new development in Chinese agriculture. The rapid spread of virus diseases is avoided, and long-distance transport of large volumes of seed tubers is circumvented. Over 5,000 hectares of potatoes are now devoted to this type of cultural propagation.

Another new development for China is the micropropagation of virus-free plants (Figure 3) derived from the culture of meristems (see Chapter 32, "Test Tube Plants"). There are now disease-free seed farms in the northern and northeastern provinces which meet local demands as well as the needs of central and south China.

Figure 3. Extra-early potato variety NEA 303.

FOR FURTHER READING

International Potato Center. 1982, 1983, 1984. *Annual reports*. Lima, Peru.

Keshan Agricultural Institute of Heilongjiang Province. 1976. *Potato breeding and seed production*. Beijing: Agricultural Press. (In Chinese)

Li Jinghua, and C. T. Shen. 1979. *Production of marketable seed tubers from botanical seeds in the People's Republic of China*. Report of a Planning Conference--Production of Potato from True Seed. Manila, Philippines.

Li Jinghua. 1982. *Prospects for the true seed to grown potato*. Report of an International Congress, Research for the Potato in the Year 2000. Lima, Peru.

Stone, B. 1984. An analysis of Chinese data on root and tuber crop production. *China Quarterly* 99:594-630.

20
DIVERSE SOURCES OF EDIBLE OILS

by Wang Lianzheng

Oil seeds (rape, peanut, sunflower, sesame, and flax) play a prominent role in Chinese food supplies. In fact, stir frying, which conserves both energy and time and seals in flavors and nutritional values, is highly dependent on them and is the most common method of Chinese cookery. Soybean oil is also used extensively in northeast China, while cotton and hemp seeds are used as vegetable oil sources in other areas.

From 1980 to 1985 the land area devoted to oil crop production increased by about 40% and the total output upwards of 86% (Table 1). Per capita output of oil bearing crops was 15.2 kilograms in 1985 for an all time high and up from 11.6 kilograms from the previous year. These production increases have improved the dietary levels and the living standards of the people and are becoming increasingly important in meeting the needs of light industry, especially food processing. The outlook for oil seed production in China calls for continuing growth and expansion, with record levels of output for every crop except cotton, which will be subject to planned reduction because of current surpluses.

In 1980, the most productive provinces for oil crops (exclusive of soybeans and cotton) were Henan, Shandong, Anhui, Sichuan, Inner Mongolia, Hebei and Guangdong. Shandong, with its extensive fields of peanuts, leads in planting area, total production and yields per unit land area. Sichuan, with its concentrated production of rapeseed, follows in yields as well as output. Many changes in planting areas, total output or production and yields of China's major oil crops occurred between 1949 and 1985.

Rapeseed

Historical. The first reference to the rape plant in Chinese literature was in the Eastern Han Dynasty of the second century A.D. It was then

TABLE 1
The Oil Seeds of China

Oil Seeds	1980	1981	1982	1983	1984	1985	1986 (projected)
Rapeseed							
Millions Hectares	2.8	3.8	4.1	3.7	3.4	4.6	---
Yields-Tons/Hectare	0.8	1.1	1.3	1.2	1.2	1.2	---
Production MMT*	2.4	4.1	5.7	4.3	4.2	5.6	5.9
Peanuts							
Millions Hectares	2.3	2.5	2.4	2.2	2.4	3.4	3.6
Yields-Tons/Hectare	1.5	1.6	1.6	1.8	2.0	1.9	---
Production MMT	3.6	3.8	3.9	3.4	4.8	5.6	7.0
Sunflower							
Millions Hectares	0.9	1.0	0.8	0.7	0.8	1.2	---
Yields-Tons/Hectare	1.1	1.3	1.6	1.8	2.1	1.7	---
Production MMT	0.9	1.3	1.3	1.3	1.7	1.9	2.2
Sesame Seed							
Million Hectares	0.8	0.8	1.0	0.8	0.8	1.0	---
Yields-Tons/Hectare	0.3	0.6	0.4	0.4	0.6	0.7	---
Production MMT	0.3	0.5	0.3	0.4	0.5	0.7	---

*MMT = million metric tons

that Fuyu recorded in "Tong Shu Shu" or the Common Book the word "yuntai," which in Chinese means rape.

Min Yao Shu (a Chinese agricultural encyclopedia), written by Jia Sixie in the latter part of the Northern Wei Dynasties, describes spring rape planting experiments in China as follows:

> The best time for sowing rapeseed is in February and March when rainfall is enough. It is better to use border planting and water when the land is dry. The rapeseed can then be harvested in May.

During the Yuan Dynasty winter rape was grown in South China, and by the time of the Ming Dynasty it was grown throughout China.

Present Status. Rape, China's most important oil crop exceeded only occasionally by peanuts, has grown in importance over the last thousand years. China leads the world in rapeseed production with an all time record of 5.5 million metric tons in 1985, up from 4.2 million in 1984. The projection for 1986 is 5.9 million tons. Attractive prices plus an increase in demand were responsible. By 1981 and through 1985, the planting area for rape was well over 40% of the total for all oil crops (excluding soybeans and cotton), and the production of rapeseed was almost one-third of the total for all oil crops in China.

Rapeseed oil is nutritious, easy to digest, and is reported to improve the function of the gallbladder. According to Chinese tradition, the fatty acids in rapeseed oil can normally be metabolized without any liver disorders, while fatty acids of animal origin cannot. The rapeseed oil cake, following oil extraction, is rich in protein, nitrogen, phosphorus and potassium.

Rapeseed oil is also an important industrial raw material, widely used in producing soap and paints. It is a good animal feed, and in some locales in China, it is used as an organic fertilizer. Rape also occupies an important role in crop rotation. Because of its short growing season and adaptability to cold temperatures, it can be grown during the winter months in central China and harvested in late May or early June. This utilizes the land throughout the year. The cropping index is thus increased and the soil enriched. Rice planted in the spring after rape grows earlier, produces more tillers, is vigorous and results in fewer blighted grains.

Chinese rape is classified as winter rape or spring rape according to the production areas. The production areas (Figure 1) are much larger for winter rape than for spring rape and are mainly in or near the Yangzi River Valley. This planting area accounts for more than 90% of the total rapeseed produced in China. The main growing areas for spring rape are the northern parts near the Great Wall, the western parts of the Yellow River valley, the Xinjiang Autonomous Region, Inner Mongolia and the Qinghai Province. The total planting area of spring grown rape is more than 335,000 hectares.

Yields of rape can be improved in many ways. The first priority is the use of improved varieties, especially F_1 (first generation) hybrids. The Sichuan Academy of Agricultural Sciences and the Central China Agriculture College at Wuhan have developed several superior yielding rape hybrids of low erucic acid content, resulting in much higher production in those areas.

The second is ensuring the appropriate level of soil fertility. A basic application of manure or other forms of organic matter is adequate, although manure combined with chemical fertilizers is better. For winter grown rape, fertilizer application before the beginning of winter followed by supplementary applications in early spring and during flowering can significantly increase yields.

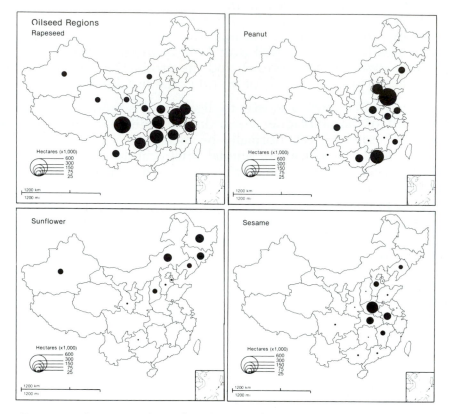

Figure 1. The geographical distribution of oil crops in China.

Other methods of yield enhancement include the development of strong winter rape seedlings through close planting, loosening the soil, disease and insect control, and irrigation. Winter rape seedlings and roots can be protected in the open land by covering with grass. Timely weeding, artificial supplementary pollination and removal of old yellow leaves from seedlings are also helpful. Cutting the peduncles off the main stem is a long historical tradition used by Chinese farmers for improving rape production. It increases branching and spreading of the plants. Because of a short growing period for spring rape, it can be planted more closely than winter rape. Otherwise, the cultural and management procedures for spring rape are the same as for the winter crop.

Peanuts

The peanut was the first American food crop to be introduced into China; this occurred during the early part of the 16th century. Today the peanut is a challenger to rapeseed as the number one oil crop in China (Figure 2). Production of these two oil crops in China for 1985 was equal at 5.6 million metric tons each. (Prior to 1984 rapeseed was the leader). Peanuts originated in the tropics and are a thermophilic (responsive to high temperatures) crop. The heat sums or accumulated temperatures for crop maturity range from 2500°C to 4800°C. Thus, peanut cake after oil extraction contains 50% protein along with phosphorus, potassium and other mineral nutrients, making it an excellent feed for livestock and poultry. China is among the main peanut producing countries in the world, second only to India in area planted. In 1985 there were 3.4 million hectares planted, with an average yield of 1.87 metric tons per hectare. Both total production and yields have since (1980) increased by over 25%. China annually exports more than 200,000 metric tons of shelled peanuts. The year 1985 was a bumper one for peanut production throughout China. The prospects for 1986 were even better (Table 1).

According to geographical areas, cultural conditions and planting schedules, peanut production in China can be divided into three regions (Figure 2). The first, the double-cropping southern area where both spring and autumn crops are produced, includes the Guangdong, Guangxi, Fujian and adjacent provinces. The second is the Yangzi River Valley including Sichuan, Anhui, and Jiangsu provinces and neighboring

Figure 2. A peanut threshing ground.

areas. The third includes the Shandong, Henan, Hebei and North-Jiangsu areas.

The early maturing peanut production region includes Liaoning, Jilin and the Heilongjiang provinces. In 1980 Shandong Province ranked first in area planted, yields per hectare and total production. Zhejiang ranked second in area planted and production, with Hebei third. Provinces other than Shandong and Guangdong which had planting areas of more than 75,000 hectares of peanuts were Henan, Hebei, Anhui, Guangxi, Liaoning, Sichuan, Jiangsu and Fujian.

A prime objective for peanut production in China is to increase yields. Many new and improved varieties, which yield in excess of 10% more than traditional varieties, have recently been introduced by the Agricultural Research Institutes in Shandong, Guangdong and other provinces. Another step toward larger yields is to maintain high levels of soil fertility using both organic and inorganic fertilizers. Phosphate fertilizers are particularly beneficial if applied at the time of planting and during flowering. Further means of yield enhancement include transplanting seedlings to unused land, timely cultivation, weeding, hilling, irrigation and pest control.

Finally, plastic soil mulching can significantly increase yields of peanuts and improve the quality (see Chapter 31, "The Plastic Revolution"). According to extensive, two-year experiments on plastic soil mulching now completed at Dalian and Jinzhou City, yields were more than doubled over an experimental area of 67,000 hectares. During 1985, over 1,250 hectares were sown with peanuts in Yanchuan County of Shaanxi Province, of which 1,000 hectares were covered with plastic mulches.

Current efforts in China to improve processing (crushing, oil pressing) with genetic improvements in peanuts for food and confections should increase demand and production of this important crop.

Sunflower Seed

The sunflower originated in North America and was introduced into Europe about 1510 A.D. It is estimated that the sunflower came to China from the Western World about four hundred years ago. The earliest documented record was in 1621 (Ming Dynasty) in the book *Register of Beautiful and Fragrant Flowers* by Wang Xiangjin. The sunflower was then called "Wenju," meaning "gentle chrysanthemum" and "Ying Yaing Hua" meaning "facing sunlight flower.

Sunflower production has increase rapidly in China during the past thirty-five years. Production expanded from 20,000 hectares and 33,000 metric tons in 1949 to over 1 million hectares and 1.33 million metric tons in 1981, and on up to over 1.7 million metric tons in 1985, with a projected 2.2 million tons in 1986. The growing area dropped to near 0.9 million hectares in 1985 but total production increased above the 1980 levels because of significant gains in yield. Sunflower seed production in China doubled from 1979 to 1984. China is now fourth among the world's sunflower-producing nations, exceeded only by the U.S.S.R., Argentina and the U.S.A.

As an important oil crop in northern China, sunflowers have wide use. The seeds have a high (35-50%) oil content. Sunflower oil is a semi-drying type of good quality and storage tolerance. In addition to being an excellent edible oil, it is also used for making paints, soaps and dyes. After extraction of the oil, the cake and flower disks make good animal feed. The sunflower plant is also important for honey. Seed varieties different from those grown for oil are used as human food (Figure 3). The snapping and shelling of sunflower seeds for consumption is as common in some of the northern provinces as the shelling and eating of peanuts in the south and central areas.

Figure 3. Sunflowers are an important oil crop in nothern China.

Sunflower plants have a high degree of cold, salt and alkali resistance and will produce crops under low soil fertility. They are found throughout all of China. Small plantings can be seen in all provinces, autonomous regions and municipalities. Extensive plantings, however, are limited to the northern provinces and autonomous regions. The largest planting area and total yield are in the Heilongjiang Province. There the planting area was over 300,000 hectares in 1980, with a total production of 400,000 metric tons and a yield of about 1.3 metric tons per hectare. The Heilongjiang Province was followed by Jilin with 200,000 hectares planted. The northern parts of China dominate in sunflower production (Figure 1).

Sunflower plants have huge root systems which require large amounts of water and soil nutrients (fertilizers). While the plant is widely adaptive to varying soil nutrient levels, fertile soils increase yields significantly. It also grows well in highly saline and alkaline soils. Recently introduced F^1 hybrid sunflowers resulted in impressive yields. The Baikuiza No. 1 hybrid, recently released by the Baiceng Prefecture of the Agricultural Research Institute of the Jilin Province, produced nearly 3.0 metric tons of seed per hectare in experiments conducted in the Hulan County of Heilongjiang. The Peledovik variety, an introduction from the U.S.S.R., is also grown widely in China. The productivity of sunflowers has also been increased by applying additional organic nitrogen and phosphorus fertilizers at sowing. Other procedures for achieving higher yields are timely plant thinning, weeding, pest control and rotation with other crops.

Sesame Seed

Sesame is one of China's edible oil crops which was originally found only in tropical and subtropical zones. It probably originated in Africa, but since wild sesame was native to Java, that island is considered the site of origin.

Sesame seeds have many uses. They have the highest oil content of all oil crops, averaging about 54%. The oil is fragrant and delicate. The seed is an excellent condiment. The ancient Chinese plant encyclopedia *Shen Nong Ben Cao Jing* maintains that sesame can give people energy, grow muscles and benefit the brain. Sesame oil is also believed to prevent vitamin decomposition, benefit digestion and increase digestive absorbability. It is also high in vitamin E, which is reported to reduce disease susceptability and prolong life. Sesame meal and cake, after extracting the oil, can be used as a highly effective manure or fertilizer for melons, fruit trees and tobacco which, according to Chinese tradition, makes watermelons sweeter and more delicate and improves the fragrance and color of tobacco.

The area devoted to sesame seed production in China is second only to that of India. The world's largest producer, however, is China. In 1984 China had 800,000 hectares of sesame with a total output of 467,000 metric tons. Figure 1 shows the distribution of sesame production in China. The provinces leading in production are Henan, Hunan, Anhui, Jiangxi and Hebei. In 1984 the Henan Province had the largest planting area and the highest yields.

Many cultural and climatic factors affect sesame yields. Sesame should follow a legume or other crop that will provide residual soil nutrients. Continuous cropping with sesame must be avoided because of disease problems. Sesame should be planted in well-drained soils. Since the seeds are small and good emergence of seedlings is essential, the soil's surface should be fine and plain. Sesame is a thermophilic (heat-loving) crop. The most suitable temperature for seed germination is 24°C. Sesame seeds, therefore, should not be planted too early or too late. In northern China, seeds should be sown in mid May. During early seedling growth, the soil should be loosened for easy emergence. Early thinning, transplanting young plants where needed and timely pest control throughout the growing season are important.

As with other oil seed crops (rape, peanuts, sunflower) both organic and chemical fertilizers are effective. Chemical fertilizers are used both in top-dressing and as foliar sprays. The most desirable sesame varieties are those which mature early, are disease-resistant and high yielding.

Flax Seed

Flax is produced for oil primarily in Inner Mongolia, Gansu, Shanxi, Hebei, and the Xinjiang Autonomous Region of northern and northwest China. The total planted area in 1981 was 668,000 hectares with production of 215,000 metric tons. The world area now devoted to flax production is about 4.7 million hectares, with a total production of about 2.65 million metric tons and an average yield of about .56 metric tons per hectare. India, the U.S.S.R., Canada, Argentina and China lead in flax production.

Other Sources of Edible Oils

The soybean is of great importance as a source of edible oil in the northeast provinces of China. In other regions hemp, perilla seed and castor bean are used as oil sources. Castor bean oil production, in particular, expanded in 1985 over previous years both with higher yields and larger producing areas. The tung-oil tree, originally grown in China, is an essential oil-bearing tree, with seeds containing 20-35% oil. Nutritionally, it is one of the best because it is high in unsaturated fatty acids. It is also used for industrial purposes. The oil palm tree is also found in the most southern provinces of China and on Hainan Island. It is known as the "Oil King of the World." The oil is edible and is a major source for shortening and margarine, in addition to being useful for many industrial purposes.

FOR FURTHER READING

Baiceng Prefecture Agriculture Research Institute. 1982. *Sunflower culture*. Beijing: Agricultural Press. (In Chinese)

Edit Group of Sesame Culture. 1983. Agriculture Publishing House. (In Chinese)

He Kang, ed. 1980, 1981, 1982, 1983, 1984. *Chinese agricultural yearbook*. Beijing: Agricultural Press. (In Chinese)

Oil Crop Research Institute of Academy of Agricultural Sciences of China. 1979. *Cultural technique of rape*. Beijing: Agricultural Press. (In Chinese)

Shih Sheng-Han. 1974. *A preliminary survey of the book "Qi Min Yao Shu": An agricultural encyclopedia of the 6th century*. Beijing: Science Press.

U.S. Department of Agriculture. Economic Research Service. 1985, 1986. *China outlook and situation reports*. Washington, D.C.: Government Printing Office.

Yianti Prefecture Peanut Research Institute of Shangdong Province. 1972. *Peanut culture technique*. Beijing: Agriculture Press. (In Chinese)

21

VEGETABLE ABUNDANCE--FROM YARDLONG COWPEAS TO BITTER MELONS[1]

by Sylvan Wittwer

One of the most conspicuous aspects of Chinese life, especially around all the major cities and settlements, is the production, transportation and marketing of huge quantities of every conceivable vegetable. The Chinese people are fond of vegetables, which constitute an important part of their diet. In quantity consumed, vegetables are second only to rice in the daily diet of the people, and are often its only accompaniment at meal time. An estimated 4.1 million hectares are devoted to vegetable production in China annually, with several crops often being produced on the same land in a single year. National estimates for consumption are 400 grams per person per day or 146 kilograms per year for people in the cities. (Three hundred to 350 grams per day are sufficient to meet dietary requirements.) This is far above U.S.A. and European consumption levels. Accurate vegetable production and consumption records are almost impossible to obtain, since marketing is at the local level and records are not collected.

Vegetable farming in China is unique as to its origin, the intensity of its culture, the quantities produced, its geographical distribution and the number of species consumed (over one-hundred). Also included in the uniqueness is the role of private plots and free markets in vegetable production and distribution; the high cropping index (number of crops per year on the same land); the hundreds of crop combinations that exist for their culture; the interlacing of one crop with another; the training and trellising of vine crops; hybrid seed production; the methods of organic and inorganic fertilization; integrated pest control; the extensive

---

[1]The author is deeply indebted to Li Shuxuan (S. H. Lee), former Chairman of the Horticulture Department and now Professor of the Zhejiang Agricultural University in Hangzhou, for many details concerning genetic resources and production systems for vegetable crops in China.

use of chemical growth regulators; and finally, the vast areas where plastic soil mulches, row covers (tunnels), row tents or greenhouses are employed in many different types of controlled environment agriculture.

Truly, among all nations, vegetable farming in China today is the epitome of traditional organic gardening on the one hand, and a remarkable influx of new chemical and cultural technologies on the other. It combines all traditional and modern technological approaches and thus admirably fulfills the Chinese philosophical approach of "walking on two legs." The result is an intensive utilization of limited land, water and energy resources in the production of a multiplicity of crops, upon which the Chinese are highly dependent for both their nutritional contributions and their medicinal properties.

If one is seeking to optimize returns from the land, to observe the most intensive farming systems of the world and view sustainable food-producing systems, examples can be witnessed in the vegetable gardens of China. As many as ten crops may be harvested from the same land in a single year, and up to eighty different kinds may be grown in a single year, in a given area. Emphasis is on quantity, quality, diversity and seasonality. These goals are accomplished through optimal water control, appropriate fertilization, intensive cultivation, interplanting and protected cultivation. Extremely high annual yields are obtained with levels in some areas ranging from 50 to 200 tons per hectare. Furthermore, some of the production systems had their origins forty centuries ago.

Historical

China is one of the earth's oldest centers for vegetable production. Its vegetable genetic resources in the wild, semi-wild and cultivated state exceed that of any other country. Of the 160 vegetables grown in China, of which 100 are commonly grown, about half are native varieties, the others imported stock. Many native types, such as the Chinese cabbage, yam, the cocoyam (taro), garlic, Welch onions, soybean and radish, have spread to other lands where they have assumed world-wide importance. *Brassica* species are widely grown, some of which originated in North China (*B. pekinensis*) and some in central and southern China (*B. chinensis*). They later spread throughout Japan and Southeast Asia. Leaf mustard (*Brassica juncea*) is also a popular vegetable, especially in South China. The first discovery of vegetable spaghetti (*Cucurbita pepo*) as a popular food was in northern China. It is especially popular in the northeast. How it got there from its presumed home in South America, however, is one of the great mysteries of horticulture.

Abundant experiences in vegetable production have been accumulated by Chinese farmers during a history exceeding forty centuries. Emphasis has been on high yields within a small land area ranging from

0.1 hectare in the south to 0.3 hectare in the north. The focus has been on self-reliance with little emphasis on transportation to distant markets. The major production areas were and still are in the suburbs around the cities.

Another historical tradition, persisting to this day in Chinese vegetable production and consumption, is that all parts of a plant can be used for food. These include young leaves, shoots, tubers, roots and buds, as well as the whole plant. Some parts may be of good taste and produce a high yield in fresh weight but may have little nutritional value.

Vegetables in China Today

Of the approximate 125 species of plants grown as vegetables in China (one report lists 115 and another 154), over half are of commercial importance. Most of them originated in China. As to the parts of the plant used for food, 60% of the species are leafy vegetables, 37% fruit vegetables, 20% stem vegetables, 16% seed vegetables, 7% root vegetables and 4% flower vegetables. With many vegetables, more than one part of the plant is used for food.

There are aquatic vegetables in addition to those grown on land. They include lotus roots; arrowhead; aquatic sweet potato (*Ipomoea aquatica*), also known as swamp cabbage; Chinese water chestnut (*Eleocharis tuberosa*), sometimes called "matai"; and water bamboo or wild rice (*Zizania caduciflora*). Two species of luffa, *Luffa acutangula* and *Luffa cylindrica*, are known as Chinese okra and sponge gourd, respectively. There is also the bitter melon or balsam pear (*Momordica charantia L.*). *Benincasa hispida* is known at the wax melon, wax gourd or the Chinese "winter melon" so highly prized as a delicacy during the fall and summer months. While it is called a "winter" melon it is actually a warm season crop grown in the summer. it is called "Dong Kwa" in Chinese, which means fuzz melon, a variety of *B. hispida*. Other vegetables include bamboo sprouts, Chinese chives, daylily buds, several kinds of beans, yardlong cowpeas (*Vigna sesquipedalis*), gourds, tubers and greens, many of which are still peculiar to China.

Around the major cities a vast array of vegetables are available, unregulated and cheap. A total of forty different primary vegetables are grown in the Shanghai municipality alone. In order of importance they are: Chinese cabbage (four kinds), tomato, cucumber, eggplant, pepper, ordinary cabbage, spinach, swamp cabbage or water sweet potato and green beans. Others are the potato, stem lettuce, radish, cauliflower, amaranth (Chinese spinach), the garland chrysanthemum (*Chrysanthemum coronerium*, var. *Spatisum*), celery, leek, onion, garlic, shallot, gourds, Chinese winter melon (*B. hispida*), squash (Figure 1), luffa, cantaloupe, watermelon, yardlong cowpeas, vegetable soybeans, peas, wild rice (water bamboo), arrowhead, taro, leaf mustards, and broad beans.

Among some forty additional secondary vegetables are carrots, beets, rutabagas, Chinese yam, Jerusalem artichoke, broccoli, Chinese kale, curly mallow, the Welch or Chinese onion, bitter melon, lima bean, cattail, watercress, water chestnut, lotus roots and seeds (*Nelumbium nucifera*), asparagus, Chinese wolfberry, mushrooms, snow peas, mung bean sprouts, daylily buds (golden needles), globe artichoke, and perilla.

For vegetables in the Beijing area, the following is the order of importance as to area devoted to production and value: Chinese cabbage, cucumber, tomato, cauliflower, sweet pepper, eggplant, snap bean and Chinese radish. Additional vegetables in the Beijing area, not listed for Shanghai, are: coriander (Chinese parsley), fennel, mallow, malibu or vine spinach (*Bassella* sp.), and calabash gourd (*Lagenaria* sp.). For South China, in the Guangzhou (Canton) area of Guangdong Province, the number one vegetable is the flowering Chinese cabbage (*Brassica chinensis, parachinensis* group), which is produced the year around. Other important vegetables are: ordinary cabbage, cowpeas (yardlong), swamp cabbage or the water sweet potato, Welch onions, Chinese chives (*Allium tuberosum*), squash, melons, sponge gourds, Chinese okra, Chinese kale, cucumbers, bitter melon, arrowhead and water bamboo (wild rice).

Figure 1. Trellised winter squash are common in the Shanghai and Beijing areas.

The important vegetables in Zhejiang Province, in the vicinity of Hangzhou, are: tomatoes, peppers--both hot and sweet, eggplant, beans, yardlong cowpeas, French and common beans, vegetable soybeans, melons, cucumbers, winter melon, the sponge gourd, the white flowered, gourd (*Lagenaria leucantha*), leaf mustards, Chinese cabbage (both *B. chinensis* and *B. pekinensis*), Chinese chives, onions and potatoes. In the northeast, the number one vegetable is Chinese cabbage (*B. pekinensis*), with emphasis on the cool season leafy vegetables, root crops and potatoes, snap beans, early maturing vine crops including watermelons, and tomatoes, peppers and eggplant. Tomato production throughout China, both in the open and in greenhouses, is increasing very rapidly. In the far northwestern parts of China (Xinjiang Autonomous Region), the air is dry and there is an abundance of sunlight. This area is particularly adapted to the production of high quality watermelons and muskmelons (Hami type).

China is a home of the radish. There are more varieties of radish here than in any other country on earth. It has been bred over long periods of time and adapted to many habitats. Likewise mustard is a special product of China. Most varieties are grown for their leaves but others for their roots and stems.

Rich, new germ plasm resources for cucurbits, beans, peppers, yams and onions are being found from surveys of wild species in China. An inventory, still in progress, of wild onions in Inner Mongolia has thus far identified a collection of eight species of *Allium*. The most popular species of onion throughout China is known as Chinese chives (*A. tuberosum*), followed by *A. fistulosum*.

There is a local exotic vegetable known as "facai" or the "hair vegetable." It is a kind of fresh water algae, *Nostoc commune* var. *flagelliforme*, belonging to *Cyanophyta*. The blue algae is dark green in color, composed of numerous unicellular cells connected together like hairs, and distributed in the running water of Inner Mongolia and the Gansu, and Shaanxi provinces. It is also called the "get rich" vegetable. Overseas Chinese are able and willing to pay very high prices for it. The vegetable looks like hair and grows parasitically on grasses. It is much relished as a Chinese delicacy and usually served in soups.

Two widely grown vegetables of considerable significance in the U.S.A. but heretofore of little interest in China are broccoli and sweet corn. Both crops produce excellent harvests in China. Broccoli varieties of high quality are now on extensive trial at the Beijing Vegetable Research Institute and are especially desired by an expanding tourist trade in the major cities. Sweet corn was first introduced into China in the 1950's, but never really caught on because of low yields. Recent studies with new strains at the Guangxi Autonomous Region Agricultural College, however, resulted in yields approaching fourteen metric tons per hectare. Sweet corn is now readily accepted by the people.

Cropping Indices

The cropping index (number of crops per year) for vegetables in China will vary from one in the northeast provinces of Heilongjiang, Jilin and Liaoning, where the growing season is short, to more than three or four in the south. In the north, which has a frost-free period of only three to four months, both warm and cool season vegetables are grown during the summer. For the North China Plain, two crops are produced, one in the summer for warm season crops like tomatoes and beans, and one in the autumn for cool season root crops and cabbage. In the Yangzi River valley, cool season leafy crops can be grown during the winter, warm season crops during the hot summers, and cool season crops again in the autumn. The area south of the Yangzi River valley is suitable for some vegetables at every season of the year. Three to four crops a year can be grown in succession.

The cropping index is increased and growing period shortened for many vegetables by the use of transplants. Seedlings are started in seedbeds, often covered with plastic, and then transplanted to the production field. This is true not only for peppers, eggplants, tomatoes, melons, squash and cucumbers, but also for snap beans, onions, all kinds of cabbages and tuber crops. Wetland taro, for example, can be started in dry seedbeds and then transplanted into wetlands to save water, as well as a month of the field-growing period.

For aquatic vegetables such as water bamboo, Chinese water chestnut and lotus, which are grown in lakes, ponds and flooded paddies, sequential and intercropped plantings are different than on dry land. Water bamboo can be intercropped with early rice and the Chinese water chestnut can be grown after the early rice harvest, while lotus can be intercropped or grown after rice. Seed corms of the Chinese water chestnut may be started in seedbeds, following which they are transplanted into paddy fields after the harvest of early rice.

Unique Features of Vegetable Production in China

Several unusual features characterize vegetables and their production in China. *First* is the generation of F_1 hybrid seed used extensively for Chinese cabbage, ordinary cabbage, tomatoes, peppers (hot and sweet), eggplant, watermelons, cucumbers, and white radish. The results are increased yields, greater uniformity and improved disease resistance, earlier maturity and an increase in the cropping index. Many disease-resistant F_1 hybrids of tomatoes, cucumbers and Chinese cabbage have been developed, not only for outdoor production but for both autumn and early spring plantings in plastic greenhouses.

Hybrid seed fits the Chinese model for both resource utilization and enhancement of productivity. It is labor intensive but sparing of natural resources with optimization of genetic inputs. The result is stable production at high levels.

Companion to the use of F_1 hybrid seed is the move toward clonal or tissue culture propagation, which is even more labor intensive but potentially more important than F_1 hybrid seed for yield improvement and disease control. Tissue culture (using meristems) is now seriously employed for the clonal propagation of super males of F_1 hybrid asparagus, virus-free garlic, disease-free potatoes and tomatoes, and for uniformity and early maturity of Chinese cabbage, ordinary cabbage and eggplant. Anther culture (new plants from pollen grains derived from anthers) is being anticipated for new varieties of tomato, Chinese cabbage, ordinary cabbage and eggplant. While the cost of hybrid seed and tissue culture-propagated clones of vegetables is often a serious constraint to their use in the U.S.A., this is not so in China. There the effort required for hybrid seed production or tissue culture propagation is of secondary importance. The primary consideration is trained labor, which is readily accessible. Little is needed in the way of special equipment or facilities.

Figure 2. Trellised yardlong cowpeas in Zhejiang Province.

Secondly, all vegetable crops that can be staked, trained or trellised are grown accordingly. This is true of pole beans, yardlong cowpeas, tomatoes, cucumbers, melons, squash, luffa and gourds (Figure 2). It is known as vertical growing. With the training of these and other vegetables on trellises, usually using bamboo stakes, a second or sometimes third or even fourth crop is grown in the understory and at various distances from the ground level. One exception is with vegetables that are grown in the northeast, the north and the northwestern regions, where land areas are extensive.

Vegetables such as green beans, tomatoes, cucumbers, squash and melons have either bush (determinate) or climbing (vine or indeterminate) plant types. Seldom are the bush types used in China. By training tomato, bean, cucumber or other plants on stakes or trellises, yields may be 20 to 25% higher than on nontrained plants. This is because more plants per unit area can be used, sunlight reception is increased, and irrigation and crop fertilization is facilitated. Also, fruit quality is improved, the harvest season is prolonged, there is less damage from plant diseases, and a second or third crop can be grown simultaneously on the same land. Most importantly, the leaf area index (the ratio of leaf area per unit land area) is greatly increased and often doubled by a trellised canopy. The sunlight intercepted by leaves is positively correlated with the leaf area index. Crops such as tomatoes are staked or trained by several methods (Figure 3). There is sufficient hand labor, if necessary, to prune and tie every branch or vine to stakes or strings to catch as much sunlight as possible. Here, again, is another example of a Chinese model for resource allocation. In this instance, the resource is sunlight. The technology is labor intensive, but through optimizing the input of sunlight the result is stable production at high levels.

Getting more food from less space has resulted in a *third* Chinese innovation for increasing vegetable production. It is known as bed culture. Almost all vegetable seedbeds and those used for crop production in China, especially in the south, are planted on beds raised to various heights with narrow furrows or ditches of various depths separating or dividing the beds, depending on the need for irrigation and drainage. Trellised crops such as tomatoes, beans, yardlong cowpeas, bitter melons, cucumbers or luffa squash are planted on the edges of the beds. When these vine crops are trained over the ditches they may be intercropped with both aquatic crops and other vegetables.

The beds upon which vegetables are grown are usually one and one-half to two meters wide and have irrigation furrows on each side to maintain appropriate moisture levels. In this way the centers can be reached conveniently from either side to plant, irrigate, weed, and conduct pest control and harvest operations. Even though water tables are maintained in the furrows only 30 to 40 centimeters below plant levels, much hand watering is necessary to maintain a moist soil surface and to allow evaporative cooling during the heat of summer days. Water is scooped out of the furrows or channels with shovel type ladels and flicked over the plants.

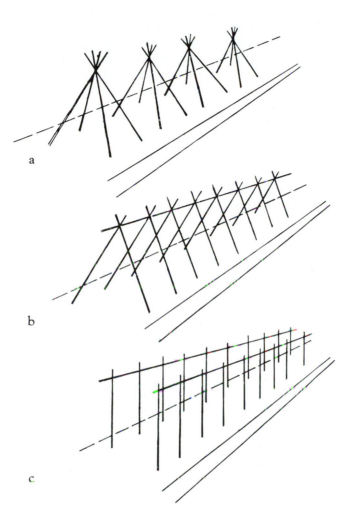

Figure 3. Tomatoes are staked or trained by three different methods: *a*, tetrapod type; *b*, leaning trellis type or A frame; *c*, straight trellis type.

Intercropping is a *fourth* practice which has long been used in China to increase yields in small land areas. Intercropping is almost universal. For hundreds of years it has increased the yield per unit of land. Intercropping gives better yields than growing a single crop but, again, is more labor intensive. Two or more kinds of crops are grown simultaneously on the same land. Mixed, relay, strip and hill cropping are among the many patterns of intercropping. Mixed cropping is a mixture of plants of different growth and branching habits, leaf size, shape, spacing and maturity. Short season and early maturing crops such as Chinese cabbage (the *B. chinensis* group), amaranth (Chinese spinach), stem lettuce and garland chrysanthemum are intercropped or mixed with tomato, pepper and eggplant. Tall growing vegetables are intercropped with the dwarf. Tomato, cucumber and the white flowered gourd are intercropped with bush beans, celery or amaranth. In the Yangzi River valley, melons and wax gourds can be intercropped with soybeans, corn or onions.

Relay intercropping is where two or more crops coexist during part of the growing period for each. Usually the second crop is seeded or transplanted after the first crop has reached the technically mature stage or the middle to latter part of its growth period, and before the first crop is harvested. An example is the triple cropping of the sponge gourd (*Luffa cylindrica*), eggplant and amaranth (Figure 4). In this triple system, amaranth is harvested first, followed by eggplant and finally the sponge gourd. Other relay cropping examples are the yardlong bean with taro and water sweet potato, and the sponge gourd, taro and flowering Chinese cabbage.

For the strip intercropping and hill or ridge intercropping systems, vegetables are intercropped with each other or with field crops. In North China, strips or beds of spinach, celery or onions may be planted on the south side of a windscreen or windbreak made of corn or sorghum stalks. In the Yangzi River valley, watermelons are intercropped in rows or hills with wheat, rape or fava beans (*Vicia faba*). This creates a warm, wind-free microclimate for growth in late spring and early summer. Windbreaks, either artificial or natural, are widely used for vegetable production in China.

There are literally hundreds of possible vegetable crop combinations for intercropping (Figure 5). This, coupled with the 80 to 120 different kinds and varieties of vegetables grown throughout the year, provides remarkable diversities for intercropping, crop rotations and sequential cropping. Again, this is part of a Chinese cropping model for optimizing natural resource inputs in a labor intensive food producing system that increases productivity. Bed culture, trellising and intercropping do present formidable obstacles to mechanization of any kind, but until now, the importance of increasing food production in China has far outweighed that of any problem from increased labor inputs.

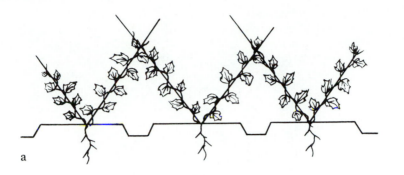

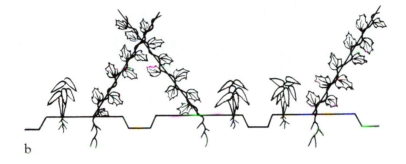

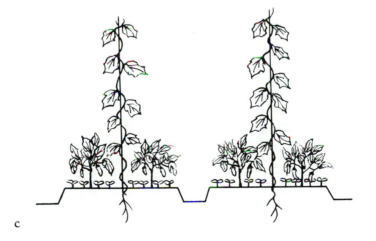

Figure 4. Tripple cropping: *a*, sponge gourd only; *b*, sponge gourd and eggplant; *c*, sponge gourd, eggplant and amaranth.

Figure 5. Intercropping of Chinese cabbage, sweet potato, rice and mulberry in Sichuan Province.

An additional and *fifth* unique practice in vegetable culture in China that has endured for hundreds of years is the sand, gravel or rock mulch. It is used extensively, particularly over hundreds of thousands of hectares in the Lanzhou area of Gansu Province where the climate is very dry.

There are two kinds of sands or pebbles according to size that are used for soil mulching. The first is the large sand or gravel, where each is oval in shape like a goose egg. This is called stone sand and may be referred to as rock mulching. The other consists of a small gravel the size of a mung bean. The sand or gravel is laid by hand on the soil surface to form a layer, and the crops are planted between the rocks or pebbles of sand. Such rock or gravel mulches (both sizes) are used for vegetable production under the extremely dry conditions of northwest China. They are used both as an irrigated or wet sand mulch for muskmelon, Chinese cabbage, eggplant, tomato, pepper, bean and other crops grown with irrigation, and as a dry sand mulch for muskmelons and watermelons with no irrigation. The small-sized sand is also used for mulching (covering) nonirrigated orchard soils and the large-sized pebbles for non irrigated field crops, such as cotton and peanuts.

The sand- or gravel-mulched field serves many useful purposes. It prevents evaporation from the soil surface and the rise of salinity from the subsoil. It regulates the soil temperature, facilitating a maximum growth response. Weed growth is arrested and soil erosion prevented during the late summer and early autumn rainy periods.

Again, we witness in China an ancient but unique labor intensive technology that optimizes the utilization of the most critical natural resource (water) in northwest China. The result is an enhancement of both the stability and magnitude of production. The current plastic revolution in China may, in the future, continue to substitute plastic for gravel, rocks and pebbles.

A *sixth* unique feature of vegetable production in China is the ever increasing use of plastic. It is used for seedbed covers to force earlier germination and growth of seedlings. All vegetables that can be conveniently transplanted, as well as many of those with some difficulty, are transplanted. This reduces the time required to mature a crop on a given piece of land and extends the growing and harvest seasons. Plastic soil mulches and row covers enable earlier transplanting, reduce water requirements, hasten crop maturity, protect from environmental hazards, extend the boundaries of production, reduce soil erosion, repel some insects, and increase yields. Plastic greenhouses, both heated and nonheated, have greatly expanded vegetable production, prolonged the harvest season and increased the stability of production. (See Chapter 31, "The Plastic Revolution"). Once more, the Chinese model for getting more food from less space is repeated. Transplanting and the use of plastics for soil mulching, covering seed beds, row covers or greenhouses are all labor intensive (Figure 6). However, both the stability and magnitude of food production from a fixed land area and water resource are greatly increased.

A *seventh* unique feature of vegetable production in China is the extensive use of both organic and inorganic fertilizers, pesticides and plant growth substances, applied in all possible combinations, where there is some promise for increasing crop yields. There is still a heavy dependence on organic manures for vegetable growing. Animal manures, especially from the pig, night soil, river and canal mud and sludge are combined with all conceivable crop residues, city wastes and soil to make a rich compost for vegetable production. Organic manures of up to 75 tons/hectare (10,000 jin/mu) are used annually to produce the desired high yields. Meanwhile, there are ever increasing quantities of inorganic chemical fertilizers being used, especially on vegetables, almost all of which are also irrigated. Pig production (see Chapter 26, "Three Hundred Million Pigs") is closely associated with vegetable growing. Pigs are fed on crop wastes and aquatic plants. Pig manure, in turn, becomes an important component of the composting operation. The use of inorganic fertilizers in China had the fastest rate of growth from 1978 to 1982 of any country using large amounts of it during a comparable period. Micronutrient sprays, along with night soil

Figure 6. Plastics have extensively increased the production of vegetables.

solutions, are regularly applied to the foliage of green leafy vegetables and to tomatoes, beans and cucumbers. These "solutions" not only fertilize the crops but add a complex of microorganisms and growth-promoting substances, the effects of which cannot be understood fully other than that they produce luxuriant growth on crops so treated. Ethylene-releasing growth regulators are used to increase the number of female flowers on gourds and to enhance the uniform ripening of tomatoes. Individual flowers of the tomato are hand-dipped on daily rounds into solutions of ten parts per million of 2, 4-dichlorophenoxyacetic acid (2, 4-D), or sprayed with 15-25 ppm of 4-cholorophenoxyacetic acid (4CPA) or other plant growth regulators, to facilitate early and more complete fruit setting. As before, the model for production is labor intensive, but the result is optimal utilization of renewable as well as nonrenewable resources, with a touch of modern technology, resulting in greater dependability of production at high levels.

Crop Protection

The production of vegetables is highly dependent upon applications of chemical pesticides, but pesticide resistance problems have arisen. A good example of extensive pesticide use and acquired resistance to pesticides is in the control of the diamondback moth on brassicas, including Chinese cabbage (see Chapter 30, "Warring With Pests," for additional examples). Induction of male sterility by ionizing radiation may be a possible alternative control measure for this pest. There is also a real problem in the use of chemicals when so many different crop species are planted together. Monocultures of vegetable crops seldom, if ever, exist. However, devastation from one pest rarely results in total crop failures. What may pose a problem in one area may provide the answer in another. Insect problems are generally more prevalent in the south than in the north. Virus problems cause the most severe diseases on tomatoes, Chinese cabbage and peppers, and are the limiting factors in production. *Bacillus thuringiensis*, resulting in a bacterial infection of the larvae of harmful insects, is widely used for the control of the cabbage worm. There are many examples of biological control in vegetables, as with other crops (see Chapter 30, "Warring with Pests"), and some go back for centuries. Just as there are vast genetic resources for vegetables in China, there are equally important opportunities in the coordinated use of natural enemies for disease and insect control.

There is little emphasis on chemical weed control for vegetables in China. Careful and timely hand removal will undoubtedly be practiced for many years to come. Successful chemical weed control would require plant groupings according to herbicide resistance. There is little opportunity for weeds to flourish in the complexity of the current intercropping systems.

Pest management for vegetables has received serious attention in China. Thus, we see a fascinating mix of ancient and modern pest control practices for vegetables. Some have evolved over the centuries and are aimed at specific insects or diseases. These are now being integrated with control methodologies that require "on-line, real-time" introduction of biological agents and chemical controls.

A unique feature of vegetable utilization in China, aside from production, is their preparation for eating. Seldom, if ever, are they served raw, except those such as tomatoes and melons that are consumed as fresh fruit. Here vegetables are stir-fried, which means cooking quickly in hot oil in a wok. The method is fast, uses little oil, preserves vitamins, heat-sterilizes the product, and preserves the juices and flavors by quickly searing and sealing the outer surfaces. All of those features, each in its order, fill important niches in resource conservation, food acceptability, safety and good nutrition.

Future Potentials and Human Resources

Vegetables are the objects of the most intensive crop cultivation in China and perhaps the world. Opportunities for genetic improvement and greater disease resistance through breeding for F_1 hybrids and micropropagation via tissue culture are being vigorously pursued. The goals are greater productivity, earlier maturity, improved quality for both fresh and processed products, and more uniformity. Growing high value vegetable crops with plastic soil mulches, under plastic row covers and in plastic greenhouses will continue to expand. New fertilizers and water management technologies, as well as unique approaches to integrated pest management and chemical growth regulation, will not only stabilize and enhance production of many vegetables but will also extend both the geographical boundaries for their culture and the duration of the seasons in which they can be produced and utilized.

Research for improvement of production is strongly centered at the Vegetable Research Institute of the Chinese Academy of Agricultural Sciences in Beijing, established in 1958. The purpose of the Vegetable Research Institute is to conduct research that local institutes cannot conduct. There is also the Beijing Vegetable Research Center, established in cooperation with the United Nations Development Program and the Chinese Government in 1981. The latter institute, in addition to conducting research on production methods, includes studies on postharvest physiology and pest control. China has demonstrated great and unique capabilities in vegetable production. The challenge for the future will be to utilize more effectively that which is produced. This means reducing postharvest losses, improving handling, storage and transportation facilities, and more effectively utilizing surpluses through modern processing, marketing and delivery systems.

Continued progress in the production and utilization of vegetable crops can be expected in the decades ahead. Meanwhile, the vast pool of genetic resources and production technologies for vegetables in China, as they are shared with others, can have major impacts on global food availability and the nutritional well-being of peoples from many nations.

FOR FURTHER READING

Brooklyn Botanic Garden Record. 1983. A dictionary of oriental and vegetables. *Plants and Gardens* 39(2): 65-76.

He Kang, ed. 1984, 1985. *Chinese agricultural yearbook*. Beijing: Agricultural Press. (In Chinese)

King, F. H. 1911. *Farmers of forty centuries*. Emmaus, Pa.: Rodale Press, Inc.

Li Shuxuan (S. H. Lee), et al. 1965. The community structure in relation to light utilization of eggplant. *Acta Horticultural* 4(3): 135-36. (In Chinese)

Li Shuxuan (S. H. Lee). 1979. *Physiology of vegetable crops*. Shanghai: Shanghai Science and Technology Press. (In Chinese)

———. 1982. Vegetable crop growing in China. *Scientia Horticulturae* 17:102-9.

Plucknett, D. L., and H. L. Beemer, Jr. 1981. *Vegetable farming in China*. Boulder, Colo.: Westview Press, Inc.

Quebedeaux, B; M. Faust; and F. D. Schales. 1985. Opportunities for horticultural food crop production improvements in China. In *Proceedings on agriculture in China*. Vol. 1, *Challenges and opportunities*, 196-203. Beltsville, Md.: Institute of International Development and Education in Agriculture and Life Sciences.

Wittwer, S. H. 1982. Vegetable production in China. *American Vegetable Grower* 30(4): 36-38.

———. 1983. *Frontiers for science and technology in vegetable production*. 10th Annual Monograph Series. Shanhua, Taiwan: Asian Vegetable Research and Development Center.

22

CHINESE CABBAGE--YEAR-ROUND[1]

by Sylvan Wittwer

When foreigners think of China, they usually think of rice. But from the Vietnamese border in the south to the northeast provinces and from January to December, it's cabbage--specifically, Chinese cabbage--boiled, pan-fried, stewed, cut up and served with rice or in dumplings, pickled, fresh from the field, or retrieved from storage. It's China's vegetable "VIP." Harvesting the crop before the first killing frost ends the growing season is vital for the winter's food supply in all of North China and many plastic greenhouses have been constructed in recent years to protect the crop and extend the growing season. By contrast, in the U.S.A. and many other parts of the world, this vegetable is largely unknown and remains a novelty.

Half the vegetables produced and consumed in China belong to the *Cruciferae* or cabbage family. The single most important representative is Chinese cabbage. With its many forms, a diversity of tolerances to seasons, locations and extremes of environment are provided, as with no other vegetable. Nutritionally, it is an excellent source of dietary fiber and vitamins A and C. Of all the vegetables that temporarily fill the city streets of China and the adjoining countryside with abundance during the summer, Chinese cabbage is the most prominent and has the longest availability. Everyone seems to buy it in small quantities from summer to winter in the south where it is eaten immediately. In autumn in the north, they purchase large quantities for winter storage. China does not have a regular transportational system that in winter will bring adequate fresh

---

[1]The author is indebted to Shu-Hsien Lee, former Chairman of the Horticultural Department, and now Professor Emeritus, Zhejiang Agricultural University in Hangzhou for his review of this chapter and many helpful suggestions, including the map illustrating the geographical distribution of the various species of Chinese cabbage.

vegetables from the south to the north. The heading type of Chinese cabbage, with its preservability and value as a source of freshness in winter, fills a niche provided by no other vegetable. The old Chinese saying that winters will not be hungry if there is lots of cabbage is literally fulfilled each year in the homes of hundreds of millions of Chinese. It is the one vegetable in its many diverse types and forms which has universal acceptance and is consumed in large quantities. Each year in the Beijing area alone, over 200 million kilograms of the heading types of Chinese cabbage are placed in storage for winter consumption. There is no heading type of Chinese cabbage available during the summer time (April to September) even in North China. These nonheading types of Chinese cabbages are harvested in the "immature stage" during the summer months in the southern parts of China.

Origin and Types

There are two main types of Chinese cabbage. Both originated in China. *Brassica chinensis*, the nonheading type, is most important south of the Yangzi River. *Brassica pekinensis*, the heading type, is predominant north of the Yangzi. (The Yangzi River is generally considered the dividing boundary between North and South China.) Many types of both species of Chinese cabbage, however, are grown everywhere.

The heading group of Chinese cabbage (*B. pekinensis*) is called "Pe-Tsai; the nonheading group (*B. chinensis*) "Pak Choi." The names "Pe-Tsai" and "Pak-Choi" both mean "white vegetable" in Chinese but Pe-Tsai is the Beijing (Peking) dialect, while Pak-Choi is the Cantonese.

There are many varieties and cultivars of Chinese cabbage. *B. pekinensis* is the most popular and widely grown vegetable crop in North China. It is characterized a leafy head with winged petioles (Figure 1). Three main varieties have been defined, according to the shape and size of the head and the characteristics of the wrapper leaves. The first variety, *laxa*, forms a loose open head known as the "flowery hearted type." The second, descriptively known as *cylindrica*, forms a compact head which is erect, elongated and cylindrical, like a stalk of celery. (It is sometimes called celery cabbage.) It does not have wrapper leave over the top. The heads are pointed at the top and spirally wrapped. The third and most commonly known variety is *cephalata*. This has large compact heads, ovate to obovate in shape. The wrapper leaves and outer head leaves curve inward and overlap on the top. Head shapes may be described as round, ovoid, or flattened types. Some early varieties in this group will mature fifty to sixty days after sowing. They form small heads with only sixteen to twenty wrapper leaves.

Brassica chinensis is the most commonly grown type of Chinese cabbage in South China. It forms no leaf head but a leaf rosette with

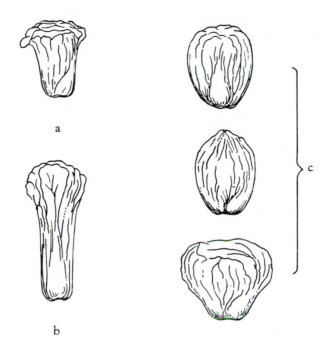

Figure 1. Main types of Chinese cabbage (*Brassica pekinensis*): *a, laxa* or open head; *b, cylindrica* - errect or cylindrical; *c, cephalata* - round, ovoid (egg shaped or pointed) or flattened heads.

upright leaves. It produces few or no leaf wings and has narrow or broad petioles. There are several distinctive varieties *Communis* is the most important group currently grown in Central and South China. The leaf blades are entire or complete and the petioles are prominent. Superficially, it resembles Swiss chard. Another variety, *Rosularis*, forms a tight and small rosette of numerous dark green leaves. There is also an annual fast growing type (*parachinensis*), with one or more fleshy flowering stems called "Tsai-Sin," and many flowering stems produced from each leaf axil called "Tsai-Tai." This type of cabbage is relished in the Guangdong and other southern provinces and is consumed flower, stems and all (Figure 2).

Climatic Requirements and Adaptability

The growth and eating quality of Chinese cabbage is greatly affected by temperature. It is basically a cool season biennial but is cultivated as an

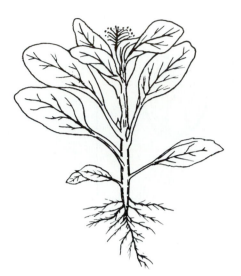

a. *parachinensis* - a flowering fleshy stem.

b. *communis* - leaf blades complete and petioles prominent.

c. *rosularis* - a small rosette of dark green leaves.

Figure 2. Types of chinese cabbage (*Brassica chinensis*).

annual. Some will flower the first year with minimal exposure to cold or cool temperatures. Chinese cabbage is also tolerant of frost and freezing temperatures but not hard freezes such as occurred in the Beijing area in the early fall of 1979, destroying some 50,000 tons while still in the fields. High temperatures (above 20°C), especially at night, do not favor the growth of rosette leaves in *B. chinensis* or heading in *B. pekinensis*. Ideal growing temperatures for young plants range from 16-25° and from 10-18°C for head formation. High light intensities and low temperatures also favor heading and the growth of broad leaves. High temperatures tend to promote the production of narrow leaves. The best quality for Chinese cabbage in the north is with *B. pekinensis* ("Pe-Tsai"), grown to maturity as a fall crop, and with *B. chinensis* ("Pak-Choi") when grown south of the Yangzi in the fall, winter and spring (Figure 3). Early or premature flowering ("bolting") is heightened in all types of Chinese cabbage when they are exposed to cool or cold temperatures follwed by a combination of long days and high temperatures.

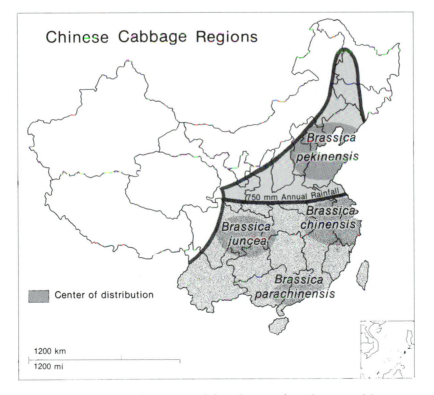

Figure 3. Regions and centers of distribution for Chinese cabbage.

Challenges in Research and Future Potentials

There are many opportunities for further improvements in the breeding, culture, handling and storage of Chinese cabbage. Beginning with the Zhejiang Province and extending southward, there is little opportunity for common storage. But the intent is to have fresh cabbage the year-round. This requires varieties that have early maturity, heat tolerance, cold tolerance and late maturity, depending upon the season. The nonheading types of Chinese cabbage to be harvested in September and October must be planted by the end of July and early August.

How to produce good Chinese cabbage all summer long is still a challenge. All the heading types of Chinese cabbage are still produced during the fall. Greater heat resistance is earnestly being sought. Early spring-sown Chinese cabbage is invariably exposed to cold or cool temperatures which, when followed by long days and high temperatures, will cause it to bolt and produce flowers prematurely. Bolting-resistant Chinese cabbages for summer production, without a serious decline in quality, is an achievable goal being pursued by many provincial academies of agricultural science, colleges of agriculture, the Asian Vegetable Research and Development Center in Taiwan with its 846 accessions, and the Vegetable Research Institute of the Central Academy of Agricultural Sciences in Beijing. Hundreds of selections of Chinese cabbage are currently on trial. In field production, F_1 hybrid varieties of Chinese cabbage derived from male sterile and self-incompatible lines are widely used. Ninety-five percent of the Chinese cabbage grown in the Beijing area is of F_1 hybrid origin.

FOR FURTHER READING

Bennett, A. 1983. Old Chinese adage: No hungry winters if lots of cabbage.*The Wall Street Journal*, 6 December, 1, 29.

Jiang Minchuan. 1981. *Culture of Chinese cabbage*. Beijing: Agricultural Press. (In Chinese)

Li Shuxuan (S. H. Lee). 1982. Vegetable crop growing in China. *Scientia Horticulture* 17:102-9.

———. 1984. Factors affecting the leaf growth and leaf head formation of Chinese cabbage. *Gartenbauwissenschaft* 49:112-16.

Talekar, N. S., and T. D. Griggs, eds. 1981. Chinese cabbage. *Proceedings of the 1st International Symposium*. Asian Vegetable Research and Development Publication no. 81-138. Tainan, Taiwan: Hong Wen Publishing Works.

SUGGESTED FURTHER READING

23

INDIGENOUS AND EXOTIC FRUITS

by Sylvan Wittwer[1]

There is an ancient Chinese story which goes as follows: An emperor of the Tang Dynasty (about 700 A.D.) had a favorite concubine, Yang Guifei. She liked litchi, one of the most exotic of tropical fruits grown in South China. At that time, the fastest means of transportation was by horseback. Litchi fruit is very perishable and will not survive long distance shipping. After many failures, a method was devised by cutting a hole in a bamboo stalk large enough to insert the litchi fruit. The hole was immediately sealed with wax. Carried on the back of the rider, the litchi fruit was "pony expressed" in good condition from Sichuan to the imperial palace in Changan. This experience appears to have been the forerunner of controlled atmosphere storage, now successfully used to preserve the flavor and freshness of the newly harvested fruit of the litchi, with promise for many other tropical fruits. It was the Chinese poet Su Dongpo (1036-1101 A.D.) of the Song Dynasty who declared, "Let me eat 300 litchi every day and I am willing to stay in Guangdong forever."

Domestication of fruit production is of great antiquity in China. Almost all known fruits on earth--temperate zone-adapted, subtropical and tropical--can be successfully cultured here. Many had their origin in this vast land, rich in genetic resources. They include the exotic longan, its relative the litchi, persimmon, and kiwi fruit. Also native to China are many types of citrus, plums, apricots, peaches, pears, crabapples, cherries and strawberries. Many others, such as pomegranates, carambola, bananas, jujubes, grapes and melons were mentioned in some of the oldest of Chinese classics. There are also mangos, avocados and papayas.

---

[1]The author is deeply indebted to Shen Tsuin, Professor of Pomology, Department of Horticulture, Beijing Agricutlural University in Beijing, China for many details concerning the history of fruit growing in China.

Locally adapted fruit and melon plantations now extend from the most southern and southwestern provinces--with their delightful harvest of the delectible litchi, longan, banana, and citrus--to the central provinces with their apples, peaches, pears, loquats, jujubes and pomegranates; from the far northern, northeastern and northwestern regions--where some of the hardiest of pears, apples, plums, apricots, peaches and grapes are produced--to the Xinjiang Autonomous Region, home of the world famous Hami Melons, seedless grapes and raisins.

It is estimated that fruit trees in China, including the wild species used for rootstocks and other purposes, comprise 59 families, 158 genera and more than 300 species. The exchange of fruit germplasm between China and other countries of the world dates back 2,000 years. Peaches, apricots and citrons were carried to Iran (Persia) via "The Silk Road" and from Iran to other European countries. Meanwhile, grapes, pome-granates and walnuts came back via the reverse route.

History of Fruit Growing in China

As far back as 4,000 B.C., in the Neolithic Age, inhabitants collected the fruits of the chestnut and hazelnut for food. This has been revealed by recent excavations from Banpocun in the vicinity of Xian, Shaanxi. Walnut fruits were also present in ruins dating back to the Neolithic Age in Yuyao County, Zhejiang and in Zhengzhou of Henan.

The earliest record of fruit growing in China is found in *Shijing* written during the Zhou Dynasty. It is an extensive compilation of folk songs and mentions the peach, pear, chestnuts (*Castanea mollissima* Bl.), hazelnut (*Corylus heterophylla* Fisch.), jujube (*Zizyphus jujuba* Mill and *Zizyphus spinosus* Hu), plum (*Prunus salicina* Lindl.), Mume (*Prunus mume* Sieb., Zucc.) and kiwi (*Actinidia chinensis* Planch).

The cultivation of citrus dates back 4,000 years. The tangerine, mandarin and sour orange were mentioned in such ancient literature as *Yu-gong* (900 B.C.), *Shanhaijing* (300 B.C.), *Zhuangzi* (about 369-286 B.C.), and *Hanfeizi* (about 280-233 B.C.). The subtropical fruits litchi, longan, loquat, (*Canarium album, Canarium pimela* and *Myrica rubra*) have been cultivated in China for at least 3,000 years.

By the time of the Qin and Han dynasties of 2,000 years ago, large fruit orchards had been established on the slopes along the Yellow and Yangzi rivers. According to *Shiji* (100 B.C.): "Those who grow 1,000 trees of jujube or chestnut or pear or tangerine are as rich as those barons who possess 1,000 families of tenant farmers." Such profit from fruit growing could have come only from improved cultivars and cultural practices. Noteworthy among the ancient Chinese literature on fruit growing are the following.

Li-zhi-pu, a monograph on litchi, was written by Caixiang about 1,059 A.D. during the Northern Song Dynasty. It was the earliest monograph on fruit growing in China. Caixiang was a magistrate in the Fujian Province and his descriptions were confined to that area. Fujian remains today as one of the main production centers for litchi (Figure 1). A total of thirty-two cultivars were described. For each was given the history, distribution, climatic and edaphic requirements, fruiting habits, biennial bearing and methods of processing. Accounts are given of exports--presumably in the dried form--to Japan and Arabia.

Figure 1. Harvesting litchi.

The earliest monograph on citrus fruits in China was written by Han Yanzhi about 1178 A.D. during the Southern Song Dynasty. It consisted of three volumes. The first two described twenty-seven cultivars under cultivation in and around Wenzhou in Zhejiang Province. Morphological characteristics were given along with time of ripening, and for each locality that cultivar which would do best. The third volume dealt with methods of grafting, cultural practices, harvesting, storage and medicinal values of the fruit. It is remarkable that an account was given of setting (planting) the trees on high broad ridges for better rooting and with furrows in between the rows of trees for irrigation and water drainage. This method is still in common use today in many citrus regions having clay soils and high water tables. A recommendation also is found for the cultivar Zhuju, a tangerine, stating that it could be propagated by seeds and still come true to type. Polyembryony seems to have been observed at that very early date.

Qi Min Yao Shu, translated as "important measures to improve the living of people," was written by *Jia Sixie* during the Northern Wei Dynasty (533-544 A.D.). This contains ten volumes. The fourth volume deals with fruit trees. It is a comprehensive compilation of cultivars and cultural practices for a large number of crops grown along the middle and lower reaches of the Yellow River. Passages are cited from 150 sources. Seventeen different kinds of fruit are described giving cultivars, methods of propagation, cultural practices, storage and processing. Notable among the cultivars are a seedless jujube, a peach ripening in winter, a pear with fruit weighing 1.3 kilograms and a large-fruited chestnut. In Volume Ten of *Qi Min Yao Shu*, brief mention is also made of fruits in Central and South China such as litchi, logan, citrus, banana, coconut, carambola, loquat and *Myrica rubra*.

Many of the arts practiced in modern fruit production in the Western world may have had their roots in China. The earliest detailed description of grafting is found in *Qi Min Yao Shu* of the sixth century. Since this volume is an extensive collection of cultural experiences prior to that time, that practice of grafting fruit trees much have preceded the sixth century, though how much earlier is not known. One sentence in the book *Zhou Li Dong Kao Gong Ji* written around 500 to 300 B.C., gives indirect and debatable evidence that grafting may have been practiced at that time. It states, "Tangerines grown in the south of the Huai River, when planted in the north of that river, change to trifoliate orange (*Poncirus trifoliate*)." The Huai is located between the Yellow and the Yangzi rivers. From this sentence it may be inferred that tangerines had, at that early date, been grafted on trifoliate orange, known to be a cold-resistant rootstock. Planted north of the Huai River, the scion cultivar tangerine is killed by low winter temperatures, while the trifoliate orange root stock survives and grows up to be a tree. Should such interpretation prove correct, the art of grafting originated before 500 B.C. This is much earlier than the descriptions of grafting by M. T. Varro in *Rerum Rusticarum*, (36 B.C.), by Columella in *De re Rustica* (60 A.D.), and by Plinius in *Historia Naturalis* (almost 70 A.D.), which are currently accepted in the Western world as the earliest records of grafting.

Other fruit growing arts were practiced at early dates in China. Flower thinning is described for jujube in *Qi Min Yao Shu* It says, "The over abundant flowers should be removed at blossoming time by striking the branches with a pole, otherwise they will not set." Biennial bearing was noted in *Yantielum* (100 B.C.): "With plum and mune, a heavy crop will result in low yield the following year." The importance of pruning is discussed in *Hanfeizi* (about 280-233 B.C.) and the time and methods of pruning in *Shiji* (100 B.C.). Notching, ringing and the bending of branches to promoted flower formation and fruit set were mentioned in *Tsee-ming-yao-su* and have been given reemphasis in the last fifty years.

Fruit Crops in China

Fruit plantations and orchards in China cover about 3.6 million hectares, 32% of which are apples, 16% citrus and 18% pears. These three crops constitute the major cultivated fruits of China. Other economically important fruit crops for which there is improved research include peaches, grapes, jujubes, the Chinese gooseberry or kiwi fruit (named after a bird in New Zealand), litchi, longan and the banana. The limitation of research to this small number of species reflects their importance for China. Between 1950 and 1980, more than 150 cultivars were introduced for the commercial production of deciduous fruit trees in China, among which were 55 apples, 30 pears, 38 peaches and 23 grapes. Fruit trees in China--apples, peaches, pears, grapes, and citrus-- are often planted with other crops, particularly legumes. This builds soil fertility, reduces weeds and provides additional food. Biological control of pests is also enhanced because predators and parasitic insects can find shelter in the ground covers.

The *apple* is the major fruit crop. Total production was 3.8 million tons in 1985 or about one-tenth of the world's supply (Figure 2). It is grown in many places and cultivated over a wide area. Crabapples are planted in the most northern part of China while large apples are grown from Liaoning in the north to Sichuan in the southwest, and from Shandong in the east to Tibet in the west. Shandong and Liaoning

Figure 2. The apple is the major fruit crop of China and cultivated over a wide area.

provinces produce more apples than all other regions, followed by Hebei and Henan provinces. Apple production in China has a bright future because the trees can be planted in mountainous regions as well as on hilly lands in which China abounds.

Research efforts in China have been to increase productivity per hectare and improve dessert and storage quality. The dominant varieties are Golden Delicious, Red Delicious, Starking Delicious, Ralls, White Winter Pearmain, American Summer Pearmain and Jonathan. These varieties have a familiar American ring. Some newly introduced ones are Red Mutant Fuji, Starkrimson and Jonagold.

Like many other countries, China has given much attention to dwarfing rootstocks which provide optional early output per unit land area; but the Malling and Malling-Mertin rootstocks, so commonly used in America and Europe, are not suited to China. They will not withstand the cold winters in North China. Here the Chinese have been remarkably innovative and successful in using species other than the apple (*Malus*) for rootstock grafting. The evergreen shrub *Dichotomanthes tristaniae-carpa*, which grows at altitudes of 1400-2100 meters, is used in Yunnan Province. In the Shanxi Province of North China, two species of cotoneaster (ornamental shrubs with bright red flowers) are used as rootstocks to attain dwarfing and early fruiting. The trees bear earlier and are even more dwarfed than the best of the Malling types.

The *pear* is grown over an even larger area in China than is the apple. Total output, however, is only two million tons, or half as much. Nevertheless, China is number one in pear production with over twenty percent of the world's total. The cold-resistant Ussurian pear (*Pyrus ussuriensis*) group is found in the most northeastern and northwestern regions, while the less cold-resistant White pear (*P. bretschneideri*) is grown in north and northwestern China, and the humidity-resistant Sand pears (*P. pyrifolia*) are grown south of the Yangzi River. The Dangshan, the Ya and the Laiyang pears--the top varieties--are distributed throughout North and Central China. Historically, Chinese pears are sweet and juicy and have crisp-textured flesh, little aroma and, in some, abundant stone cells. These latter are traditionally known in the Western world as "Sand Pears." Some of the goals of breeding are improvement of eating quality, more cold hardiness in the north, and lower chilling requirements in the south. The Bartlett pear, in China called the "Western Pear," has been used in some variety improvement programs to impart its buttery flesh, texture and aroma to native types.

Some of the Asian (Chinese) type pears have become a recent attraction in the U.S.A. Their apple-like appearance and roundness of shape, and their being crisp and juicy with the flavor of a pear when ripe, make them attractive to both consumers and growers. They also ripen on the tree and are ready to eat when you pick them, and come into production earlier than European types.

Pears in China, unlike apples, are all grown on their own rootstocks. No attempt has been made, as in the U.S.A. to use the quince for dwarfing. However, recent reports indicate that another species of pear--*Pyrus xerophila*, which grows wild in the northwest--is a promising dwarfing rootstock. It is deep-rooted and highly resistant to drought and pear rust.

The science and art of pear production in Taiwan has reached a high level. Multiple fruiting of temperate zone pear varieties under essentially tropical conditions has been achieved by a combination of special pruning, grafting and chemical regulator treatments. Up to three fruit crops a year are produced on the same trees.

The *jujube*, a native to China and sometimes referred to as the "Chinese date," has received relatively little attention from research workers but is the third most important deciduous fruit in North and Northwest China (Figure 3). Its production, however, is not as well organized as for apples and pears. They occur as small plots or as individual backyard trees in hill and mountain country and even on alkaline flat lands. Drought near the time of flowering improves fruit set and increases yield. Cropping is markedly biennial with heavy crops in "on" years and little, if any, fruit during "off" years. There are many varieties. They vary in size from 25 to 50 mm. in diameter, with skin colors from green to brown and great differences in flavor, texture and stone size. Harvesting is done by shaking the trees or knocking off the fruit with bamboo poles. The fruits may be eaten fresh, dried or cooked and made into cakes or a form of porridge.

Figure 3. The jujube or Chinese date.

Citrus are the most important fruits in South China. The original home of many citrus fruits, of which there are many domestic varieties and types (large and small, edible and ornamental, may well have been China. They are produced in Sichuan, Zhejiang, Guangdong, Hunan, Guangxi, Hubei, Jiangxi, Fujian, Jiangsu and, in fact, all fifteen provinces and districts south of the Yangzi River. The quality is especially high in the Bashan Mountain area of Sichuan and in the Zhujiang delta of Guangdong. While the potential for production is great, the annual output is only 1.8 million tons. This compares with a U.S.A. yearly output of 15 million tons for oranges and tangerines.

The best type is the mandarin, which constitutes about 70% of China's citrus species and is represented by the varieties "Tankan," "Ponkan," "Hong Gu," "Ben Oi Zao" and "Satsuma." Oranges ("Xinhui," Willow Leaf and "Jin Cheng") in Sichuan account for 27% with pomeloes, kumquats and some newly introduced varieties, such as the Washington Navel and Valencia Orange making up the balance of about 3%. The Chinese much prefer mandarines and tangerines over grapefruit, limes and lemons. Grapefruit are not well liked in China. Many good quality varieties of citrus are grown in Sichuan, Guangdong, Guangxi and Fujian. Pomeloes can be kept for approximately half a year (from October to April) because of the thick layer of "albedo" in the rind. Kumquats are usually preserved in syrup.

Peaches in China are of many types, flesh and skin colors, sizes, and shapes and of varying times for maturity. There are also North China and South China types. White fleshed, brightly blushed types are common during June, July and August in the Shanghai area, Zhejiang, Jiangsu and throughout the provinces in the lower reaches of the Yellow and Yangzi Rivers including the Beijing area. Recent investigations have confirmed that the peach is indigenous to China, that it has been cultivated since antiquity, and that it probably had its origin in the northwest provinces penetrated by the Yellow River.

Peach breeding in China has been centered on early maturing types suitable for processing. A very early peach variety--"Wu-005" or "Shanghai 005"--has been obtained that reaches maturity 56 days after bloom. In the Shanghai area it is harvested in late May or early June. The fruit has white flesh, a semi-cling stone which is soft, and an average weight of 70 grams.

Grapes were introduced, via the Silk Road, into China during the Han Dynasty (second century B.C.). Yearly production has increased substantially (doubled) since 1980 with expansion of the wine industries and improved marketing of the table quality types. Approximately 360,000 tons are now produced annually on about 86,700 hectares in areas north of the Yangzi River. The principal grape producing area remains the Xinjiang Autonomous Region, where excellent raisins from the "Wuhebai" or "Thompson Seedless" are produced. Fresh Thompson Seedless table grapes (*Vitis vinifera*) are harvested in late August and early September and shipped to many of the major cities of China from this world-famous irrigated desert area which centers around Grape Valley of Turpan known as the hottest and lowest elevation spot in China.

Unlike the Thompson Seedless grapes of California, those grown in the deserts of Xinjiang Autonomous Region of China are not now treated with gibberellin to increase the size and quality of the berries. Initially they were treated, but the practice was discontinued because of the lower sugar content. Almost comparable size and berry quality are achieved naturally under the cultural conditions and the favorable grape-growing environment of this region. Grape varieties in this region are not confined to the Thompson Seedless. Many other *V. vinifera* type varieties (those with a delicious flavor and soft crisp skins) were noted as typical of the many seeded and seedless red, blue and white skinned types produced in California and other southwestern areas in the U.S.A.

Wine and table grapes of many varieties and origins are found elsewhere in China. The "Longyan" ("Dragon's Eye") is a purple, late season type grown extensively on the hillsides of North China. It is both a table and wine grape. "Niunai" ("Cow's Nipple") has large conical clusters of yellow grapes of sweet and delicate flavor that ripen in late midseason in the Hebei Province. They are grown principally in Hebei, Liaoning, Shandong, Shanxi, Gansu, Henan, Anhui and Jiangsu provinces and in the Beijing and Tianjin areas.

One of the primary breeding objectives for grapes in China is improved winter hardiness. Crosses of cultivated varieties such as the "Muscat Hamburg," the most important table grape which was introduced many years ago, have been made using *Vitis amurensis* Rupr. as the chief source of resistance. The results are cultivars which will survive temperatures of from -20° to -25°C. To prevent bud freezing in the northern parts of China, the vine of many commercial vineyards must be manually removed from their trellises during the winter months, buried in deep trenches and covered with straw and soil. This is very labor intensive but essential for survival and dependable production.

Hawthorn (*Crataegus pinnatifida* Bunge. var major N.E.Br.), a shrub or small tree about seven meters high having deep red fruit 2.5-3.0 cm in diameter, has been receiving much attention during the past decade. Indigenous to China and with a history of 3,000 years, this fruit tree is widely distributed in the hills of many provinces from the Northeast to the Southwest. Despite the insipid eating quality of the fresh fruit, it is very rich in iron and calcium and its vitamin C content is seventeen times that of the apple. Believed to be an effective cure for the hardening of the arteries and for hypertension, it has been in great demand by the public which, in turn, has promoted a rapid increase in new plantings. Processing methods are diverse. They include the conventional coating of the fruit with crystalline sugar, a favorite of children and teenagers in the winter; jelly cakes, which also have a long history; and more recently, preserving whole fruit in syrup, juice and wine. A nation-wide cooperative research program has been organized to explore superior cultivars with large fruits, high vitamin C content and better processing cultivars with large fruits, high vitamin C content and better processing properties. Meanwhile, experiments are being conducted on improved methods for propagation, on cultural practices which will increase productivity, disease and pest control, and on processing and utilization.

The *Hami melon* is one of the most exotic of fruits in all of China and the world. It is produced as a counterpart of the Thompson Seedless grape in the valleys and depressions around the fringes of the Gobi desert in the Northwest Xinjiang Autonomous Region. These valleys are fed with waters transported through the underground "Kan-Er-Jin" from the snowfields of the Tianshan Mountains. The Hami melon, like the seedless grapes reaches maturity in late August and early September. With its sweetness, aroma, crisp green or yellow flesh, and green or tan, slightly netted rind color, the Hami is unlike the U.S.A. muskmelon. Many domestic and foreign tourists frequent the hot-dry Urumqi (pronounced OO-LOO-MOO-CHE) and Turfan areas in late summer just to eat their fill of these melons. As for taste and texture, they have few equals on earth today. The nearest counterpart in the Western world is the Honeydew melon.

The delectable *Litchi* of the Guangdong, Guangxi, and Fujian provinces grows in large orchards of the south and ripens in late June and early July. The fruit is borne on an evergreen tree, native of subtropical and tropical China, where it has been cultivated for over 3,500 years. It is one of the most attractive and delicious of all fruits (Figure 4). It is still cultivated in its native environment. Super varieties of dessert quality have recently been developed in the Guangzhou (Canton) area that have very small and often only residual seeds. No fruit is more refreshing on a hot summer day. It is easily managed for eating fresh but, as with many tropical fruits, shelf life is very short, even with good refrigeration. The fresh fruit can now be kept longer with controlled atmosphere (CA) storage whereby the carbon dioxide content of the air is increased and the oxygen content greatly reduced.

Future Potentials

There are vast genetic resources of cultivated, semi-cultivated and wild fruits in China. For no food-producing area is the future potential for exploration, conservation, protection, further development and utilization of these resources more exciting.

It would be particularly challenging to explore further such areas of opportunity as improvement of resistance to environmental stresses, competing biological systems, dwarfing potentials, and the differential absorption and accumulation of various mineral nutrients. Under the administration of the Chinese Academy of Agricultural Science, there are three National Fruit Research Institute. The first is Xingcheng in

Figure 4. The litchi fruit is native to subtropical and tropical China.

Liaoning; the second is Zhengzhou in Henan (both are for temperate) zone fruits); and the third is Beibei in Sichuan (for citrus fruits). There is not yet a research institute for tropical or subtropical fruits, nor is there a germplasm repository. Recently, however, a plan for establishing fruit germplasm repositories in selected locations has been initiated by the Ministry of Agriculture, Animal Husbandry and Fishery.

Many opportunities exist in China's northwest for fruit development. In the province of Qinghai and in Tibet, there are also vast fruit germplasm resources hidden in the forests, the mountains and along the rivers. A recent two-year survey in two regions of Tibet produced specimens belonging to 18 families, 33 genera and 106 species and/or varieties of fruit. The more important genera included *Malus* (apple), *Pyrus* (pear), *Prunus* (peach, plum, cherry), *Fragaria* (strawberry), *Rubus* (raspberry) and *Vitis* (grape). Trees of *Prunus mira* more than 1,000 years old were identified with heights of 20 meters and a trunk circumference of 10 meters, growing at altitudes ranging from 1,700 to 4,200 meters. There were also widely distributed species of *Rubus* and *Fragaria*.

Kiwi fruit (*Actinidia chinensis*), usually called "Mi Hou Tao" in Chinese and sometimes "Yang Tao," and formerly called the "Chinese Gooseberry" is an important native fruit of China. The annual yield of kiwi from plants growing in the wilds of China is about 100,000 tons.

Trees producing much larger fruit with higher vitamin C content, have recently been selected, and some chemical growth regulators will also remarkably increase fruit size. While the fruit normally has a hairy surface, a hairless type has also been found. Kiwi is now cultivated on plantations in many provinces in China and has excellent possibilities for an expanding export market. It is probably the most recent of important native fruit plants to have been domesticated. Until 1900, kiwi fruit was just another plant growing wild in the hills and mountains of southern and central China.

The Chinese *Yangtao* (*Averrhao carambola* L.) is also called the carambola. In transverse section, it looks like a star. It is grown primarily in Guangdong and Guangxi. The light green, sometimes yellowish green fruit, is produced on an evergreen tree that grows up to eight meters in height. The fruit is both sour and sweet, agreeable to taste, and the raw product may be used for wine, juice, jam or as a preserved fruit. While the kiwi (*Actinidia chinensis*) is sometimes called "Yangtao" in China, Yangtao is an entirely different fruit from kiwi.

There have been other new developments and discoveries with fruit crops. From the northwest, three new forms of peaches have been reported. One is a hairless flat type with an average fruit weight of 30-45 grams and a clingstone with nonmelting flesh. The other two are varieties not of *Prunus persica* (the common peach) but of P. *ferganensis*, one being flat, the other hairless (no fuzz). All three occur at altitudes between 1000 and 1400 meters. There is still much evidence of great variability in the peach yet to be explored in Northwest China. In the most northern parts of the northeast, there are large areas of "Du-si" blueberries (*Vaccinium uliginosum*), which vary greatly in fruit size, fruit shape and vine height. The fruits are collected for wine making. Much could be done to improve yield and fruit quality. In northwest Xinjiang there are extensive stands of a wild apple (*Malus sieversii*) covering an area of 15,000 hectares. In its natural habitat, it is tolerant of temperatures ranging from -30° to -35°C, and it is drought resistant. Some of the trees are over one-hundred years old.

Production of "wax apples" (*Byzygium Samarangense*, Merr. and Perry) is a recent development. This is a new fruit crop commercially grown in Taiwan. Production for the domestic market expanded almost exponentially from 1980 to 1985. Over 7,000 hectares are currently devoted to its culture. Flowering and fruiting originate from adventitious buds. Manipulations of soil moisture levels, pruning and the use of growth regulators enable near year-round production, with great improvements in appearance and fruit quality.

Considering all fruits now produced in China, the watermelon, if it can be considered a fruit rather than a vegetable, is the most important in total volume consumed. It is grown in every province with the possible exception of Tibet. Clear plastic mulches and row covers are now being used both for earlier production and to extend the northern limits of production. No "fruit" is relished more by the Chinese during the hot summer months (Figure 5). Production has expanded enormously in recent years to an estimated volume of over five billion kilograms in 1985. The area sown in 1986 was one-third over the previous year and an all-time high.

Figure 5. The Chinese love watermelons.

The Chinese love watermelons. They help satisfy the desire the Chinese have for sweets and are a fruit they can afford. New high quality, high-yielding early varieties are being developed to meet the increasing demand. As an example, farmers of thirty-two households in the village of Dali of Shexian County of Anhui Province formed an association in the spring of 1985 to produce (using latest technologies) and market early watermelons. By all counts the project was a success in that 500,000 kilograms were sold beginning June 6 and ending June 22, when all of the crop was gone.

Continued explorations of genetic potentials for the improvement of fruit crops in China is only one promising avenue for the future. The enhancement of cultural techniques for orchards would also be rewarding. Yields of fruit per unit area are still very low and fruit quality could be greatly improved. With China having reached a new stage in its fruit crop industry, there is a need for a revolution in cultural techniques for fruit production and handling. Fruit is still relatively rare and expensive in China, especially in the winter months in the North. Annual per capita consumption, exluding watermelons, is only six kilograms. With the grain, oil seed and cotton needs of the state and society now being exceeded for the first time in recent history (1984 and 1985), new emphasis may well be directed toward increasing the production of fruits, vegetables and animal products.

FOR FURTHER READING

Ferguson, A R. 1984. Kiwi fruit: A botanical review. *Horticultural Reviews* 6:1-64.

The fruits of Taiwan. 1985. Taipei: Provincial Department of Agriculture and Forestry. (In Chinese)

Huang Huibai. 1980. Viticulture in China. *HortScience* 15(40): 461-66.

Menzel, C. M. 1985. Propagation of litchi: A review: *Scientia Horticulturae* 25: 31-48.

Shen Tsuin. 1982. Research on deciduous fruits in China. *Proceedings of the 20th International Horticultural Congress* 1:222-30.

Zhuang Enji; Xu Zhuying; Wu Yuliang; and Cai Xiping. 1982. *The breedings of very early-ripening peaches.* Shanghai: Academy of Agricultural Sciences, Institute of Horticulture.

24

FROM MONKEY HEADS
TO WOOD EARS

by Yu Youtai

China could just as well be called the land of mushrooms as the land of rice, fish, Chinese cabbage and pigs. Mushrooms, in addition to being delicious, have almost no fat, sugar or sodium--the dietary "no-no's" of Westerners. Yet they provide a healthful complex of carbohydrates and fiber. They also contain calcium, iron, potassium, phosphorus, magnesium, thiamine, riboflavin, niacin and folic acid. They are truly a food fit for kings and were called the "divine fruit of immortality" in ancient China. They have become one of the most popular foods in China.

From Gathering to Artificial Cultivation

Mushrooms are large fungi. They are either gathered from the wild or cultivated for eating. At least 300 kinds of edible mushrooms are grown in forests, grasslands and open fields throughout China. As many as 83 types of mushrooms in China are now known to be poisonous. No foolproof method exists for identifying the poisonous mushrooms, so extreme care must be exercised in the gathering of wild mushrooms.

The medicinal value of mushrooms was recorded in ancient Chinese literature before the tenth century. More recently, it has been discovered that some types of edible mushrooms contain substances which improve human health and increase resistance to disease. What the Chinese don't eat for pleasure they will take for medicine. So it is with mushrooms.

The collection of mushrooms for food in China had its historical beginnings in the tenth century. Domestication goes back to the artificial cultivation of "wood ears" in the early seventh to eighth centuries (Tang Dynasty)--almost a thousand years earlier than the first cultivated mushrooms were recorded in the Western Hemisphere (in France around 1700 A.D.). Since China's liberation in 1949, the artificial cultivation of mushrooms for both domestic and international markets has expanded enormously. China now dominates the world export market for cultivated mushrooms.

Monkey Heads

Foreigners are intrigued by the descriptive names of Chinese mushrooms. Two of the most important edible mushrooms are called "monkey heads" and "wood ears"--remarkably fitting names because of their unique shapes.

Monkey head mushrooms (Figure 1) are also called hedgehog fungi. Since the seventh to eighth centuries, they have been collected as food from forests in China. Monkey heads are pulpy, half-spherical or head shaped, and five to twenty centimeters in diameter. They are white in color when fresh, light to brownish yellow when dried, and thorny on the surface. In China, it is said that "mountain delicious the monkey head, and seafood delicious the sea cucumber." The monkey head mushroom together with the sea cucumber, "sea bird's nest" and "bear's paw" are cited as the four most famous delicacies in a Chinese banquet. The monkey head is also the most nutritious of all the mushrooms.

Figure 1. The monkey head mushroom.

Wild monkey heads are scarce and are found mainly in the mountain forests of the northeastern provinces. They grow primarily on the dead branches of broad leaf trees such as oak and walnut. Since the monkey head is an aerobic fungus, it can be found more frequently in the forests where tree density is low, the air circulation is good and temperatures are high. The wild monkey head is found most frequently during August and September.

Chinese scientists have recently succeeded in domesticating monkey heads by cultivating them in wood sawdust, cotton seed hulls, rice stalks and sugarcane bagasse. If properly cultivated, one kilogram of the raw plant material will produce one kilogram of fresh monkey heads. The monkey head fungus is also highly resistant to bacterial diseases. A recent trend toward cultivation by bottle culture further facilitates disease control and ease of operation and management.

Monkey heads are used successfully as cures for digestive disorders and for arresting tumor growth without harmful side effects. Boiled monkey head soap and "monkey head tablets" are sold on the market for such remedies.

Wood Ears

Wood ears (Figure 2) are also called black wood ears. They are the most popular of all mushrooms for Chinese food preparation. Artificial cultivation dates far back in Chinese history and they are currently produced in almost every province and autonomous region.

Figure 2. The wood ear mushroom.

The name derives from the fact that they grow on wood and their shallow dish shape resembles an ear. The fresh wood ear is gummy, semi-transparent, dark brown in color, smooth on the surface and elastic. The diameter of the fresh wood ear is generally five to six centimeters; the largest may reach ten to twelve centimeters. Wood ears grow in clusters on the trunks and branches of broad leaf tree species such as oak, birch, poplar, banyan and scholar. The weight of the dried wood ear is about one-tenth that of the fresh weight. The original shape reappears when the dried wood ear is soaked in warm water.

Wood ears are nutritious, containing a number of amino acids as well as gums. According to Chinese medicine, they provide protection for miners and textile workers as they clear away residues in the stomach and intestines, soothe lung infections and cure hemorrhoids. It has been noted recently that wood ears also hasten blood coagulation or blood clotting and arrest tumor growth.

Wood ears are now produced in the mountainous regions of China by the traditional tree trunk culture method. Tree trunks suitable for wood ear culture are called "ear trees," of which there are numerous varieties in China. The export of black wood ears reached 1,272 tons in 1983, an increase of 31% over 1982.

Other mushrooms closely related to wood ears include the "hair wood ear" and "silver ear." The hair wood ear belongs to the same wood ear genus of fungi as wood ears. They are very similar except that the hair wood ears are thicker, hairy, more brittle and not so tasty as wood ears. They are produced in almost all provinces of China but sold at a lower price than wood ears.

Silver ears (Figure 3), also called white wood ears, have a milky white color. They belong to the silver ear genus of fungi, consist of clusters of petals four to ten centimeters in diamter, and are soft and semi-transparent when fresh. They will shrink when dried but recover their original shape when soaked in warm water. Silver ears, produced mainly in the southern and southwestern provinces of China, are one of the most famous of Chinese traditional medicinal plants. They are widely used as a blood tonic and for nourishing the brain. As a sweet dish for a banquet they are superb. Until recently silver ears were much more expensive than wood ears, but successful artificial cultivation has reduced their cost.

Figure 3. The silver ear or white wood mushroom.

Lingzhi--A Life Saving Mushroom

There is a mushroom known by almost all Chinese even the little children. It is a part of a very famous fairy tale known as "The White Snake." In ancient times, a white snake became a beautiful white queen called Bai Niang Zi and married Xu Xian. During a celebration, Bai Niang Zi drank a bottle of yellow wine and returned to her original snake form. This was so shocking to Xu Xian that he died of anguish. As soon as the queen recovered, she risked death because of her great sorrow to steal a piece of lingzhi, the fairy grass mushroom from the top of Kunlun Mountains which were guarded by the crane and deer fairy spirits. After her husband, Xu Xian, smelled the lingzhi, he came back to life and drank the lingzhi soup. Although no one believes that lingzhi could really rescue a person from death, lingzhi was considered a very rare and valuable medicine, found only among forests on high mountains.

Since lingzhi has now been produced by artificial cultivation, it has become more popular than ever. It has been given the good names of "fortune mushroom," "fairy grass," "longevity mushroom" and "monkey chair," since it is so big a monkey can sit on it.

Lingzhi is dark reddish brown in color and round or heart shaped (Figure 4). Its woodiness and bitter taste defy palatability. It is used for medicine, as an ornament, in wine and for cigarettes. (See Chapter 25, "Plants to Keep People Healthy," for further information on medicinal plants.)

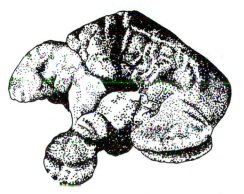

Figure 4. The lingzhi or life saving mushroom.

Other Famous Mushrooms

The koumo (Figure 5), named for the city Zhangjiakou where it originated, is the best mushroom produced in the grasslands of northern China. It is white in color and grown chiefly in Inner Mongolia. Accordingly, it is also often called the white mushroom or the Mongolian mushroom. Koumo is widely distributed in Hebei, the northeastern provinces and Inner Mongolia. During late summer and early autumn these mushrooms break through the soil in large numbers. Their color and thick flesh embellish the landscape with shining white rings in a sea of green grass (see Chapter 5, "The Potentials of Grasslands"). The koumo is small or medium sized and hemispheric in shape with thick, fine flesh and a good taste. It is commonly used in cooking in China and is a traditional export commodity.

Xianggu, meaning the "mushroom with flavor," is one of the most famous artificially cultivated mushrooms (Figure 6). It is flat rather than

Figure 5. The koumo mushroom.

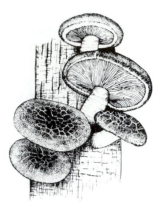

Figure 6. The Xianggu or donggu mushroom.

round and larger than the koumo. The color is reddish dark with a white, thick flesh that is very delicious and deeply flavored. Because it is grown in winter and spring, it is also called "donggu," which in China means "winter mushroom." Wang Zhen's agricultural book of 1313 (see Chapter 2, "Agricultural History Over Seven Thousand Years, Table 2") bears a record of the method for the artificial cultivation of xianggu. Xianggu also grows naturally on the trunks of broad leaf trees and is widely distributed in the southern provinces of China. While it is considered valuable for food, experiments have shown that it also inhibits the growth of tumors.

The caogu or "straw mushroom" is another popular cultivated mushroom with a very long history in China. In the southern provinces during the autumn, it is grown artificially in rice straw where it appears in large clusters. Large and gray or brown in color it is one of the most traditional of mushrooms both in China and in other countries.

Jichong or "chicken meat mushroom" is a wild, medium to large sized mushroom. It has fine meat and is especially delicious when cooked with chicken. "Ji" means "chicken" in Chinese, hence the name jichong. It is brown to dark brown in color, although the most delicious type has a black skin. There is a long history of its collection for food. It is distributed mainly in the southwestern provinces of China.

The huangu or yellow mushroom is another well-known wild type of mushroom widely distributed in China. It is flat, medium sized and yellow in color. Clusters of huangu appear in autumn on the rotten trunks of broad leafed trees.

FOR FURTHER READING

Ding Shuqun. 1964. *Fungi in China.* Beijing: Science Press. (In Chinese)

Du Zijiang. 1974. *Artificial cultivation techniques for edible mushrooms.* 3d ed. Taiwan: Fing Nian Book Series. (In Chinese)

Ying Jianjian, et al. 1982. *Edible mushrooms.* Beijing: Science Press.

25

PLANTS TO KEEP PEOPLE HEALTHY

by Wang Lianzheng

There is a saying that "What the Chinese do not use for food they may well take as medicine." The Chinese make little distinction between food and medicine. What is good for the body is both a food and a medicine. Thus, the Chinese have used plants as sources of medicine for thousands of years. In primitive times human beings, hunting and struggling against nature and often fighting for survival, found that eating some plants protected their bodies against infection, reduced suffering, controlled diseases and healed wounds. After prolonged study and practice, it became known that certain plants could be used to cure diseases, and thus early medical treatments were developed.

Historical

According to ancient Chinese history, three legendary emperors--Fu Hsi, Shen Nong and Huang Di--were associated with the origins of Chinese or herbal medicine. Fu Hsi formulated the Yinyang doctrine of opposites, the cornerstone of Chinese philosophy. Shen Nong was the father of agriculture and credited with the first Chinese *Materia Medica*. It was Huang-Ti, the Yellow Emperor reigning from 2697-2595 B.C., who contributed the treatise *Huang Di Nei Jing Su Wen* which was translated as *The Yellow Emperor's Classic of Internal Medicine*. It was written over 4,000 years ago and is considered the world's oldest extant medical book.

It was during the Western Zhou Dynasty in China that some professional doctors noted for "curing diseases with its poisons" began to appear. Concoctions of herbal medicines and liquors were formulated as drugs.

Many naturally occurring plants in China produce valuable medicines when their culture is altered. Knowledge of these medicines was spread by word of mouth before they were recorded in writing. Some medicinal knowledge appeared in Chinese historical books by the time of the Qin and Han dynasties. Accounts of traditional Chinese pharmacology appeared in an embryonic form as early as the Western Han Dynasty. There were 240 medicines recorded in a book copied on silk found in the Han Tomb of Ma Wang Dui of Changsha.

By the time of the Eastern Han Dynasty, the first complete collection of works on traditional Chinese pharmacology known as the *Compendium of Materia Medica* had been published. Recorded therein were about 365 kinds of Chinese medicines. This document contains a rich and accurate account of the curative effects of various medicines, as well as their medicinal properties, names, and prescriptions. The *Compendium of Materia Medica* also gives a complete account of basic medicinal theories and summarizes medicinal knowledge and experience up to that time. Here is laid the foundation for the development of traditional Chinese pharmacology.

Sometime during the Jin Dynasties and the Liang Dynasty the famous medical scientist, Tao Hongjing, wrote the book *Shen Nong Compendium of Materia Medica Ji Zhu*, which was based on the *Compendium of Matria Medica*. It is divided into seven volumes and records 730 kinds of medicines derived from plants. This book also summarizes developments in traditional Chinese medicines during the 300 years after the Jin Dynasties.

With expanded trade and improved communication, cultures from other countries were introduced into China, along with an influx of herbal medicines. During the Tang Dynasty a total of twenty-two persons contributed to the book *Xin Xou Ben Cao*, also called *Tang Ben Cao*. Divided into twenty volumes, it records 844 kinds of medicines from home and abroad. Its composition and illustrations provided a bilingual textbook and created a new world precedent for the publication of medical works. In 731 A.D., it was introduced to Japan through the book *Yan Xi Shi*. *Xin Xou Ben Cao* became the earliest work on pharmacopoeia, not only in China but also in the world.

Zhen Lei Ben Cao was written in Sichuan Province by the renowned doctor Tang Zhenhui, who finished his works during the Song Dynasty in 1082 A.D. Sichuan was rich in native medicines, and Tang Zhenhui collected a large number of medicinal plant materials and conducted folk prescription experiments there. His work, divided into 31 volumes, recorded 1,746 kinds of medicines and 300 folk prescriptions and greatly enlarged on the content of *Chinese Materia Medica*. Revised three times during the Song Dynasty, this book has a wealth of information on pharmacopoeia and is of great practical value in field work.

The most famous Chinese work on traditional medicines was the *Compendium of Materia Medica* written by Li Shizhen (Figure 1), the celebrated Chinese medical scientist and botanist of the Ming Dynasty. Li Shizhen (1518-1593) was born into an aristocratic medical family from Jichun county in Hubei Province. During his lifetime he summarized the activities of medical sciences from the ancient practices to his time. In preparation of the *Compendium of Materia Medica*, he spent thirty years reading 276 copies of reference materials, 440 volumes of economic history and the historical accounts of hundreds of scholars; collected all kinds of theory; and wrote three drafts. He finished his book in 1578 A.D. and published it in Nanjing in 1596. This two-million word is divided into fifty-two volumes and contains 1,160 maps. It describes 1,892 kinds of medicines, including 374 new ones and 11,096 folk prescriptions and proven recipes. The book, which provides accurate classifications, clear articles and practical uses, is a summary of all herbal medical sciences up to the beginning of the sixteenth century. It was soon circulated to foreign countries and had a tremendous influence not only on medical science but on the development of botany. Aside from its value as a source book for pathology and therapeutics, it gives classifications for vegetable, mineral and mineral products as well as geographical information. In 1606 and again in 1929, it was translated into Japanese, and in 1659 was translated into Latin. It has also been translated into French, German and English.

Figure 1. Statue of Li Shizhen and the flower of *Datura*. Jiangsu Institute of Botany.

The medical scientist Zhao Xuemin of the Tang Dynasty completed *Ben Cao Gang Mu Shi Yi* in the thirtieth Year of Qian Long of the Qing Dynasty (1765 A.D.). This work, divided into ten volumes, recorded 921 different medicines including 716 new ones.

Zhong Yao Da Ci Dian, published in China in the 1970s, describes a total of 5,767 different kinds of herbal medicines, far surpassing the number in the earlier volumes. Chinese traditional medicine stands today as the result of countless centuries of valuable practical experience which should be vindicated by research for enriching modern medical knowledge throughout the world.

Chinese Herbal Medicines--A Brief Listing

A very brief listing of some plants and plant parts, or products of plants, used for medicinal purposes are found in Table 1. It should be emphasized, however, that Chinese remedies usually consist not of one herb but of a principal plant, root or other plant part and at least three or more assorted herbs, roots or other natural products. Several difference medicinal herbs are usually combined to treat a specific disease or disorder. The theory of opposites--"Yin and Yang"-- is used. According to the theory, medicine does not itself cure anything but works to support and assist the organism in healing itself through the use of natural food products. There is a Chinese proverb: "Nature cures the disease, the doctor collects the fee." Occasionally a domestic remedy may consist of a single botanical or other product such as the ginseng root, royal jelly or garlic. The single product, however, is more typical of Western prescriptions and not traditional Chinese medicines.

It may also be noted that among almost all crops and commodities used for food in China, there are those specifically designated as having medicinal properties. References to those are found in many other chapters. Among the fruits are the hawthorn, the loquat and the persimmon. Medicinal vegetables include the onion and garlic. Many species of mushrooms are accredited as having medicinal properties and in ancient times some were even considered life-giving. Rapeseed and sesame seed oils have healthful properties, as do some types of rice. Finally, with food animals one of the chief values of meat from black-boned chickens and rabbits purportedly is their health-giving properties.

Modern Day Assessments

In very modern times (1985) *A Barefoot Doctors Manual* put forth by the government of the People's Republic of China, has been translated into English (see "For Further Reading"). It describes both modern Western medical practices and traditional Chinese methods of diagnosis

TABLE 1
Examples of Traditional Chinese Herbal Medicines
as Related to Modern Usage

Genus and Species	NAMES English	Chinese	Modern Application	Plant Part
Aguilaria sinensis		Peimoshan	Asthma Cardiac	Bark Exudate
Allium sativum	Garlic		Pulmonary disorders Hypertension Reduces infection Cardiac	Bulb
Amomum villosum		Sahlun	Stomach ache	Seeds
Angelica polymorpha and sinensis	Angelica	Tangkuei or Danggui	Analgesic Sedative Boils	Root
Artemisia annua L.		Qinghaosu or Aihao	Malaria	Aerial parts
Begonia finbristipula	Begonia	Zhibeitienquai or Qiuhaitang	Heat or Sunstroke	Leaves
Catharenthus roseus, albus or flairus		Changchunhwa	Anti tumor	All parts especially flowers
Cephalotaxus haenensis		Sanjiansan	Leukemia Lymph node Tumors	Whole plant (stems best)
Chrysanthemum morifolium Ramat.	Chrysanthemum	Chuhua or Juhua	Cold or Influenza	Flowers
Datura metel L.f. alba	Jimson Weed	Naoyanghua	Anesthetic Pain killer	Flowers, roots and leaves
Eriobotrya japonica	Loquat	Pipa	Pulmonary disorders	Fruit
Eucommia ulmoides	Rubber-tree	Tuchung or Duzhong	Hypertension Lumbago	Bark

Genus and Species	NAMES English	Chinese	Modern Application	Plant Part
Ganoderma lucidum	Fortune mushroom	Linzee (Lingzhi)	Nervous breakdown	Mushroom
Gastrodia elata		Tienma	Dizziness Headache	Tuber
Lonicera japonica	Japanese honeysuckle	Chinyen Hua or Jinyinhua	Fever Cold	Flower and vine
Morus alba	White mulberry	Sang	Diuretic Pulmonary soother	Leaves
Panax pseudo ginseng	Ginseng	Jenshen	Old age/ Longevity	Roots
Polygonum multiflorum	Cornbind	Hoshouwu or Hesnouwu	Tonic Turns grey Hair black	All plant parts
Rauvolfia verticillata		Lufumo	Hypertension	Whole plant (seeds best)
Trichosanthes kirilowii maxim		Tienhwafen	Reduce infection	Fruits, seeds
Zingiber officinale	Ginger	Shengjiang or Jiang	Cardiac	Rhizome

and healing. It is particularly timely in coming forth with the dismantling of the collectives and cooperative medical care systems and the emergence of the family responsibility contract initiatives. Some 197 prevalent diseases are described along with a listing of 522 medicinal herbs accompanied by 338 illustrations. Throughout China today there of plants which continue to be evaluated for their medicinal and herbal applications for both man and beast (Figure 2). Many hospitals using traditional medicines have also been set up in almost every province and large city. They are investigating the advantages that may result from the integration of traditional and Western style medicine--another example of the basic Chinese philosophy of "walking on two legs." Much of what has been practiced for centuries in China is now being examined by the modern world's medical professions. A major pharmaceutical company in the U.S.A. is presently conducting research in both the laboratory and the clinic on the possible health-giving and medicinal properties of ginseng as an herbal medicine.

Figure 2. A collection of medicinal plants at a research institute in Hohhot of Inner Mongolia.

FOR FURTHER READING

Anonymous. 1986. Therapeutic value of garlic. *World Farmer's Times* 1(5): 31-32.

Chao Young. 1983. Traditional Chinese medicine. *Plants and Gardens* 39(2): 60-64.

Duke, J. A. 1981. *Medical plants in China*. U.S. Department of Agriculture, Office of International Cooperation and Development, Scientific and Technical Exchange Division. Washington, D.C.: Government Printing Office.

Huxley, A. 1984. *Green inheritance*. Garden City, N.Y.: Anchor Press.

Hyatt, R. 1978. *Chinese herbal medicine: Ancient art and modern science*. New York: Schocken Books.

Klayman, D. L. 1985. Qinghaosu (Artemisinin): An antimalarial drug from China. *Science* 228: 1049-55.

Lucas, R. 1977. *Secrets of the Chinese herbalists*. West Nyack, N.Y.: Parker Publishing Co.

Subhuti Dharmananda. 1986. Royal jelly. *Bestways* 14(2): 38-41.

Xu Huiquang. *Chinese medicinal herbs most in use*. Shanghai: Shanghai Press of Science and Technology. (In Chinese)

26
THREE HUNDRED MILLION PIGS

by Yu Youtai

Pigs Come First in Meat for China

Pigs can be seen everywhere in China. They are about as universal here as are people--in proximity to households, being hauled to market, or as carcasses. They may be raised under the most primitive of conditions or in the most ultra-modern housing. There are now, under the new responsibility production system, many professional pig-raising households that specialize in the full-time raising of pigs.

According to ancient Chinese mythology in the sixteenth to seventh century B.C. there was a specialist in the Chinese Slave Society named Weishi whose expertise was in pig breeding and improvement. And as early as the third century B.C., the physiognomy of domestic animals was recorded in ancient Chinese books. Those observations, together with additional study (including morphology), established ancient methods for measuring the productive performance of domestic animals. These methods were simple and easy to learn but important for improving the quality of the local pig breeds, some of which were of high quality. The earthernware models of the South China Small Ear pig and the Northern China Big Ear pig unearthed recently are typical examples (Figure 1). Pig bones unearthed from ancient ruins date back 6,000 to 7,000 years or more.

Although pig raising in China has had a very long history, it has declined during the past hundred years and decreased significantly during the two decades before the establishment of the new China in 1949, when there were only three-fourths the number of pigs produced in 1934. Since then, pig raising has developed rapidly corresponding with the recovery and development of Chinese agriculture and the rural economy (Figure 2). Although pig production has experienced periodic setbacks since 1949, as reflected by changes in the economic structure of the country, a remarkable upward trend is noted. The number of pigs increased from 50-60 million in 1949 to nearly 300 million in 1975,

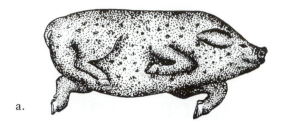

a.

b.

Figure 1. Earthenware models found recently in ruins dating back approximately 7,000 years: *a*, South China small ear pig; *b*, Northern China big ear pig.

where it stabilized for about eight years. The number topped 300 million for the first time in 1978--a fivefold increase in less than 30 years. In 1984, the total number of pigs increased to 306.7 million, and in 1985 to 331.5 million.

According to world statistics, the total number of pigs on earth is about 800 million, of which over 300 million-or 38%-are in China. Of these, only 2% and 7% are owned by the state and collectives, respectively. The balance belongs to individual families, for whom pigs are the primary meat source. World pork production is about 60 million tons, with China accounting for about 16.5 million tons or 27% of the world's supply.

There are other statistics of interest regarding pig production in China. During the decade from 1971 to 1981, the number of pigs worldwide increased by 37.5% and pork production by 43.4%--only a slight increase in the rate of pork production above the number of pigs. In

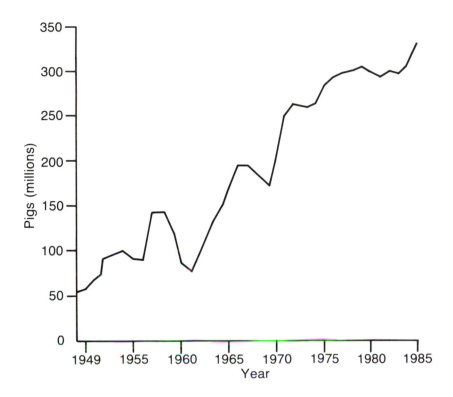

Figure 2. The number of pigs on hand since the establishment of New China.

China, by contrast, the number of pigs increased by only 2.27% from 1976 to 1981 but pork production increased by 78.65%. This increase in pork production with little change in pig numbers continued through 1984. These remarkable increases in pork production suggests a transition from a strong emphasis on numbers of pigs to improved techniques and scientific inputs which have enhanced productivity and the value of individual pigs.

Meat production in China for the year 1985 shows the primary emphasis was on pork production, with sheep and cattle playing very weak seconds (Table 1). In China pork constitutes 94% of the red meat consumed annually. Such statistics do not include ducks, chickens or rabbits.

Chapter 2, "Agricultural History Over Seven Thousand Years" gives the traditional order of importance of the "Six Animals": horses, cattle, sheep, chickens, dogs and pigs. Horses and cattle came first because they

TABLE 1
Number Of Food Animals And Meat Production In China (1985)

	Horses	Cattle	Asses and Mules	Goats and Sheep	Pigs
Number (Millions)	11	87	15	156	332
Meat Production (1000 Tons)	--	373	--	586	16,495

were the main draft animals for thousands of years, and horses were of great military value. Although the pig was last on the list, the statistics above (Table 1)--both in numbers of animals and in total meat production--show the pig is now by far the most important for China. Of the total amount of meat consumed by nations in 1981, exclusive of poultry, the world average for pork was 38.72%. In the U.S.A. it was 28.54%; in the U.S.S.R., 34.11%; in West Germany, 57.86%; and in China, 97.21%. The Chinese are a pork-eating people! While it is now energetically advocated in China to raise grass-eating animals such as cattle, sheep, and rabbits, the pig's leading position as a food animal will not likely change significantly in the decades ahead.

Breeds of Pigs in Different Regions

Within China's vast geographical area, the climatic, agricultural and economic conditions are highly variable. The many indigenous pig breeds now present were developed according to the requirements of regional and local conditions and through long periods of domestication and selection from a wide variety of wild types. China's indigenous pig breeds can be roughly divided into six types according to their origin, distribution, reproductive performance and morphological characteristics. There are, however, up to sixty native breeds of pigs in the whole of China, with only ten being used in swine improvement programs. Their regional distribution is shown in Figure 3.

North. Distribution is over the vast regions north of the Qin Ling Mountains and the Huai River. The climate is rigorous, and feed supplies are limited and not as good as in South and mid-China. Historically, extensive grazing was practiced using a predominance of green and coarse fodders. The combination of open shelters and grazing is still practiced in some places.

The North China pig has a high and large body with sturdy legs, a long mouth, drooping ears, many longitudinal wrinkles on the forehead, a thick skin with many wrinkles, coarse and thick hair and well developed bristles. Most are black in color with fine brown hair that develops in

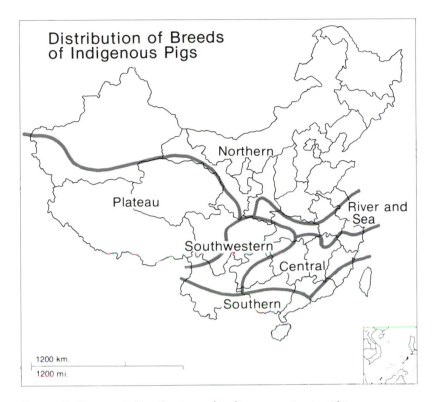

Figure 3. Regional distribution of indigenous pigs in China.

winter to resist the severe cold. Sexual maturity is early and there is good reproductive performance. The sows, which have good nursing ability and a high fostering rate, have about eight pairs of nipples and will mother more than twelve piglets in one litter. They have a firm meat which is highly flavorful. Famous indigenous breeds of this type include the Northeast Ming (Figure 4-A), the Northwest Bamei and the Huanghuaihai Black.

South. Distribution is in the tropical and subtropical regions along the southern Chinese border. In this region three harvests of grain or other crops in a single year may be produced on the same land by growing around the calendar. Thus feed (especially the green and juicy types) for raising pigs is usually plentiful. The South China-type pig is healthy and strong and of early maturity. It has a short, round body with a swayback, thin skin and hair, little bristles and upright or level ears. Most are black

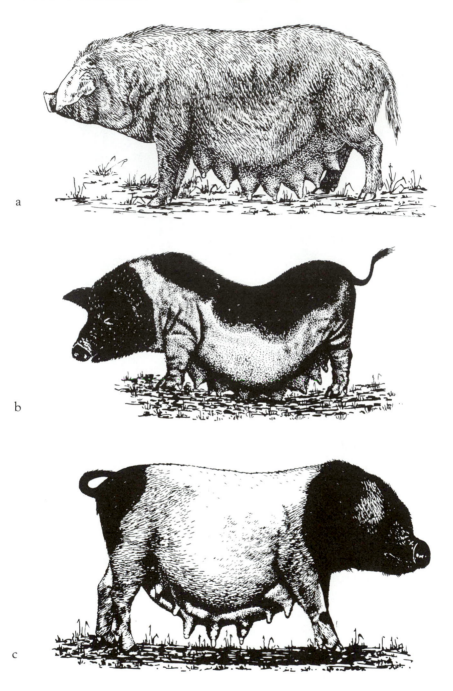

Figure 4. China's indigenous pig breeds: *a*, The Northeast Ming pig; *b*, The Guangxi Small Spotted pig; *c*, The Zhejiang Jinhua pig.

Figure 4. China's indigenous pig breeds: *d*, The Jiangsu Taihu pig; *e*, The Sichuan Rongchang pig; *f*, The Zang pig.

or black and white. They are easy to fatten and have a finely textured meat. Sexual maturity is early but they are much less prolific than the North China type. Sows have five to six pairs of nipples and can support only eight to eleven piglets per litter. Well-known breeds of this type include the Tainnan Small Ear, the Fujian Huai, the Guangdong and Guangxi Small Spotted (Figure 4-B) and the Hainan.

Central. Distribution is in the region between the Yangzi River and the Tropic of Cancer or in south Central China. These pigs have a cylindrically shaped body which is larger than the South China type with its sunken back and waist, short legs and drooping belly. Central China pigs have thin hair, and larger and more drooping ears than the South China type. They mature early and are easy to fatten. Most are black and white in color. Reproductive performance is intermediate between the North and South China types. Sows have 6 to 7 pairs of nipples and will sustain 10 to 12 piglets in one litter. The piglets grow rapidly and have meat of a fine texture. Famous indigenous pig breeds of the this type include the Guangdong Big White Spotted, the Zhejiang Jinhua (Figure 4-C), the Hunan Ningxiang and the Central China Two Top Black.

River and seashore. Distribution is mainly along the middle and delta regions of the Han and Yangzi rivers and the southeast shore including the west plain of Taiwan. The shape is intermediate between the North and Central China types. They have black hair with occasional white spots, a broad forehead, many diamond-shaped wrinkles, long and big drooping ears and a flat or slightly sunken back and waist. Sexual maturity is early, and they are the most prolific of all Chinese pigs with the highest reproductive capacity. They have more than eight pairs of nipples and give birth to thirteen or more piglets per litter. It is not unusual to have more than twenty piglets in one litter. Famous indigenous breeds include the Jiangsu Taihu of the Tai Lake valley (Figure 4-D), the Taiwan Taoyuan, the Zhejiang Hongqiao and the Jiangsu Jiangquhai.

Southwest. Distribution is mainly in the Sichuan Basin and the Yun Gui Plateau. These pigs have big heads, short and sturdy legs and foreheads. Other features include whirling hair, horizontal skin wrinkles, swaybacks and curved bellies. Most are entirely black or "six white" (one white spot for each leg, the tail and the forehead), but some have black and white or red hair. They give birth to eight to ten piglets per litter. The indigenous breeds include the Sichuan Neijiang, the Sichuan Rongchang (Figure 4-E), Guizhou Guanling, and the Wujin in the Yun Gui Chuan contiguous areas.

Plateau. Distribution is mainly in the Qing Zang Plateau, at elevations of more than 3,000 meters and in very cold, dry climates. They graze the year around since more concentrated feed resources are in very short supply. They are small in size, and have short, sturdy legs; a long and pointed mouth; small, erect ears; a slightly bent back, tight belly, and

sloped buttocks; a thick skin with long dense hair; and well developed and elastic bristles interspersed with fine hair. Sexual maturity is late. Sows of this type have five pairs of nipples and usually give birth to five to six piglets per litter. They are the least prolific pig type in China. Distribution is, however, over a vast area. There are only a few indigenous breeds of this type in the region. The Zang (Figure 4-F) is the most typical.

Successful International Exchange of Pig Breeds

China's indigenous pigs are famous worldwide for their early sexual and growth maturities, ease of fattening, utilization of coarse fodder feeds, resilience to adverse environments, high quality meat and the prolific reproductive capacities of some breeds.

During the third century B.C., the Roman Empire imported a large number of South China breeds to improve their indigenous breeds. The result was a much improved Roman breed which later had great impact on the breeding and selection of the now famous Western English breeds, including the Yorkshire and Berkshire. These were hybrids of the indigenous pigs and the Chinese Guangdong pig introduced at the beginning of the eighteenth century. Less than one century later, breeds with Chinese parentage have replaced almost all the indigenous English breeds. The Poland-China and the Chester-White were also the results of crossing with Chinese pigs which were introduced into the U.S.A. at the beginning of the nineteenth century. These famous pig breeds of Chinese parentage have had an important impact on pig breeding throughout the world, contributing significantly to modern day pig genetics and to global pig production.

China has also utilized many important pig breeds from other countries since the end of the nineteenth century. Among them are the Berkshire, the Yorkshire, the U.S.S.R. Big White and the Landrace. These breeds have had a significant influence on modern day pig enterprises in China. China has recently introduced from abroad large numbers of the Duroc and Hampshire breeds.

Berkshires were introduced into China from England at the beginning of the twentieth century. Desirable characteristics are the "six white" hair spots and strong adaptability. They are now widespread in China and have combined well when crossed with Chinese indigenous breeds. Several new pigs breeds have been developed by such crosses and include the Northeast Xinjin, the Fuzhou Black and Ningxia Black.

The Yorkshire pig was also introduced into China at the beginning of the twentieth century. After domestication, crossing and selection, many new Chinese breeds were developed such as the Shanghai White (Figure 5-A) and the Xinhuai.

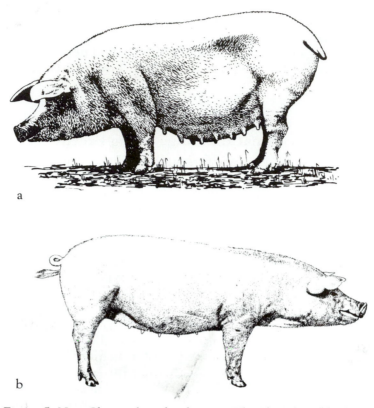

Figure 5. New Chinese breeds of pigs: *a*, The Shanghai White pig; *b*, The San Jiang White pig.

The U.S.S.R. Big White or simply the U.S.S.R. White and the Kemerove were introduced into the northeastern region of China in 1950 and 1958, respectively, and then to other regions. After crossing with indigenous breeds and further selection, significant improvements were obtained. For example, the U.S.S.R. Big White played an important role in developing the Harbin White, the Yili White and the Hanzhong White. Crossing native breeds with the Kemerove produced the Northeast Spotted breed.

The Long White, originally named the Landrace, was introduced into China in 1964. Since it has an especially long body with all white hair, it is commonly called the Long White pig. It is now widely distributed in both the northern and southern parts of China. The impacts of crossing vary with different feeding conditions. The Long White has played an important role in breeding the first new meat type, called the San Jiang (Three-River) White (Figure 5-B).

On the basis of biological and economic traits of Chinese indigenous pig breeds, Professor Xu Zhengying of the Northeast Agricultural College in Harbin has pointed out that the traits of early sexual maturity and obvious estrus should be preserved in modern day pig breeding. The potentials for improving world pig production by retaining and utilizing such beneficial traits in cross breeding are great. Some Chinese indigenous pig breeds have an extremely strong adaptability to adverse conditions compared with present world-famous breeds. Such traits will be found highly beneficial in developing pig industries in third world countries. Also, the better quality of the meat in taste, flavor and texture, resistance to both cold and heat, the obvious estrus and especially docility would be of great value for the development of flourishing pig industries in many countries.

Traditional Chinese Experiences in Raising Pigs

The "Poor Method." Because of the large amounts of green and coarse (vegetative) feedstuffs consumed, this method is in contrast to the so-called "rich method" of raising pigs using fine or rich feedstuffs (grains) and thus neglecting cost considerations.

As early as the third century A.D., there was criticism of the "rich method" of raising pigs. In agricultural reports published in the seventeenth century, cost-accounting studies provided great detail to illustrate that the "rich method" of raising pigs used by feudal nobles and landlords was not economically sound. Meanwhile, the broad masses of people had been raising pigs by "poor methods" suitable to local conditions, which had resulted in many worthwhile observations. For example, it was pointed out (see reference to *Fan Shengzhi's Book*, written at the end of the first century B.C., in Chapter 2, "Agricultural History Over Seven Thousand Years" that the flesh of melons could be used a feedstuff for pigs. In Jia Sixie's book, *Key Skills for People*, published in the sixth century A.D., many detailed experiences on pig culture were recorded. It was emphasized that the limited fine feedstuffs (grains) should be used for piglets following weaning and for pigs housed for fattening. In between, grazing and edible herbs and weeds should be used insofar as possible with a minimum of fine feedstuffs. These methods are not only economically sound for raising pigs, but also most appropriate for meeting nutritional requirements.

Experiences in China have shown that the development of pig production was dependent, first of all, upon adequate feedstuffs. Wherever and whenever the problems of the feed supply are solved according to designated standards, pigs for breeding stocks have a greater reproductive capacity. For fattening, they will have a greater rate of gain in weight and will sell at a premium price. The traditional Chinese approach in solving the feedstuff supply problem for pigs is the recognition that pigs are omnivorous animals which eat both animal and vegetable products. The "poor method" of raising pigs is encouraged on the basis of both efficiency in crop production and good animal husbandry.

The "poor method" can be summarized in five words: "reserving," "planting," "collecting," "storing" and "processing."

"Reserving means to reserve or save certain amounts of grains and legumes (beans) for fine feedstuffs.

"Planting" means to plant green and juicy feed plants, especially for pigs. Green feeds are numerous and vary with different locations in China. They include many aquatic plants, leafy plants such as the sweet potato, green manure plants, and green cut soy beans and corn plants. The juicy feeds include many kinds of root and tuber plants such as the sweet potato, different types of squashes and melons, and various waste and cull fruits, melons and squash.

"Collecting" means to collect various kinds of herbs, terrestrial or land weeds, aquatic weeds, tree leaves and fruits.

"Storing" means to ensile and to use fermented and dry feeds for winter and spring time.

"Processing" means to use for pig feed the byproducts of processing agricultural products such as in grain processing, oil pressing and starch manufacturing; sugar plant residues and byproducts; and winery and bean curd by-products. All of the above are important sources of feedstuffs for pigs in China.

Raising Pigs for Collecting Manure. Raising pigs for supplying manure is an unalterable principle everywhere in China. In Chapters 2 and 9, "Agricultural History Over Seven Thousand Years" and "Organic Farming--Growing Plants the Organic Way," it is emphasized that use of organic fertilizers is one of the significant historical characteristics of Chinese agriculture. The most important source of organic fertilizer in China is pig manure, with a mature pig producing approximately two metric tons per year. The production of farm crops requires not only large amounts of various nutrients but also large amounts of organic matter. Both are found in pig excrement and urine. The raising of pigs for the production of manure is one of the radical approaches used to raise soil fertility levels and improve crop yields. The pig is actually used as a pipeline or conduit to convert or digest coarse vegetation and other materials to a well rotted mix that will fertilize crops for food production. Water hyacinth is a good example of coarse vegetation being converted to something useful. While it is considered a noxious weed choking waterways in the U.S.A., in China it is managed, harvested, dehydrated and used as a feed supplement for pigs. Thus, raising pigs for the production of manure embodies a complete cycle for utilizing as well as improving land and water resources.

There are many methods for collecting pig manure. The most commonly used is to bed down animals with dry soil and straw to reduce loss of water (urine) and gaseous ammonia. Another method involves enclosing the manure piles with mud or plastic to make waterlogged composts.

An additional type of integrated farming system or cycle is very commonly used in the southern part of China. Pigs are produced for both farm products and byproducts (Figure 6). The droppings or pig excrement and urine are cycled to fish ponds and fed to fish. The ponds are later drained and the pond mud is used to fertilize the soil, thus increasing crop production.

Figure 6. An integrated pig farming system.

Castration Techniques. Castration of pigs has been used extensively for several thousands of years in the Chinese countryside. Castration improves both the quality and flavor of the meat and increases the rate of feed conversion. The "cutting off of the ovary of the little sow" or spaying of females is also common practice, the technique being both simple and effective. The practice is welcomed and widely practiced by farmers as it is performed quickly (in one or two minutes) with simple tools and with no technical assistance.

Records of castration are found in the most ancient of Chinese characters inscribed on bones and tortoise (land-roving turtle) shells. It is believed that primitive castration techniques were invented early in the sixteenth century B.C. in China and used extensively thereafter. There is a tradition that the first man who castrated animals was Shao Hao, a mythological character of the New Stone Age too far back to verify.

Drying and Curing Techniques. Drying and curing techniques for preserving pork were developed in the primitive Chinese society of 4,000-5,000 years ago. In *Key Skill for People* (Jia Sixie), a special chapter is found on how to dry and cure meat (see Chapter 2, "Agricultural History Over Seven Thousand Years"). Many specialized methods created in different regions were handed down through generations. Among the most famous of the dried and cured meats are the Jianghua ham, the Rongfeng ham and Sichuan bacon, produced in the Zhejiang, Yunnan and Sichuan provinces, respectively.

Applying Modern Techniques to Raising Pork Production

To satisfy an ever-increasing demand for both quantity and quality, China's goal is to increase pork production using less grain by combining traditional experience with ultramodern technologies. The basic aims are to increase significantly 1) meat yield per pig, 2) human productivity, and 3) economic returns, while sustaining or even reducing the number of pigs.

To increase the production of pork, the main approach will be to increase the number of litters per sow per year and the number of weaned piglets, the number of fattened pigs for sale, the carcass weight of each butchered pig, and the percentage of lean meat.

One of the ultramodern technologies is artificial insemination for rapid genetic improvement, which is now universal for pigs in China but has made only a small beginning in the U.S.A. Through this technique only genetically superior boars are used for breeding purposes.

Improved labor productivity will come from an increase in feed production and improvement of feed-processing industries, increased levels of mechanization in feeding and total industrialization of the pig industry. China has a long history of low grain supplies for human consumption, with little grain available for livestock feeding. With grain self-sufficiency being achieved and surplus production now a reality, an expansion of livestock production is now a top government priority. There is currently a big expansion in China's processed feed industry with increasing availability of feed grains, most of which go for pig production. It started in the mid-1970s along with the increased number of mechanized poultry and pig farms. The country's first compound feed mill was designed and built in Beijing in 1976. The pig sector which has contributed about 94% of the red meat output in recent years consumed 45 million tons of grain in 1980 and about 60 million in 1984 for an estimated 60% of the total mixed feed produced, the balance going mostly to poultry and fish. These averages, however, are still far less than the amounts of grain used for hog production in the U.S.A. Nevertheless, much of the increase in pork output in China can be attributed to the increasing availability of feed grains and the elimination of fixed pork prices at the beginning of 1985. Improved economic returns in the furuter will also be the product of better standards and price policies for purchasing pigs for the producers.

FOR FURTHER READING

He Kang, ed. 1980, 1981, 1982, 1983. *Chinese agricultural yearbook*. Beijing: Agricultural Press. (In Chinese)

Hoefer, J. A., and P. J. Tsuchitani. 1980. *Animal agriculture in China*. Committee on Scholarly Communication with the People's Republic of China Report no. 11. Washington, D.C.: National Academy Press.

Shanxi Agricultural Universtiy, and Jiangsu Agricultural College. 1982. *Raising pigs*. Beijing: Agricultural Press. (In Chinese)

Tuan, F. C. 1986. *China's livestock sector* (draft). U.S. Department of Agriculture. China Section. Asian Branch, International Economics Division. Economic Research Service. Washington, D.C.: Government Printing Office.

U.S. Department of Agriculture. Economic Research Service. 1985, 1986. *China outlook and situation reports*. Washington, D.C.: Government Printing Office.

Xu Zhengying. 1985. On the biological and economical traits of ten Chinese indigenous breeds of swine. *Pig news and information*. Commonwealth Agricultural Bureau, U.K.

Zhang Zhongge. 1980. Accomplishments in pig raising science and technology of my country. *Chinese ancient science and technology of agriculture*. Beijing: Agricultural Press. (In Chinese)

27
CHICKENS, DUCKS, GEESE AND RABBITS GALORE

by Wang Lianzheng

There are more domesticated chickens, ducks, geese and rabbits in China than in any other country. They also appear to be of greater diversity. Chickens range from San Huang (the "Three Yellows") to those that have black meat and bones. Ducks include the Beijing, Grass Muscovy and other species, as well as, Shitou Lionhead geese. As a source of animal protein for the Chinese people, poultry products are second only to pork, and rabbits now follow poultry. Rabbits, which have long served as meat producers, are now also being raised for fur, wool, and even medicine.

Of the poultry in China, scarcely more than ten percent are ducks and geese. The total number of poultry in 1984 was estimated at 1.67 billion with retail sales of 305 million. They are predominately laying hens, of which China produces over twenty percent of the world's total. This is about equal to its percentage of the world's people. The numbers of poultry have increased rapidly since 1980, and egg production went from 2.8 million tons in 1982 to 5.3 million tons in 1985, exceeding (1985) production in both the U.S.A. and the U.S.S.R. This represented almost a doubling of production in three years. Egg production increased by 23 percent from 1984 to 1985. Leading provinces in poultry (egg) production are Shandong, Henan, Hunan, Sichuan, Guangdong and Jiangsu.

Most Chinese families now eat eggs daily. They are prepared in many ways and are used in soups and other traditional Chinese dishes. They are also pickled and served at banquets. In many provinces, especially in the south and in Central China, brown-shelled eggs are preferred over the white. Current per capita consumption of eggs in China is about one-third that of the U.S.A. The raising of chickens for their meat alone is just beginning to develop.

Until recently, poultry production has been largely a household, backyard activity. Modern facilities and confinement housing both for egg production and broilers may now be observed, on some state farms and around large urban centers such as Beijing. Feathers from the chickens and down from ducks and geese now constitute a major export item for the Chinese--and a major import item for the U.S.A.

CHICKENS

Breeds and Types

Many breeds of laying hens are found in China. Some resemble the White Leghorn so commonly found in other parts of the world and appear to be selections from it. The Harbin White and Beijing White are among them. The Leghorn type predominates in North China. The white-feathered Leghorn type of breeds have a high performance, producing 230 to 250 eggs per laying hen per year. Another chicken breed, introduced into North China in 1981 by the Canadian Shavers Company, is the Shingburo Hybrid 579. It consists of four lines of a medium-sized laying bird. The males have brown feathers, the female white. Another breed of laying hen is the Rose. It was introduced from Britain by the Shanghai Breeding Stock Farm in 1981. It is of medium size and is found in East and South China.

A somewhat exotic and unusual breed is the "New Yangzhou" chicken. It was developed at Yangzhou in the Jiangsu Province from a local species and is used for both meat and eggs. It is also called the "Three Yellows" and has gained fame in the Yanzi River basin and in Guangzhou. Consumers in Hong Kong prefer it above other breeds. It has yellow feathers, yellow legs and a yellow beak (Figure 1). A fourth yellow could be added because it produces yellow brownish eggs.

All meat chicken breeds in China have been introduced from other countries. They include the Shingburo from Canada, propagated in Harbin and Shanghai, and the "AA" from West Germany and the U.S.A. Meat chickens in China are produced mainly in or near the large cities along the eastern coastal areas.

White turkeys have only recently been introduced into China. There were no white-feathered turkey flocks prior to 1980, although there were a few broad-breasted bronze. As yet, they play no significant economic role as a domestic source of meat or for export. Turkey production is being considered, however, because the birds grow rapidly and can be ranged with very little shelter.

BLACK-BONED CHICKENS

Origin

Unlike the mythological sphinx of ancient Egypt, the modern day Chinese "Black-Boned Chicken" and "White Phoenix Pill" are real.

Figure 1. The New Yangzhou or "Three Yellows" chicken.

The black-boned chicken, recognized internationally as a standard breed, is also called the Silk-Feather, or the Taihe or Wushan chicken as it originated in Wushan, Taihe County of the Jiangxi Province.

Uses and History

Black-boned chickens, increasingly known for both their nutritional and medicinal values, have a long history of use in China. A thousand years ago in the Tang Dynasty the "White Phoenix Pill," derived from black-boned chickens and a symbol of longevity, was used as a medicine for the women of imperial families. In the Qing Dynasty, the Palace Pharmacy *Tong Ren Tang*, carefully prescribed traditional Chinese medicines including the "Black-Boned Chicken" and "White Phoenix Pill." Some of the conditions for which black-boned chickens are considered an effective treatment or cure include: anemia, asthenia, deterioration of the organ functions, loss of memory, insufficient body fluids, hepatitis, irritability, thirst, irregular menstruation and constipation. They reportedly also promote rapid recovery after an illness.

Characteristics

Black-boned chickens have ten distinctive characteristics: a Phoenix comb, green or blue ears, silk feathers, five talons, feathered legs, a black skin, black bones, black meat, a tasseled head and a growing beard

(Figure 2). Because of their many unique features, they are in great demand and widely distributed in foreign countries. They are classified as playing (pet) pattern chickens. Black-boned chickens move slowly and in a crouching position, preferring flat ground rather than elevated positions. They are timid, easily frightened, and appear to be very sensitive creatures.

Figure 2. The black-boned chicken.

The black-boned chicken's body is frail and small; its bones tenuous. It has a lower digestive function (lower feed conversion rate), less than usual disease resistance, limited adaptability, and a lower incubation rate than regular breeds of chickens. It is not easy to manage, and care must be exercised in all operations. Nevertheless, its hatching ability is very high.

The adult body weight of the cock is 1.25 to 1.5 kilograms. Hens weigh 1.0 to 1.25 kilograms. When commercially produced for meat, the black-boned chicken reaches 0.75 to 1.0 kilograms at four to five months of age, when it is marketed. Adult hens lay 70 to 90 eggs per year. The average egg weight is 35 to 45 grams, and the egg shell is a light brown color.

Approximate daily growth rates for chicks are give in Table 1.

TABLE 1
Rates of Gain and Body Weights
of Black-Boned Chickens

Age in Weeks	Rates of gain per day (Grams)	Approximate Total Weight (Grams)
1 - 2	1	---
3 - 4	2	129
5 - 8	4-6	384
9 - 17	8	715
18 - 21	---	906

At 132 days of age, the hens begin to lay eggs. Egg production peaks at about 188 days; 15 to 20 days after the peak laying, rates may be at 30% but decrease sharply thereafter. The egg-layig period is of short duration. After a black-boned chicken has laid 20 eggs, it begins to incubate and wants to become a brooding hen. If a delay in this brooding instinct could be achieved, egg production would be greatly increased.

Black-boned chickens require complete feed rations both day and night; the more frequent the feeding, the better. The feed is cooked for young chickens, while fresh wet feed can be used for adults. These chickens require a constant supply of drinking water and seek out well aerated shady spots, where they adapt to group rearing. Black-boned chickens raised in the northern provinces require supplementary lighting during the winter to extend the length of day. Eighty percent of the black-boned chickens currently survive to 120 days of age. Good management should increase this survival rate, as well as the current 80% dressing-out rate. Black-boned chickens are slaughtered and marketed between 120 to 150 days of age.

DUCKS AND GEESE

Ducks abound in China, crowding the waterways, ponds and lakes. They are attractive to old and yound, and fill important niches in the economy for pest control, the environment and the food chain. Like ducks, geese are also prominent in China as the Chinese relish the eggs and meat of both. While many breeds of ducks and geese are found in China and the "Gao You duck" is famous nationally and internationally for its eggs and meat, nothing approaches in fame the Beijing duck (Figure 3) with its worldwide renown as a favorite among all Chinese and as a delicacy. One of the highlights in China is to visit the Beijing Duck Restaurant in Beijing and partake of the delectable morsels that are served daily.

Figure 3. The Beijing duck.

History

China was one of the first countries to domesticate wild ducks. Over two thousand years ago, the word for wild duck--pronounced "Wu"-- was recorded in the ancient books for the Zhou Dynasty. People in ancient times called the wild duck either "Wu" or "Yieji." During the Northern Wei Dynasty (386-534 A.D.), Jia Sixie described duck raising methods in detail in his famous agricultural book *Qi Min Yao Shu*. He suggested, for instance, that 1 to 5 was the best ratio of male to females, and that ducks 60 to 70 days of age were the best for meat purposes. He also described at that early date a method for force-feeding ducklines. Thus, duck-raising technologies were well developed 1,400 years ago.

During the Ming Dynasty, the technology for raising ducks was further perfected. Another famous Chinese scientist, Li Shizhen, recorded the following in *Ben Cao Gang Mu* (Compendium of *Materia Medica*). According to the studies of *All Things on Earth*, it reads:

> Drakes have green heads and graceful wings and female ducks have yellow spots. Some female ducks are pure black or pure white. The ones that have white color and black bones are good for medicine. All drakes crow huskily and female ducks crow sonorously. After the Double Ninth Festival (9th day of the 9th lunar month), duck's meat becomes fat and delicate. But after Pure Brightness (5th solar term) ducks lay eggs and become emaciated.

Li Shizhen goes on in this remarkable book, devoted to classifications of living things and to medical science, to give a minute description of types of ducks, sex identification and artificial hatching methods. The record reveals that even in the Ming Dynasty, duck raising was widespread.

BEIJING DUCKS

Origin

There is nothing more uniquely Chinese than the Beijing duck. As a roasted delicacy, no food has attained greater popularity with visitors from abroad, the elite at home and the masses. Roasted Beijing duck is truly the flagship of Chinese cuisine.

The history of the Beijing duck, according to known records and documents, goes back more than three hundred years. In the fifteenth century, the capital of the Ming Dynasty was moved from Nanking (Nanjing) to Peking (Beijing). To transport grain from the southern Yangzi River area northward, large numbers of laborers were forced to repair the Grand Canal. Great quantities of grain were spilled along the banks of the canal. The peasants along the canal used this grain to raise ducks. Thus, from this unusual diet the body form and meat quality of what was to become the Beijing duck was greatly improved.

There are two different accounts of the origin of the Beijing duck. One reports that boatmen along the Grand Canal brought white ducks from the south and domesticated them in Beijing; the other records that the Beijing duck originated from a "small white-eyed duck" or the "White Hepu Duck" produced in the Chao Bai River located in the eastern suburbs of what is now Beijing. In the Ming Dynasty some of these ducks were moved to Yuquanshan Mountain region, now in the western suburbs of Beijing, and were raised there. Both "Western Beijing Rice" and "Beijing Ducks" were reserved for the use of the emporer. There are rich water resources, luxuriant grasses and an abundance of fish and shrimp near Yuquanshan. This area is also surrounded on the northern and western sides by mountains which keep out the cold winds from the north. Most of the river water originates from springs and has a relatively constant, moderate year-round temperature. These year-round conditions of suitable climate, water, luxuriant grasses, and food resources were an ideal environment for what was to become of the Beijing duck. Through careful breed selection over a long period of time, the quality and produtivity of the ducks were gradually improved.

Dissemination

Prior to 1949, the raising of Beijing ducks was a small scale endeavor confined largely to the Yuquanshan area, the City Moat Zone and the Chao Yiang Men Wai. In 1926, there were only three hundred duck-raising families producing about 4,500 breeding ducks. After 1949, several million force-fed ducks were produced each year in Beijing.

Beijing ducks are now produced not only in Beijing but throughout all of China. Since 1973, for example, the Yian Jia Gang farm located in Harbin, Heilongjiang Province introduced a large number of breeding Beijing ducks from Beijing and has been in continuous production since then. These Harbin-Beijing ducks are cold-tolerant, disease-resistant and highly adaptable. Epidemic diseases have been no problem on this farm since it was established. In Harbin, egg production per Beijing duck per year is 165 or 14.8 kilograms. This compares with the daily production of the local Sheldrake duck breed of only 80 eggs or 6 kilograms per year. In addition to Heilongjiang, Beijing ducks have now been popularized and mass-produced in many provinces, municipalities, and cities. They have become a treasure trove in Chinese poultry husbandry.

More than a hundred years ago, Beijing ducks found favor in many other countries. They were introduced into the United States and in 1873. Reports from Japan recorded that Beijing ducks were introduced there in 1888, and they finally reached the Soviet Union in 1925. Meanwhile, Soviet breeders developed a "Moscow White Duck" by hybridizing Beijing ducks with the British Khaki-Campbell ducks.

Beijing ducks have now become an important breed throughout the world because of their productivity and adaptability. Many countries have used the Beijing duck to hybridize with their indigenous duck breeds, thus greatly improving local selections. For example, the Australian Shiagao duck, prized for its superior meat production capabilities, was developed from crosses with the Beijing duck.

Uses of Beijing Duck

Meat. The Beijing duck is particularly valued throughout the world for its delicate meat. Roasted Beijing duck is classified internationally as one of the finest foods. Large quantities of Beijing force-fed frozen ducks are now shipped to many foreign countries. Foreign visitors in Beijing should not fail to visit the Quan Ju De Roast Duck Restaurant, the shrine of Beijing's best known dish (Figure 4). Roasted Beijing duck is also a delicacy among the Chinese people.

Figure 4. The Quan Ju De Roast Duck Restaurant in Beijing.

Eggs. Beijing duck egg production is almost equally as important as the popularity of its meat. Egg production for breeding flocks averages from 50 to 200 eggs per duck per year, while some ducks lay 300 or more eggs per year. Female ducks can, on the average, lay 230 eggs per year and may be retained for egg laying for three years. This egg-laying capacity of the Beijing duck is equal to or exceeds the best of the flocks of laying hens or chickens in the United States.

Pest Control on Crops. Ducks serve a third very important purpose, in that they fill an ecological niche in the food and agricultural systems of China. In addition to providing meat and eggs, they are raised for the biocontrol of insects, being a natural enemy of insect pests that devastate crops (especially rice) and more specifically of the brown planthoppers which destroy rice. An example is given for what was the Pu Feng Township, Yuanjiang County of Hunan Province. Here scientists dissected 25 ducks following their grazing in a rice paddy field and found, on the average, 27 rice delphacids, 636 rice leafhoppers, 40 larva, pupa and adults of lepidoptera, and 20 mole-crickets and beetles in the gullet of each duck. Also, at the Qi Yiang Rice Disease and Insect Control Experimental Station of Qi Yiang County, 13 young ducklings under 0.5 kilograms in weight were dissected and 206 insects on an average were found in the gullet of each. As many as 712 insects were found in the gullet of one duck. Another accout from the Meizhitang No. 1 production team of the former Pu Feng Township reports that 700 ducks were herded into a field of 20 mu (1.33 hectares). After six hours the density of insect populations in the paddy fields was decreased by 88%. Thus, ducks directly control insects that infest crops-- a unique biological control and an approach that saves pesticides, labor, power and money. It also reduces environmental pollution, lessens human health hazards, and provides a high protein feed supplement for the ducks which in turn makes a part of the human food chain. Appropriately, the ducks are called "living insecticides" (see Chapter 30, "Warring with Pests").

A Source of Soil Fertility

Each mature duck can produce 150 grams of droppings (manure) per day and more than 50 kilograms per year. Duck excreta is high in phosphorus, and when used as a fertilizer for crops can play an important role in preventing flower and fruit drop, reducing excessive vegetative growth, and hastening maturity with earlier fruiting.

Other Beijing Duck Uses

More extensive utilization of duck products in China has promise for the future. Duck feathers and down can be used for down coats, eiderdown quilts and other duck down products. Duck skin can be used to make gelatin. The brain, blood, gallbladder, liver, intestines, pancreas and spleen, just as with rabbits and black-boned chickens, can be used to make various biomedicines such as cephalin, lecithin, serum syrup and Vitamin B^{12}. Ducks eggs can be used to make dry egg powder. Egg white (albumen) is used to make white protein and dry albumen tablets.

Feeding Requirements

The main duck feed in China is grass grown on land used for agriculture, forestry and fisheries. The duck, like the pig, is omnivorous. It eats almost anything of animal or plant origin. Beijing ducks relish cereal grains and utilize plant protein feeds as well, including the soybean, black bean, and soybean meal. The ducks are especially fond of aquatic plants such as goldfish algae, shrimp algae, duckweed, water calabash and *Azolla*. Ducks eat grass weeds and their seeds and are thus helpful in weed control. The tenth production team of the fourth branch of the Qian Shan Hon Farm, Hunan Province, noted that the growth of grass weeds in paddy fields was reduced by 60% when 710 ducks were tended therein.

Description and Performance

Beijing ducks have a large body form with compact snowy white feathers over the entire body (Figure 5). They have chubby, upward-projected breasts and a deep-wide abdomen, with the back lightly inclining downward. A fine outward appearance--which includes short, strong legs and orange-red webbed toes--compliments their strong and healthy constitutions, high adaptability and tractable temperament. They are socially adapted to living in groups, are peaceful and do not like moving about. All these characteristics are conducive to intensive culture and the industrialization of each production phase.

Figure 5. Beijing ducks are socially adaptive to living in groups.

The Beijing duck has no brooding tendency or habits. Thus, artificial hatching has been used for reproducing the young. Beijing ducks prefer water, and laying ducks are given access to ponds for swimming. If, however, no lakes or rivers are present they can be raised by using small ponds for bathing. They lay their eggs at night. They like clean and dry, shady conditions and shy away from wet and dirty places. Peasants who are master duck producers have an expression: "Beijing ducks like both wet (water) and dry."

Forced Feeding

Beijing ducks grow and develop rapidly, especially with forced feeding. In the Beijing area, the life cycle is as follows: there are 28 days from incubation of the eggs to hatching; the ducklings are then fed for 45 days, followed by 15 days of forced-feeding before slaughter, thereby making an 88-day lifecycle.

They are fed by machine every six hours during the last 15 days. With forced-feeding, the ducks are grabbed by the nape of the neck, their mouths forced open and a plastic tube shoved halfway down the gullet (Figure 6). A healthy mixture of a grain soup is pumped in. The ducks waddle away and sometimes a sprinkling of water is necessary for them to regain their composure and to clean them up.

Figure 6. Beijing ducks are force-fed for 15 days prior to slaughter.

After forced-feeding the ducks weigh 3 kilograms, half of which was gained during the forced feeding. In the Harbin area, the body weight of Beijing ducks from the time of hatching to 50 days of age can reach 2.5 kilograms. Followed by 10 days of forced feeding, a weight of 3 to 3.33 kilograms per bird can be achieved. It is at this time that both the quantity and quality of the meat becomes optimal. The muscle fibers are fine and smooth, and the fat is well distributed under both the skin and muscles so that it is not oily. It is then that the roasted Beijing duck is the most delicious and enjoys the greatest popularity. If cooked properly, the outside meat is scorched and the inside is tender, which results in its distinctive, delightful taste and fragrance.

RABBITS

Introduction

Of all nations, China is the most populous for people and for rabbits. The consumption of rabbit meat here is surpassed only by pork and chicken. Half of the rabbit meat of the world comes from China. It takes 1,000 rabbits to produce a metric tons of rabbit meat, of which the Chinese produce a million tons a year and annually export 23,000 metric tons. This is exporting roughly the equivalent of 23 million rabbits. Italy, France and Spain are also big producers of rabbits but their combined total is less than 50 percent that of China.

A second product of the abundant Chinese rabbits is the wool or fur which comprises about 10% of their weight. Between 30 and 40% of the rabbit fur entering international markets has its origin in China. Much of the rabbit fur is exported to Hong Kong where it is processed for use in mattresses, overcoats, collars, fur coats and caps.

Types of Rabbits and Their Uses

There are three main types of rabbits in China: those produced primarily for their wool or fur, the long-haired (meat) rabbits, and the dual purpose fur and meat rabbits. The Angora is the most famous wool or fur rabbit (Figure 7). Different breeds of Angora have been introduced from West Germany, France, England and Japan. The fur or wool of the Angora rabbit is removed three times a year for a total yield of about 750 grams. A total yearly weight of one kilogram represents top production.

Dual purpose rabbits (for both meat and fur) include the Belgian Gray and the California White. The latter has white fur and eight black points. They include the four feet, two ears, the nose and tail. Long-haired rabbits are the newest introduction. Breeds of these meat rabbits include the native Chinese and those imported from Belgium, Denmark, the

Figure 7. The Angora fur rabbit.

U.S.A. and Japan during the seventeenth and eighteenth centuries. The Danish White has distinctively big ears.

Rabbit production is spread throughout China. Long-haired rabbit production has become very popular in both the southern and northern provinces, but especially in the north. The wool and fur types are found principally in Jiangsu and Zhejiang, and the meat-producing rabbits in the more northern provinces of Shandong, Gansu and Hebei. In recent years, the demand for meat rabbits has gradually decreased in importance (international markets are greatly depressed), while that for wool and fur has increased.

Rabbits occupy another important economic and social niche, which is in traditional Chinese medicine. The pattern follows that of black-boned chickens and ducks. Medicinal concoctions are extracted from rabbit livers, gallbladders, eyes and testes. These extracts are used for treating high blood pressure, heart disease and atherosclerosis. Moreover, rabbit meat is higher in protein and contains less fat than pork, mutton or beef. In China, it is considered the very best meat for people who are troubled with obesity and heart disorders.

Conclusions

There is a growing interest among Chinese in rabbit production. The demand is increasing for the natural fabrics of rabbit wool, fur and hair.

It is thin and dense at the same time, and can be dyed in all colors. From it can be made cold-resistant clothing, shawls, fur collars and caps. Rabbits thrive on forages and byproducts. They are prolific reproducers. As a profit motive, the investment is low with the offer of quick returns. Furthermore, rabbit manure enriches cropland and, according to Chinese traditions, imparts disease and insect resistance to crops and reduces soil alkalinity. The meat provides not only a high grade protein but is very low in cholesterol, and the organs have medicinal properties. The Chinese may rightfully declare, "All parts of the rabbit are treasured objects."

FOR FURTHER READING

Bai Yucheng, et all. 1985. *Technology of practical animal husbandry.* Harbin: Heilongjiang Bureau of Animal Husbandry. (In Chinese)

He Kang, ed. 1980, 1981, 1982, 1983, 1984. *Chinese agricultural yearbook.* Beijing: Agricultural Press. (In Chinese)

Mathews, J., and L. Mathews. 1983. *One billion, a Chinese chronicle.* New York: Random House.

Qui Xiangpin. 1982. *Fowl culture.* Chongqing: Sichuan People's Press. (In Chinese)

Tuan, F. C. 1986. *China's livestock sector* (draft). U.S. Department of Agriculture, China Section. Asian Branch, International Economics Division, Economic Research Service. Washington, D.C.: Government Printing Office.

U.S. Department of Agriculture. Economic Research Service. 1986. *China outlook and situation report.* Washington, D.C.: Government Printing Office.

Zhangjiakou Agricultural Technical School. 1981. *Rabbit culture.* Beijing: Agricultural Press. (In Chinese)

28

FISH CULTURE--THREE THOUSAND YEARS OF HISTORY

by Sun Han

China has long been known as "The Land of Fish and Rice." All richly endowed agricultural areas of China teem with fish and rice. The Chinese characters for delicacy consist of two--one for fish, the other for sheep. The Chinese love fish and believe it to be most delicious. It is a seeming coincidence that "fish" in the Chinese language is *yu*, which is homophonic with part of the word *jiyu* (which means accumulating surplus) and *fuyu* (meaning prosperous). To the Chinese, fish are lucky objects. They are always served in a family dinner on New Year's Eve and during the Chinese lunar calendar. Fish symbolize *"there is surplus every year."*

China's Fish Resources

China has been and remains the world's leader in freshwater fish culture. Twenty-five percent of the world's fish production is accounted for by China, of which 60 percent is generated from highly integrated freshwater pond systems. The annual catch of freshwater fish has reached 1.8 million tons--the highest in the world--and is still increasing. China has more than 4,000 freshwater and shallow lakes on the lower and middle reaches of the Yangzi River, but they are still grossly undeveloped. Only 3 of the 5 million hectares of inland waters suited for aquaculture have been utilized. All this is in addition to the 16 thousand square kilometers out of a total of 49 thousand that have been developed for marine fish farms along China's coastlines. Many natural endowments and economic reasons account for the development of freshwater areas of lakes, rivers, streams and ponds covering 26 million hectares. More than 3 million hectares can be used for fish culture. Secondly, the "standing on two legs" approach is utilized by coupling rich traditional experiences with the most modern developments in science and technology. These include the popularization of techniques for artificial incubation (spawning) of domestic species and for intensive pond culture, ranging from grass-eating carp to most exotic species. Also, fish farming is often integrated with conventional farming, using organic wastes from the land to fertilize ponds and provide the fish with a food supply. Thirdly, the rapid decline in the fish taken from the oceans and natural waters of the interior have placed a new emphasis on intensive artificial culture.

Historical

Fish were probably caught and used for food in China dating back to prehistoric times. For example, large quantities of fish bones have been found in the Upper Cave Cultural Layers at Zhoukoudian, where the fossil remains of primitive Peking man (*Sinanthropus pekinensis*) were unearthed. This suggests that fish were caught as food in prehistoric ages. Fishing spears, well designed fish hooks and fine stylized paintings of fish have been excavated from the Yangshao Cultural Ruins of the Neolithic Age at Banpo, near Xi'an. Fish hooks made of bronze date back to the Shang (sixteenth-eleventh centuries B.C.) and Zhou (eleventh century - 221 B.C.) dynasties.

Hence, fish culture in China dates back to being the earliest in the world. It actually began in the western Zhou Dynasty of 3,000 years ago. There is a song in the classic, *The Book of Songs*, describing a pond which was dug by removing earth to build a sacred terrace as ordered by an Emperor of the Zhou Dynasty. Fish were raised in the pond. While the fish were cultured for ornamental purposes rather than for large-scale food production, this is still the world's earliest historical record of fish culture. Fish culture for food production began in the Spring and Autumn periods during the Warring states 2,500 years ago.

Fan Li--The Father of Fish Culture

It was Fan Li, a minister in State Yue (now Zhejiang Province), who first advocated raising fish. He wrote the first book on fish culture. To help Gou Jian, the King of State Yue, to revenge and restore his conquered state, Fan Li followed a policy of encouraging production to strengthen his state. Fish culture was one of the measures adopted. Fish culture also developed in State Wu (now Jiangsu Province) after it was annexed by State Yue.

Meanwhile, Fan Li's accomplishments continued. He believed that after the victory, Gou Jian would become envious and seek to do him harm. Accordingly, Fan Li ran away to State Chi (now Shandong

Province) with his lover, Xishi--a famous beauty of ancient China. There he became a rich nobleman and embarked upon the large-scale raising of fish and pigs.

The classic on fish culture written by Fan Li about 473 B.C. has long since been lost. There are quotations from it, however, in another agricultural encyclopedia classic, *Qi Min Yao Shu*. Topics covered are expositions on raising fish for profit; discussions on construction of fish ponds; modifying the ecological environments to accommodate the development and growth of fish; and techniques for collecting and hatching roe (eggs) under natural conditions.

Artificial Propagation

The Chinese specialize in carp production. Roe are inherently spawned in rivers, and traditional fish culture has long been dependent on collecting the fry (very small fish) from rivers. Dependability of supplies, as affected by natural conditions, has been the problem. Quality control is difficult because species may be mixed. Moreover, long-distance transport is costly, mortality rates may be excessive and labor requirements are high.

A key step in large-scale fish production is artificial propagation. This was achieved in China during the 1950s with the major domesticated species of black, grass, silver and big head carp. The first step is to select and rear superior parental fish. They should be of good body shape, have rapid growth, and be disease resistant and of high reproductive potential. Selections for propagation are made annually from the progenies of each generation. Meanwhile, parental fish are periodically exchanged with those from other regions to avoid deterioration and inbreeding decline. The parental fish are then raised in special ponds. Here feeding regimes, disease control measures and oxygen levels can be maintained conducive to good health and rapid maturation.

The second step in artificial fish culture is to chemically induce estrus, followed by spawning and fertilization. Estrualizing agents are injected into selected, mature, parental fish, both male and female (Figure 1). The most widely used materials are human chorionic gonadotropin (HCG) and pituitary gland (PG) and luteotropic hormone analogues (LTH-A). The effects of the several agents vary with the different species. Round spawning ponds, 30 to 100 square meters in area and 1 to 1.5 meters deep, are constructed with facilities for drainage, inlet and outlet water tubes for rinsing the roe (eggs), and a roe-collecting pit and box. The estrualized parental fish are then admitted into the spawning pond where the roe are fertilized with the spermatozoa. It is critical that spawning (egg or roe laying) of the females coincide precisely with

Figure 1. Injecting an estrualizing agent into mature parental fish.

ejaculation of sperm by the males, because the survival times for both the roe and spermatozoa are very short.

The final stage is incubation. Here, the fertilized roe are collected and placed in an incubation vat with flowing water. After the swim or air bladder is formed, the young fish fry are transferred to rearing ponds for further development.

Artificial propagation has been successful with many species including crucian carp, mud carp, Tilapia, Wuchang fish, bream, triangular bream and eel. This is in addition to the four major domesticated species of black carp, grass carp, silver carp and big head carp. There are also pending breakthroughs for shrimp, crab and clams.

Intensive Fish Culture in Ponds

Fish culture in China varies with the nature of the water resource. It is extensive in reservoirs and on both balustraded sides of navigable rivers. Fry are also placed in large lakes for propagation and in netted cages installed in both large- and medium-sized bodies of water.

Fish raising, however, is most important in ponds, either man-made or the improved natural ones (Figure 2). Such freshwater ponds produce the highest yields and provide two-thirds of the total output in fish production. The culture is highly intensive, with annual yields in excess of 750 kilograms per hectare. The highest average yields have exceeded ten tons per hectare and were obtained at Helie Township in Wuxi, Jiangsu Province.

The usual design for a fish pond is 0.5 hectares in area and 2-2.5 meters deep, and separated from other ponds by 5-10 meter-wide dykes. There are both water inflow and outflow channels. Nutrients are added to the ponds to encourage the growth of plankton, algae and a variety of aquatic plants which serve as feed for the fish. Supplemental materials or special nutrients (feeds), however, must be supplied for the culture of some fish. They are necessary to produce snails for black carp and the large quantities of fresh grass required for grass carp. In some of the major regions of fish culture, the nutritional requirements for various fish species are now being met by the industrial formulation of special feedstuffs. The increasing availability of formulated feeds will serve as a catalyst for further expansion of intensive fish culture in China. The oxygen supply in the pond water is critical for fish development. Aeration devices are necessary for increasing the oxygen content of ponds of high fish density, along with periodic replacement of the fresh water.

Another effective and ingenious technique for increasing the yields of fish in a pond is a mixed culture of different species in the same pond. Fish of different species live and thrive best at varying water depths. Each has specific feeding habits and nutritional requirements. Only with

Figure 2. Fish culture near Chongqing in Sichuan Province.

mixed cultures of different fish species, at reasonable densities, can the full advantage of feedstuffs and water use be realized. A typical example of a mixed fish pond culture is where grass carp and bream live in the upper water layers. They feed on aquatic plants and weeds produced along the dykes. Silver carp and big head carp live in the intermediate water layer. They feed on the plankton and the feces of the grass carp and bream. The black carp and other carp which live on the bottom feed on the benthon, such as snails.

According to records in ancient books, these mixed fish cultures or polyculture technologies have a history of nearly 1,000 years. In the beginning, it was an unconscious practice to collect mixed fry. With observations extending through many generations and following careful study by fish culturists, it became a successful practice. It has now become a scientifically-based, high-yielding technology.

Efficient Artificial Ecosystems

Fish ponds with mulberry trees planted along the dykes which separate them are a common scene in the countrysides of south and southeast China (Figure 3). It is a classical example of a typically efficient and successful artificial ecosystem. Plant materials and energy conversion are combined with farming practices both in water and on the land

Figure 3. Fish ponds of the Tai Lake area.

to produce crops, fish or other food animals for the greatest benefit. By planting mulberry trees on the dykes and feeding the silkworms, *in situ*, with mulberry leaves, the feces and pupae from the silkworms drop or can be scraped into the ponds. Hence the silkworms provide not only silk but highly quality feedstuffs for fish. But that is not all! Each year the ponds are drained and cleaned of mud, which is collected as a natural fertilizer rich in organic matter and minerals. The mud is then placed around the mulberry trees. The practice is most popular in Shunde County, a major area for fish culture in Guangdong Province. There the temperature is high, and up to seven crops of silkworms can be harvested annually. The cultures are high yielding and there are good returns. The system is, however, very labor intensive.

Another good example of an integrated food-producing, resource-sparing system in China is where fish culture is combined with food grain production and pig raising. A piggery is constructed on top of one corner of a fish pond. This allows the feces of the pigs to drop directly into the pond to feed the plankton and fertilize the aquatic plants therein. After a season, the pond is drained and the mud at the bottom collected and used as a basal manure for food grain production. The byproducts of the food grain crops are then fed to pigs. This completes the cycle. Many wastes or byproducts are utilized in such a food system, and high yields result for food grain production, pig raising and fish culture.

There are many other examples of integrated farming systems in China involving fish culture. In the most populated areas, further development of fish culture by more fully utilizing both the inland water and sea areas is still an important frontier to provide the people with more high-protein food. To establish even more elite artificial ecosystems, in which fish culture is combined with other farming activities to absorb surplus labor while pursuing food production with high economic benefits, remains one of the numerous challenges in feeding a billion and beyond.

FOR FURTHER READING

Aquacultural Science Society of China. 1985. *High-yielding techniques of fresh water fish culture*. Beijing: Popular Science Press. (In Chinese)

Aquatics Products Bureau of Jiangsu Province. 1985. *Practical techniques of fresh water fish culture*. Beijing: Agricultural Press. (In Chinese)

Chang, W. Y. B. 1986. Aquaculture research in China. *China Exchange News* 14(2): 13-16. Committe on Scholarly Communication with the People's Republic of China. Washington, D.C.: National Academy of Science.

Chen Naide. 1983. *Basic information of fish culture*. Nanjing: Jiangsu Press of Science and Technology. (In Chinese)

Clayre, A. 1985. *The heart of the dragon*. Boston: Houghton Mifflin Co.

Hanson, J. R. 1986. Chinese Fisheries. In *China's economy looks toward the year 2000*. Vol. 1, *The Four Modernizations*, ed. U.S. Congress Joint Economic Committee, 431-50. Washington, D.C: U.S. Government Printing Office.

He Kang, ed. 1985. *Statistics of China's agriculture*. Beijing: Ministry of Agriculture, Animal Husbandry and Fishery. (In Chinese)

———, ed. 1986. China agricultural yearbook 1985. Beijing: Agricultural Publishing House (English Edition).

Pease, R. 1986. Harvesting fish in China. *The Christian Science Monitor*, 24 June, 23-24.

Qui Feng. 1982. A brief history of fresh water fishery in China. *Agricultural Archaeology*, no. 1. (In Chinese)

Summarization Committee. n.d. *Proceedings: Experiences of Fresh Water Aquaculture in China*. Beijing: Science Press. (In Chinese)

29

PEOPLE AND MACHINES

by Yu Youtai

Selective Agricultural Mechanization

Machines may be called extensions of the human body. From the beginning, people have sought to develop new types of power and improve or design implements which would reduce human labor and increase productivity.

Agricultural production has thus evolved from the use of human labor alone to the use of draft animals, and finally to mechanical/electrical power, combining both simple and complex implements. In some areas, it has even reached the level of automation. But while mechanization is an extension of the skills of people, automation replaces people. Choices have been based on the urgency for production, available technology and profitability.

Prior to 1949, hand tools and animal-drawn implements were primarily used in Chinese agriculture. Except for a few modern pumps used to lift water for crop irrigation in limited areas, there was no mechanization. Since the early 1950s, China has stressed the extension of improved, animal-drawn implements, called semi-mechanization. More recently there has been renewed emphasis on the mechanization of Chinese agriculture.

The history of agricultural mechanization in China is characterized by significant parallel developments in several areas, all essential for improved food production and handling.

1) Irrigation, drainage and water management
2) Grain threshing, husking, milling and processing
3) Field cultivation--plowing, drilling of seed, and transplanting
4) More recently, the use of tractors, trucks and harvesters

A brief review is given of the origin and description of the ancient Chinese farm implements and recent developments in the use of modern machines.

Crop Irrigation--From the Dragon-Bone Water Lift to the Axial-Flow Pump

Historically, low precipitation and a lack of water in North China led to an old farming proverb: "It depends upon fertilizer to get a good or bad harvest, but water will determine whether you get any harvest at all." Thus, the first priority for machines in China was to improve water supplies and help meet water requirements for increasing both the output and stability of crop production in the plains of North China, where agriculture had its first beginnings (see Chapter 2, "Agricultural History Over Seven Thousand Years").

Rice is the most commonly grown crop in China. Most of it is irrigated. Timing of irrigation during dry weather is as important as draining the crop land during the rainy season to avoid excess flooding. Currently, about 50% of the cultivated land in China is irrigated and half of that is done with modern pumps. The horsepower used for irrigation and drainage constitutes about a third of the total horsepower used in Chinese agriculture, so water pumps play an important role. The dragon-bone water lift and the axial-flow pump are good examples of the ancient human- and animal-powered pumps on the one hand, and the modern mechanically and electrically powered pumps on the other.

Among the most ancient of Chinese water-lifting implements are the water-drawing level, windlass, bailing bucket, dragon-bone and the bamboo tube wheel. The water-drawing level (Figure 1), used to draw water from shallow wells, was invented 3,700 years ago. The windlass water lift for drawing water from deeper wells originated more than 3,000 years ago. The bailing bucket (Figure 2) was used for bailing water when differences in water levels were small. The dragon-bone water lift was invented by Bi Lan more than 1,700 years ago. In the beginning, it was called the water-turning lift. Since the water-drawing paddles are mounted in series on a chain called a dragon-bone, its name was changed accordingly. This water lift was first operated by the hands or feet. Later, mechanisms were invented to utilize oxen power (Figure 3) and wind power. The dragon-bone water lift has been the most popular and most effective water-lifting implement in China for almost 2,000 years. The bamboo tube water lift wheel (Figure 4), which utilizes the impulse or force of water flow to lift water automatically, was invented 1,100 years ago. The dyke raises the water level and leads water to the bottom of the tube wheel. The water flow then causes the wheel to rotate and fills the tubes with water. When the water-filled tubes turn to the upper side, water is poured into a trough which leads to the field to be irrigated.

All of these ancient water-lifting implements were improved in efficiency by using modern materials and bearings during the 1950s. The machines most commonly used at the time were the dragon-bone water lift, the largest of which is 10 meters in length; the bamboo tube water lift

Figure 1. The water-drawing level.

Figure 2. The bailing bucket.

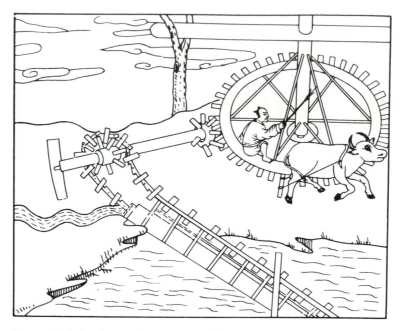

Figure 3. The dragon-bone water lift.

Figure 4. The bamboo tube water lift wheel.

wheels, which may reach 20 meters in diameter with about 80 tubes; and the tube-chain and bucket-chain water lifts, used for drawing water from shallow wells and swills. Modern pumps were later substituted for most of the lifts, although in certain areas lifts are still used as supplements to the modern pump systems. Figure 5 is a drawing of a series of dragon-bone water lifts being driven by windmills in the Yangzi River delta.

Figure 5. A series of dragon-bone water lifts being driven by windmills.

Modern water pumps were first used in the region of the Yangzi River basin and Pearl River delta areas. At that time, industrial pumps were the only ones available. Later, water pumps were designed especially for agricultural purposes. Today many different kinds of water pumps are used in China, in regions with water from rivers and lakes as well as in areas irrigated by wells. For flatlands and low-lying fields, axial-flow pumps with lifts of less than ten meters are the most common, along with some mixed-flow and centrifugal pumps. In hilly areas, the mixed-flow and centrifugal pumps with lifts of more than 40-100 meters predominate. Water turbine pumps can be used if there are water power resources. In areas that are irrigated by wells, there are multi-stage centrifugal pumps, deep well pumps and submersible pumps to choose from. Since the 1970s different kinds of sprinkling units are also being used in many places, including suburban areas and on state farms.

Axial-flow pumps are simple in structure, convenient to operate and maintain, and have the advantages of low lift, high volume discharge and superior efficiency. The big axial-flow pumps are especially suitable for irrigating large areas and for drainage along the Yangzi, Pearl and Yellow rivers. There are many large pumping stations in these regions. In 1983, when the water level was especially high, the amount of discharge by 2,000 electrical pumping stations of different sizes in the Hubei Province (the middle part of the Yangzi River Valley) reached 400 million tons daily during the peak of drainage, thus playing a very important role in flood control. By comparison, when flood control depended on dragon-bone water lifts, farmers were helpless during high flooding. It can be said that the "fierce and cruel water dragon king" is being controlled to a considerable extent by modern science and technology, and a good harvests are now assured by the use of these large pumps. The smaller axial-flow pumps with diameters smaller than 25 cm. are light, easy to install, and may be substituted for the dragon-bone water lifts with very good results.

Husking Rice and Grinding Wheat without Oxen

Rice must be husked and milled and wheat ground before being eaten. This is also true of most other grains. Implements are, therefore, very important for processing grains in the countryside.

The earliest grain-processing implement used in China was the stone mortar and pestle (Figure 6). It was a product of the New Stone Age and dates back more than 4,000 years. About 2,200 years ago, the Chinese invented a treadle-operated tilt hammer (Figure 7) by applying the principle used in the mortar and pestle. Somewhat later, a tilt hammer operated by draft animals and water power was invented. The tilt hammer, which works intermittently, was not efficient. This led, about 2,000 years ago, to the rice huller and wheat grinder which could work continuously (Figure 8). The machine for separating the rice grain and hull is the winnower (Figure 9), invented in the tenth century. The horse tail was first used in the flour separator (Figure 10) to separate the flour from the wheat bran. Later, the horse tail was exchanged for silk. These hullers, grinders, winnowers and flour separators, with gradual improvements, constituted a system of grain-processing machines used in the Chinese countryside for many centuries

The ancient grain-processing machines made of wood and stone were operated mainly by oxen, donkeys and a few horses. The work input was intense, productivity was low and the quality of the processed rice and wheat was less than satisfactory. Accordingly, engine-operated grain-processing machines were designed and became widespread in most provinces in the 1960s. Today in China, there are modern rice and wheat mills in most cities, and also many small and simply constructed grain mills in the countryside. Many small, modern hullers and grinders are also used to process not only rice and wheat but corn, barley, millet and sorghum as well.

Figure 6. The stone mortar and pestle.

Figure 7. The treadle-operated tilt hammer.

Figure 8. The rice huller and wheat grinder.

Figure 9. The winnower

Figure 10. The flour separator.

The importance of pulverizing, crushing or rolling grains for animal feed is second only to processing grains for human food. Only recently has the forage industry begun to commercialize the processing of animal feeds, although animal feeds were processed locally for a long time in the Chinese countryside. Along with the development of animal husbandry, feed processing machinery--with the grain crusher as the key unit--has been developed. Among the different types of grain crushers, the hammermill is the most popular.

From the Live to the Iron Ox

Animals were used very early in Chinese agricultural field operations. Throughout the feudal society, there was little improvement either in farm power or implements. Chinese agriculture prevailed for almost 2,000 years with animal-drawn plows, harrows and drills in addition to hand tools such as hoes and sickles.

As with water lifting and grain processing, field work for crop production has evolved from human- and animal-operated implements to power machinery. About 7,000 years ago, all farm work was accomplished by human labor. Plowing with oxen began during the later part of the Slave Society, approximately 3,200 years ago. As oxen were more expensive laborers than slaves, the practice of ox plowing was not greatly extended until the historical change from a slave to a feudal society--about 400-500 years after oxen were first used.

Accompanying the development of the agricultural economy in the second to fourth centuries (A.D.), plowing, harrowing and leveling--with the corresponding tillage implements drawn by oxen--were gradually introduced in the northern part of China. About 500 years later, tillage practices with appropriate implements were introduced for rice paddy fields in South China. These ancient pictures show that the straight beam of the plow had been changed to a bent one. This important improvement in plow design occurred in the eighth century.

The animal-drawn grain drill was invented in China about 100 years B.C. Figure 11 and 12 show the operations of a two-legged grain drill drawn by an ox and a pair of stone rollers drawn by a donkey.

Different draft animals can be seen in the illustrations. The water buffalo was used mainly in South China since irrigated paddy fields predominated. Most of the cultivated land in North China is for dryland cropping. Here oxen, donkeys and horses are the important agricultural animals.

To meet the urgent needs created by the agricultural production rehabilitation of the 1950s, various hand tools and improved animal-drawn implements such as the walking plow and grain drills were

Figure 11. The two-legged grain drill.

Figure 12. Stone rollers drawn by a donkey.

produced. The national output of agricultural machinery products was only 79 million yuan in 1953. Since then, more and more factories for making agricultural diesel engines, tractors, and various kinds of farm implements have been established in most of the provinces. By 1978, the total output value for farm machinery had increased to 7.9 billion yuan, a 100-fold increase over 1953, and to 8.5 billion yuan by 1983. Figure 13 illustrates the progressive increase in total horsepower of agricultural machinery and shows that the largest investment of horsepower for farm machinery is for drainage and irrigation equipment, followed by tractors, grain processing and trucks. The development of the large modern tractors preceded that of the hand or walking tractors. Since the 1970s, however, the number of walking tractors has increased more rapidly than the number of large tractors.

Tractors and their complementary implements were first brought to the countryside in the late 1950s. Farmers excitedly and affectionately called them the "iron oxen." Since then, these "iron oxen" have been substituted gradually for the live oxen which had been successfully used as draft animals for over 2,000 years. Thus, Chinese agriculture entered a period of mechanization a step equal in importance to the transition from human labor to draft animals.

Today in China, tractors being manufactured in the different provinces range from the small 4-wheel and walking types of 5 to 10

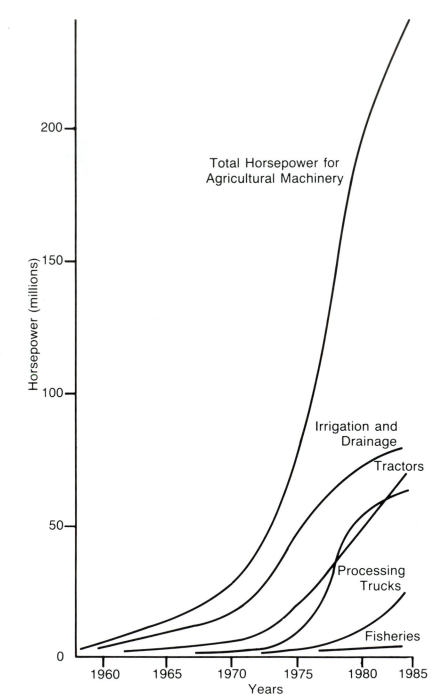

Figure 13. Progressive increase in total horsepower of agricultural machinery (1958-1985).

horsepower all the way up to the wheel and crawler types of 30 to 160 horsepower. All kinds of farm implements now needed can be manufactured domestically. A great deal of farm machinery is being produced in series, including the southern paddy field and northern dryland series of plows and harrows, and series of water pumps, grain-processing machines and feed crushers.

That which cannot be purchased abroad must be created locally. The production of rice, China's most important food crop, offers a good example of selective mechanization. Getting power-driven tractors into muddy rice paddy fields has posed a problem. One possible solution is the boat-tractor or the mechanical plowing boat (Figure 14). Modifications of conventional wheel tractors to work in rice paddy fields are other possibilities. With the boat tractor, the weight of the tractor is supported mainly by the body of the boat. It can be operated in a deep paddy field without sinking and in a shallow, muddy field without breaking the hard pan. The hard pan is an impervious layer in the subsoil which prevents the depth of mud from increasing each year. This unique creation may effectively solve the problem of getting tractors into paddy fields. Generally the boat tractors are equipped with 5-12 horsepower diesel engines and are used mainly for plowing, harrowing and roto-tilling the paddy fields. With modifications, the boat tractor may be used for other operations on dry land, including transportation.

Figure 14. The boat-tractor or mechanical plowing boat for use in muddy rice paddy fields.

Rice-transplanting machines are another example of labor-saving machinery. Rice transplanting is the most difficult, labor-consuming work in the countryside, but is indispensable in China for rice production. In the middle 1950s Chinese agricultural engineers succeeded in designing and building a rice-transplanting machine operated by human labor. Both semi-automatic and engine-propelled versions were later developed that were many times more efficient than manual transplanting. By the end of the 1970s, the numbers of mechanical rice transplanters operated by human labor had reached 510,000 and there were approximately 100,000 engine-propelled units. Engine-propelled transplanters were used for more than 100,000 hectares of paddy rice in 1976. Yet by 1981, these rice transplanters were used on less than four-tenths of one percent of all the rice in China, and there has since been no substantial change. Labor was, and remains, abundant, land is scarce, and machines are expensive. There were also problems of reliable performance of the transplanters and their effective integration with other rice seedling operations. Large-scale mechanical transplanting of rice is still a hope for the future.

A Dramatic Shift Since 1979

Before 1979, farm families were not allowed to own tractors or other farm machinery. These restrictions have since been lifted. Dramatic shifts have since occurred in the ownership, control, operation and types of farm machinery. The kinds of tractors being manufactured and used have also changed.

By the end of 1983, 43% of all tractors in use were privately owned, 29% were owned by production teams but contracted to households, and only 28% were owned by state or collective farm machinery stations.

TABLE 1

Year	Number of Tractors Owned by Farmers	Percent of Total Tractors in Countryside
1980	38,000	1
1981	384,000	14
1982	991,000	32
1983	1,500,000	43
1984	3,120,000	78

Fewer large- and medium-sized tractors were manufactured in 1985 than in 1981, because farmers were working small plots of land under the *Chengbao* system which requires hand-guided or small 4-wheel tractors that are inexpensive and versatile. Of the 3,120,000 tractors privately owned by farmers in the countryside in 1984, 87% were of small size. However, a large part of them and up to 85% of the operating time was used for rural transportation and the hauling of goods rather than for direct agricultural operations. Farmers invested an estimated 30 billion yuan in various kinds of farm machinery from 1979 to 1984. Of the 427,000 total trucks in the countryside in 1985, 75% were of small size. Along with rural people operating their own machinery, custom work centers for farm machinery have grown rapidly.

The Chinese Model of Agricultural Mechanization

China, with over one billion people, does not have, comparatively, much cultivated land. There are over 800 million people living in the countryside, including more than 300 million agricultural laborers, and only 0.1 hectares of cultivated land per person. This about one-eighth that of the U.S.A. and one-third that of France. Thus, there has been a reluctance to mechanize. The high cost of machinery is also a problem. Additionally, the cultivated land of China is very diverse with vast differences among provinces and regions. These factors, combined with minimal inputs of technology and economic investment in the country-side, shortages of petroleum, and the new responsibility production system, have put a damper, at least temporarily, on significant expansions in agricultural mechanization. Machine-plowed areas fell about 16% from 1981 to 1986, and machine-sowed areas decreased by more than 19%. There is now, however, a reversal of the downward trend.

All of these points show the need for resource-conserving models of agricultural mechanization which are aimed at increasing the stability of yields at high levels, improving the cropping index, and utilizing integrated biological and engineering technology approaches with low capital investments. Any investments in energy and machines should be accompanies by higher economic returns and increased agricultural productivity. As mechanization in China is expanded, human labor and draft animals must be utilized according to the overall conditions of different regions. There should be an effective combination of mechanization and semi-mechanization. Big, medium and small machines should be integrated, with the primary focus on medium and small sizes. The requirements for good quality, low prices, small sizes, energy savings, timeliness of operations, and multiple uses--as desired by farmers following the adoption of China's new "responsibility production contract system"--must be fulfilled as far as possible. Appropriate technology should be used to assure both technical and economic effectiveness. Agricultural mechanization should be combined with the development of a more diversified economy, including sideline

industries and the integration of various complexes, to assure a flourishing rural economy and transfer of farm labor. Mechanization will
become urgent and necessary when labor becomes expensive, undepend-
able, and in short supply, and when farmers become rich enough to buy
and operate farm machinery.

In 1983, about 245 million mechanical/electrical horsepower units
were used in Chinese agriculture, of which about 35% went for irrigation
and drainage, about 25% for processing grain, cotton and oil crops, and
about 30% for tractors, trucks and self-propelled machines. This is the
approximate distribution of farm operations that are mechanized in
China, although it will vary with the region and province. For instance,
South China led the way in the mechanization of irrigation and drainage,
while the mechanization of field operations proceeded much earlier and
more rapidly in the northeastern provinces and the suburbs of large
cities. Chinese agricultural mechanization has progressed according to
the principle of selective mechanization, with the order, degree and
speed varying with the region. From an agroeconomic point of view,
China's agricultural mechanization program thus far has been compe-
tent and practical.

The Agricultural Mechanization Regions of China

According to geographical, natural, agricultural and economic
conditions, there are nine primary regions of Chinese agricultural
mechanization. Here, however, they will be described as the following
four integrated regions (Figure 15).

The *first* is the northern plains, which includes the flatlands and wide
open spaces in the northeastern, northern and northwestern provinces
and autonomous regions. Food production is the priority in these areas,
which are the most advanced for agricultural mechanization in China. At
present, there are more than 700 horsepower units for every one
thousand hectares of cultivated land. Mechanization of all major farming
operations could be realized by the end of the twentieth century. In
China this is called the stage of basic agricultural mechanization. More
than 80% of the cultivated land of state farms is located in the northern
plains region. Many farms have already attained a high level of
mechanization and labor productivity (see Chapter 8, "From Bare Lands
to Bread Baskets"). Some of the state farms and the wheat-soybean
growing regions in these areas and in the suburbs of large cities such as
Beijing and Tianjin (and also Shanghai in the second region) may soon
approach the stage of complete mechanization. Figure 16 shows wheat
harvested by a domestically manufactured, self-propelled combine in
the northeast.

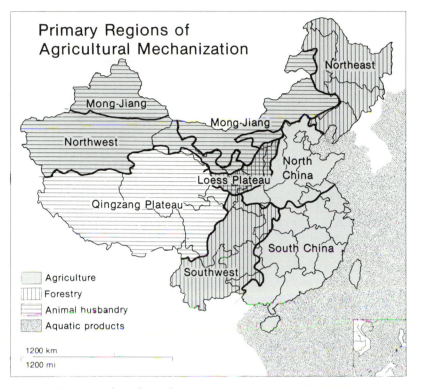

Figure 15. Agricultural mechanization regions.

The *second* is the basins and plains in the southeastern and southwestern provinces, the main land base for food production in China. In these areas, the ratio of people to land area is very high, with less than ⅕ hectare per person. However, the high index of intercropping has created an urgency comparable to that in the northern plains to proceed with agricultural mechanization. There are many large cities in this region, and general economic conditions, diversification and sideline industries are all further developed than elsewhere. This applies both to transferring farm labor as well as to financing investments for developing agricultural mechanization. Currently, the level of farm power is even higher in some places than on the northern plains, but the degree of agricultural mechanization is less. After an adequate system for mechanized rice production has been developed and accepted, agricultural mechanization could proceed rapidly. Some predict that the stage of basic agricultural mechanization might be reached by the end of this century.

Figure 16. Self-propelled combine for wheat harvest in the Northeast.

The *third* is the hilly areas, which are still mainly used for crop production. This is changing to integrated farming systems of crop production, forestry and animal husbandry. The field plots are small and the differences in the altitude among the plots is extreme. Here it is difficult to mechanize field operations. Much power is also required for transportation, and many local products must be collected and processed. For this region more emphasis should be put on machines for transportation, and for processing local products as well as on small water power plants. The integration of mechanization with semi-mechanization should especially be encouraged in this region.

The *fourth* is the region of forestry, animal husbandry and interior fisheries. In the northeastern forestry region, mechanization of tree cutting and wood transportation is well advanced. It is necessary, however, to accelerate the mechanization of reforestation and maintenance of forests. In the southwestern forestry region, there are numerous gorges and high mountains. Emphasis should be put on building cableways and machines for reforestation and composite utilization of wood products. Urgently needed for animal husbandry is the building of machines for water lifting, grassland renovation, hay making, and wool and milk collecting; as processing equipment for animal disease control; and for slaughtering, transportation, handling and storage. The interior fishery area includes the rivers, lakes, reservoirs, ponds and pools for fish production. Oxygen-adding equipment for ponds and machines for feeding and catching fish should be developed. Intensive and high density fish culture demands an advanced degree of mechanization.

Conclusions

One of the needs for agricultural mechanization in China is to break the labor intensive bottleneck inherent in the traditional and even now increasing number and complexity of multiple cropping systems. The Chinese have developed a vast array of cropping systems involving the integration of more than one crop in a given field at the same time. This is to maximize total output or production from a given land area. Intercropping is everywhere, whether it's corn with soybeans and sweet potatoes, or rice interlaced with soybeans, fruit trees, and vegetables. Relay cropping, where one crop is planted into a field before the first is harvested, is commonplace. Rice follows wheat, watermelons follow winter wheat, and barley or rapeseed and cotton follow barley, rapeseed or wheat.

Mechanization for labor efficiency in China should not be a priority to the same degree as it has been in the U.S.A., where affordable, dependable and adequate farm labor has been and remains a major constraint. Labor-saving technologies in the U.S.A. have been accompanied by some losses as well as gains in both production and quality. As for the future, some modification in multiple and relay cropping systems may need to be accepted in China to accomodate further mechanization of tillage, sowing, transplanting and harvesting operations as rural labor becomes more expensive, less dependable and less available.

Hopefully, integrated biological and engineering systems can be developed that will not only maintain but even increase total food output by retaining multiple cropping systems, and that will further encourage their development and permit an orderly transfer to labor-saving equipment.

Constraints, still inherent in further developments of Chinese agricultural mechanization, are excessive human labor, an undeveloped rural economy, limited land resources, and a lack of money to purchase and operate machines. The hope and challenge for the future is in the development of a more diversified rural economy, with sideline industries that will absorb the excess labor and provide the necessary land and money. The intent is that "farmers leave the soil but not the village; farmers enter factories but not the city."

FOR FURTHER READING

Beijing Agricultural Mechanization Institute. 1983. *The regionalization of agricultural mechanization.* Beijing. (In Chinese)

Binswanger, H. P. 1984. *Agricultural mechanization.* World Bank Staff Working Paper No. 673. Washington, D.C.: The World Bank.

Chen Wenhua. 1978. A brief diagramatic history of Chinese ancient agricultural science and technology. Beijing: Agricultural Press. (In Chinese)

Chinese Agricultural Regionalization Committee. 1981. *A comprehensive regionalization of Chinese agriculture.* Beijing: Agricultural Press. (In Chinese)

He Kang, ed. 1980, 1981, 1982, 1983, 1984. *Chinese agricultural yearbook.* Beijing: Agricultural Press. (In Chinese)

———, ed. 1986. *China agricultural yearbooks.* 1985. Beijing: Agricultural Publishing House (English Edition).

Hsu, R. C. 1983. *Food for one billion.* Boulder, Colo.: Westview Press.

Hua, Gouzhu, et al. 1985. *The regionalization of agricultural mechanization.* Beijing: Agricultural Mechanization Institute. (In Chinese)

Liu Xianzhow. 1963. *The invention history of Chinese ancient farm machinery.* Beijing: Science Press. (In Chinese)

Perkins, D., and S. Yusuf. 1984. *Rural development in China.* Baltimore: Johns Hopkins University Press.

Qiang, D. Z. 1986. Rice seedling transplanters in China. In *Small farm equipment for developing countries.* Los Banos, Philippines. International Rice Research Institute.

Shi Senghan. 1981. *An outline of Chinese agricultural heritages.* Beijing: Agricultural Press. (In Chinese)

Song Yingxing. 1637. *Skillful hands create the world, China.* (In Chinese)

Stavis, B. 1978. *The politics of agricultural mechanization.* Ithaca, N.Y.: Cornell University Press.

U.S. Department of Agriculture. Economic Research Service. 1984, 1985, 1986. *China outlook and situation reports.* Washington, D.C.: Government Printing Office.

Wu Shuren. 1985. Progress in rural mechanization. *China Reconstructs* 34(9): 3-33.

Yao, Jianfu. 1983. *To develop agricultural mechanization steadily and selectively.* Beijing: Chinese Agricultural Regionalization Committee. (In Chinese)

Yu Youtai, and Xue Chaogui. 1985. A review of the development of Chinese agricultural mechanization. *Transactions of the Chinese Society of Agricultural Engineering* 1(2): 1-13. (In Chinese)

———. 1986. Forecast of the prospects of the development of Chinese agricultural mechanization. *Transactions of the Chinese Society of Agricultural Machinery* 17(1): 1-9. (In Chinese)

Zhoa Jizhu. 1983. Agricultural machines. In *Ancient China' technology and science*, 419-28. Beijing: Foreign Language Press.

———. 1986. On the objective principle and Chinese way of the development of agricultural mechanization. *Transactions of the Chinese Society of Agricultural Machinery*. 17(1): 1-9. (In Chinese)

30
WARRING WITH PESTS

by Sylvan Wittwer

Historical

There is a modern-day Chinese slogan: "The more you work, the more you get. Things foreign and ancient should be used to serve modern China. We must weed through the old to bring forth the new;" and from Party Leader Deng Xiaoping, "The cat would be a good one so long as it catches mice, no matter whether it is black or white."

China has a long history of warring with agricultural pests. The "Book of Poems" written in the 11th century B.C. lists a decree issued by an ancient ruler to mobilize peasants for locust control through the use of fire. Physical methods of insect control have been used more extensively in China than anywhere else. Along with the use of heat were listed lime, plant ashes and insecticidal plants as control measures as early as 240 B.C.

"*Qi Min Yao Shu,*" an ancient Chinese agricultural encyclopedia of the sixth century, abounds in descriptions of protecting crops from pests. The remedies were often simple but effective. For example, wheat grains were singed with fire. This treatment no doubt destroyed most of the ova and pupae of storage insects present in the grains. "Cereal fields abutting of thoroughfares were usually violated by passing animals. This was corrected by planting sesame or female hemp plants on the boundaries. Cattle never touch sesame, and female hemp plants, when browsed upon, branch only the more produsely, and both produce oil seeds good for illumination." For melons, the seed was washed with water and mixed table salt which protected the vine from mildew and safeguard against fungal diseases. If melon vines were plagued by ants, the recommendation was to place a few pieces of "marrowy" ox or sheep bones by the melon stock, wait till ants assembled, then pick up and cast both away. This process was repeated until all ants were gone.

The Chinese fill a unique historical niche in the war against pests. They first conceived the idea that some insects could be intentionally used to suppress populations of other insects. During the third century A.D., predator ants (*Oecophylla smaragdina*) were used as natural enemies against, and to reduce the number of, mites and leaf-feeding insects on citrus, among which were leaf beetles, curculios, scarabaeus beetles and stink bugs. This use of predatory ants by the ancient Chinese agriculturists to control pests was not accomplished without ingenuity. Not all ants are predatory. Farmers who grew oranges in groves went to market at certain times of the year and purchased little bags containing a special kind of ant which they hung in the orange trees.

The Chinese were very early aware of the food web, and had a concept of nature based on an organismic philosophy. They looked at nature as a whole rather than as dissected into pieces. This philosophy has prevailed to the present day and is particularly applicable to the control of pests. Plant protection in China today embodies a fascinating mix of ancient insect and disease control practices, derived empirically over centuries and aimed at specific diseases or insect pests, coupled with modern methodologies that require precise timing in the introduction of biological agents and chemical pesticides. Integrated control is the rule.

The "walking on two legs" concept for pest control appears again and again. Modern methods are integrated with old ways of doing things. Principles are combined with commodities and recipes with the ingredients.

There are two impositions--one environmental, the other biological-- that farmers fear most: the vagaries of weather or climate and the ravages of insects and plant diseases. More has been done in China to "weather-proof" farming than in any other major food producing country. Varieties of crops (soybeans, rice, wheat, barley, fruits and vegetables) have been developed which are remarkably resilient to the harshest of environmental stresses. Nearly half the cultivated land is irrigated, establishing China as the top nation in the world in the magnitude of irrigated cropland. Mechanized irrigation covers over half the land supplied with water. On hundreds of thousands of hectares of staple crops (cotton, peanuts, sugar beets, corn, sugarcane) as well as on large areas devoted to fruit and vegetable production and to watermelons, the soils are mulched with plastic for weed control, water conservation, alleviation of erosion, warming the soil and for protection against frost and freezing temperatures (see Chapter 31, "The Plastic Revolution"). This also helps to repel insects that carry virus diseases, encourage earlier crop maturity and increase production. The ancient sand mulch technology is similarly used over vast cropping areas in the northwest desert areas. The boundaries for successful crop production have been extended to the north, the northeast and the northwest. Tens of thousands of hectares are covered with plastic greenhouses, and plastic tunnels cover crop rows and rice seedling beds to protect tender high value crops from pestilence, adverse temperatures and natural disasters.

There is increased water and fertilizer use efficiency. The harvest seasons have been lengthened and there is an enhancement of both the stability and magnitude of production.

The battles being waged against the devastation invoked by insects and plant disease parallel those directed toward controlling the ravages of climate. Pestilence problems are often linked with the vagaries of weather related natural disasters (floods, typhoons, drought, frost). The two are simultaneously manifest in the agriculture of China.

Biological Controls

Anyone having an interest in gardening or farming with minimal use of chemical pesticides should observe the Chinese systems. Pest management has received serious attention here. The Chinese have adopted multifaceted pest control programs that rely heavily on the use of improved varieties, cultural practices and natural enemies, coupled with local and countrywide networks for crop protection. There is a vegetable disease network for cucumbers, tomatoes and peppers. A network has also been established for biological control of vegetable diseases and insects. The Chinese have developed and adopted many different methods of pest control which, when used in combination, not only reduce pest damage but are environmentally sound, conserve natural resources, and are economically viable and acceptably safe for human health. A good example is minimum tillage, now being used on over 300,000 hectares in Jiangsu Province alone. This practice reduces weed problems, lessens chemical usage and is more energy and resource efficient.

Many of the early U.S.A.-Chinese agricultural exchanges of scholarly tourism in the late 1970s and early 1980s focused on the potential for biological pest control. American scientists observed Chinese expertise in the culture or rearing of insect species, both as hosts and parasites, and many integrated pest control methodologies. There was also widespread use of pesticides on some crops then and a beginning awareness of pesticide resistance, the rise of secondary pests and the need for pesticide resistance management.

Some classical examples of success in biological control follow, for which the words of Pu Zhilong, a Cantonese entomologist, are appropriate. "It is a pity that, because natural enemies and their role in insect control is still far from being recognized, these nameless heroes are often overlooked or even harmed by some irrational production practices." Ducks were used to control pests in paddy fields in China as early as the mid-seventeenth century, and a decree was issued by a ruler of the Han Dynasty to protect such insect predators as birds and frogs.

The most popular biological control for insects on major crops in China is the mass rearing and release of billions of *Trichogramma* species, (Figure 1), a tiny wasp that parasitizes the eggs of the corn borer, the sugarcane borer, the rice leaf roller, the rice case worm, the pine caterpillar and many other pests. It is referred to as a "living insecticide." These parasitic wasps, for which there are thousands of rearing or production stations, are applied to fields and forests in all the 26 provinces and the three municipalities. Formerly, in the corn-producing provinces the counties stored the wasps, the communes propagated them and the production brigades released them. These duties are now performed by the various county, township, village and family enterprises. Large numbers of the *Trichogramma* are bred on eggs of the giant silkworm moths, rice grain moths and other hosts, which in turn must be cultured. This parasite release method has generally been 70-80% effective, with many pests held to acceptable populations. Because of local availability of labor and raw materials for rearing and breeding, production costs are usually less than those encountered in the use of chemical insecticides, and there are no hazards to human health, issues of food safety or adverse impacts on the environment.

One of the most successful biological control programs has been with the stink bug (*Tessaratona papillosa*, Drury) on litchi (*Litchi chinensis*, Sonn) in Guangdong Province. Between 1962 and 1967 the usefulness of a parasitic wasp (*Anastatus*) was explored and the effectiveness demonstrated. The wasps are now propagated on a large scale in laboratories and released as an effective control measure (Figure 2).

Some species of green lacewings (*Chrysopa*) that feed on aphids are also artificially propagated and released on a much smaller scale than *Trichogramma*. But like *Trichogramma*, they have a wide host range of pest insects extending from aphids to the cotton boll weevil. *Bacillus thuringiensis*, an entomogenous bacterium, is now widely known as a

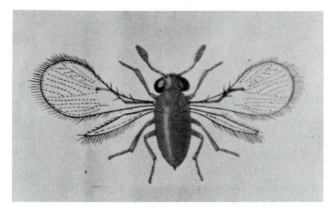

Figure 1. The Trichogramma parasitic wasp.

bacterial control for insects. It is also used successfully against the cotton bollworm and the small cotton measuring worm. Several beneficial organisms are also unharmed by *B. thuringiensis*. A combination of *Trichogramma* and *B. thuringiensis* enhances control. Ladybird beetles are the primary control against the cotton aphid, the major cotton pest in North China.

Microbial control is also exemplified by the use of *Beauveria bassiana* for control of the corn borer (affecting corn, millet and sorghum), the pine caterpillar, the pine moth, the rice leafhopper and the brown planthopper. Applied to corn in spring and autumn it kills the European corn borer and its overwintering larvae in both North and South China. Local farm byproducts or even waste materials may be used for its culture. It may also spread spontaneously and rapidly. Caution must be exercised, however, since it may cause allergic reactions in persons directly involved in its production and dispersal.

Figure 2. Parasitization of the stink bug on litchi.

Other unique technologies have been developed by the Chinese for biological control of pests. Spiders are natural predators on many rice insects and other pests and are greatly revered. Before flooding the rice paddies, peasants provide places of refuge for spiders on the tops of poles or sticks well above the water level. As the water rises the spiders gain access to shelter while many of the harmful insects are drowned. Army mortars and other firing devices are sometimes used to disperse organisms that spread diseases on insects. Armies of women and other workers are available for distributing the predators through the fields and, at times, to individual plants.

Pest control is particularly labor intensive in China. It involves cleaning up plant residues and debris, intensive monitoring for early detection, hand dispersal of parasites, hand removal and treating of affected spots, hand bagging of fruit to prevent insect ovipositing, and the use of light traps. Chemicals are usually applied by hand with portable airblast or compressed air sprayers. Often only the infected parts of fields are sprayed. Workers wear mouth covers and step backwards to avoid walking into the spray.

Insect-eating frogs are also used in China for pest control. It has been reported that, in Fujian Province, 800 frogs per mu (1/15 hectare) effectively eliminated damage from the brown planthopper and the yellow rice borer. Ducks, in addition to providing meat and eggs, are also raised for biocontrol of insects. Flooding of rice paddies to a depth of 8 centimeters when rice is 20 centimeters high forces mobile pests, including planthoppers, to the tips of the plants. Ducklings are then released to eat the insects. Ducks are a natural enemy of insect pests that devastate rice fields (see Chapter 27, "Chickens, Ducks, Geese and Rabbits Galore"). Within two hours after being herded into rice paddies, at a density of 300 per hectare, they will have eaten up most of the insects on the water. While the herding of ducks from field to field for pest control is labor intensive, it often provides much needed employment opportunities (Figure 3).

Light traps as physical control measures for insects have been used directly since 1970. Prior to that time, they were used only to monitor pest populations. Ultraviolet radiators attract a greater variety and number of pests than all comparable lamps. They have been especially effective for control of cotton and rice insects. Transistor instruments

Figure 3. Ducks are a living insecticide for control of many insects in China.

recently developed for low voltage, direct current save on expensive energy and cables. Bright reflecting plastic is used for repelling insects on many vegetable crops and watermelons in Zhejiang Province.

Catching or repelling insect pests is not an end in itself. There is usually a completely integrated system. Thus, insects caught in light traps may be dumped in ponds to feed fish. Later, the pond may be drained, the fish harvested and the pond mud hauled to fields as fertilizer. Similarly, plant materials collected in fields are piled up and covered with plastic. The solar heat drives the insects to the surface but the plastic cover confines them to the inside. Chickens or ducks are then herded to the piles and feed on the insects. The plant material then goes for making compost and the insect fed ducks are eventually eaten.

Resistant Varieties

Breeding for resistance to insect pests and plant diseases is still much in its infancy in China. There are, nevertheless, some major success stories resulting from improved strains, better cultural practices and the use of insecticides. Spring wheat varieties in the 1950s were highly susceptible to stem rust and head blight or scab, and winter wheat to strip rust. Varieties resistant to these dieases have since been developed, and there are now winter wheat varieties resistant to "stinking bunt." Yellow wheat rust has also been entirely eliminated, damage from rice stem borers greatly reduced and armyworms brought under control. Strains of *Indica* rice have been developed at the Jiangsu Academy of Agricultural Sciences with resistance to both brown planthoppers and thrips. For corn, a combination of resistant varieties, crop rotations, removal of plant residues and chemical pesticides have been successful in controlling most of the insects and diseases. Resistance to bacterial wilt is now being sought. Virus diseases are becoming increasingly severe on many crops. Particularly serious are those on cowpeas, tomatoes, potatoes, peppers, garlic, cucumbers and all members of the cabbage family, including Chinese cabbage. Genetic resistance may become the best solution.

Many reasons may be listed for the increasing severity of insects and diseases in China. The ever increasing numbers of greenhouses and plastic structures being used throughout the country provide an ideal environment for carryover from one season to the next. There have been changes in cropping systems with less rotation. More chemical and less organic fertilizers are being used. Chemical pesticides (insecticides, fungicides and bacteriocides) are causing an increasing number of resistant biotypes. Finally, there is a reduction in natural enemies.

It would appear that China's pest control problems are becoming less and less those of traditional Chinese agriculture. Rather, they are the result of modern inputs. This is being manifested in cultural practices, control technologies and the inadvertent promotion of new pest problems and populations by chemical destruction of natural enemies, as well as the introduction of highly susceptible new varieties. An example of the latter is the introduction of dwarf rice varieties in the early 1960s. They provided an improved food source for brown plant-hoppers, since the rice leaves were more fleshy while the high leaf density and cold mircoclimate were less favorable for natural enemies such as spiders.

Diseases for which genetic resistance is being sought include a cucumber blight (*Phytophthora*), blackrot on cabbage, late blight (*Phytophthora infestans*) on tomatoes and potatoes and *Fusarium* wilt on cucumbers and eggplant. Here the potential is great when related to the policy of self-sufficiency in vegetable seed production. The simultaneous presence and coexistence of wild, semi-wild and cultivated types provide a diversity of germplasm in each vegetable species that is not likely paralleled anywhere in the world. This diversity also provides an important long-term stability derived from genetic heterogeneity, and it can likely be maintained with the almost 100% use of F_1 hybrids.

Cultural Practices

In China the cultural approach is basic and the chemical supplementary. One of the most significant deterrents to the spread and prevalence of bacterial diseases in vegetables is the use of ditches or trenches for furrow irrigation as an alternative to overhead sprinkling systems. Surprising to Western observers, nematodes apparently pose no recognizable problem. The periodic flooding of rice paddies, extensive crop rotations and deep furrow irrigation systems apparently suppress the multiplication of many diseases and nematodes to avoid epidemic proportions. Perhaps more than in any other nation, the Chinese are in a position to provide alternatives to chemical control of vegetable diseases and insects. The collective nature of China's agriculture has in the past placed it in a unique position for the control of pests and for farmers to carry out and coordinate pest control activities. Entire labor forces could be mobilized, if necessary, for pest control. How successful this will be under the new responsibility production contract system recently enacted remains to be seen. Pests usually infest a geographical area rather than individual farms, and they do not confine themselves to man-made boundaries.

It is well known that pest infestations in rice and cotton fields can be reduced by changes in cultivating techniques and by altering the sequence of plantings. The almost universal practice in China, with occasional exceptions for rice, wheat, corn and cotton, is to intercrop or multiple-crop. Mixed cropping is also practiced. These technologies constitute the establishment of natural barriers for rapid migration of pests; are built-in plant rotational systems; impose variable cultural practices at the same time in a given area; and provide some assurance that despite the failure or severe loss of one crop from pestilence, others will survive and be productive.

Chemical Control

During the 1950s, chemical control was prominent and dominated China's warring with pests such as locusts, corn borers, armyworms and boll weevils. Production of high quality fruits and vegetables in China, as in most countries, was and still is heavily dependent upon the application of chemical pesticides. Visitors in China are often advised to peel fruits and vegetables before eating them raw because of potentially dangerous pesticides residues. It was not until 1978 that the chlorinated hydrocarbons, DDT and Benzene Hexachloride (BHC), were banned for use on medicinal plants, grains, fruits and vegetables.

Irrespective of advanced technologies for numerous biological control mechanisms, cultural practices, and built-in genetic resistance, chemical pesticides are still applied to many crops in China. While they are important components for insect control, they are not of primary reliance as is true for the U.S.A., Japan and much of Europe. Fungicides are seldom if ever used for control of plant diseases such as rusts and smuts on cereal crops. Chemical (fungicidal) seed treatments, however, are still widespread in China and date back well before the first century A.D., but residues are minimal. Many insect pests cannot be effectively controlled or populations reduced to acceptable levels without chemical pesticides. These include planthoppers and borers in rice fields, the armyworm, the cotton boll weevil and pink bollworm in the north, the carmine mite in cotton fields and several apple and vegetable pests. Chemicals (insecticides) are commonly used as a supplement to cultural and biological methods to control vectors (aphids) of viral diseases.

Chemical pesticides alone, however, are not the ultimate answer. The Chinese recognize this truism as well as anyone in the world. In the rice fields of China one can observe, again and again, that the number of pest insects significantly decreases after pesticide application; however, soon thereafter the number increases and then surpasses the original level. Yet, there are agricultural areas in China such as the Xinjiang Autonomous Region of the far northwest where disease and insect problems on the major crops are essentially nonexistent.

Chemical herbicide usage is increasing in China, especially on rice, wheat and cotton. About one-third of the rice farms in the Jiangsu and Guangdong provinces use herbicides. They are also used extensively on wheat in Heilongjiang, and about 30 percent of the cotton farmers are now using herbicides. The levels of herbicide usage for major food crops (rice, wheat, corn, soybeans, potatoes, sugar crops), however, are still far below those in the U.S.A. Meanwhile, Chinese agricultural scientists have been actively engaged in devising integrated pest management programs for all crops.

Insecticide resistance has not yet reached serious proportions in China, except for the diamond back moth in crucifers, the hawthorn spider and European red mites on apples, and some cotton and fruit insects.

Finally, pest control possibilities are also being pursued in China with the relatively effective natural insecticides produced from a number of locally grown plants. One of the more noteworthy is Derris, the source of rotenone, a relatively safe but highly effective material for the control of many insect pests. Roots of *Derris elliptica* normally contain about 6% rotenone. Genetic strains have now been selected at the South China Agricultural University in Guangzhou that produce 13% rotenone, or more than double the normal level of the active ingredient.

The decrease in the use of chemical pesticides in China is reflected in the peak of nearly 500,000 tons produced and marketed in 1979-80 and a decline to nearly 200,000 tons in 1985. This compares with the approximate 500,000 tons of pesticides used annually in the U.S.A. Products are now being manufactured that are more effective and less harmful to the environment. A specific example is the widespread and effective use of synthetic pyrethroids which have, at least partially, accounted for the phenomenal increases in cotton yields in China during the past 5 years (Figure 4). Alternative methods of pest control (biological, including natural parasites), cultural practices and genetic resistance) are playing an increasingly important role in Chinese agriculture with positive financial, environmental, food safety and human health dividends. Chemical pesticide usage will probably continue to decline.

Conclusions and Projections

China has a high priority for the development of fully integrated pest control programs and for improved crop protection. There is also a policy of keeping prices low for essential agricultural production inputs. In fact, prices to the producer for pesticide products were lower in 1984 than in 1966. The need for stability and dependability of crop production is recognized as second only to the enhancement of production itself. The diversity of natural parasites now being cultured and released, with the high labor inputs but minimal investments for equipment and facilities, probably exceeds that of any other nation. Similarly, the diversity of genetic materials--wild, semi-wild and domesticated--provides a remarkable setting for achieving built-in

Figure 4. Phenomenal increases in yields of cotton have been achieved through improved insect control.

resistance to many fungal and viral pathogenes that now are exacting serious losses for rice, cotton, and many fruits and vegetables. There are elaborate pest control networks. An example is the vegetable disease research network, which deals with cucumbers, tomatoes and peppers. Coordinated by the Central Beijing Vegetable Research Institute, it has linkages to all the Provincial Academies of Agricultural Science and the Colleges of Agriculture. The Beijing and Nanjing Agricultural Universities have been designated as the lead institutions in China for the future development of integrated pest management programs.

Until recently, the unusually successful integrated pest control programs in China have been implemented and funded by collectives--communes and their subunits. With changes in China's economic and social structures as well as strengthening of household and family units through the responsibility production contract system and the dissolving of communes, brigades and production teams, one may well as what will become of integrated pest control efforts, which tend to be most effective when applied over large areas? Can and will individual households shoulder their new responsibilities for the community as a whole, for protection of the environment, for reductions in cost and for food safety and human health?

Will the old Chinese adage still hold? "Help your brother's boat to yonder shore, and your boat will arrive there also." The new economic incentives for farmers, with the responsibility production contract system now extended to virtually all of China, will likely serve as a catalyst for seeking out and putting to use the latest in new technologies for crop improvement and protection. The future paths to be followed for warring with pests in China will be of no small interest.

FOR FURTHER READING

Anonymous. 1986. New method lessens bollworm damage. *Beijing Review* 39(20): 30-31.

Chiang, H. C. 1976. Pest control in the People's Republic of China. *Science* 192: 675-76.

———. 1978. Why China's crops have fewer pests. *Horticulture* 56:32-36.

Chin, A. N. 1986. Pesticides in China: present status and prospects. *Proceedings on agriculture in China*. Vol. 2, *Macro issues in Chinese agricultural development*, 114-41. Beltsville, Md.: Institute of International Development and Education in Agriculture and Life Sciences.

Guyer, G.E. 1977. *Insect control in the People's Republic of China*. A trip report of the American Insect Control Delegation, CSC PRC Report no. 2. Washington, D.C.: National Academy of Sciences.

He Kang, ed. 1985. Beijing: Ministry of Agriculture, Animal Husbandry and Fishery. *Statistics of China's agriculture*.

Integrated control of major insect pests in China, An informal report. 1983. Trans. by R. G. Wanger. Beijing: Zoological Institute, Academia Sinica; Ithaca, N.Y.: Cornell University. (In Chinese, with English summary)

Ministry of Agriculture, Animal Husbandry and Fishery. 1985. *Statistics of China's agriculture*. Beijing.

Tsai, J. H. 1982. Entomology in the People's Republic of China. *New York Entomology Society* 90(3): 186-212.

U.S. Department of Agriculture. 1982. *Biological control of pests in China*. Washington, D.C.: Government Printing Office.

U.S. Department of Agriculture. Economic Research Service. 1985, 1986. *China outlook and situation reports*. Washington, D.C.: Government Printing Office.

Van Der Bosch, R.; P. S. Messenger; and A. P. Gutierrez. 1982. *Biological control*. New York: Plenum Press.

31
THE PLASTIC REVOLUTION

by Sylvan Wittwer

A dramatic transition is now occurring over much of China's countryside. Polyvinyl chloride (PVC) and polyethylene plastic films glisten in the sunlight. Plastic greenhouses, plastic-covered frames, plastic plant row tunnels or tents, and plastic soil mulches may be viewed in shining resplendence over the vegetable-growing areas as far as the eye can see around the major cities of north and northeast China as well as in the fields. The suburbs of Beijing and Tianjin, the major cities in the Jilin and Liaoning provinces, and Harbin in the Heilongjiang Province abound in plastic. Tens of thousands of hectares are covered with newspaper-thin layers, mostly of clear plastic, which protect the crops against the adversities of climate and weather. Many of the greenhouses are temporary structures, as are frames and row covers (tunnels), using local materials such as bamboo sticks and poles for support of single-layer plastic films (Figures 1 and 2).

Plastics are revolutionizing the production of many crops in China. They increase returns from the land and extend the growing seasons, enable the production of more crops per year, conserve water, improve fertilizer availability, raise soil temperatures, and utilize an ever increasing labor supply. Controlled environment agriculture in China, made possible by the use of plastic covers and soil mulches, is fittingly adapted to a country with a vast rural labor force and limited land, water, energy and fertilizer resources.

Plastic covers transmit sunlight for plant growth while at the same time protecting plants from cold and freezing temperatures, hot drying winds, and excessive downpours of rain and hail--all recognized as long-time hazards for agriculture in China.

The Chinese are intent on achieving stable yields at high levels and increasing the output per unit land area during a given year. They have

Figure 1. Plastic covered frames for starting vegetable seedlings in the Shanghai area.

Figure 2. The space between plastic greenhouses is used for growing hardy leafy vegetables.

long recognized the value of crop irrigation to achieve such objectives. Now they have found that plastic sheets placed over the plants and the soil effectively increase both the stability and magnitude of crop production.

Historical

China was probably the first country on earth to use protected areas for growing fresh vegetables. It began as early as the Western Han Dynasty. Among the luxuries enjoyed by the rich were "winter mallow" and "hothouse chives." Special houses were heated both day and night to grow green onions and chives, and there is a legend that during the reign of Qin Shi Huang (221-207 B.C.) melons were grown in winter, heated by the hot springs of Lishan. There are also accounts of where the warmth of hot springs was utilized for "out of season" production of vegetables during the Tang Dynasty, and where cold frames were used for growing chives during the Yuan Dynasty.

Rice Seedbed Covers. The first agricultural use of plastics in China began in 1958 as covers for rice seedling beds. By 1965, their use had spread to all provinces, autonomous regions and municipalities for promoting earlier crop production. There was a fivefold increase in their use between 1965 and 1973. The production advantages in using plastics for growin rice provided much of the technology that followed for its used on vegetable, fruit and field crops.

Plastic film covers for rice made it possible to plant rice seedbeds earlier and to grow plants to maturity prior to frost, thus extending the northern boundaries for rice production. It also became possible to produce two rice crops per year in some southerly regions where before only one had been possible. The use of plastic for rice seedbed covers also reduced labor requirements, increased efficiency of water use, and reduced losses from birds, nematodes, insects, diseases and problem soils. Other advantages were the saving of rice seed and more vigorous seedlings. Additionally, protection was provided from downpours of rain, sleet, hail, and snow as well as against frost and freezing temperatures. The plastic covers reduced moisture loss and surface drying and encouraged more uniform seedling emergence, seedling growth, and crop maturity. The use of plastic films for rice seedbed covers stands today as the most universal use of plastics in Chinese agriculture and in much of oriental agriculture. It is all the more important because most of the early rice produced in China is from seedlings that are started in seedbeds and then transplanted to the field.

Row Covers, Tunnels and Greenhouses. The large-scale use of plastics for agricultural crop protection in China is a development that has occurred in less than a decade. Some of the first documentation of protected cultivation, particularly plastic-covered structures used for growing plants in Chinese agriculture, was by the U.S. National Academy of Science team that reviewed vegetable resources in 1977. It was then reported that in the Beijing area alone, there were 130,000 plastic-covered cold frames being used to induce earlier production of vegetables. Beyond their use for covering rice seedling beds, plastics in Chinese agriculture were first used on a large scale for greenhouse construction and row tunnels in the early 1970s and finally, beginning in 1979, as soil mulches for the production of high value vegetables. Their use now extends to some of the major food and other agricultural crops. With the exception of some 130 hectares of glass structures, crop production in greenhouses is relatively new in China.

Following the use of plastic seedbed covers for rice was their application as row covers, row tunnels and greenhouses. The purpose was to extend the harvest season for vegetables grown in the suburbs. In China, there is limited transportation capacity for fresh produce. Any practice that will extend local availability and improve the volume of fresh vegetables in winter is important. Plastic greenhouses in China help accomplish these objectives. They are now found mostly in the northerly and central areas, particularly in the northeast. Here the early interest in development was related to Japanese influence and technology and the early availability of the Japanese polyvinylchloride (PVC).

Most greenhouse structures in China are used simply to extend the growing season and are not equipped for either heating or ventilation (Figure 3). Many have no doors. Entry and exit of workers is under the sides or at the ends. Most are constructed with flexible bamboo frames and often with the northside being a solid earthern or brick wall. Some plastic greenhouses are heated using briquettes of coal dust, straw, and mud.

Crops initially grown in plastic greenhouses were cucumbers, tomatoes, eggplants and peppers. Other crops now include Chinese cabbage, bush and pole beans, white gourds, calabash gourds, melons, cantaloupes, and grapes. Use of plastic greenhouses has progressed very rapidly since 1979.

The total area for protected vegetable crop production in China was estimated at 16,000 hectares in 1984. There were 30 hectares of modern glass greenhouses, and 1,400 hectares of traditional Chinese greenhouses with the earthen wall on one side. The traditional Chinese greenhouses are heated in the winter. They were formerly covered with glass which has now been replaced by plastic. There are also 4,000 hectares of large plastic greenhouses and 15,000 hectares of small and medium sized plastic greenhouses. In the Beijing area, there is a total growing area of 15,300 hectares, of which there are 300 hectares of glass greenhouses and traditional Chinese greenhouses along with 675

Figure 3. Most plastic greenhouses in China are not equipped for either heating or ventilation.

hectares of large and medium sized plastic greenhouses that are not heated, and an additional 2,000 hectares of protected growing which includes windbreaks. In the vicinity of Harbin, there were eighty hectares of plastic greenhouses in 1984, which was increased to nearly 200 hectares in 1985. There were also sixteen plastic factories in Harbin alone, with many of them specializing in the production of agricultural plastics. There is truly a "plastic revolution" occurring in China today. Numerous family and countryside enterprises now carry the name of "evergreen," made possible by year-round production of vegetables in plastic greenhouses. They center on the production of high value crops in plastic greenhouses under the new production responsibility contract system. Under this system, each family may have one or two greenhouses in which they produce a crop of tomatoes or cucumbers and derive therefrom, an income.

Plastic Soil Mulches

The technology for soil-mulching with plastic film was first introduced into China from Japan in 1978. The purpose was for earlier maturity and higher yields of vegetable crops. Initially, only 50 hectares of crops were mulched or covered with plastic. This was increased to 5,000 hectares by 1980 and 15,000 hectares in 1981. By 1982 there were at least 118,000 hectares of row crops in 26 of the 30 provinces utilizing plastic mulching. This grew to 655,000 hectares in 1983, 1,267,000 in 1984, and a projected estimate of 3,000,000 hectares by 1990 (Figure 4).

Figure 4. Plastic soil mulches are used extensively for high value crops and for cotton, peanuts, and even corn.

Plastic soil-mulching has been extended beyond its original use for vegetables and other high value crops such as strawberries. It is now used extensively on cotton, peanuts, corn, sugarcane and sugar beets. Peanuts and cotton, warm season crops formerly grown only in the southern provinces, are now found in the northern provinces where plastic soil mulches are used extensively. Of the principal crops for which plastic soil mulches are used, 64% of the plastic mulch is used on cotton, 12% for peanuts, 10% for vegetables and fruit and the balance for such crops as sugarcane, sugar beets, corn, and root and tuber crops.

Plastic soil mulches are used more extensively in China than in any other nation. Plastic covers and mulches generally increase plant growth which is followed by increased yields of crops. They provide an effective means of weed control and achieve a higher and more constant soil temperature. These mulches warm the soil in early spring and thus enable earlier planting, higher yields, and a means of achieving earlier maturity. This is occurring at latitudes of 45° north in the Xinjiang and Inner Mongolia Autonomous regions, in Heilongjiang and in southwest Hubei for corn production at marginally cold-high altitudes.

Cotton. Approximately 12% or 810,000 hectares of the 6,800,000 hectares of cotton in China was covered with plastic soil mulches in

1984. The thin clear plastic is preferred over white, opaque, black or white-over-black plastic. Where the crop is directly seeded, the film is laid over the entire surface after seeding and then holes are punched into the film so seedlings can emerge. A pre emergence herbicide is applied before the plastic is laid down. Over 25% of the cotton in China, however, is transplanted; this may be as high as 80% in some provinces such as Jiangsu. For transplanted cotton, the plastic film for soil-mulching is laid after the plants are set in the field. For cotton that is transplanted, a clear plastic film is used for covering the seedbeds. This is true also for rice seedbeds and for mulching in between the rows of seedlings.

Plastic soil mulches used on cotton increase yields by 25 to 30%. They hasten maturity, and produce a significant improvement both in fiber quality and on productivity of crops which follow the cotton. China became the number one cotton producer of the world in 1984-85, and plastic soil mulches contributed significantly to that accomplishment.

Peanuts. Second only to cotton, peanuts are the crop on which plastic soil mulches are used most widely. Nearly 2% of the total cropped area, or about 50,000 hectares, was covered with plastic in 1984. There were 37,200 hectares in 1983, double that for 1982.

The use of plastic soil mulches as an aid in peanut production has progressed rapidly in the northern parts of China such as in the Liaoning and Hebei provinces, where yields of up to four metric tons per hectare were achieved with plastic films in 1983. The advantages are an increase in and maintenance of higher soil temperatures, a retention of soil moisture with increased drought resistance, improved chemical and physical soil properties, weed control and, of most importance, earlier maturity and higher yields. Early experiments with clear plastic soil mulches which were initiated in 1979 produced yield increases of 30 to 50% of 1.0 to 1.5 metric tons per hectares.

Corn. A significant new development in the use of plastics for improving agricultural production in China is with corn. During 1986 a high altitude plastic covering technique was used on over 250,000 hectares in southwest Hubei Province and over considerable areas in Heilongjiang. The plastic soil mulch raised the soil temperature, improved soil nutrient availability and yields were advanced from 2.2 to 3.7 metric tons per hectare. The results were similar to those noted for thousands of hectares of corn grown since the early 1970's in France where early summer growth is often retarded by cold soil temperatures.

Fruits, Vegetables and Melons. Vegetables were among the first crops to be considered for plastic soil mulches in China. A hastening of maturity and increased yields were the primary considerations during the 1970s. Vegetable crops for which plastic soil mulches are now extensively used in China include the tomato, pepper, eggplant, cucumber, squash, cabbage, cauliflower, beans and peas.

A surprisingly widespread development in the use of plastic film for soil mulching is with watermelons. They were produced on 850,000 hectares in 1986, and are rapidly becoming one of China's most important "fruits." Early varieties dominate and are important in all the northerly provinces. Mulching with thin clear plastic was on 60-70% of the total area. First, these mulches increase the soil temperature. Second, they enable watermelons to mature and ripen fully three weeks earlier than otherwise allowing them to be grown further north. Third, they are effective for weed control. It gets so hot under the clear plastic that weeds are scorched by the sun, and they have difficulty growing in the very confined space. Fourth, the plastic mulch prevents surface evaporation of soil moisture, thus greatly reducing the loss of water by acting as a sort of solar still. Fifth, the mulch reduces soil erosion and compaction from heavy rains. The area sown to watermelons in the Beijing area in 1986 was near 10,000 hectares--a 25% increase over 1986. The output was near 250,000 tons. Ninety percent of the melon farms used plastic film covering techniques.

Currently, the Chinese are experimenting with plastic soil mulches on a great variety of crops and under a wide range of environments. The most dramatic effects can be observed in the most northerly provinces on high value crops and in desert-drought areas where evapotranspiration levels are high and water use efficiency is critical.

The use of plastics for covering seedbeds and constructing greenhouses has now been extended in a limited way to the production of flowers and ornamentals. Some former communes, now countryside and family enterprises in the vicinities of Beijing, Tianjin, Shanghai and Nanjing, have extensive plantings of flower crops and ornamentals for which plastic-covered cold frames and greenhouses are used.

Constraints and Problems

Plastic film covers and mulches for crop production in China are not without problems. Several large plastic factories in the major metropolitan areas of China now produce films for agriculture; but petroleum products, essential for plastics manufacturing, are often in short supply. short supply.

"Plastic pollution" is also a serious problem since most plastic films now used in agriculture are not biodegradable. The disposal of plastic residues poses the same problems, but is more severe than that encountered in the United States, Israel, Jordan, Japan, and several European nations. Waste piles of plastic are beginning to dot the countryside. Residual plastic materials can be serious obstacles in soil tillage operations as well as being unsightly. Biodegradable plastics have not, as yet, proven either effective or acceptable on a wide scale, although there has been much discussion as to their use and hopeful availability. Developments include the mixing of new plastics with corn starch to foster biodegradation by soil organisms, and plastics that will self-destruct after predetermined times of exposure to the ultraviolet wave lengths in sunlight. One unique approach the Chinese have employed is to recycle or maximize the use of agricultural plastic. It is used the first year for covering greenhouses and the following two years as a soil mulch. It is then factory recycled.

Another problem related to the use of plastic soil mulches is the control of weeds and soil-borne diseases. Herbicides (chemical weed killers) are not generally or popularly used as yet in China. Fungicides and fertilizers are difficult to apply after the mulch is laid down. In the U.S.A. and some other countries, this problem is resolved by the use of drip irrigation lines beneath the mulch through which fertilizers, fungicides and herbicides may be simultaneously applied with water.

International Concerns and the Future

The widespread adoption within a decade of the use of plastics in agriculture is an example of a new technology adapted to increase vertical productivity (output per unit land area or yields) for a nation with over 800 million people in the countryside and where further growth is constrained by land resources. This technological development is, at the same time, labor intensive. The large scale use of plastics in agriculture, along with other technological developments discussed in this book, set China apart from other agriculturally developing nations.

Until now little international visibility has been given to China for its vast cultivated areas of high value and conventional crops grown under plastic greenhouses and other plastic protected structures, or for its widespread use of plastic soil mulches for cotton, peanuts, corn, watermelons and a great variety of vegetables. There is every indication, however, that the use of plastics in Chinese agriculture will increase greatly in the future and be given added visibility, and that additional technologies will emerge for use in food production.

FOR FURTHER READING

He Kang. 1983, 1984. *Chinese agricultural yearbook*. Beijing: Agricultural Press. (In Chinese)

Houmin Yuan. 1980. Resume of applications of plastics in China's agriculture. *Proceedings 8th International Agricultural Plastics Conference*, 1:287-94.

Proceedings (subject abstracts) of the 9th International Congress of Plastics in Agriculture. 1983. Guadalajara, Jal, Mexico, 6-12 November.

Quebedeaux, B.; M. Faust; and F. D. Schales. 1985. Opportunities for horticultural food crop production improvements in China. In *Proceedings on agriculture in China*. Vol. 1, *Challenges and opportunities*, 196-203. Beltsville, Md.: Institute of International Development and Education in Agriculture and Life Sciences.

Romanowski, R. R. 1981. Environmental control structures. In *Vegetable farming systems in China*. A report of the visit of the Vegetable Farming Systems Delegation to China, June 1977, ed. D. H. Plucknett and H. L. Beemer, Jr., 119-27.

Wells, O. S., and J. B. Loy. 1985. Intensive vegetable production with row covers. *HortScience* 20(5): 822-26.

32
TEST TUBE PLANTS

by Wang Lianzheng

The wonders of biotechnology are nowhere more visible than in the laboratories, research institutes and countrysides of China. Of great interest is plant tissue culture. The Chinese are particularly adept at tissue culture techniques which require a minimum of expensive equipment and facilities and are labor intensive. Most importantly, the results of many basic research findings are easily applicable to field usage, crop improvement and increased food production.

Chinese plant scientists have, in recent years, developed early-maturing, high-yielding and disease-resistant varieties of hybrid rice. Through haploid culture (growing plants from pollen grains), new highly uniform selections of rice, wheat and tobacco have been obtained. Using tissue culture and special micropropagation techniques, they have developed genetically superior and disease (virus)-free selections of garlic, onion, sweet potato, tomato, asparagus, sugarcane, bananas, cassava and many other fruits and vegetables. The Chinese have regenerated new plantlets from somatic (vegetative) cells of rice and tobacco. Somatic embryogenesis (getting embryos from vegetative cells) has been achieved with ginseng, a precious medicinal plant (see Chapter 25, "Plants to Keep People Healthy"), and very recently with soybean cells. Mutation breeding is commonplace in China because masses of people are available to take part in the selection process. Chinese scientists have contributed greatly to the production of test tube plants, but only in recent years have their contributions been recognized beyond the borders of China. The Chinese have been very clever at developing innovative approaches in the micropropagation of a great variety of economically important food crops.

Test tube plants are obtained from the culture of pollen grains, anthers, meristems, buds, or sections of leaves, stems or roots grown in test tubes or other suitable containers. The goal is to rapidly reproduce, by vegetative propagation or by cloning, super strains or disease-resistant plants of economic importance. The plant tissue--meristem, pollen, stem or root section--is first placed in a sterilized nutrient medium or culture solution with the necessary minerals and growth hormones until a callus forms. (A callus is soft tissue from which roots or new plants can develop). The calluses are then transplanted into test tubes with additional growth media so that little plants are formed from them. These plantlets or propagules are called test tube plants. At an appropriate growth stage, they are carefully removed from their home in a tube and gradually adjusted to outdoor conditions by moving to partially controlled environments in a greenhouse or other protective structure and eventually to the field.

Meristem Culture

The classical example of meristem culture in China, as well as in many other countries, is the production of virus-free seed potatoes, with the technique now being extended to many other crops. Another example is the large-scale production of Panama (*Fusarium* wilt) disease-free banana plants being propagated by meristem culture at the Banana Research Institute in Taiwan.

Anther Culture

Anther or pollen culture is also an important way to produce test tube plants. It was first used in China to produce haploids (plants with half the normal number of chromosomes) in the mid 1960s. The technique has since been refined. Much attention has been given recently to the production and utilization of haploids for crop improvement and for studies of basic genetics. Haploids, started by pollen culture, have been produced on over 250 species of plants belonging to 88 genera and 34 families. Forty species including 6 cereals (rice, wheat, corn, sorghum, millet and triticale), 13 trees (such as rubber and poplar), 6 fruits (such as orange and grape), and other crops (such as sugar beet, sugarcane, Chinese cabbage, flax and soybean) were first obtained by anther culture in China. Some of the achievements of Chinese scientists who were the first to regenerate specific food crops from anther culture are listed in Table 1.

Anther culture had its origin in India with the culture of *Datura* pollen. The procedure is to tease out immature pollen grains from anthers of various crops and then carefully transfer them to an appropriate culture medium in a test tube (Figure 1). The pollen them germinates and a haploid plant is regenerated with half the chromosome

TABLE 1
Food Crop Species in Which Regenerated Plants from Anther Culture Were First Obtained in China (Hu Han, 1983)

Species	Year	Author
Wheat (*Triticum aestivum* L.)	1971	T. W. Ouyang, et al. C. C. Wang, et al. C. C. Chu, et al.
(*Triticale triticole*)	1971	C. S. Sun, et al.
Wheat-wheat grass hybrid (*T. aestivum* X *Agropyron glaucum*)	1973	C. C. Wang, et al.
Sugar beet (*Beta vulgaris* L.)	1973	Institute of Sugar Beet
Chinese cabbage (*Brassica pekinensis* Rurp.)	1973	L. P. Teng, et al.
Corn or Maize (*Zea mays* L.)	1975	Institute of Genetics Academia Sinica
Chinese cabbage (*Brassica chinensis* L.)	1977	C. H. Chung, et al.
Sorghum (*Sorghum vulgare*)	1978	W. B. Zhao, et al.
Flax (*Linum ustitalissimum*)	1979	H. T. Sun
Sugarcane (*Saccharum sinensis*)	1979	Z. H. Cheng
Orange (*Citrus microcarpa*)	1979	Z. G. Cheng
Alfalfa (*Medicago denticulata*)	1979	Hui Shu
Soybean (*Glycine max*)	1980	G. C. Yin, et al.
Job's tears (*Coix larxyma*)	1980	Z. C. Wang, et al.
Grape (*Vitis vinifera*)	1981	C. Z. Zhou, et al.
Chinese wolfberry (*Lycium barbarum*)	1981	S. Y. Gu
Strawberry (*Fragaria orientalis*)	1981	G. Y. She

number. The result can be a progeny of extremely uniform plants with all having exactly the same (homozygous) genetic constitution. Even though it is particularly difficult to culture anthers of the grain species, such as wheat and maize, and other plants, (such as the rubber tree, cotton and rapeseed), they were chosen for study in China because of their value as staple foods, their economic importance and their need for improvement. Regenerated plants from pollen cultures have been produced, and represent in many instances greatly improved varieties. Even wider applications of anther culture have been found by linking it with other breeding methods such as wide crosses of cereals and induced mutations, and with hybrid rice development.

For rapid crop improvement, the anthers of hybrid progenies--especially the F1 hybrids--are used. Through anther culture of F1 hybrids, the most desirable complementary characteristics of the two parents can be combined, and homozygous plants obtained directly in a single generation. Breeding cycles may be shortened to three generations when the pollen haploid breeding method is used. Alternatively, ten years or more may be required by conventional cross breeding. New varieties arise from doubled haploids, being derived from either spontaneous or chemically induced conversion of haploids back to diploids.

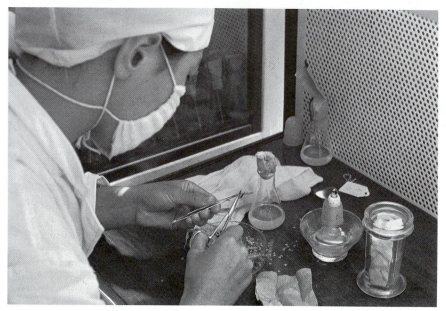

Figure 1. The first step in anther culture of rice is to tease out the immature pollen grains from the anthers.

Rice Haploids. More than eighty rice varieties and strains have been developed through anther culture in China. In no other country has comparable progress been made. Many new varieties have been released for growing in the suburbs of Beijing, Tianjin and Shanghai. The Huayu No. 1 rice is high-yielding (7.5 metric tons/hectare for a single crop in some areas), resistant to bacterial blight, and widely adaptable. "Danfong 1," developed jointly by the Institute of Botany, Academia Sinica, the Institute of Crop Breeding, the Heilongjiang Academy of Agricultural Sciences (HAAS) and the Sunghuajiang Rice Experiment Station of HAAS, is high-yielding, disease-resistant, stiff-strawed, resistant to lodging, and has compact, erect plants and a uniform canopy.

"Xin Xiu," a rice variety developed through anther culture, is grown on more than 100,000 hectares in the eastern part of China, and "Tonghua No. 2" is cultivated on over 6,000 hectares. Both the Xinxiu and Tonghua No. 2 varieties are high-yielding.

High-yielding rice varieties with blast (a highly destructive fungus disease) resistance are usually bred in the rice-growing regions of North China by backcrossing, which is a lengthy process. By using anther culture and the gene for blast resistance (Pi-2^t) found in Toride No. 2 and in Zhonghua No. 8 and No. 9, only two years were required to produce a variety with blast resistance, high yields and good quality. By contrast, the development of Toride No. 1 and No. 2 with the Pi-2^t gene by reciprocal crossing required twelve years in Japan.

Anther Culture of Hybrid Rice. Creating new varieties from hybrid rice by anther culture truly is a revolutionary development. Both Nanhua Nos. 5 and 11 rice lines, developed from the hybrid rice Nanyu No. 2, had 17 to 23% higher yields than the original parent Nanyu No. 2. Six strains have been selected from pollen plants derived from the F$_1$ anther culture of the hybrid rice "Shanyu No. 2." The phenotype, and some economic characters of four lines among them, are similar to the donor plants. These strains show promise for replacing the parent "Shanyu No. 2," and would avoid the cross-pollination difficulties and low seed yields currently associated with hybrid rice seed production (see Chapter 11, "Miracles of Rice"). These haploid-derived plants are not only high-yielding but uniform.

Haploid (anther) culture of rice, both in the test tube and in the field, has been observed at the Shanghai Academy of Agricultural Sciences and in the Shanghai Municipality. Plots of rice, one hectare in size, and each generated from plants derived from a single anther, produce extremely uniform and high-yielding plants (Figure 2). Chromosome doubling of the haploids was first achieved with colchicine but now occurs spontaneously.

The Development of Wheat Varieties. By 1982, more than twenty new wheat varieties and strains of both spring and winter wheat had been developed through anther culture by sixteen different research institutions in China. The spring wheat variety "Huapei No. 1," developed by the Kunming Institute of Agricultural Sciences and the Institute of Genetics, Academia Sinica in Beijing, has vigorous tillering, cold resistance, early maturity and good milling quality. It is cultivated on approximately 700 hectares in the Kunming Suburb of Yunnan Province. "Yunhua No. 1" and "Yunhua No. 2," additional spring wheats developed jointly by the Kunming Institute of Botany and other research institutions, mature early, are rust-resistant and have a high grain weight. In 1983 they were cultivated on about 70 hectares in the Kunming area. Another spring wheat, "Longhua 1," was developed by

Figure 2. A rice variety derived from anther culture which is very uniform and high-yielding.

the Institute of Crop Breeding at the HAAS and the Botanical Institute, Academia Sinica. These new spring wheat varieties, adapted for culture in one of the most southern of the Chinese provinces, constitute a significant breakthrough for wheat production in the lowland tropics.

Anther culture has also been combined with complex hybridization to produce the new winter wheat variety "Jinghua No. 1," which has a large spike and many grains, vigorous tillering, and resistance to stripe rust and powdery mildew. In the autumn of 1983, Jinghua No. 1 was being cultivated on about 5,000 hectares.

The Development of Inbred Lines of Corn. Pollen-derived corn plants are valuable in developing inbred lines for hybridization. Many such plants have been produced in China since 1975. Among them is the "Qunhua" line. It is an excellent variety with good combining ability. The "411 x Qunhua" cross is both high-yielding and disease-resistant. Seeds from regenerated maize plants derived from anther culture were obtained in a cooperative program of the Botanical Institute, Academia Sinica, the Institute of Maize, the Guangxi Autonomous Region Academy of Agricultural Science and the Dongbeiwang Township, Haidian District, Beijing. This technique should produce a large number of maize inbreds of pollen origin in the near future. Large investments of time and resources have gone into anther culture investigations of corn inbred lines. The results of research on utilization of heterosis in anther culture of maize may advance corn production to a new level (Figure 3).

Figure 3. The utilization of heterosis in anther culture
of corn in China is advancing production to new levels.

Other Crops. Improved tobacco varieties have been developed by
anther culture. The "Danyu No. 1" tobacco was jointly introduced by
the Shandong Institute of Tobacco and the Botanical Institute, Academia Sinica. This variety has now been released and is cultivated on more
than 8,000 hectares in regions along the Yellow and Huai rivers.

Improved varieties of both rubber trees and sugarcane plants have
been derived from pollen or anther culture. The tallest pollen plant of
the rubber tree has reached more than six meters. A sugarcane pollen
plant containing high sugar content and a tall stem has also been
produced.

Mass Propagation and Cloning by Plant Tissue Culture
For Some Major Food Crops

The "totipotency" of single cells has been scientifically demonstrated
for many plant species. Totipotency means that, through test tube
culture of a single protoplast or cell, a new plant--complete with all the
parts and organs--can be regenerated. Plant tissue cultures can now be
used for the mass propagation of economically important crops. This is
one of the most exhilarating achievements of the "new biology." It is
leading to rapid progress in improvement of many basic food crops,
horticultural species and the tree crops of forestry. The production of
millions of plantlets via suspension culture or embryogenesis, beginning
with the multiplication of clones or explants in a test tube, is now
possible. Plant tissue cultures serve as the pathway from the laboratory
to the field in the genetic engineering of new super crop plant varieties.
Techniques for improved handling of the so-called *in vitro*-produced
"test-tube seedlings" and their transfer to field conditions need to be
improved and the process automated and programmed. Nevertheless,
cell, meristem and tissue culture propagation has already found com-

mercial application for orchids and economically important varieties of strawberries, potatoes, bananas, cassava, sweet potatoes, yams, oil palm, garlic, onions, sugarcane, papaya, citrus and asparagus. The potential exists for almost all tropical fruits. Test tube propagation of many ornamentals, several economically important food crops listed above (rice, wheat, corn and potatoes) and some species of seaweed have been carried out in China.

Potato. Recently, the quality of potato seed stocks in China deteriorated greatly and yields were depressed significantly as a result of virus disease infections. At great cost, the government distributed disease-free seed potatoes from the North to the South. Virus diseases can be detected in the field in the northern cool climates but not in the South except at the higher elevations. Meanwhile, the Botanical Institute Academia Sinica at Beijing cooperated with other concerned institutes and designed a system for obtaining virus-free seed potatoes.

A virus eradication program using meristem culture has now been established in ten provincial institutes and the findings disseminated to the countryside. Tiny stem tips from virus-free plants containing one or two leaf primoidia are used. These are cut off mother plants and placed in a basic culture medium. The resulting plantlets are in due time subjected to virus disease assays. These include the indexing of each plant and running serological tests. After establishing that the plantlets are virus-free, they are cut into segments and cultured in a medium containing nutrients and various growth-promoting substances. Plantlets with three to five leaflets are regenerated after about two weeks. The rate of multiplication can be 10^7 to 10^8 a year. Before transplanting from the culture or test tube, a plant growth hormone at a few parts per million is added. Survival rates approach 100%.

Large numbers of virus-free seed potatoes have been produced by this stem tip culture technique at various agricultural research institutes and distributed throughout the countryside. This is an example of a massive program of biotechnology in action for improvement of a major food crop. Yields of potatoes have been significantly increased by planting "virus-free" seed stocks, derived from "virus-free" seed farms. Yields of one cultivar in the Heilongjiang Province using virus-free seed potatoes approached 38 metric tons per hectare. This compared with only 24 metric tons per hectare the the virus infected fields.

Sugarcane. This is an important economic crop well known for its ease of vegetative propagation. One-half to one ton of seedcane clones, stems or stalks is sufficient to plant one hectare. Tissue culture techniques or test tube cultures provide many potential advantages. The large volume of seed cane is greatly reduced which, hopefully, will lessen virus disease transmission and, more importantly, provide a means for selecting disease-resistant clones. Portions of the stem apex or lateral buds as well as young leaves may be used for the initial explant or culture material. A callus is first induced from which young seedlings are regenerated. Scientists at the Guangdong Academy of Agricultural Sciences have reported that the yields from test tube-raised sugarcane plantlets compare favorably with those obtained by ordinary field culture.

Citrus. It has recently been discovered that the nucellus (the part of the ovary that contains the embryo sac) or fertilized seed, or even the nonfertilized, abortive and seedless nucellus, of citrus may be used for tissue culture. Citrus carry many virus diseases which destroy hundreds of thousands of trees. With nucellus-derived embryoids, however, virus diseases can be avoided. Triploid citrus plants have been derived from endosperm (the triploid nucleus) culture. The requirements for endosperm culture of *Citrus grandis* (Osbeck) have been established. The results are seedless fruits and a new technique for breeding by culturing the hybrid endosperm. Callus tissue formation can be induced from the young endosperm at the cellular stage with a culture medium supplemented with specific plant growth regulators. Embryoids at various developmental stages are differentiated from the endosperm callus. These embryoids, in turn, produce roots and shoots and develop into plantlets. Chromosome counts of root tip cells show that they are triploids. Again, this is a unique breakthrough based on tissue culture for the propagation of superior disease-free citrus varieties.

Apples. The results are equally as exciting as for citrus. Scientists at the Shandong College of Agriculture have produced triploid plants from endosperm culture of the cultivar "Jingsui." New plants were also derived from meristem culture of Malling 7 dwarf apple rootstocks. Scientists at the Botanical Institute in Beijing have produced new plants by meristem culture from five cultivars of dwarf apple seedling rootstocks, and seedlings from the endosperm callus of immature seeds.

Other plants. Activity in test tube plant production has been intense within many Chinese research institutes. Scientists at the Botanical Institute, Academia Sinica and the Heilongjiang Academy of Agricultural Sciences (HAAS) have obtained seedlings derived from both the callus of soybean and pea hypocotyls. The Shandong Academy of Agricultural Sciences has reported callus formation from endosperm tissues of grape, apple, pear, apricot, peach, walnut, date and cherry. Both the Guangxi and Hainan Institutes of Tropical Crops have obtained plantlets from the callus of *Agave nisalana*. The Shandong College of Oceanology has developed a somatic propagation system for both female and male gametophytes of kelps. Tobacco fertilization experiments have been conducted in test tubes where, after thirty days of culture, ripe capsules and seedlings were produced from the germinated seeds.

The Shanghai Institute of Plant Physiology cooperating with the Shanghai Longhwa Nursery has succeeded in regenerating the Chinese orchid cymbidium cultivar "Tai-I-Pei" through tissue culture. Protocorms were differentiated from both apical meristems and lateral buds. Plantlets were then produced by the culture of small cut pieces of the protocorm tissue. Occasionally and within a year, some of the small orchid plantlets flowered in the 100-milliliter culture flasks. Other young orchids started in test tubes were successfully grown to flowering after transplanting to a nursery.

Medicinal Plants. A preliminary report in 1963 from the Shanghai Institute of Plant Physiology, Academia Sinica described the cultivation of ginseng and *Datura* callus tissue. Meanwhile, the Beijing Pharmaceutical Institute cultivated ginseng callus, proliferated from young stems and roots. The saponins in the test tube-grown ginseng were the same as those of ginseng grown in gardens. The *in vitro* cultivation of *Pritillaria* has been simultaneously conducted at several institutions. Both callus tissue and bulbils were useful for propagation. The Zhejiang Medical Institute and the Beijing Pharmaceutical Institute, in 1975, succeeded in obtaining a callus tissue culture of the Chinese *herbscorydaris*. The essential alkaloid was in the cultured tissue. Soybean plantlets have been produced from anther culture by scientists of the Heilongjiang Academy of Agricultural Sciences (Figure 4).

Methods for Improving the Production of Test Tube Plants from Anther Culture

Several variables are important for the induction of new plants (plantlets) from pollen grains. These include the culture media, culture conditions, genotypes of donor plants and the stage of microspore development when prepared for culture.

Culture Media. The culture medium is the chief factor for induction and control of development, especially of intact plantlets produced from pollen grains. The sucrose concentration is a critical factor. Sucrose not only regulates the osmotic pressure of the medium but is often the most effective carbohydrate source. A 9% sucrose solution is appropriate for anther culture of wheat, with 12% recommended for corn, rapeseed, triticale and barley.

New media plays a prominent role. One called "N6" has been developed. A large number of experiments revealed that the induction frequency of plantlets from pollen plants of rice, wheat, triticale, rye, and corn was higher on the N6 medium than on the Miller's or the Murashige-Skoog (MS) Medium.

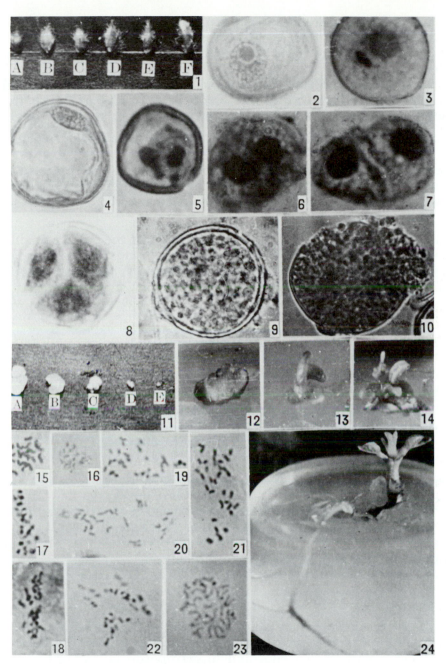

Figure 4. Developmental stages in the anther culture of soybeans. 1. Pollen of the early and mid-uninucleate stage, 2-10. Androgenesis of anthers, 11-14. Callus from anthers, 15-23. Chromosome number of callus and pollen plantlets, 24. Plantlets from anther culture.

Plants were successfully induced from pollen of *Triticum dicoccoides* and from the hybrid between *Triticale* and *Triticum aestivum* in the N6 medium. Pollen calli were also obtained from anther cultures of *Triticum durum* and a hybrid between *Triticum aestivum* and *Secale cereale*. The Potato-II medium contains 10% aqueous potato extract and one-half the microelements of the MS medium. Frequency of callus induction from pollen in this medium was higher than that in other synthetic media.

Improving the Cultural Conditions. Temperature has a marked influence on the frequency of induced pollen callus and the formation of embryoids. A cold pretreatment of pollen before placement in the culture medium may increase the frequency of plantlets induced for rice and wheat. The frequency is doubled when wheat anthers are pretreated at 1° to 4°C for 48 hours.

An elevation or alteration in the temperature of the culture medium increases the frequency of callus formation for both wheat and rapeseed. When wheat anthers are cultured at 33°C for eight days and then transferred to 24°C, not only is the frequency of induced callus increased but the frequency of the differentiating green plantlets as well.

Floating the anthers in a liquid medium has improved results for the culture of some plants, such as tobacco, Datura, wheat and barley. Floating cultures also increase the induction frequency of rice plants derived from pollen grains. In keng rice, the induction frequency of callus is greatly increased by a floating culture.

The Genotype of the Donor Plants. This has a significant influence on the effectiveness of anther culture. Both callus formation and the production of plantlets from callus are heritable characteristics quantitatively controlled by multiple genes.

The Stage of Microspore Development. This also determines the effectiveness of anther culture. Although the pollen-derived calli may be induced in cultured anthers inoculated at any stage from pollen mother cells to mature pollen, the best results are achieved with anthers containing mid-to-late uninucleate microspores. At these stages the induction frequencies of callus were the highest.

The Future

There is great potential in China for future achievements in biotechnology. The resource base resides in rich genetic plant resources, both domesticated and in the wild, and in germplasm collections now in progress. This is coupled with a rising human capital that is current with or becoming so with the latest in advanced training and knowledge of tissue, anther and meristem culture and with somatic fusion. Many plant scientists, some who have received training from abroad in micropropagation of genetically superior disease-resistant crops, are now associated with the Botanical and Genetic Institutes of Academia Sinica in Beijing, the Shanghai Institute of Plant Physiology, the universities, and many of the Provinical Academies of Agricultural Sciences. Such research institutes and many others now have or plan to have tissue culture laboratories for crop improvement programs. Many now have the facilities and the people to do the work, and programs are already in progress. All this is coupled with a record of past achievements conducive to the support of continuing and future exploratory research.

It is expected that the future of biotechnology in China will include the use of recombinant DNA, construction of plasmid vectors, cloned DNA fragments and transposable elements. The crown gall (*Agrobacterium tumefaciens*) Ti plasmid system for incorporation of useful germplasm into crop cells, is already in use, along with other approaches to plant cell transformations. Severe problems of salt tolerance, and stresses from cold, heat, drought, and other environmental constraints, have been long-time hazards for crop production in China. Research now in progress is designed to develop cultivars that will be resistant to these and other environmental and biological limitations.

FOR FURTHER READING

Hu Han. 1978. Advances in anther culture investigations in China. In *Proceedings of Symposium on Plant Tissue Culture*. 3-10. Beijing: Science Press. (In Chinese)

———. 1984. Crop improvement by anther culture. New Delhi: In *Proceedings of the 15th International Congress on Genetics*. Vol 4: 27-84. (In Chinese)

Hu Han, and Shao Qiquan. 1981. Advances in plant cell and tissue culture in China. *Advances in Agronomy* 34: 1-13.

Hwang, S. C.; C. L. Chen; and H. L. Lin. 1984. Cultivation of banana using plantlets from meristem culture. *HortScience* 19(2): 231-33.

International Symposium on Genetic Manipulation of Crops (Abstracts). 1984. Third International Symposium on Haploidy. First International Symposium on Somatic Cell Genetics in Crops, 22-26 October. Beijing.

Loo Shihwei. 1978. The present status of the practical application of plant tissue and cell culture in China. In *Proceedings of Symposium on Plant Tissue Culture*, 449-53. Beijing: Science Press.

National Academy of Sciences. 1985. *New directions for bioscience research in agriculture. High reward opportunities*. Washington, D.C.: National Academy Press.

Nickell, L. G. 1986. *Plant growth regulation, biotechnology and world food production*. Chicago: VS Crop Protection Corporation.

Tao, K. C., et al. 1978. Meristem culture of potatoes and the production of virus-free seed-potatoes. In *Proceedings of Symposium on Plant Tissue Culture*, 459-62. Beijing: Science Press. (In Chinese)

Wang Lianzheng, et al. 1984. A study on tumor formation of soybean and gene transfer. *Scientia Sinica* (Series B) 27(4): 391-97. (In Chinese)

Wang Tuyan, and Chang Chinjen. 1978. Triploid citrus plantlets from endosperm of plant tissue culture. In *Proceedings of Symposium on Plant Tissue Culture*, 463-68. Beijing: Science Press. (In Chinese)

Yin Guangchu, et al. 1976. A study of the new cultivar of rice raised by haploid breeding method. *Scientia Sinica* 19(2): 227-42. (In Chinese)

———. 1980. A study of anther culture of *Glycine max*. *Kexue Tongbao* 25(18): 916-81. (In Chinese)

33

ACUPUNCTURE AND MOXIBUSTION FOR FARM ANIMALS

by Yu Youtai[1]

No practices in China are surrounded by more mystery, suspicion and intrigue than those of acupuncture and moxibustion. These techniques are used not only for disease control and the correction of disorders in humans but also for treating sick farm animals and for the improvement of animal health.

Historical

The development of traditional veterinary medicine in China has paralleled that of human medicine. Both have a very long history, dating back several millenia, and both are characterized by an integral conception and dialectical approach in the prevention and treatment of diseases. This unique theoretical and somewhat philosophical system allows for prescriptions of medicinal herbs along with the use of acupuncture and moxibustion.

Acupuncture and moxibustion are similar therapies developed by the ancient Chinese and are often considered as one. No drugs are needed in either treatment. They are, however, two distinct methods for treating animal diseases extensively, efficiently, rapidly and safely with little if any medication. The curative effects are obtained by puncturing or applying heat to certain points of the body. Because of the simple equipment needed and the ease with which it can be used, these methods are easily adapted to disease control and surgery for horses, cattle, camels, sheep, goats, pigs and chickens. Positive results with farm animals have ruled out what could be attributed to the psychological factor with humans.

---

[1] The author is deeply indebted to Professor Jiang Cisheng, Head of the Laboratory of Chinese Traditional Veterinary Medicine, Zhejiang Agricultural University in Hangzhou for details concerning the channels and collaterals and the therapeutic mechanisms of acupuncture and moxibustion.

Ancient Records

The history of Chinese traditional veterinary medicine and surgery is recorded in two ancient medical works: the *Canon of Internal Medicine* and *Classics on Shen Nong's Medicinal Herbs*. Written in the third and second centuries B.C. (Han Dynasty), respectively, they cover both human and animal care. In practice, veterinary activities were carried out at the very beginning of domesticated livestock production, going back to primitive societies. In the ruins of the Yangshao culture of the New Stone Age (about 5,000 years B.C.), there were unearthed in Henan Province, not only the skeletons of pigs, cattle and horses but also stone knives, bone needles and earthenware designed for treating sick animals and for animal surgery.

During the age of China's Slave Society (twenty-first to the fifth century B.C.), from the Xia to the Spring and Autumn dynasties, there were records inscribed on animal bones and tortoise (land-roving turtle) shells that depicted not only pigpens, cowsheds, sheepfolds and horse stables, but also the cures for illnesses generally found in both human beings and domesticated animals. These include gastrointestinal diseases, parasitosis and teeth disorders. Bronze knives and needles were also among the historical relics from that same age. Gold pins and needles were found in excavations dated a few centuries later.

The earliest accounts of professional veterinary activities in China were in the eleventh century B.C. (Zhou Dynasty). Animal diseases were then categorized as either of an internal nature or as requiring surgery. Disorders were treated through oral administration of medicines, surgery and comprehensive nursing and rearing procedures.

A complete system of Chinese traditional veterinary medicine did not take shape until the fifth century B.C. (the Warring States), when China entered into a feudal society. A specialized volume on veterinary medicine, *Key Skills for the People*, was written by Jia Sixie in the sixth century A.D. (Southern and Northern dynasty). Yuan Heng's work on the *Treatment of Equine Diseases*--with supplements on cattle and camels by Yu Benyuan Yu Benheng, two renowned veterinarians--appeared in the seventeenth century A.D. (Ming Dynasty). This classical work on traditional Chinese veterinary medicine became widely known both in China and abroad. Many other more recent monographs on diagnosis, prescriptions of medicinal herbs, and acupuncture and moxibustion have contributed to the world's knowledge of veterinary medicine.

For several decades before the establishment of the new China in 1949, traditional veterinary medicine as well as traditional human medicine were denigrated as unscientific and much of the literature was destroyed. After that, however, through a policy of combining traditional and Western medicine, they developed rapidly like "spring comes to the withered tree."

Acupuncture

Acupuncture is a therapy which treats diseases by puncturing the animal (or human) body at certain critical or sensitive areas ("acupoints"). Very thin metal needles, much thinner than the more familiar hypodermic needles, are inserted to varying depths at a great variety of acupoints. Stimulations are then induced by various manipulations. Acupuncture is clinically used to treat over 300 animal diseases. There are no uniform specifications for the needles and they vary with regional traditions and preferences of the operator. The most commonly used needles for treatment of animal diseases and for surgical anesthesia are shown in Figure 1. Four main techniques are used in the practice of acupuncture:

1) *Naked Needling.* This is the most common method. Here the operator pricks at certain acupoints using both the naked round and sharp needles (Figure 1-B) or the broad needle (Figure 1-D), according to the depth of stimulation desired.

2) *Fire Needling.* Here the operator pricks at certain acupoints (apart from those on or near the blood vessels and joints) with a fire needle, which is heated to a specified level to produce a burned spot that confines the stimulations to the acupoint. This method combines the effects of acupuncture and moxibustion.

3) *Blood Needling.* A broad or three-edged needle is used for pricking the blood vessel at the acupoint (Figure 1-D).

4) *Air Needling.* The air needle is used to inject subcutaneously an appropriate amount of air or oxygen at the acupoint. This stimulates the nerve endings and the blood vessels, resulting in improved blood circulation.

Moxibustion

The moxibustion treatment applies a burning stimulation at the acupoints by fumigating or burning a "moxa-wool stick" or other heated substances to treat the disease. "Moxa" is made of dried and shredded leaves of the Chinese Mugwort (*Atemisia argyi*) which is highly fragrant, burns rapidly and evenly, and has a therapeutic effect on vital body functions. The points chosen are the same as for acupuncture. The amount of heat applied can be mild or provide a powerful counter irritant.

Ironing and cauterization are types of moxibustion which have long been popular for veterinarian practice in the Chinese countryside. The ironing treatment employs a mixture of vinegar and wheat bran (1:4 by weight) which is heated (fried) to about 40°C and then put on the affected, cloth-wrapped part of the animal. While ironing (pressing with a hot flat iron) the affected part, vinegar and 70% alcohol are used

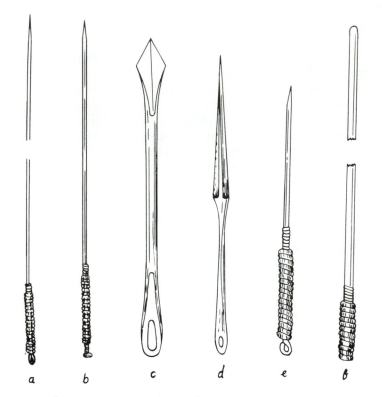

Figure 1. The most commonly used needles in veterinary acupuncture practices: *a*, filiform needle; *b*, round and sharp needle; *c*, three-edged needle; *d*, broad needle; *e*, fire needle; *f*, air needle.

alternatively to moisten the back and waist. This area is then set on fire and sprinkled alternatively with vinegar and alcohol to control the fire strength (heat) until the patient (animal) begins to sweat. These methods are effective for relief of rheumatism of the waist and hip. Cauterization involves branding the affected part with a heated knife-shaped iron, interrupted at times with a sprinkling of vinegar until the fur becomes scorched.

Acupoints and "Channels and Collaterals"

An acupoint is a specific spot on the body surface at which needling or moxibustion is applied to produce therapeutic effects in certain body parts or viscera. By connecting acupoints that have similar or closely related functions, lines of acupoints are established, thus giving rise to the concept of "channels and collaterals." The vertically distributed "trunk lines" are described as "channels," implying "passages." The large and small branches of these "channels" or "passages" are referred to as "collaterals," meaning a "network." These concepts are usually used to describe the patho-physiological connections between the acupoints and the respective viscera (Figure 2).

The therapeutic effects of both acupuncture and moxibustion are directly dependent upon the accuracy of precisely locating the acupoints. There are many acupoints on the animal body. Some can be located by the exterior anatomical appearance, others by proportional distances between parts on the animals body, and still others by measuring distances with the fingers. "Two horizontal fingers" means the total width of the forefinger and middle finger, which equals about 3 centimeters. "Four horizontal fingers" means the total width of all fingers, which is about 6 centimeters. There are different acupoints with different names on different animals for different diseases (Table 1).

TABLE 1
Commonly Used Acupoints for Different Farm Animals

Number of Acupoints

Animal	Total	Head and Neck	Foreleg	Rearleg	Body
			Both legs		
Pig	43	14	10		19
Horse	97	23	25	26	23
Cattle	60	13	13	11	23
Sheep	43	12	7	12	12
Camel	37	--	--	--	--
Poultry	28	--	--	--	--

Traditional Chinese veterinary medicine maintains that the basis of acupuncture and moxibustion for treatment of diseases is this concept of "channels and collaterals." The stimulations induced at the acupoints are transmitted through the "channels and collaterals" to the respective internal organs and vital areas. These unusual methods of therapy are effective because they can dredge the channels and collaterals, regulate the energy and blood, and readjust the functions of the affected viscera to restore good health.

Chinese clinical practice and records have demonstrated that acupuncture and moxibustion are effective for more than sixty kinds of animal diseases including sunstroke, equine colic, the forestomachic disease of cattle, rheumatism, neuroparalysis, catarrheal gastroenteritis of pigs, and the so-called distemper and common cold.

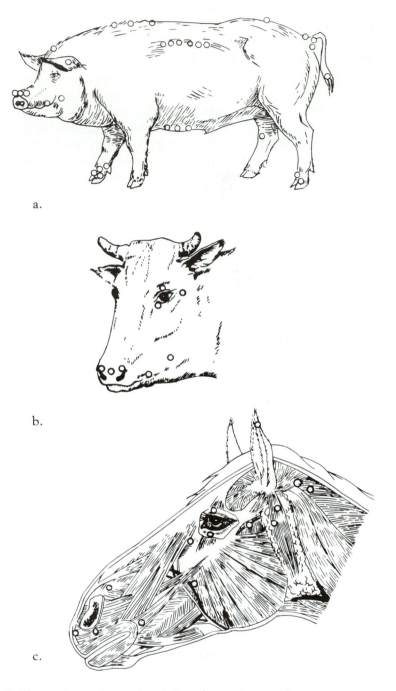

a.

b.

c.

Figure 2. Illustrations of acupoints (o) on domestic animals: *a*, acupoints on the pig body; *b*, acupoints on the cow head; *c*, acupoints on the horse head.

New Developments of Acupuncture

Many advances in acupuncture have occurred in recent years through the use of naked needling. For acupuncture-induced anesthesia, properly selected acupoints are pricked to obtain the necessary anesthetic effect for various surgical procedures (Figure 3).

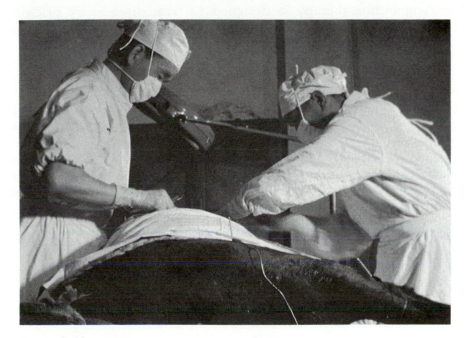

Figure 3. Veterinarian acupuncture anesthesia.

Laser Acupuncture is a significant new development referred to as "high-tech acupuncture." In this process metal needles are replaced by laser beams which have the advantages of no pain, no infections, simplicity, safety and strength adjustability. For China, laser acupuncture is considered a new direction in animal disease control and health improvement. The many opportunities for laser acupuncture are now being pursued throughout China's many colleges of agriculture and veterinary medicine and provincial academies of agricultural science. The most commonly used laser beam is generated by the He Ne laser.

Electro-Acupuncture is stimulation at the acupoint by using a small electric current in a filiform needle (Figure 1-A) therapy. It is used both for treating diseases and for electro-acupuncture anesthesia.

Modified or Renewed Acupuncture involves using filiform needles to prick the acupoint to a depth of six to ten centimeters, about twice the usual depth of acupuncture. According to this new therapy, several acupoints beyond the selected one can be passed through at one time by a single needle. The therapeutic effect is greater and there is less injury to the therapeutic tissue, since the filiform needle has a very small diameter.

Aqueous Acupuncture therapy requires that measured amounts of prescribed medicines be injected at the acupoint. A dual advantage results from combining the physical effect of acupuncture and medicine.

Ear Acupuncture therapy is designed to treat diseases by pricking special acupoints located on the ear shell or lobe. It is based on internal relationships between different parts of the body and the ears.

Veterinary Acupuncture in America

While acupuncture had its origin in China perhaps 5,000 years ago, its use in America hardly dates fifteen years. Today, there are some fifty veterinary acupuncturists in the U.S.A. officially certified by the International Veterinary Acupuncture Society, although many more practice the technique. Measurable success has been achieved in the relief of musculoskeletal disorders such as arthritis, skin diseases, chronic gastrointestinal diseases, neurologic problems, chronic pain syndromes, infertility problems and respiratory arrest.

FOR FURTHER READING

Chinese Academy of Agriculture. Institute of Chinese. Traditional Veterinary Medicine. 1979. *Lately edited Chinese veterinary medicine*. Lanzhou, China: People's Press of Gansu Province. (In Chinese)

Gansu Provincial Institute. 1981. *Acupuncture and moxibustion in veterinary medicine*. Beijing: Agricultural Press. (In Chinese)

Langone, J. 1984. Acupuncture: A new respect for an ancient remedy. *Discover* (August): 70-74.

Lanzhou Institute of Veterinary Medicine. 1983. *Handbook of veterinary medicine*. New ed. Lanzhou, China: People's Press of Gansu Province. (In Chinese)

Ma Jixing. 1983. Acupuncture and moxibustion. In *Ancient China's technology and science*, 345-51. Beijing: Foreign Language Press.

Needham, J. 1981. The history and rationale of acupuncture and moxibustion. In *Science in traditional China: A comparative perspective*. 85-106. Cambridge: Harvard University Press.

Pitcairn, R. H. 1982. Veterinary acupuncture. *Prevention* 34:65-67.

34

RETURNS BEYOND THE LAND

by Wang Lianzheng

There is an old Chinese proverb:

> Those living on the mountain live off the mountain,
> Those living near the water live off the water.

So it is in China today with crop production, forestry, animal husbandry, sideline industries and fisheries--all developing simultaneously. Agriculture, industry and commerce overlap. In recent years the importance of animal husbandry, forestry, sideline industries and fisheries has been gaining with each passing day in answer to rising demands of people in both the cities and the countryside. As agriculture, industry and commerce develop together, they enliven the economy in the countryside. Accordingly, farmers encouraged by the production responsibility contract system are receptive to the development of village and township enterprises involving light industries, transportation and trade as well as crop and livestock production.

Thus, Chinese farmers today not only rely on their crops to increase their incomes and improve their lives but are also seeking returns beyond the land. Farmers are becoming increasingly engaged in diversification and a broadening of interests. The result has been that China's economy has rocketed upward during the early 1980s. In 1982 China's GNP gained over 7%, 9% in 1983 and a spectacular 13% annual growth rate in 1984, exceeding that in all other major countries. The driving force has been a thriving farm sector prompted by economic incentives.

A survey by the National Agricultural Commission in 1979 showed the composition of production in eleven select counties in China. Included were those close to large cities and those more distant. The results are summarized in Table 1.

For the counties (Table 1) in the vicinities of large cities such as Jiading (close to Shanghai), Tong (close to Beijing) and Wuxi (close to Wuxi City), sideline industries are much higher because they support agriculture. In Jiading County, the labor for sideline industries was 30%

TABLE 1
Comparative Percentages of Crop Production, Forestry,
Animal Husbandry, Sideline Industries and Fisheries
of Selected Counties (1979)

Counties	Crop Production	Forestry	Animal Husbandry	Sideline Industries	Fisheries
Tong	34.2	1.0	17.7	47.0	0.1
Jiading	23.1	0.0	6.6	70.0	0.3
Wuxian	51.8	0.4	14.0	30.6	3.2
Wuxi	36.1	0.2	12.8	50.0	0.9
Taoyuan	66.7	3.6	12.3	16.9	0.5
Luancheng	79.6	0.2	0.8	19.4	---
Hailun	80.3	4.3	10.3	5.1	---
Guanghan	70.0	1.2	18.1	9.9	0.1
Beluo	70.2	2.1	9.0	17.6	1.1
Cangji	71.2	1.5	20.5	6.8	0.0
Yanchi	47.6	6.0	35.8	10.6	---
Average for China	66.9	2.8	14.0	15.1	1.2

of the total but the value of output was 70% of the total. Here the labor input for crop production was 61.4% while the output was only 23.1%. In Tong County, each person earned about 103 yuan from crop production, 1,090 yuan from forestry, 1,296 yuan from animal husbandry, 440 yuan from fisheries, and 2,894 yuan from sideline industries. The value of crop production was nearly three times greater in the Hailun County of the Heilongjiang Province and Luancheng County in Hebei. Here the proportion of crop production predominated and approximated 80%, accompanied by low levels for forestry and animal husbandry. The average income for each person was also low.

Forestry and Afforestation

Forestry differs from the production of cultivated crops. It centers on mountainous or semi-mountainous areas and is apart from afforestation on the plains (Figure 1). Forests now cover about 120 million hectares or 13% of China's land surface. In 1979 there were 220,000 forestry centers operated by communes and brigades, with a total area of 13 million hectares of managed forests and 0.4 million hectares devoted to nurseries for raising forest tree seedlings. The reforestation area assigned to farmers in 1981 was 3.2 million hectares. With the establishment and implementation of the production responsibility contract system, the farmer's enthusiasm for reforestation has been greatly stimulated.

Figure 1. Afforestation in the mountains of China.

The fourth session of the Fifth National Congress on December 13, 1981 passed "The Decision About the Movement of Voluntary Reforestation in the Whole Nation." The decision stipulated that every Chinese citizen other than the old, weak or disabled who was eleven years of age or older must plant three trees each year according to local conditions, protect the seedlings and make the countryside green. The reforestation movement has in recent years been activated throughout China with the participation of the state, the collective farm units and the individual. This has already added to the farmer's incomes and will do so increasingly by supplying wood for construction, cooking, heating, furniture and paper products. Moreover, in the northern areas where the forests are scanty, there is a notable reforestation movement by the state. In 1981, the reforested areas totaled 4.1 million hectares which included 0.64 million hectares for firewood, 0.63 million hectares for economic trees and 0.64 million hectares for windbreaks. The total area reforested by 1984 was 6.32 million hectares, a 41% increase over 1982. By any measure, this was a remarkable achievement for improvement of natural resources.

The afforestation program in China has met with great success and has the potential for supplying needed energy resources (firewood) to replace the traditional crop residues as fuels. The option is emerging whereby, in many parts of China, crop residues can once again be recycled to enhance the organic matter in long impoverished crop lands.

A serious problem, however, persists in Central and North China within the reaches of the Yellow River on the Loess Plateau. Here it has been difficult to establish trees because of a lack of water, the removal of forest and brush cover for firewood, and the grazing of goats, leaving a continuing problem of massive silting of rivers and reservoirs.

Animal Husbandry--Livestock in Transition

The growth of animal husbandry, including livestock and poultry but exclusive of pigs, has more than kept pace with gains in crop production. The production of cow's milk and eggs essentially doubled from 1981 to 1985. Milk production in 1985 rose to 2.5 million tons, up 14% from the previous year, while egg production in 1985 was 5.3 million tons--almost 23% above 1984. Poultry production, including both eggs and meat, has been one of the most rapidly growing sectors in Chinese agriculture (Figure 2). The efficiency in feed conversion, rapid developments in the feed industry, rising personal incomes and household incentives for production, and a government supportive of making livestock and poultry production a top priority in agricultural development have all contributed to these gains. The pig inventory rose to 331.5 million head in 1985 after remaining at around 300 million for many years. Pork production, which has traditionally contributed roughly

Figure 2. Poultry production has more than kept pace with increases in crop production from 1978 to 1986.

94% of China's red meat output, reached 16.5 million tons in 1985. The balance of red meat is provided by beef and mutton with contributions of about 2 and 4%, respectively. The increased demand for lean meat has continuously exceeded the supply, especially in the cities.

Special reference is made to recent developments of the pig industry in China (see Chapter 26, "Three Hundred Million Pigs"). The number of hogs butchered increased from 170 million in 1978 to nearly 200 million in 1981, 219 million in 1984, and 239 million in 1985. The average weight of pigs marketed has also increased from 37.5 to 45 kilograms for an average annual gain of 2.5 kilograms by the time of butchering. The annual slaughter rates for hogs have made impressive progress from 55.2% in 1978 to 73.3% in 1984. Farmers are feeding more grain to hogs and, as a result, hogs have become marketable in a shorter feeding period. For the three-year period 1978 to 1981, pork production increased by 47% or 4.04 million tons. Another 10% increase was recorded from 1981 to 1983. The per capita consumption of pork in both city and country increased from 7.5 kilograms in 1978 to 11 kilograms in 1981 and to nearly 17 kilograms in 1983 and is still rising.

There is still much opportunity for the growth of animal husbandry in China. At present there are 1.6 million dairy cows (Figure 3) with the previously indicated production of 2.5 million tons of milk. This compares with 11 million cows in the U.S.A. and 70 million tons of milk, with per capita annual consumption levels of approximately 2.1 kilograms of milk in China and 97.7 kilograms for the U.S.A. Milk production levels per cow and in total for China are far below those of the U.S.A. Livestock in China currently constitutes about 20% of the gross agricultural output, while in the U.S.A. it approximates 50%. The populations of horses, mules, donkeys, camels, sheep and goats in China have stabilized during the past five years.

Total meat production including pork, beef and mutton grew from 12.6 million metric tons in 1981 to 15.4 in 1984 and on to a new record of 17.6 million metric tons in 1985. While the greatest total increase was in pork production, a significant increase in beef as well as pork production was also registered, going from 249,000 tons in 1981 to 463,000 tons in 1985, with some likely contributions from an expanding dairy cow industry. China made the first successful shipment o 1,000 beef cattle, mostly from Shandong and Hebei provinces, to Japan in 1984. This export market is likely to increase in the future. Rabbits constitute an additional component of animal husbandry with remarkable increases in the production of both fur and meat, much of which is exported (see Chapter 27, "Chickens, Ducks, Geese and Rabbits Galore"). The production responsibility system encourages individual care of animals with a resulting reduction in mortality rates.

Figure 3. Most of the dairy herds in China are near the large cities and in the municipalities of Beijing, Shanghai, and Tianjin.

In recent years, much attention has been given to establishing cooperative enterprises with industry and animal husbandry for the processing of agricultural and sideline products. This will give added value to raw products (meat, hides, skins, furs, wool) and help to enhance trade, improve distribution and marketing, and introduce modern principles of farm management. Policies have also been implemented to promote the development of animal husbandry among the minorities in the autonomous regions.

In summary, animal husbandry will increasingly contribute to the economy of China by providing high quality protein food (meat, eggs and milk); draft power (water buffalo, yellow cattle, horses, mules, donkeys, camels and yaks) for farming and transportation; raw products (meat, hair, skins, hides, bristles, feathers) for processing industries; manure, particularly from pigs, as a supplement to chemical nitrogen fertilizers; supplemental incomes for farmers via sideline production; and export sales of live animals and livestock products for foreign exchange.

Fisheries

Farmers profit not only from crop production, forestry, and animal husbandry but also from fish culture, a primary source of income in China. Farmers who are primarily engaged in fish culture are appropriately called fishermen (Figure 4).

China has abundant inland water resources (see Chapter 28, "Fish Culture--Three Thousand Years of History"). Of the 26.7 million hectares of inland waters, more than 5 million hectares are devoted to the artificial and concentrated production of fish (aquaculture). There are also 0.5 hectares of shallow sea saltwater used for the same purpose. Over 2.88 million hectares of freshwater were also devoted to fish farming in 1981. There is an increasing importance attached to aquaculture.

In 1981, the production of aquatic products was 4.6 million tons, a gain of almost 10% over 1980. By 1983 production had grown to 5.46 million metric tons, with the greatest growth in freshwater fisheries. Of the total aquatic products harvested in 1981, 3.23 million tons came from saltwater with the balance (1.37 million tons) from freshwater. The provinces (all bordering the sea) which led in the harvest of aquatic products in 1981 were Zhejiang (842,000 tons), Shandong (589,000 tons), Fujian (484,000 tons), Liaoning (446,000 tons), Jiangsu (441,000 tons), Shanghai (190,000 tons), Hainan (179,000 tons), Hubei (150,000 tons) and Guangxi (117,000 tons).

The production responsibility contract system has also motivated fishermen. Many family fish farms have been established and fish breeding has developed on the outskirts of cities. The result is an increasing supply of fresh fish and shrimp. There are now 0.28 million hectares of water to breed and produce fish for most of the 106 large and medium sized cities.

Figure 4. Many farmers in China are engaged in fish culture.

Wuxi in Jiangsu Province is a city with long experience in fish breeding and production. Its fish breeding area in 1981 was double that of 1978. Large areas have also been reserved for fish production in Hunan, Hubei, Jiangxi, Jiangsu and the Heilongjiang provinces. In 1981 these areas produced 25,000 tons of fish, double that for 1980. As more and more aquatic products are required and the profits increase, fishermen are renewing and improving their breeding techniques.

The production of fish from the sea has also been refined and strengthened. For the protection and production of croacker and hairtail fish, two reserve areas for young fish have been established in the Eastern and Yellow seas of China. The artificial reproduction of prawn has also met with great success and established a new production level.

Moreover, with the emphasis on preservation, processing and utilization of aquatic resources, many cold storages have been built. In 1981 over 900,000 tons of aquatic resources were preserved by canning, pickling or drying.

Sideline Industries and Village Enterprises

These have developed rapidly in recent years. Sideline industries, as overall sources for rural incomes in China, rose from 27% in 1978 to over 50% in 1986. Total output of sideline industries and village enterprises in Jiangsu Province alone surpassed 40 billion yuan for 1986, when this province ranked first in the nation. In some advanced prefectures or counties, the village enterprises accounted for 80% of the output value in the economy. Where crop production is severely reduced by natural disasters (drought, floods, hail and frost), the sideline industries compensate and assist in maintaining the living standards of the people. Village enterprises include building construction, food processing, fish culture, forage crop production, mining (coal and minerals), the manufacture of construction materials, electronic products and weaving. Beside the local industries in rural areas, farmers are engaged in the transport, marketing and delivery of commodities, thus increasing their incomes while the meeting the demands of society.

All over China there is an explosion of rural industries. Price incentives, farming diversification, advanced technology, and a growing government investment as well as a continuing and expanding agricultural trade and professional exchanges with the U.S.A. are all playing a part. Concerning specialization, commercialization and modernization of agricultural and sideline activities in the countrysides of China, there were (in 1985) more than 4.25 million specialized households and nearly 180 million peasant families under the responsibility program with long-time contracts on land, along with over 6 million town and countryside enterprises. The output of these enterprises was 143 billion yuan in 1984, and they provided employment for 52 million peasants. The figure in 1986 approaches 100 million people employed. This may be compared with 1.33 million town enterprises involving 30 million people and outputs of 49 billion yuan in 1978 and 68 billion yuan in 1981. (The average U.S. dollar was equivalent to 2.32 yuan in 1984.) Great progress is being made in enabling farmers to work in factories in the countryside rather than in the cities. Many now draw double incomes by working in industry during the day and cultivating the land by early morning and late afternoon.

Through production controls, the manufacture of long line complex equipment and products for heavy industry has been curtailed. Meanwhile, the production of short line products for agriculture and sideline industries such as light weaving, labor-saving services, food services and raw materials production have been encouraged.

The government's organizational structure for sideline industries and village enterprises enhances cooperation. Newly built enterprises are placed in desirable locations. There is cooperation among similar enterprises. Attention is now being directed toward new technological transformations, improvements in management, and programming for the future to avoid blind progress. Management, technicians and workers receive technological training. The deposition of profit varies with the enterprise and its location, but the primary beneficiaries are the farmers.

FOR FURTHER READING

Dajun Liu. 1986. Developments in rural economy and reformation of agricultural universities in China. In *Proceedings on agriculture in China*. Vol. 2, *Macro issues in Chinese agricultural development*, 17-31. Beltsville, Md.: Institue of International Development and Education in Agriculture and Life Sciences.

Dickerman, M.B., et al. 1981. Forestry today in China. *Journal of Forestry* 79(2): 65, 71-75.

He Kang, ed. 1980, 1981, 1982, 1983, 1984. *Chinese agricultural yearbook*. Beijing: Agricultural Press. (In Chinese)

———. 1986. *China agricultural yearbook*. Beijing Agricultural Publishing House.

Tuan, F. C. 1986. *China's livestock sector* (draft). U.S. Department of Agriculture, China Section. Asian Branch, International Economics Division, Economic Research Service. Washington, D.C.: Government Printing Office.

U.S. Department of Agriculture. Economic Research Service. 1984, 1985, 1986. *China outlook and situation reports*. Washington, D.C.: Government Printing Office.

World Resources Institute. 1985. *Tropical forests, a call for action: Case studies*. Washington, D.C.

Xiaotan Zhu; L. M. James; and J. W. Hanover. 1985. *Timber production potential in China*. East Lansing: Michigan Agricultural Experiment Station.

35

MORE AND BETTER FOOD FOR THE FUTURE--PROSPECTS TO THE YEAR 2000

by Sun Han

The most important consideration for over one billion Chinese people is to eat. Food supplies in China have always been precarious. For the past severl millennia, millions of Chinese have not known where their next meal would come from. Famines from droughts and floods have ravaged China. According to an ancient Chinese proverb, "Food for the people equals heaven." No other people lavish so much thought and attention on food--its production, distribution, preparation and consumption. No effort is being spared in promoting grain production and developing a diversified agriculture. Eating is so linked with well-being that all over China a standard greeting among friends is "Have you eaten?", not "How are you?" (Figure 1).

The rural economy in China is now growing by leaps and bounds. The Chinese have basically solved the problems of food production and have eliminated hunger. Twenty-two percent of the world's people--in a country periodically racked by famine--now have enough to eat. They are now working hard to improve their standard of living. Three short phrases currently used by the people to project China's agricultural development to the year 2000 are "one target, two transformations, and three reforms." The one target is that by the year 2000, the national value of the total annual output for agriculture and rural industries will have increased fourfold. The two transformations indicate that agriculture will be transformed first, from a self-sufficient or semi-self-sufficient economy to large-scale commodity production, and second, from a traditional to a modernized agriculture. The three reforms refer to the rural economic systems, agricultural technologies and rural industrial structures. These three phrases precisely describe the pathway for the development of China's rural economy to the end of this century.

Reaching the target will not be easy. The policy will be that of "walking on two legs" to "build a socialist country with Chinese character-

Figure 1. In China, the food may also be a piece of art.

istics." With the high enthusiasm of 800 million supportive farmers, these goals can be realized. While the ultimate objective will be common prosperity for all, some farmers will become prosperous first and bring the others along later. Wealth is worthy of imitation. It may require fifty years into the next century for rural China to reach the level of prosperity of what are now the world's developed countries, but the hope is there.

A Magnificent Goal

The 12th Congress of the Chinese Communist Party proclaimed in September, 1982 that:

> In the forthcoming years (from 1981 to the end of the century), the general objective of our struggle in our national economic reconstruction under the prerequisite of increasing continuously the economic benefit, is to strive for making the annual total output value in industry and agriculture of the whole nation increase by four times, that is, to increase from 710 billion yuan in 1980 to about 2,800 billion yuan in the year 2000.

This magnificent goal has become a strong driving force for the Chinese people to bring about an economic reconstruction of the entire nation. By the end of 1984, the nation's total annual output for agriculture and industry was over 1,000 billion yuan. The annual average growth rate during the Sixth Five-Year Plan (1981-1985) was over 10%. There is confidence that the goal for the year 2000 can be reached even with lower growth rates than those thus far experienced. The current reform of the economic system is one of the strategic measures for realizing this goal. What is now happening in the privatization and diversification of Chinese agriculture may become the most far-reaching and systematic economic and social transformation of the latter part of the twentieth century.

The recent high growth rate in China's economic reconstruction began appropriately with agriculture. It started in rural China. The transformation is still going on in the countryside, where 80% of the people reside. Agriculture, however, is different from other industries and enterprises. The rapid growth experienced over the past five years is exceptional under any conditions, and will be difficult to sustain. In this light, a realistic goal for development of the rural economy is that, for agricultural production, the output should be increased by 2.8 times, from 222 billion yuan in 1980 to 622 billion yuan by the year 2000. With the addition of the rapidly increasing countryside enterprises, the total rural output hopefully could be increased fourfold, from 250 billion yuan in 1980 to 1,000 billion yuan for the year 2000. A yearly average increase of 5.3% and 13.9% for agriculture and rural enterprises, respectively, will be required. The rate of rural development experienced in China during the last five years suggests that this target can be reached. If such a target is realized, the average per capita net income for farmers throughout the country would be 800, and possibly as high as 1,000 yuan.

Reforms in the Rural Economic System

A series of agrarian reforms have characterized the People's Republic of China since its founding in 1949, which promoted the restoration and development of agricultural productivity. The country then suffered from both stagnation and decline during the so-called "Great Leap Forward," followed by the "Movements of People's Communes" launched in 1958-61 and the ten-year "Great Cultural Revolution," which started in 1966. The Third Plenary Session of the 11th Congress of the Central Committee of the Chinese Communist Party in December, 1978, recognized the disadvantages of overcentralized management in running people's communes and equalitarianism in payment for labor. These practices were corrected and replaced by an output-related system with different forms of contracted responsibilities (the "production responsibility system"). Individual households were placed in charge of production, and the rights of individual farmers were enlarged in the rural cooperatives. The result has been a simultaneous increase in individual initiatives and a strengthening of the collectives.

In 1985, further adjustments in the agricultural management system eliminated the state of monopoly for the purchase and marketing of major agricultural products and introduced a contract system for farmers. While the land is collectively owned, plots for farming are distributed to individual families (Figure 2). According to the production responsibility contract, farmers are asked to deliver a quota of farm products at a fixed price and pay to collective economic organization an amount of money for a common accumulation fund. With the payment of that obligation, farmers can grow anything they want and sell competitively for whatever price they can get. Formerly they worked to meet the quota; now they work to meet the demands of the market.

Reform of the rural economy will continue. The target will be to facilitate an orderly transformation to a self-sufficient or semi-self-sufficient economy. What was formerly controlled by an overly centralized

Figure 2. Intensively gardened family plots in Sichuan.

management will move into a planned coordinated commodity economy. It is believed that promotion of such a cooperative system, inbred with the enthusiasm of farmers who have the right to determine production and make management decisions, will direct them in the socialist path of planned development. It will also further develop the economy and put farmers on the road to prosperity.

The essential component of the Chinese production responsibility contract system is household autonomy. This involves specialization, commoditization and diversification. These are related to, or come with, household autonomy. Attractive farmgate prices have made it profitable to produce. There has also been increased availability of inputs; for example, between 1978 and 1985, the quantity of applied chemical fertilizers rose from less than 9 to 18 million metric tons. Many advanced technologies have been used in China to enhance agricultural output since it became profitable to produce, and the availability of many new consumer goods has increased. Another key to increased food production in China during the early 1980s was a favorable climate.

The following policy measures will be adopted to point the direction for increased productivity.

1) Continuously promote and develop the output from the contract responsibility system and other related forms of management; and on the basis of individual household management, encourage farmers to move cooperatively and jointly forward under the principle of voluntary participation and mutual benefit.

2) Under the guidance of state planning, increase market regulations in agricultural production; adjust prices of agricultural commodities and sideline products; facilitate rational development fo rural industrial infrastructures; and develop the commodity economy.

3) Encourage rural cooperative economic organizations and farmer-operated rural enterprises; build up rural infrastructures and facilities for commodity production, storage and distribution; and promote the development of a production base for special local and export items.

4) Speed-up agrotechnical transformations and the development of rural intelligence or information systems.

5) Increase state support for agricultural development and reduce the financial burdens of farmers.

Major reforms in the rural industrial structure and the long-standing emphasis on grain production are called for as the key directives in agriculture. Much labor should be moved from the limited farmland to areas with more potential.

The family planning program is proving effective. It is now estimated that by the year 2000 the population will reach 1.2 billion, with 450 million rural or countryside laborers. With increased but selective agricultural mechanization and development of the social service system, it is projected that 30% of the laborers will be producing crops; 20% will be in forestry, animal husbandry and fisheries; and 40% will be employed in rural industries. This leaves only 10% who would migrate to cities. This program of profitability, engaging the people in primary production in the countryside through gainful employment, will add to the wealth of society and ease the heavy population burdens in the cities.

Emphasis on Increasing Crop Yields

An all-time record for grain production was achieved in China in 1984. The national output was a whopping 407 million metric tons. This was the equivalent of about 400 kilograms per person, resulting in grain self-sufficiency--with some to spare--and no need for imports. This amount of grain, however, will not be sufficient to support the rapidly expanding livestock, poultry and food processing industries which are projected for the year 2000. The anticipated population growth, rising incomes and desires for improved diets will begin to put great pressure on grain production. The agriculture of China is not sufficiently productive to both meet those future needs and withstand the major hazards of drought, freezes, floods, drying winds, hail and typhoons-- limitations which have always existed. Hence, "Never slacken grain production" is a policy that must continue. Annual output of grain has been set at between 425 and 450 million tons by 1990, and by the year 2000 should reach 500 million metric tons. This will annually provide 300 million tons for the average grain ration of 250 kilograms per person for 1.2 billion people; 175 million tons for livestock, poultry and stock for food processing; and 25 million tons for seed purposes. To reach such targets of production, the area under cultivation must be stabilized at 113 million hectares, the level which currently exists. All future gains in food production must, of necessity, be achieved by an increase in yields per unit land area and possibly from an increase in the cropping index (Figure 3).

Cotton output also reached an all-time high in 1984 at 6.25 million tons. This resulted in self-sufficiency and nearly half of the world's total cotton stocks. There is no need to increase cotton production, the annual needs of which can likely be provided at an annual production level of about 4.25 million tons. Stress will be on quality improvement and expanding export markets for the best cotton. Hereafter, the output of edible oils, sugar, fruits and vegetables will be doubled or greater to meet demands for improved diets, higher incomes and changes in consumption patterns. For oil crops, annual production is planned at 17 million tons with a goal of 18 million tons by 1990. Increasing demands for high quality Chinese silk and tea will be met through an expansion of export markets.

Improvements in crop production, through higher yields, will come from the already highly productive and richly endowed river basins and alluvial plains of the middle and lower Yangzi, the Pearl River delta in Southeast China and the Sichuan Basin in southwest China. Attention

Figure 3. A threshing ground for grain.

will also be directed to achieving high yields in what is now the moderately productive Huang He (Yellow)-Huai-He-Hai-He river valleys and the plains of the northeast.

China has but few additional level land resources that can be reclaimed for agricultural production in the coming years. Any reclamation efforts will merely balance those lands which will be diverted to urbanization, industrialization, recreation and developments in transportation. There will be no net increase in tillable land. Something can yet be done, in addition to what has already been accomplished with controlled environment agriculture (greenhouses, row tunnels, plastic mulches, windbreaks and irrigation), to increase the cropping index. Emphasis must be on increasing crop yields per unit land area and on the improvement of quality to meet the demands of consumers who are becoming increasingly discriminating and whose consumptive patterns are changing. These are the greatest challenges confronting the Chinese in future agricultural development.

Animal Agriculture

A great leap forward in animal agriculture is anticipated. Meat production is expected to reach 23 million tons by 1990, which will be up 20% from 1985. Milk production will climb to over 6 million tons or double the 1985 figure, and egg production will move up to nearly 9 million tons or 65% above the 1985 level. Per capita output by the year 2000 is expected to be 25 kilograms each for meat and milk and 12.5 for eggs. Regions for development are still overwhelmingly in the agricultural areas. The pig population is now over 300 million; there is no reason to increase that number. Emphasis should be on improving rates of gain for meat production, increasing the dressing-out (the marketable carcass) percentage and promoting higher feeding efficiency. Technologies for improving the productivity of milk cows, beef cattle and chickens (both for meat and eggs), as well as ducks, geese and rabbits, are urgently called for.

The key to livestock improvement will be the establishment of a modernized fodder production and feed industry, along with genetic improvements in yields and greater digestibility of nutritionally superior forage crops and legumes. More attention must also be given to means for rapid genetic improvements of food animals through artificial insemination, embryo transfer, and better disease control through breeding for genetic resistance and improved environmental adaptation. Particular attention should be given to improving China's vast expanse of native grasslands--introducing new species of grasses and legumes, developing man-made or artificial grasslands according to local conditions, determining the appropriate carrying capacity, and reversing the degenerative trend of the pasture land resources of the past decade.

Fisheries--Aquatic Resources

The water resources of China are enormous. China has been the world's leader in aquaculture for 3,000 years, but there could be much more effective onshore, inland and seawater use for fish production. Fish can be raised like livestock and poultry in many parts of China by using natural and artificial ponds and lakes and flooded land. The target is to produce 15 kilograms of aquatic products annually per person by the year 2000. This is still well below that of pork and poultry. The output for the entire country is expected to reach 9 million tons by 1990, which should be 30% above the 1985 level. This will be an important means of increasing high volume animal foodstuffs. The policy will be to further develop fish production in both sea and fresh water with the greater emphasis on the latter for the near future. For China, only 60% of the inland waters and 12% of the sea shoals available for fish production are being used. Before the end of this century, these vacant, nonproductive areas should be utilized as fully as possible and the yield per unit area greatly improved. Fish farming could become the "blue revolution" of the twenty-first century. Fishing must be improved in both the onshore and inland water, but the aquatic resources must simultaneously be preserved. Artificial reproduction techniques for exotic species must be developed and water productivity capabilities enhanced. Deep-sea fishing deserves similar attention.

Forestry

The land area in China currently covered with forests amounts to 12.7%. For several years, there has been a national movement for reforestation in which all the people in the country participate. This has resulted in six million hectares of reforestation each year. The program is expected to continue to the year 2000, when forest cover will exceed 20% of the land surface area. By 1990, forests should cover 14% of the country's land. Destructive lumbering (log cutting) will be banned in the two major forest areas--the Northeast and the Southwest. Here, the cutting rates will not exceed the growth rates. Where clear cutting occurs, there will be rapid and protected replanting. A focal point for reforestation will be in the hilly regions in the subtropics of south China, where climatic conditions favor rapid growth and where a new resource base for both commercial and economic forest ventures may hopefully be established within this century. More attention will also be given to farmland shelter belts and windbreaks and to small woodlots in rural areas. The existing tree cover in the semi-arid and arid regions should be energetically protected. Plantings of grass, hedges, windbreaks, and sand breaks should be vigorously pursued (Figure 4). The renewed effort in reforestation will increase and preserve valuable timber and special local products; reduce soil erosion; improve land reclamation and stabilization; protect food crops from wind and sand damage; greatly improve the agro-ecological environment; and, with appropriately selected tree species, increase food supplies from fruit, nuts and edible oils.

Industrial Development and the Rural Economy

Currently 60 million people or 20% of the rural laborers are employed in rural industries with a total output value surpassing 230 billion yuan annually. With the expectation that the output of the rural economy will increase fourfold by the end of the century, a vast number of surplus workers must be relocated. Funds for rural reconstruction can be accumulated and the economic income increased. All depends largely, however, on the development of rural and affiliated industries.

Development should proceed according to local economic conditions, natural resources and available technology. There should be emphasis on food and feed processing, feed mills, small mining industries, processing of agricultural byproducts, building materials and the building industry; and on transportation, commerce and service trades. In the vast areas surrounding cities, cooperative efforts between the

Figure 4. The "green walls" of China. Trees for windbreaks, fuel, and timber are becoming increasingly important.

cities and the countryside should be encouraged. Rural industries should become the base to produce components and parts for city industries and commodities which are not produced in the cities. Art and handicraft production, which are labor intensive, should be encouraged and rural tourism developed.

The development of rural industries and those affiliated with urbanization will speed the construction of rural townships and small cities. City-like towns will merge. It is projected that by the end of this century, one-third of the total rural population will live permanently in rural townships and small cities, which will make them the centers for culture, technology, education and the countryside economy. They will provide the connecting link between the big cities and the vast rural areas, and the base for development of the rural commodity economy. This will prevent a mass migration of the people in rural areas to the big and middle-sized cities, and will be one of the characteristics of Chinese countryside modernization.

Improvement of the Agricultural Environment and New Technology Inputs

Protection of the natural resource base and environmental improvement will become increasingly important. The illegal occupation of farmland must be controlled. Lands with soils that now are low-yielding, shallow, fragile and erosive and which account for one-third of the tillable area must be improved. Highly erodible soils cover an area of about 1.5 million square kilometers. Desert-like areas cover approximately 0.33 million square kilometers. Many of these hostile and low-producing regions could be reclaimed through grass planting and reforestation. Increased attention must be given to the improved protection and utilization of forest, grassland and water resources, avoiding the current overdraft of groundwater. Needless exploitation of these endowments through poor management and administration must end.

Attention must be given to protection of the agricultural environment. Soil and water pollution as a result of industrial developments in towns and cities is serious and must be brought under control. The intent will be to strengthen the agricultural material and technological bases, and to practice modernized intensive farming. Agriculture will benefit greatly from an expansion of irrigation networks to extend the cropping area under irrigation to 53 million hectares. There will be major schemes for controlling big rivers and lakes as well as other major projects, such as the "transfer of waters from south to north" (see Chapter 4, "Water Resources--the Lifeline of Chinese Agriculture"). Mechanization will expand both for water management (drainage and irrigation) and in the development of machinery for animal production, forestry, aquaculture, food processing and transportation (see Chapter 29, "People and Machines"). Use of chemical fertilizers for crop production more than tripled between 1975 (5.37 million tons) and 1983 (16.6 million tons) and it will double again by the year 2000 to an estimated annual level of 30 million metric tons. Integrated systems for pest control will increase, and the plastic soil mulch revolution for cotton, peanuts, vegetable crops and corn will continue to roll on. New sources of energy for rural China will be sought which will include solar energy, power, wind, marsh gas (methane) and biomass from forest trees.

Chinese farmers must have at hand the latest in science and technology to achieve these goals by the year 2000. Nine years of compulsory education will be popularized. A large-scale, in-service or continuing technical educational program is being initiated. By the end of this century, many young farmers will have received a middle agricultural technical school education and will become a new breed of farm operators and managers. Agricultural research and extension programs will be expanded. Chinese farmers will be "walking on two legs." They will be blending traditional Chinese agricultural practices with the latest developments in biotechnology and genetic engineering to make Chinese agriculture provide more and better food for future generations of a billion people and more.

FOR FURTHER READING

Clayre, A. 1985. *The heart of the dragon.* Boston: Houghton Mifflin Co.

He Kang. 1984. Construction of socialist modernized agriculture with Chinese features. *Honggi [Red Flag]*, no. 19. (In Chinese)

———. 1986. Agriculture. The Chinese way. *Beijing Review* 29(19): 23-25.

Huang Shumin. 1986. The strategy of prosperity in a Chinese village. Paper presented at a symposium: China Update: The Four Modernizations, 28 April-1 May, at Oakland University, Rochester, Mich.

Lu Liangshu. 1985. The path toward food self-sufficiency in China. In *Food for the Future*, 73-81. Proceedings of the Bicentennial Forum of the Philadelphia Society for Promoting Agriculture, 6 November.

Major economic indexes. 1986. *Beijing Review* 29(14): 27-28.

Mathews, J., and L. Mathews. 1983. *One billion, a China chronicle.* New York: Random House.

Nu Ruofeng. 1985. Grain for a billion people. *China Reconstructs* 34:3-6.

Rural Development Center, the State Council of China, ed. 1985. *The strategy of rural development in China.* Beijing: Agricultural Science and Technology Press. (In Chinese)

U.S. Department of Agriculture. Economic Research Service. 1984, 1985, 1986. *China outlook and situation reports,* Washington, D.C.: Government Printing Office.

Smil, V. 1985. China's food. *Scientific American* 253(6): 116-24.

Sun Han. 1982. Some strategic problems of agricultural development in China. *Scientia Agricultural Sinica*, no. 1. (In Chinese)

Walker, H. R. 1984. Chinese agriculture during the period of readjustment, 1978-83. *China Quarterly* 100:783-812.

Wang Mingzheng. 1985. China's growing food industry. *China Reconstructs* 34:30-33.

World Bank. 1985. *China: Agriculture to the year 2000.* Washington, D.C.

World Resources Institute. 1985. *Tropical forests, a call for action: Case studies* Washington, D.C.

Zhong Jing. 1986. China's new five-year plan. *China Reconstructs* 35:24-28.

36

CHINESE AGRICULTURE IN THE EYES OF AN AMERICAN

by Sylvan Wittwer

China has been a world of strong family traditions--of loyalty to kin, wariness toward strangers and obedience to authority. It has been a world barely touched by machines, yet the home of inventions--silk weaving, paper, acupuncture, the printing press, wheelbarrow, compass (magnetic needle) and gunpowder. Prosperity, even survival, has depended upon ingenuity coupled with human hands and strong backs.

The Chinese have effectively utilized resources and accumulated rich experiences in both intensive and extensive crop production; in animal husbandry, forestry, fisheries and sideline operations; and more recently, in countryside, village and township enterprises.

With more than 800 million or 80% of its people engaged in food production and other countryside enterprises, China makes up almost one-fifth of the world's population and feeds nearly one-quarter of it. The Chinese practice careful and meticulous cultivation, and probably have the most intensive farming systems in the world, especially for vegetable production. Profit or money is motivating the Chinese peasant as never before. Economic incentives have been substituted for bureaucratic control. Beijing's new slogans are "Get Rich Through Labor" and "Getting Rich is Glorious*." State Planning with Market Regulation and Individual Responsibility is the motto for the future.

The recent agricultural and rural development witnessed in China is one of the remarkable achievements of the latter half of the twentieth century. It has been more than a localized pocket of success, as was recorded from 1965 to 1975 when grain production tripled in the Punjab State of India, and when corn production in Kenya was increased to 4.8 tons/hectare in the 1960s, or when wheat yields in the Yaqui

---

*Title of a book by Orville Schell. See FOR FURTHER READING.

Valley of the State of Sonora, Mexico were increased 3 1/2-fold from 1950 to 1970.

What we have witnessed and are now observing in China has not been a phenomenal increase in a single commodity, but an across-the-board improvement. China's recent food production revolution is one involving the entire nation, affecting almost all of its commodities in practically all provinces, autonomous regions and municipalities--and this in the most populous nation on earth. It has not been the result alone of the infusion of new varieties, biological innovations, or resource inputs such as land, water or oil. Credit must also be given to the economic program called the "contract responsibility production system," (see Chapter 1, "Introduction"), which is focusing on economic incentives as well as simultaneous inputs of new government programs, a greatly improved infrastructure supporting agriculture, over a threefold increase in chemical fertilizer applications between 1975 and 1984, and a favorable climate and natural resource inputs, all of which have contributed to increased agricultural productivity. It is doubtful if a model of such magnitude has existed previously or is likely to be replicated in the future. The senior author has personally followed this model from 1980 through 1986. It is a model to be emulated, providing it can be replicated by other nations, particularly some of those in Africa which face the earth's most critical food production problems during the next two decades. Abject poverty in China cannot be observed in the countryside as one sees so often in Southeast Asia, Asia, Latin America and Africa, except in the far outlying areas. China, for the first time, has enough grain to feed a population ten times greater than Japan and four times that of the U.S.A., with some leftover for export.

Agricultural Modernization

Among the four major areas of modernization--industry, agriculture, science and technology, and defense and the military--agricultural development has been the most striking. Farmers in China, as in other parts of the world, have responded eagerly to the new production responsibility incentives and marketing opportunities.

What have been the results? Average farm income has doubled in five years, with many impacts on farmers, city factory workers and all consumers. After two decades of indifferent performance, and with vivid memories of food shortages and famines in the not too distant past, stunning production records have been achieved with not just one commodity but many. The introduction of market incentives, coupled with unusually good climatic conditions in 1982, 1983 and 1984, have resulted in a 15% increase in corn production, a 20% expansion in rice and a 40% rise in wheat production since 1982. Between 1981 and 1983, grain production rose by 62 million tons (19%) and reached an all-time high of 387 million metric tons, which exceeded--for the first time in modern history--that of the U.S.A. This progress was made even though the area sown to food grains declined from more than 120 million hectares in 1978 to 114 million hectares in 1983. Production rose to yet a new record of 407 million metric tons in 1984, but fell to roughly 379 million tons in 1985, a drop of 5%. For the first time in three decades, China is in many places grappling with grain surplus, having reached self-sufficiency with the 387 million metric tons harvested in 1983. Farmers had difficulty selling their surplus grain in 1984 and so moved to other crops in 1985. China produced the largest wheat crops in the world in both 1984 and 1985, achieving higher yields than the U.S.A. For China to be faced with significant local surpluses of grain and other agricultural commodities exceeding storage capacities is not a problem it has historically had to cope with. This will likely be a temporary phenomenon. The gains in cotton production (110% from 1979 to 1983) and in edible vegetable oil seeds and soybeans, as well as in sugarcane and sugar beets, have also been impressive. China led the world in cotton production in 1984 and 1985; and output rose a phenomenal 175% in the five-year period (1979-1984). China had, in 1985, nearly one-half of the world's cotton stock. In 1984 record grain, cotton, oil seed, sugar, jute, hemp and tea crops were produced. China's definition of grain includes wheat, rice, coarse grains (corn, sorghum and millet) potatoes, root crops (sweet potatoes and cassava) and soybeans.

Pork accounts for about 94% of all the meat consumed in China. The big gain in pork output, 55% from 1978 to 1983 and another 25% from 1983 to 1985, was not in numbers of pigs but an increase in rates of gain resulting from increased amounts of feed grains, the use of genetically improved animals and better management. A specific objective in China has been to double per capita meat consumption from the 8 kilograms per person in 1976 to 16 kilograms by 1985. The half-way mark was reached in 1983, and the goal was more than met in 1985 with a 14% increase in meat production over the 1984 record for a total of 17 million metric tons. An expansion of dairying is being encouraged near the cities of Beijing, Shanghai, Tianjin, Wuhan, Nanjing, Harbin and Xian, with black and white Holstein (Fresian)-derived cows. The number of cows as well as milk production has doubled since 1981 (Figure 1).

Two approaches are being used in the countryside of China today to increase farmers' incomes. One is to increase primary agricultural production; the other is to encourage participation in sideline industries and township, village, county and even family countryside enterprises. As with many other agriculturally developing nations, there are increasing numbers of part-time farmers or those with secondary in-

Figure 1. The number of dairy cows in China has doubled since 1981.

comes. Many formerly earth-bound peasants have become wealthy. They are drawing double incomes, being willing to work in industry during the day and in the fields in the early morning and late afternoon. There is new home building all over China. These developments and others are changing consumptive habits to less grain and more animal products (meat, milk, eggs) and fruits and vegetables in the diet. The whole intent is to keep farmers in the countryside and avoid mass migrations to cities, which are already overcrowded and teeming with unemployment. The policy is that villagers may leave the land but not the village as farm mechanization and rural industrialization proceeds. In almost all other agriculturally developing countries this has meant unemployment and the inevitable rural poverty. The rest of the world will be observing China to see if she has an acceptable alternative.

Nevertheless, the well-founded emphasis in China on having agricultural development precede industrial development is providing food for the people and raw materials for industry. It is also creating an economic surplus for investments in other segments of the economy, and producing exportable products which earn foreign exchange for imports of machines and technology for industrialization. Finally, rural markets are being created for manufactured goods, and employment opportunities are being provided which can later be channeled to industrial development.

In rural China today, there is pervasive emphasis on year-round productivity and a strong work ethic in the individual. The stress is on achieving maximum yields per unit time and per unit area and on stabilizing agricultural production at high levels. This is being done through genetically improved and early-maturing crop varieties and new hybrids; traditional and, more recently, massive irrigation and drainage works; extensive use of both organic and inorganic fertilizers; some totally integrated pest control programs; the use of plastic and rock mulches to control soil erosion; and through reforestation. But it is more than this, entailing a curious blend of the ancient and traditional with the most modern resources and technological inputs.

The Chinese are beginning to accommodate to fast-food establishments, coffee shops, Coca Cola, bell-bottom pants, high heels, disco, night life, rock music, push-button telephones, video games, golf and even American Express credit cards. Many Chinese are taking European Christian names. Oddities such as "Fast Food Duck" (Figure 2) and "Sichuan Cola" are now found in China. They realize they cannot continue to prosper while clinging to all the traditions of the past, in view of the present level of technology. Automation will come to manufacturing, industrial development and, eventually, to agriculture.

Technology Inputs--Ancient and Modern

China's agriculture is known for its long history, its vast areas, its extensive crop and livestock diversifications and its abundant resources and products. It is a sea of contrasts. All stages of agricultural development can now be seen, extending from the ancient and traditional to the ultramodern. They range from the wide open spaces of the northwest and northeast and the grasslands of Inner Mongolia, where there are fully mechanized fields of grain and soybeans, to the labor-intensive rice paddies of the Yangzi River basin; from the tropical fruit orchards and sugarcane plantations of Guangdong Province to the Tibetan barley on the "Roof of the World."

Only in China do you find nearly 30% of the rice production using F^1 hybrids and, at the same time, an almost universal retention of the back-wrenching practice of hand transplanting. Only in China do you have such massive expanses of land being irrigated to enhance both the stability and magnitude of crop production. Only in China are there over 300 million pigs, whose primary food is derived from vegetable resources (some of which we call weeds) which cannot be used for food by people, and whose manure may be worth as much as their meat. Only in China, the world's third largest soybean producer, is this crop and its products used so extensively for human food and for numerous and attractive products which are derived for human consumption. Only in

Figure 2. Roast ducks in a "fast food" establishment.

China do you see integrated farming systems which completely recycle resources usually considered wastes by other countries. Only in China do you see vegetable oil crops of many species (soybean, cotton, peanut, rapeseed, sunflower and sesame), all used extensively for food consumption. An advocacy group looking for alternative food-producing technologies, such as organic farming or sustainable or regenerative systems of agriculture, will find them in China.

It is not one unique technology, ancient or modern, that has enabled the Chinese to feed its more than a billion people with less in the way of arable land resources than in the U.S.A. It's an assemblage of many. The margins for food production are being extended in many directions.

The use of newly developed plastic soil mulches for erosion and weed control, conservation of soil moisture, and earlier and more productive cropping, and plastic covers for rice seedling beds, are probably the most intensive and extensive in all the world. Harvest seasons for vegetables are extended in both spring and fall. For staple crops such as cotton and peanuts, both the northern and western boundaries have been moved forward. Plastic tunnels and greenhouses, which abound around all the major cities in the north and northeast, are even more effective than plastic soil mulches for extending the margins--both seasonal and geographic--for successful vegetable production.

Almost all the vegetable crops and many of the staple crops (especially rice, some cotton and even corn) are started in seedling or "nursery" beds and then transplanted. This relieves the land from cropping when there is little vegetative cover. A vast labor force is utilized in this endeavor. Earlier harvests are facilitated, the cropping index is increased, and only the good plants are retained for growing to maturity. More crops are hand transplanted over wider expanses of cultivated land in China than in any other nation.

The Chinese trellis or train any crop that has a vine or will climb a pole, string or stick. Only the vining or climbing types of cucumbers, melons, squash, beans and tomatoes are extensively cultured. Training the vines on bamboo sticks or poles or trellising them upward with string increases the leaf area index and hence the sunlight-absorbing surface of the foliage, and facilitates hand harvesting, pest control and irrigation. Trellising or staking greatly increases the cropping index and in all ways optimizes the utilization of resource inputs. Along with hand transplanting, it is a traditional labor-intensive technology that substantially increases productivity.

There are hundreds of crop combinations in China. This is one of the most distinctive and impressive features in Chinese agriculture. Nowhere else on earth can one see such diversities of crops grown side-by-side, in sequence and in tall and short (dwarf) combinations. Plant densities are designed to give maximum yields over extended periods of time. Several crops may be planted together and separated at harvest. The crop combinations, mixed cropping systems and relay cropping techniques add great complexity, at least superficially, in meeting differing fertilizer and water requirements, in mechanizing operations, and in designing pest control strategies; but in reality, the system itself may, in large part, be the solution.

Mixed cropping, relay cropping and companion cropping in China are tried and proven methods that provide the maximum productivity under the existing environmental conditions, resources and technologies. Such systems reduce the failures which often result from dependence on a single crop; provide a maximum return from the land, water and labor; optimize the use of sunlight, moisture, and soil nutrients; reduce the spread and severity of pests in comparison with typical monocultures; and may substantially increase food production compared to single-crop programs. Such technologies, which increase outputs and reduce inputs, might serve as models for depressed farmers in the Western world to cut costs and reduce resource inputs. In other words, America--with its deficits (national debt, foreign trade) and depressed agricultural industries--should not ignore some possible lessons from a poor country.

All of China, however, is not using a cropping system with more than one crop a year or even intercropping. For Inner Mongolia, Heilongjiang and Xinjiang, it's a single crop a year or monocropping. In these northern outlying areas, there are large expanses of soybeans, wheat, corn, sorghum, millet and sugar beets. Mechanization of both production and harvesting is being standardized and approaches 80%. While there is much talk of future agricultural mechanization, it is only in the northeast and northwest where it may be witnessed.

Intensive cropping systems and intricate programs of water management have been developed over the centuries to cope with three critical environmental constraints--a shortage of arable land, frequent droughts in the north and floods in the south. In view of land scarcity, both irrigation and drainage (water management) take on a special significance as a means of increasing or improving the sown areas (Figure 3).

Figure 3. A pool of night soil coupled with an irrigation and drainage system.

The underground aquifiers (the *Kan-Er-Jin*) in the Xinjiang Autonomous Region transport fresh mountain water hundreds of kilometers from the snowfields of the great Tianshan Mountains to the adjoining basins of the Gobi Desert. They provide the water resources for the production of not only high grade long staple cotton, mung beans, corn, sweet potatoes and watermelons, but also the delectible Hami melon and seedless grapes. Here the margins are being pressed by bringing new land into production with a blend of traditional and modern technologies of irrigation and drainage, and mechanized production and harvesting. Water systems designed centuries ago to prevent evaporative losses during transport though desert areas have been coupled with modern methods of mechanized pumping of groundwater.

Crop irrigation in China has expanded beyond that of any other major nation. The results are twofold: first, greater stability of production, and second, an increase in the magnitude of production. There are both large regional irrigation projects and thousands of small-scale, labor-intensive irrigation schemes. Many of the small-scale systems developed in China would be appropriate for Africa with its major food production problems and where only 2% of the irrigable land is irrigated, of which Egypt and the Sudan account for more than half. Less than 12 million hectares are under irrigation in all of Africa, which is hardly one-fourth of that in China alone. A similar opportunities exists with the use of organic materials for crop fertilization; Africa presently accounts for only 2.5% of the world's consumption of fertilizer. Other opportunities reside in viewing, with some hope, the rural energy systems of China, which produce food where the people are and which, while being labor intensive, achieve high food productivity while sparing resource inputs. Merit can be envisioned for many fronts in future cooperative efforts of the Chinese with those in Africa.

Concerning plant nutrition, nowhere else have organic fertilizers attained such importance in the food system as in China, which has developed the world's most efficient systems of livestock, crop and human waste recycling. The use of waste materials from man and beast are composted with crop residues, city rubbish, sediments from ponds, canals and rivers, wood ashes, green remains, *Azolla*, *Lemna* and several legumes. An especially important ingredient is the manure from over 300 million pigs. The social constraints relative to the use of human wastes in food-producing systems in the U.S.A. are nonexistent in China. But while the basic principles of successful organic farming can be observed in China, there are also inputs from the inorganic.

Chemical fertilizers have been one of the most important resource inputs accounting for recent advances in food production in China. Current crop fertilization has a N:P:K (Nitrogen:Phosphorus:Potassium) ratio of 100:31:4, compared with a world average of 100:52:10, which is highly skewed to nitrogen. There has been a tendency in China to use excessive nitrogen to achieve maximum yields rather than the most economic amount. Some of this imbalance of P and K with N is undoubtedly being corrected by the enormous quantities of organic fertilizers which equal or surpass the nutrients supplied by chemical fertilizers. Nevertheless, this present nutrient imbalance may be reducing the benefits from the relatively high levels of nitrogen fertilizer used.

Phosphorus and potassium may now be more limiting than nitrogen in some of the more advanced agricultural areas. For the future, chemical fertilizer applications--including phosphorus and potassium as well as nitrogen--will increase due to significant reductions in the use of green manure and the availability of (labor intensive) composts and night soil. One of the most important production inputs will continue to be fertilizer, particularly potassium. China's current fertilizer industry is characterized as having few products and materials of low nutrient content.

In the U.S.A., we are attempting to rid our lakes, ponds and streams of weeds and accompanying eutrophication. In China, aquatic plants and materials from eutrophication are considered a resource, both as a green manure and for biologically-fixed nitrogen, as well as feed for snails, fish and livestock.

There are more aquatic plants used for feeding pigs, fish and even people in China than in any other country. The Chinese people have few food prejudices. They are both experimental and innovative. An old saying goes that the Chinese eat all creatures that swim or float. Some of their delicacies are the bird's nest, bear's claw, moose's nose, rattlesnakes, frogs, giant salamanders and large insects. Each has its own flavor and mode of preparation. Many aquatic plants are in this category. They include matai (*Eleocharis tuberosa*), arrowhead (*Sagittaria sagittifolia*), water bamboo (*Zizania caduciflora*), water chestnut (*Trapa natans*), lotus (*Nelumbium nelumbo*), and the swamp cabbage or water sweet potato (*Ipomoa aquatica*). Aquatic plants used for pig feed include the water hyacinth (*Eichhornia crassipes*), the water lettuce (*Pistia stratiotes*), the water peanut (*Attamanthera philoxeroides*) and Azolla.

Azolla, a miniature water fern which, with its blue green algae partner *Anabaena*, captures atmospheric nitrogen, fertilizes rice paddies and taro plantations (see Chapter 9, "Organic Farming--Growing Plants the Organic Way"). It may fix up to 320 kilograms of nitrogen per hectare per year. It also concentrates other plant nutrients. Azolla is cultured in thirteen provinces in South China, with the center of interest in Zhejiang (Figure 4). The program is one crop of azolla for one crop of rice. If there are two crops or rice, there are two crops of azolla. In the Zhejiang Province there are 240,000 hectares of rice, or 16% of the rice, fertilized with azolla. It has been termed the "Second Green Revolution." Yet it is even more important as a high protein feed for pigs. Sixty strains, from seven species of azolla, have so far been collected and are being evaluated by the Zhejiang Academy of Agricultural Sciences. Azolla can flourish in China because only limited quantitites of herbicides have thus far been used for weed control in the rice paddies. This is in contrast to many other tropical rice-producing areas where herbicides are used more freely.

Figure 4. Azolla tank culture in Zhejiang Province.

Since 1976, hybrid rice varieties have contributed heavily to improved rice production in China. The area sown to hybrid rice in 1985 was 8 million hectares or 22% of the total. This was an increase of over three million hectares from 1982, with yield increases of 18 to 30% above standard open-pollinated varieties. Special attention has also recently been directed to improving the quality of hybrid rice. Hybrid vegetables include tomatoes, peppers, cucumbers, squash, melons and practically all the Chinese and ordinary cabbage. The production of hybrid vegetable seed, as with that of rice, is with minimal investments in other than the human resource.

Biotechnology is finding its place in Chinese agriculture. Tissue culture is expanding rapidly throughout the land for the clonal micropropagation of genetically superior and disease-free selections of many tropical fruits, vegetables, potatoes, ornamental plants and flowers, and berries (black currants) in the northeastern provinces. The new technology requires little capital investment but is meticulously labor intensive, for which the Chinese are admirably adept. Haploid culture of rice has been advanced for the development of new rice varieties, and attention is now being directed to wheat.

Earliness of maturity is of primary consideration, especially for fruits and vegetables grown in northern China and for barley in Tibet. Barley is the only cereal grain early and hardy enough to mature during the growing season for most areas on the "roof of the world." Earliness in vegetables around the major cities of North and Central China is achieved through varying degrees of protected cultivation and genetically-selected varieties.

the growing season for most areas on the "roof of the world." Earliness in vegetables around the major cities of North and Central China is achieved through varying degrees of protected cultivation and genetically-selected varieties.

With no crop have the Chinese effectively pressed the margins more tightly than with the soybean. It can be grown in every province and municipality and even in some of the low river valleys of Tibet. Varieties have been developed that will mature at the 50th latitude north and at 1,500 meters elevation, and with an accumulated heat sum of only 1,900°C from a base temperature of 10°C. No crop, other than possibly rice, is more adapted to the temperature, latitude and soils of China than is the soybean. The wild genetic variants, alongside cultivated types, still offer great opportunities for further adaptation.

Rapeseed has emerged as the number one oil crop in China, achieving an increase in production of over 200% from 1978 to 1982, and has outstripped demand. Rape is a winter hardy crop which is sown in Central China (Jiangsu, Sichuan, Zhejiang and Anhui provinces) in the fall and harvested in the late spring or early summer. Unlike other oil crops (peanuts, soybeans, cotton, sunflowers and sesame), it does not compete in winter with the growth of staple crops. With newly improved varieties, it has added greatly to the food resources of China. A big problem is the shattering of seed pods during harvest and the toxic erucic acid, both of which are being successfully reduced and essentially eliminated by plant breeding. Rapeseed, which sold for three times the price of wheat in 1985, yields 3 to 4 tons per hectare.

Livestock abounds in the provinces and autonomous regions of the north. There are 60 native breeds of pigs in China, 10 of which are being used in swine improvement programs, and many different kinds of ducks (the Beijing duck is only one of them). There are numerous chickens, including the exotic black-boned. The Chinese are eating well over twice as many eggs per person as they did a decade ago. They are number one in the world in the production of rabbits for both their fur and their meat. Some of the most renowned and exotic fiber- and fur-bearing animals in the world are found in China. There are many different breeds of sheep, goats, horses, beef cattle and dairy cows. These include the Sanhe and Yili horses, the Rong (wooly or cashmere) goat, Quinchuan cattle, Meishan pigs, and Bactrian or double-humped camels known as "Boats in the Desert." There are vast water, land, plant and animal resources yet to be utilized in the grasslands of the north. A unique and dominant grazing system has been established in the Xinjiang Autonomous Region. During the summer months the herdsmen and family members follow the herds with yurts (camp tents). This lifestyle is not nomadic but is called "transhumance," since there is always a home base.

The production of livestock products is expanding rapidly. Meat production (pork, beef and mutton) increased by 9% from 1983 to 1984 and by a remarkable 14% from 1984 to 1985. Processed feed production for livestock and poultry doubled between 1982 and 1984. Production of dairy products in 1985 was up 14% above the previous year. The Chinese love ice cream but detest the sight or smell of cheese. Milk consumption is on the increase.

The forced feeding of ducks, a practice designed for rapid rates of gain and distinctive quality development, is associated with one of the most unique and treasured Chinese delicacies--Beijing duck. Highly prized beyond the boundaries of China, 120,000 Beijing ducks are exported annually, primarily to Hong Kong. Forced feeding is during the last 15 days of an 88-day growth cycle, during which half of the weight gain (1 1/2 kilograms) occurs.

Black-boned chickens are uniquely Chinese as is the Beijing duck. Their behavior, appearance, color coding and size is an Oriental curiosity, while their reputation among Chinese for both their meat and medicinal properties is at once perplexing and mysterious.

Grass-eating carp and tilapia abound in China. They grow rapidly and thrive on vegetative materials not considered edible by people. As a basic part of the fish food chain, they are, in turn, preyed upon by other more highly valued aquatic species. A given fish pond is an aquarium of many species separately inhabiting surface, middle and bottom layers. Fish occupy an important spot in the diet of the Chinese people. They supply much needed protein, and without threatening land crops or competing for the feed ingredients of poultry or livestock or food for people. The range of seafoods consumed by the Chinese is beyond that of any other people.

Reforestation, ornamental plants and flowers are changing the countryside landscapes. It could be called the "Greening of China." Descriptive also are the "Green Walls of China." Trees are being planted in the countryside by the millions, and flowers now line the streets and boulevards of cities and villages. Some production units are now engaged solely in producing bedding plants, potted flowers and ornamentals.

China is noted particularly for its azaleas, of which 600 kinds of the world's total of 800 are found in the valleys and mountains of Sichuan, Yunnan and Tibet. The genetic resources for flowers in China are truly as great as those for fruit and vegetables. Chrysanthemums were first cultivated over 3,000 years ago. The peony (*Paeonla*) has its origin in Northwest China, and some species have been cultivated there for at least 1,500 years. First used for its medicinal qualities only, it was not until the Sui-Tang period (581-907 A.D.) that it was cultivated and bred an an ornamental. Other flowers such as orchids, yulan (a Chinese magnolia) and narcissus have been grown for 1,000 years.

There is also the "Four Sides" project and the "Three Norths" program. "Four Sides" means that people are encouraged to plant trees alongside their homes, roads, fields and waterways, and as a whole for improving the ecological balance for Chinese agriculture. The "Three Norths" program arose from the 1979 Forestry Act and the National Conservation Plan to encourage forestry and pasture development in the eleven provinces of the North, Northeast and Northwest. The expectation is that six million hectares of new forests will be established by 1990.

Trees for the Chinese serve many useful purposes. They are effectively used as windbreaks for crops and livestock and for moving sand; to protect arable land, reduce soil erosion and aid in land stabilization; to provide a source of wood fuel, timber and fodder; and to beautify.

The afforestation program in China has been a success by any standard (Figure 5). Tree plantings have far exceeded those of all other developing countries. The Chinese experience in designing optimal approaches to rural forestry has been a success in maximizing both food and tree crop production. It is a model that contains much of relevance for other countries.

Figure 5. Afforestation in China has met with great success.

The Chinese people--through hard labor, extreme toil and incessant struggles against nature and periodic inputs of traditional and modern technologies--have fought for and thus far won their survival. Hopefully some of the challenges they have met and overcome in feeding themselves will merit consideration by those still striving to meet basic human needs.

Conclusions

China, with its vast composite of food-producing systems, is not only feeding its 1.06 billion people--and quite well at that-- but has much to offer the rest of the world. Approximately 80% of the Chinese people are directly or indirectly involved in the production and distribution of food. The Chinese excel in waste management and byproduct recycling, *Azolla* culture, methane generation and fish production. Their farmers are the most efficient of the world's organic gardeners. They are among the most advanced in soil management, and have been able to maintain productivity for thousands of years. Their progress in plant protection, using literal storehouses of natural parasites and integrated control methods, is innovative and impressive, and has been given high priority for crop management and to the stabilizing of production. Their plant scientists are among the world's leaders in hybrid rice developments, haploid (pollen) culture of cereal grains and new tissue culture technologies. China is the place of origin for all cultivated soybeans and still has a vast reserve of primitive types. Programs in forestry involve the exchange of seeds of tree strains which do not exist in the U.S.A. Recent developments in acupuncture and moxibustion in China for animal disease control and improved animal health are of great interest and potential benefit to the U.S.A. livestock industry. One of the more recent developments in China for these technologies has been the use of laser beams in place of needles.

China is particularly rich in vast plant and crop genetic resources of wild and cultivated species having great potential value for the U.S.A. These crops include wheat, Tibetan barley, sweet potato, soybeans, cowpeas, Chinese cabbage, leaf mustards, onions (seven species), cucurbits, and tropical, subtropical, temperate zone and winter hardy fruits. There are hundreds of medicinal herbs used in formulating concoctions of traditional Chinese medicines for man and beast.

The wild plants of China are of special international importance. There are over 30,000 species of flowering plants, gymnosperms and ferns constituting one out of eight species in the world. The plants of China are the most used and appreciated of any in the world. Those that are not eaten for food are often used for medicine. China is a center for the survival of plants that once formed a continuum across Eurasia and

North America. Most cold and winter hardy horticultural crops now grown in the U.S.A. had their origin in Manchuria (Heilongjiang).

Exotic and useful genetic resources are not limited to plants. There are at least 60 native breeds of pigs, each adapted to a particular region in China. Some are extremely prolific, with 16 to 20 piglets per litter. Chinese research in animal genetics and the extensive practice (approximating 100%) of artificial insemination for cattle and pigs are of great interest to American animal reproduction physiologists. The black-boned chicken is not only a source of food but of medicine used to relieve a score of ailments. Exotic domesticated and wild animals, some of which are not found even in American zoos, roam the grasslands of Inner Mongolia, the Xinjiang Autonomous Region, and the Xizang (Tibet) and Quinghai plateaus, where the fine cashmeres and other exotic natural fibers have their origin.

To summarize, many are the margins that are pressed in China to increase food production. They may be seen in mixed, multiple, inter-, relay, strip, hill and companion cropping. Crop irrigation has expanded beyond that of any other major nation. Earliness and quick maturity are emphasized for every major crop, whether it be rice, wheat, maize, barley, cotton, soybeans, rapeseed or a multitude of fruits and vegetables, including watermelons. Soybean varieties range from the very early "OOO" types to the very late "X." Winter-grown rapeseed has become the number one edible oil crop. F_1 hybrid seed is available for many vegetables and for rice, sorghum, millet and corn. Some of the most efficient methods of recycling human, livestock and insect wastes may be found here. Grass-eating fish (carp and talapia) abound and serve as food for more exotic types. *Azolla* culture for biofertilization of rice paddies is actively promoted in the middle and southern provinces. Crops that can climb or be trained (cucumbers, melons, squash, tomatoes and beans) are trellised or staked in a multitude of designs and techniques. Seedbeds of rice are covered with plastic for earlier maturity. Cotton, peanuts and many vegetable crops are mulched with plastic for extending the boundaries of successful production, and for water conservation, weed control and earlier maturity; and vegetable crops are covered within plastic greenhouses or row tunnels to hasten maturity and increase production. Beijing ducks are force-fed, and pigs thrive on aquatic plants (weeds). A great variety of plants and natural products, including those from marine and freshwater sources, are used for human food. The Chinese, beyond that of any other people, have achieved a high level of food production. They are now producing enough to feed themselves with some to spare.

The "standing on two legs" approach--the blending of the traditional with the modern--has permeated all Chinese food-producing systems. Examples are found in the simultaneous use of organic and inorganic fertilizers for crop production; the biological and chemical control of plant pests; the use of traditional (herbal) and modern (Western) medicines for animal disease control; the coupling of rich traditional experiences with modern methods of propagation and intensive culture for fish; the extensive use of bioenergy resources with the nonrenewable, and those that are both big and small, centralized and decentralized; the emphasis on both intermediate technology equipment and the large-scale, modern machines; the two-track enhancement of overall agricultural productivity through market incentives and supportive public services; and finally, the development of a socialist country with Chinese characteristics.

It has recently been stated that one of the most dramatic psychological turnabouts in all history is the current reharnessing of the natural industriousness of more than a billion China, 80% of whom reside in the countryside.

China has been a nation beset with wars, violence and revolutions-- the civil war, the war of resistance with Japan, the "New China," land reforms, collectivization, the Cultural Revolution and now the production responsibility contract system. But violence and revolution were accompanied by and followed with construction programs as massive as the world has ever seen. Controlling floods on the Yellow River; building massive water diversion and reclamation projects bridging and damming the Yangzi River; leveling and terracing mountains; irrigating millions of new hectares; planting billions of trees for reforestation, shelter belts and windbreaks; creating some of the world's largest industries (silk, linen, sugar, soybean technology) where no appropriate skills existed (Figure 6). All of this has been accomplished in a land where food production has expanded on a scale never equalled, providing over 100 million more tons of grain than a decade ago and on 8% less land, thereby boosting per capita consumption by almost 50% and eliminating food deficits.

The current opportunity for Chinese farmers to make their own decisions with households as the principle production unit, replacing collectives, may become the most far reaching and orderly economic, social and political transformation of the twentieth century. It is a real world living experiment, now in transition from a state-controlled economy to a market-driven one, with reliance on market forces, price incentives and personal initiatives. The speed and ease with which it has occurred has surpassed the expectations of both internal as well as external observers. China's contract responsibility output system has not only put profit into agricultural production but has created an insatiable search for, and encouraged the adoption of, the latest production improvement technologies. The net result has been a 10% annual increase in total agricultural output between 1981 and 1985.

The future annals of oriental history may also record that the most dramatic revolution the world has ever seen is that which is now occur-

Figure 6. Increases in soybean technology have been highly successful.

ring in China. What is happening may well be termed China's golden age of agricultural productivity, comparable to that which occurred in the U.S.A. during the decades of the 1950s and 1960s.

Challenges for the Future

The most important consideration for the Chinese has been and remains producing enough to eat for over one billion people. They are sparing no effort in promotion grain production. With over one billion people to feed, China cannot rely on food aid. Grain, in China, in addition to rice, wheat, corn, barley, millet and sorghum includes potatoes, root crops and soybeans and accounts for over 80% of food consumption. A diversified agriculture is now being promoted. Here, technologies imported from the Western world would be of great benefit, especially in fruit production and handling and in animal husbandry. Agriculture in China is still not productive enough to withstand major natural disasters such as floods and droughts. With the transition from a state-controlled to a market-driven economy and reliance on market forces, price incentives and individual initiatives, a smoothly operating marketing system has not yet been developed. This now constitutes a major strategic problem. Improved storage and post-harvest handling and processing would greatly reduce current food losses, but the practices are still quite primitive.

The most limiting of natural resources for food production in China will be water. Overdraft of groundwaters and shortages for irrigation, industrial and municipal uses are already serious in Beijing, Tianjin and the surrounding areas in Hebei, Shanxi and Shandon provinces. Shortages are also beginning to show in the Shanghai area.

Equally serious is the problem of water quality, with water pollution arising from the rapid expansion of rural industrialization, untreated urban wastes, millions of small enterprises and sideline industries which are coming into being, the precipitous rise in the use of nitrogen fertilizer for crop production, and the anticipated growth of animal husbandry and expansions in fisheries and aquaculture.

Grain surpluses will only be temporary in China. Expanding livestock and poultry industries will quickly absorb the slack. In 1985, grain harvest fell sharply from 407 million tons in 1984 to 379 million tons for a drop of 5%. This was partly by design, encouraged by substituting cash crops, but it lead to domestic criticism. Some 10 million acres were shifted out of grain production in 1985. With the bumper grain harvest in 1984, farmers had difficulty selling their surplus grain and so planted other crops with the hope of reaping more profit.

The challenge for the future will be utilization of what is produced, especially the surpluses. Little attention has been given thus far to post-harvest handling and physiology--precooling, packaging, storage, transportation, processing, distribution and marketing. The development of adaptive technologies for improvements in the postharvest handling, distribution and marketing of perishable fruits and vegetables--almost always in short supply--now constitutes China's immediate challenge for feeding more than a billion people.

A final challenge will be maintaining food production while large numbers of peasants are leaving the farms and arable land is being used for housing and industrial expansion. Some potentials for technological inputs reside in genetic improvements in crops and livestock, increased fertilizer usage, integrated pest management, expansion in irrigation, reclamation of arid and problem soils, the development of aquatic resources, the marshalling of hydroelectric power resources, and the use of chemical plant growth regulators, biotechnology and protected cultivation. Continuing and pervasive problems will be those of soil erosion, overdrafts of groundwaters, droughts, floods, air and water pollution, and limitations in postharvest handling, storage and food processing.

Currently the Chinese are living in a period of breathless transition-- economic incentives, innovations, modernization, mechanization, commoditization changing consumptive habits, and material progress, coupled with limitations in capital, energy supplies, fertilizers, technical expertise, a supporting infrastructure, communications and transportation. To what degree is the leadership willing to sacrifice control in order to achieve a certain degree of increase in agricultural productivity?

What is going on today in the Chinese countryside is an attempt to blend seemingly irreconcilable elements. These include state ownership of land with private operation, central planning with competitive free markets, and political dictatorship with economic and cultural freedom. What is going on in China today may be redefining what a communist society is supposed to mean--not that China is going capitalist. One cannot help but be awed, not only by the enormous progress achieved since 1978, but also by how much further China must go to realize the goals set for the year 2000 (see Chapter 35, "More and Better Food for the Future--Prospects to the Year 2000"). During the past eight years (1978-1986), China has faced obstacle courses considered by most as difficult to surmount. But she has overcome. There may well be further surprises for Western observers.

FOR FURTHER READING

Burns, J. F. 1985. China on the move. *The New York Times Magazine*, 8 December, 38.

Chen Denyi, and Hu Jishan. 1983. *Chinese economic geography*. Beijing: Zhan Wang Press. (In Chinese)

Chow, V. 1987. Development of a more market-oriented economy in China. *Science* 235:290-95.

Church, G. 1986. China. *Time* 127(1): 24-41.

Ensminger, M. E., and A. Ensminger. 1973. *China--The impossible dream*. Clovia, Calif.: M. E. Ensminger and A. Ensminger.

He Kang, ed. 1980, 1981, 1982, 1983, 1984. *Chinese agricultural yearbook*. Beijing: Agricultural Press. (In Chinese)

IDEALS. 1985, 1986. *Proceedings on agriculture in China*. Vol. 1, *Challenges and opportunities*; Vol. 2, *Macro issues in Chinese agricultural development*. Beltsville, Md.: Institute of International Development and Education in Agriculture and Life Sciences.

King, F. H. 1911. *Farmers of forty centuries*. Emmaus, Pa.: Rodale Press, Inc.

Kuan-I Chen. 1983. China's changing agricultural system. *Current History* 82:259-64.

Lardy, N. R. 1983. *Agriculture in China's modern economic development*. New York: Cambridge University Press.

———. 1986. Overview: Agricultural reform and the rural economy. In *China's economy looks toward the year 2000*. Vol. 1, *The Four Modernizations*, ed. U.S. Congress Joint Economic Committee, 325-35. Washington, D.C.: U.S. Government Printing Office.

———. 1986. Prospects and some policy problems of agricultural development in China. *Journal of Agricultural Economics*. 68(2): 451-57.

Leeming, F. 1985. *Rural China today*. New York: Longman, Inc.

Lu Liangshu. 1985. The path toward food self-sufficiency in China. In *Food for the Future*, 73-81. Proceedings of the bicentennial forum of the Philadelphia Society for Promoting Agriculture.

Lumpkin, T. A., and D. C. Plucknett. 1982. *Azolla as a green manure: Use and management in crop production*. Boulder, Colo.: Westview Press.

Perkins, D., and S. Yusuf. 1984. *Rural development in China*. Baltimore: Johns Hopkins University Press.

Schell, O. 1985. *To get rich is glorious*. New York: Random House, Inc.

Smil, V. 1985. China's food. *Scientific American* 253(6): 116-24.

Stone, B. 1985. *The basis for Chinese agricultural growth in the 1980s and 1990s: A comment on Document No. 1, 1984*. Washington, D.C.: International Food Policy Research Institute.

Surls, F. M. 1986. China's agriculture in the eighties. In *China's economy looks toward the year 2000*. Vol. 1, *The Four Modernizations*, ed. U.S. Congress Joint Economic Committee, 336-53. Washington, D.C.: U.S. Government Printing Office.

Terrill, R. 1985. Sichuan: Where China changes course. *National Geographic* 168(3): 280-317.

U.S. Department of Agriculture. Economic Research Service. 1984, 1985, 1986. *China outlook and situation reports*. Washington, D.C.: Government Printing Office.

Walker, K. R. 1984. *Food grain procurement and consumption in China*. New York: Cambridge University Press.

World Bank. 1985. *China: Agriculture to the year 2000*. Washington, D.C.

37

A VIEW OF THE 21st CENTURY

by Sylvan Wittwer

By any measurement, assessment, standard, criterion or index, what has been wrought in food production during the first half of the 1980s through the countrysides of China has had no equal in any other agriculturally developing nation. The Chinese--comprising twenty-two percent of the world's population and almost a third of the world's farmers--have been involved with across-the-board improvement programs in crop production, animal agriculture, forestry, fisheries and sideline industries.

Further structural changes in China may be even more dramatic by the turn of the century, but no more so than has already occurred in Japan and Korea (1960-1980). The differences will be in the magnitude and number of people involved. The impacts of Chinese agriculture on the world food market (economy) by the twenty-first century may well compare with that of Japanese industry on world business in the 1980s.

The expansion of agricultural production in China has depended, above all, upon intensification or increase in production per unit land area, achieved by people rather than through government policy. Present signs are that this will continue. Looking toward the twenty-first century and at the accomplishments of the past decade, agricultural production seems likely to grow at least twice as fast as population and continue to make positive advances.

There have been extensive efforts in the past to improve the land base, extend irrigation, reclaim problem soils, control flooding and increase nutrient availability for crops. There is every indication this will continue, but gains in new lands will be more than offset by the diversion of what are now agricultural land resources to roads, houses and factories.

Agricultural food production in China has arrived at a threshold. Since 1978 its performance has been remarkable and impressive. There are now issues emerging of much greater complexity for the future.

There is an urgent need for improved systems of storage, distribution, retailing, packaging, wholesaling and food processing. The farm system still cannot get perishable produce to market. The boundary of the agricultural sector in China is no longer confined to production but is going beyond the farmgate all the way to food consumption.

Environmental issues are surfacing in every major food-producing area. The extensive use of coal as industrialization grows is polluting the atmosphere and contributing to acid precipitation. Groundwater resources are being excessively depleted, especially in the north and northwest, and soil erosion continues through the reaches of the Yellow River. Groundwater pollution is becoming rampant near the major industrialized centers and progressively serious in rural areas with the rapid expansion of countryside enterprises. Energy efficiency in food production will become increasingly critical as fuel requirements increase.

The changing world economy and the complexity and competitiveness of international trade will leave its mark on China, where traditionally there has been little or no experience in dealing with food surpluses, meager statistical reporting, limited attention to marketing economics, few grain storage facilities, and an overloaded transport system.

Extensive studies are just being initiated in the collection, cataloguing, distribution and utilization of germplasm resources. Seed certification and testing will become increasingly important. Development of animal husbandry or the livestock sector will place new constraints on resources both natural and human and must be balanced with the availability of feed grains, the development of an expanding feed processing industry, and an assessment of current and potential carrying capacities of grasslands. There will be a rising need to respond to growing consumer demands for agricultural commodities associated with higher standards of living--fresh fruits, vegetables and a variety of animal products such as milk, ice cream, meat and eggs. Particularly critical will be the reduction of people engaged in agricultural production and the subsequent challenge of providing gainful employment for released workers and avoiding the hazards of decreased purchasing power and rural poverty.

China has great natural resource potentials for future agricultural development. These include reclamation of the salty and other problem soils of the North China Plain; mechanization of the wide open spaces of the northeast frontiers; development of the grasslands of Inner Mongolia and the semi-arid regions of the northwest; greater crop diversification and reclamation of the erodible red soils in the south; more effective cropping of the fertile soils of the Sichuan Basin; broader development of the abundant tropical climatic resources of Hainan Island; and finally, the harnessing of the rich land, water, climatic and human resources of minorities in the Xinjiang Autonomous Region.

Dr. T. C. Tso, Executive Director of the Institue of International Development and Education in Agricultural and Life Sciences (IDE-ALS), Beltsville, Maryland, U.S.A., speaking of China, puts it as follows for Xinjiang:

> . . . . Xinjiang is multirich--rich in arable land, pasture, forestry; rich in oil, gas, coal; and rich in sunshine, mineral resources, water resources--yes, in water resources! The *Kan-Er-Jin* underground water system matches the scale of the Great Wall in human creation. Rich in culture, Xinjiang's civilization in 200 or 100 B.C. is an equal to the intelligence of any other of the same period. Xinjiang is a reflection of wisdom and creativity. . . .
>
> Xinjiang is a state of contrast--big in area but small in population; hot by day but cold by night; rich in old traditions but new in modern spirit; rich in natural resources but poor in human resources; and last but not least, abundant in gold but in need of capital. Xinjiang is full of opportunities and challenges. . . .

For the outside world Xinjiang may be considered a Chinese "Shangri-la" with endowed advantages over other provinces and geographically located along ancient trade routes known as the "Silk Road." Xinjiang has 10.8 million hectares of arable land waiting to be reclaimed for crops, a climate favorable for the production of long fiber cotton, sugar beets, grapes and melons and grasslands that now support over thirty million fine-wool sheep. Needs are for trained personnel, funds, transportation and communications.

Conclusion

One message is patently clear for the future of China: the Chinese people want a better standard of living--improved diets, housing, communications, transportation, household conveniences, consumer goods, job opportunities and labor-saving technologies. Any action by China, a nation with 22% of the world's people, is certain to have an effect on the U.S.A. and the entire world. Strategies for future growth will include, among other possibilities, changes in production and consumption patterns, the preservation of natural resources, continued emphasis on agricultural science and technology, and the efficient use of foreign capital. Finally, China, a country that has essentially eliminated hunger, offers hope for the developing world of the twenty-first century. Of all the countries in Central and South America, Africa, the Asian Sub-continent and the Middle East, China has some of the most favorable conditions and potential for growth.

The Chinese experience of "walking on two legs"--blending the traditional with modern technologies--in all aspects of its agricultural development, coupled with it unique systems of resource management and recylcing of managed inputs, economic incentives, diversification, producing food where the people are, and providing for some farmers to leave the land but remain in the countryside for gainful employment in village enterprises, is a model that might elsewhere be emulated.

FOR FURTHER READING

Anonymous. 1986. China--new long march, new revolution. *U.S. News and World Report*, 8 September, 26-31.

Anonymous. 1986. Xinjiang opens to the world. *Beijing Review* 29(46): 6-8.

Dai Yannian. 1986. Xinjiang strides ahead while opening to the world. *Beijing Review* 29(44): 17-25.

He Kang. 1986. Agriculture: The Chinese way. *Beijing Review* 29(19): 23-25.

Lu Liangshu. 1985. The path toward food self-sufficiency in China. In *Food for the future*, 73-81. Proceedings of the Philadelphia Society for Promoting Agriculture Bicentennial Forum, 1785-1985.

Tso, T. C. 1986. Strategy for year 2000. In *Proceedings on agriculture in China*. Vol 2, *Macro issues in Chinese agricultural development*. 196-99. Beltsville, Md.: Institute of International Development and Education in Agriculture and Life Sciences.

U.S. Department of Agriculture. Economic Research Service. 1986. *China situation and outlook reports*. Washington, D.C.: Government Printing Office.

World Bank. 1985. *China: Agriculture to the year 2000*. Washington, D.C.

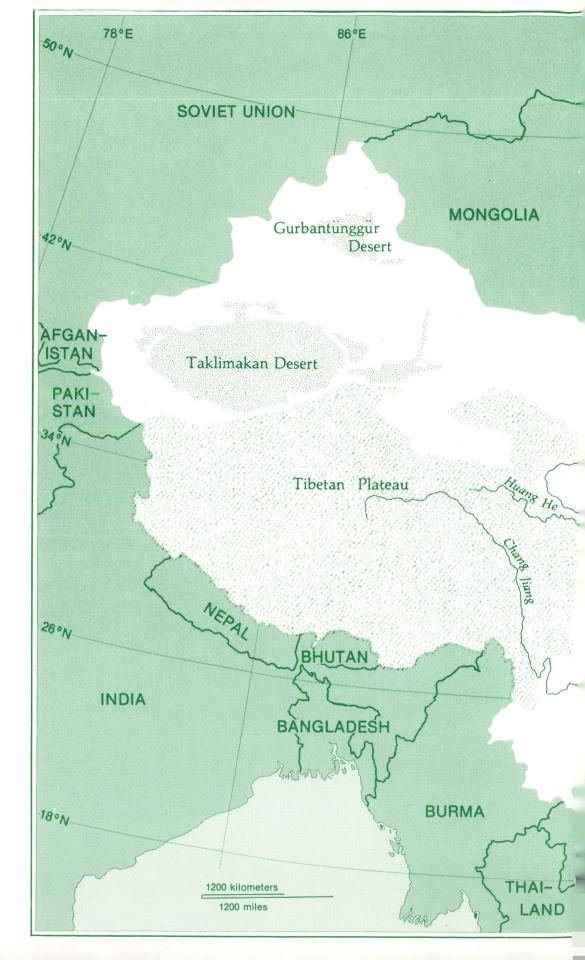